LEGAL RESEARCH SKILLS FOR SCOTS LAWYERS

LEGAL RESEARCH SKILLS FOR SCOTS LAWYERS

Third Edition

Dr Karen Fullerton
PhD, MA (Hons), LLB, DipLB
Teaching Fellow, University of Aberdeen

Third Edition by

Fiona Grant
LLB European Business Law Programme Leader,
Lecturer in Law
Abertay University, Dundee

W. GREEN

 THOMSON REUTERS

Second edition published 2007
Published in 2014 by W. Green, 21 Alva Street,
Edinburgh EH2 4PS
Part of Thomson Reuters (Professional) UK Limited
(Registered in England & Wales, Company No 1679046. Registered Office and address for
service: 2nd Floor, 1 Mark Square, Leonard Street, London EC2A 4EG)

Typeset by YHT Ltd, London
Printed and bound in Great Britain by CPI Group (UK) Ltd, Croydon, CR0 4YY

No natural forests were destroyed to make this product; only
farmed timber was used and replanted.

A CIP catalogue record for this title is available from the British Library

ISBN 978-0414-01825-9

Foreword

Legal research skills are fundamental to both the study and practice of law. The ability to identify, locate and evaluate relevant, current and authoritative legal information and to use it to construct legal argument in various forms (e.g. coursework, examinations, research projects, letters to clients, pleadings, etc.) is essential for all those working with the law.

The nature of legal research skills has evolved over time. Since the first edition of this work was published in 1999 there have been changes not only in the way legal research is carried out but also in the teaching of legal skills at Scottish universities and the expectations of graduate employers. This new edition has taken account of these changes and is designed to meet the needs of the modern legal researcher.

There have been many changes in the availability and format of legal materials with the massive increase in electronic sources. While the accessibility of legal information has increased at a terrific pace this has not meant that life has become easier for the Scottish legal researcher. In fact the opposite is true. Now that so many legal materials are available at the click of a mouse difficulty in finding information has been replaced by the problem of information overload. There are an increased number of possible pitfalls which can befall the unwary researcher and result in inaccurate research findings. Familiarity with using search engines to locate information can lead to their unquestioning use for legal materials which can result in the identification of irrelevant and out of date material which lacks any authority. The volume of electronic material can also lead to a presumption that paper sources are irrelevant—a presumption which is misplaced even in the 21st century.

It is now more important than ever for both students and practitioners to be able to appreciate the features, along with both the strengths and weaknesses, of legal sources and to evaluate their accuracy, currency and level of authority. This new edition is a user friendly guide to navigation through the sea of information sources and enables readers to develop the ability to assess their validity. In so doing it covers and clearly differentiates between subscription services available in most Scottish universities, open source material available freely on the internet and paper information sources.

In Pt II this work turns to cultivating study skills and research skills and provides a range of useful advice aimed at different stages in a student's university career, from induction through to undertaking research projects.

This edition is an excellent reference work suitable for undergraduate and post-graduate students, as well as for legal practitioners. It should prove a valuable resource for any legal research activity.

Dr Karen Fullerton
July 2014

Contents

Table of Abbreviations

A

A.C.	Appeal Cases (Law Reports)
A.J.I.L.	American Journal of International Law
All E.R.	All England Law Reports
A.P.S.	Acts of the Parliament of Scotland 1124–1707 (Record Edition)
asp	Act of the Scottish Parliament

B

BAILLI	British and Irish Legal Information Institute
B.C.C.	British Company Cases
B.D.I.L.	British Digest of International Law
B.J.Crim	British Journal of Criminology
B.Y.I.L.	British Yearbook of International Law

C

C.F.I.	Court of First Instance
C.L.	Current Law
C.L.J.	Cambridge Law Journal
C.L.Y.	Current Law Yearbook
COM	Official publication of the European Commission
C.M.L.R.	Common Market Law Reports
C.M.L.Rev.	Common Market Law Review
CoE	Council of Europe
CSIH	Court of Session Inner House
CSOH	Court of Session Outer House
Ch.	Chancery Division (Law Reports)
Cmnd,Cm.	UK Government publications presented to Parliament
Crim.L.R.	Criminal Law Review

E

E.A.T.	Employment Appeal Tribunal
E.B.L.R.	European Business Law Review
EC	European Community
ECHR	European Convention on Human Rights
ECtHR	European Court of Human Rights
ECJ	European Court of Justice
ECLAS	European Commission Library Catalogue
E.C.L.R.	European Competition Law Review
E.C.R.	European Court Reports
ECSC	European Coal & Steel Community
EDC	European Documentation Centres
Edin.L.R.	Edinburgh Law Review
EEC	European Economic Community

E.E.L.R.   European Environmental Law Review
EFTA   European Free Trade Association
E.H.R.L.R.   European Human Rights Law Review
E.H.R.R.   European Human Rights Reports
E.I.P.R.   European Intellectual Property Review
E.J.I.L.   European Journal of International Law
E.L.J.   European Law Journal
E.L.Rev.   European Law Review
E.P.L.   European Public Law
E.T.S.   European Treaty Series
EU   European Union
Env.L.R.   Environmental Law Reports

F
FLAG   Foreign Law Guide
F.L.R.   Family Law Reports
Fam.   Family Division (Law Reports)
Fam. L.R.   Family Law Reports (W. Green)

G
GLIN   Global Legal Information Network
GTLD   Generic Top Level Domain
G.W.D.   Greens Weekly Digest

H
HCJ   High Court of Justiciary
HCJAC   High Court of Justiciary Appeal
H.L.   House of Lords
Hous. L.R.   House Law Reports (W.Green)
HUDOC   Human Rights Documentation Centre

I
ICANN   Internet Corporation for Assigned Names and Numbers
I.C.C.   International Criminal Court
I.C.J.   International Court of Justice
I.C.J. Reports   International Court of Justice Reports
I.C.J. Yearbook   Yearbook of the International Court of Justice
ICLR   Incorporated Council of Law Reporting for England and
                               Wales
I.C.L.Q.   International and Comparative Law Quarterly
I.C.R.   Industrial Cases Reports
Ibid.   *Ibidem*; meaning "the same"
ILAS   Institute of Advanced Legal Studies
I.L.M.   International Legal Materials
ILO   International Labour Organisation
I.L.R.   International Law Reports
I.R.L.R.   Industrial Relations Law Reports
ISBN   International Standard Book Number
IT   Information Technology

J

J.C.	Justiciary Cases
J.C.M.S.	Journal of Common Market Studies
JCPC	Judicial Committee of the Privy Council
J.I.L.T.	Journal of Information Law & Technology
J.L.S.	Journal of Law and Society
J.L.S.S.	Journal of the Law Society of Scotland
J.R.	Juridical Review

L

LJI	Legal Journals Index (Westlaw)
LLB	Bachelor of Laws
LLI	Legal Information Institute
Loc. Cit.	*Loco citro*; meaning ' in the place cited'
L.Q.R.	Law Quarterly Review

M

M. or Mor.	Morison's Dictionary of Decisions
M.L.R.	Modern Law Review
Med.L.R.	Medical Law Reports
MEP	Member of the European Parliament
MSP	Member of the Scottish Parliament

O

O.J.	Official Journal of the European Union
O.J.L.S.	Oxford Journal of Legal Studies
Op. Cit.	*Opere citaro*; meaning 'in the work previously cited'
OQPS	Office of the Queen's Printer for Scotland
OSCOLA	Oxford Standard for Citation of Legal Authorities

P

P.C.I.J.	Permanent Court of International Justice
PDP	Personal Development Planning

Q

Q.B.	Queen's Bench (Law Reports)

R

Rep. B	Reparation Bulletin
Rep.L.R.	Reparation Law Reports

S

S.C.	Session Cases
S.C.(H.L.)	Session Cases, appeals to House of Lords
S.C. (P.C.)	Session Cases Privy Council
S.C.C.R.	Scottish Criminal Case Reports
S.C.L.R.	Scottish Civil Law Reports
Sch.	Schedule
S.I.	Statutory Instrument
S.J. or Sc. Jur.	Scottish Jurist
SLC	Scottish Law Commission

S.L.C.R.	Scottish Land Court Reports
S.L.G.	Scottish Law Gazette
S.L.R. or Sc. L.R.	Scottish Law Reporter
S.L.R. or S.L. Rev. or Sc.L.R.	Scottish Law Review and Sheriff Court Reporter
S.L.T.	Scots Law Times
S.L.T. (Land Ct.)	Scots Law Times, Land Court Reports
S.L.T. (Lands Tr.)	Scots Law Times, Lands Tribunal Reports
S.L.T. (Lyon Ct.)	Scots Law Times, Lyon Court Reports
S.L.T. (Notes.)	Scots Law Times, Notes of Recent Decisions
S.L.T. (Sh. Ct.)	Scots Law Times, Sheriff Court Reports
S.N.	Session Notes
S.P.E.L.	Scottish Planning and Environmental Law
SCOLAG	Scottish Legal Action Group
SPICe	Scottish Parliament Information Centre
Sh. Ct. Rep.	Sheriff Court Reports

T

T.C.	Reports of Tax Cases
TLD	Top Level Domain
T.S.O.	The Stationery Office

U

UK	United Kingdom
UKHL	United Kingdom House of Lords
UKSC	United Kingdom Supreme Court
U.K.T.S.	United Kingdom Treaty Service
U.N.T.S.	United Nations Treaty Series
URL	Uniform Resource Locator

W

| WIPO | World Intellectual Property Organisation |
| W.L.R. | Weekly Law Reports |

Y

| Y.E.L. | Yearbook of European Law |
| Yearbook ECHR | Yearbook of the European Convention on Human Rights |

Table of Regnal Years*

Sovereigns	Commencement of Reign	Length of Reign
		Years
William I	October 14, 1066	21
William II	September 26, 1087	13
Henry I	August 5, 1100	36
Stephen	December 26, 1135	19
Henry II	December 19, 1154	35
Richard I	September 23, 1189	10
John	May 27, 1199	18
Henry III	October 28, 1216	57
Edward I	November 20, 1272	35
Edward II	July 8, 1307	20
Edward III	January 25, 1326	51
Richard II	June 22, 1377	23
Henry IV	September 30, 1399	14
Henry V	March 21, 1413	10
Henry VI	September 1, 1422	39
Edward IV	March 4, 1461	23
Edward V	April 9, 1483	–
Richard III	June 26, 1483	3
Henry VII	August 22, 1485	24
Henry VIII	April 22, 1509	38
Edward VI	January 28, 1547	7
Mary	July 6, 1553	6
Elizabeth I	November 17, 1558	45
James I	March 24, 1603	23

Sovereigns	Commencement of Reign	Length of Reign
		Years
Charles I	March 27, 1625	24
Commonwealth	January 30, 1649	11
Charles II†	May 29, 1660	37
James II	February 6, 1685	4
William and Mary	February 13, 1689	14
Anne	March 8, 1702	13
George I	August 1, 1714	13
George II	June 11, 1727	34
George III	October 25, 1760	60
George IV	January 29, 1820	11
William IV	June 26, 1830	7
Victoria	June 20, 1837	64
Edward VII	January 22, 1901	9
George V	May 6, 1910	26
Edward VIII	January 20, 1936	1
George VI	December 11, 1936	15
Elizabeth II	February 6, 1952	–

* The Scottish Kings are not given, inasmuch as the Scots Acts are cited by year and chapter not by regal name, year and chapter.

† Charles II did not ascend the throne until May 29, 1660, but his regnal years were computed from the death of Charles I, January 30, 1649, so that the year of his restoration is styled the 12th of his reign.

Chapter 1
Introduction

Significant abbreviations used in this chapter

- ECHR—European Convention on Human Rights
- EU—European Union
- LLB—Bachelor of Laws
- O.J.—Official Journal of the European Union
- SI—Statutory Instrument
- S.L.T.—Scots Law Times

Legal Research Skills for Scots Lawyers is a user-friendly guide to researching Scots law. It will **1–01** enable the reader to identify relevant and authoritative sources of legal information with confidence, and assess which is or are the most appropriate for the task in hand. It also explains various search strategies and techniques that will assist in locating materials efficiently and provides guidance on how to comprehend and evaluate the materials retrieved. However, Scots lawyers cannot focus solely on Scots law. Law applicable throughout the United Kingdom and European Union ("EU") and indeed aspects of public and private international law are all integral to the Scottish legal system. There are therefore chapters dealing with these external but directly applicable sources of Scots law. Although *Legal Research Skills for Scots Lawyers* is primarily intended for the undergraduate law student studying on an accredited LLB programme, it will also be of interest and relevance to those studying for the post-graduate vocational qualification, the Diploma in Professional Legal Practice, trainee solicitors or advocates and even seasoned practitioners who wish to enhance their knowledge of contemporary legal research methods, techniques, resources and issues.

In the interests of consistency, the word "researcher" is used throughout Pt 1 of *Legal Research* **1–02** *Skills for Scots Lawyers* to encompass the core activity and purpose of all readers, whether they are students or practitioners.

In summation, *Legal Research Skills for Scots Lawyers* shows the reader how to use the fruits of **1–03** research to produce high quality work.

Legal research in the 21st century

Since the first edition of this book was published in 1999, the then embryonic electronic sources **1–04** of legal information have become pervasive and will often be the first port of call for legal researchers seeking primary and secondary sources of Scots law in the belief that electronic sources will, with ease and efficiency, provide all information sought. This is far from the truth—the reality is that electronic sources, although abundant and readily available, will merely retrieve large amounts of irrelevant or inaccurate information if not used properly, thereby wasting a considerable amount of the researcher's time and/or presaging the production of work of poor quality and doubtful provenance. Although a distinction can be drawn between validated information contained in subscription (paid for) legal data bases, e.g. Westlaw and LexisNexis, and (often unattributed) open source material (free) on the internet, the student and practitioner alike may not always have access to the most comprehensive or most current subscription sources and, even if they are available, it can often prove quicker and more effective to locate some information required using traditional paper sources.

1–05 It is therefore important for the legal researcher to appreciate the properties and value of a range of legal sources and develop the ability to evaluate their accuracy, currency and ultimately their validity. Thus, while electronic sources do play a vital and growing role in legal research, the challenge for the researcher is to constantly assess the most appropriate source(s) and then locate the required material efficiently. *Legal Research Skills for Scots Lawyers* provides the reader with a rounded appreciation of these differing sources and alternative ways of locating required information, whether searching for sources by name, searching with incomplete details or searching by subject.

1–06 Websites and web pages cited in *italics* in each chapter are correct at the time of publication and are collated, for convenience, in Appendix I. Whilst it is inevitable that such addresses will change, be modified or otherwise become unavailable with the passage of time, many websites making such changes will provide a "redirect" link to take the viewer to the current landing page for a resource. Neither the author nor the publisher is responsible for the content of any website or web page referred to, its owner's policies or contractual relationship with a third party.

The law as stated is correct as at June 24, 2014.

STRUCTURE OF THE BOOK

1–07 *Legal Research Skills for Scots Lawyers* is a book in two distinct parts: Part I examines different types of legal information, explaining their status thus authority as sources of Scots law, and suggested retrieval strategies; whilst Part II focuses on acquiring and developing legal research skills, as well as the appropriate presentation of the results in a variety of fora.

Anatomy of Part I

1–08 Chapter 2 discusses the utility and use of electronic legal resources and identifies strategies for searching on the internet for open source resources and how to assess the seemingly endless amount of legal information available online. It then identifies key legal information gateways, including subscription databases, and provides advice on how to search them effectively and efficiently. Chapter 2 concludes by: advising how to make best use of the materials gathered; providing criterion against which information retrieved ought to be evaluated and suggests model citation and referencing styles for electronic information sources.

1–09 The leading formal sources of Scots law are case law and legislation. Chapter 3 provides an introduction to the essence and nature of case law, the formalities of law reporting and the principal series of law reports used by Scots legal researchers. This chapter concludes by outlining the skills that require to be developed to ensure effective reading and analysis of case law and how to author a case note, which is a mainstay of the study of law and provides the foundation of any legal argument.

Chapter 4 concentrates on tracing cases and the different search strategies that can be adopted **1–10** to locate a case where the researcher only has partial information about it. It concludes by advising how to evaluate the status of a case, i.e. its impact or otherwise on the development of Scots law and therefore its currency as a component part of contemporary legal argument. Taken together, Chs 3 and 4 equip both the new and more experienced researcher to make effective use of this prime source of Scots law.

Legislation is discussed in Chs 5–7. Chapter 5 provides an explanation of the legislative process **1–11** in both the UK Parliament (referred to as Westminster) and the Scottish Parliament (referred to as Holyrood) and details the main types of legislative instruments operative in both the UK and Scotland. The layout and structure of Acts of Parliament and Statutory Instruments (SI) in both legislatures are detailed and annotated. Advice on reading, understanding and interpreting legislation per se is also given. Chapter 6 outlines search strategies for tracing legislation enacted at Westminster, while Ch.7 adopts the same approach to legislation enacted by the Holyrood Parliament in Edinburgh.

Chapter 8 contains information about further sources of relevance to the Scots lawyer. These **1–12** range from an introduction to further formal sources of Scots law, e.g. the Institutional Writers of the 17th to 19th centuries, to how to evaluate secondary (non formal) sources of legal information. Such secondary sources include;

> ➤ Journal, etc. articles written by legal academics and/or practitioners;
> ➤ Current awareness websites;
> ➤ Publications containing legal information, e.g. Government papers and circulars.

All the above may yield valuable information and comment on legal issues. However, not all such information, irrespective of whether it is published in electronic or paper form, carries the same weight or authority and distinguishing between valid and more spurious sources in an essential research skill. Although this chapter is primarily for the instruction of law students, some practitioner-orientated materials are also included.

Chapter 9 considers selected sources of UK-wide legal information which exclude, either wholly **1–13** or partially, Scots law, and builds on the introduction given to such materials in previous chapters. Primarily, Ch.9 explains the historic and contemporary influence and impact of English case law on the development of Scots law and legal reasoning by discussing the persuasive nature of judgments handed down by English courts. The sources referred to have been limited to those which are widely available in Scottish university law libraries, in either paper or electronic form

Chapter 10 explains core facets of EU law and outlines its ever increasing impact on the Scottish **1–14** legal system. Principal sources of EU law and attendant key documents are discussed prior to effective search strategies for locating information about EU law and policy. Chapter 11 briefly discusses public and private international law and the impact of the European Convention on Human Rights ("ECHR") on the domestic legal systems of all signatory States. Search strategies for locating key materials in each sphere are also discussed.

Anatomy of Part II

Part II of Legal Research Skills for Scots Lawyers discusses research skills in a broader context. **1–15** It builds on the development and honing of germane information-retrieval skills by charting the necessary stages of the legal research process and, vitally, the appropriate presentation of information. By mastering these necessary steps, researchers will be empowered to confidently undertake valid research for bespoke projects.

1–16 Chapter 12 concentrates on the investigation process by examining topic based research. Much legal research involves considering the substantive rules of a given area, i.e. examining so called black letter rules of law for the purposes of constructing essays, a written/oral legal opinion or answering problem questions typically posed in examinations, e.g. examination of the legal rules controlling dangerous dogs as enacted in the Dangerous Dogs Act 1991 will lead to an analysis of how courts have interpreted the wording of s.3 of that Act which defines the circumstances when a dog will be deemed (or not) to be dangerously out of control in a public place. However, legal research is not restricted to looking at such legal rules in isolation. Socio-legal research examines how law operates in a variety of social spheres, e.g. whether the Dangerous Dogs Act has changed the attitudes and behaviour of dog owners or persons in charge of dogs, e.g. self-employed dog walkers or kennel proprietors. In recognition of this fact, Ch.12 includes a brief discussion of mainstream socio-legal methods of data collection relevant to legal research, namely questionnaires, personal interviews and observational studies. Unlike black letter-based research, such research methods present ethical considerations, i.e. the propriety of the research in the first instance and, secondly, whether the research is then undertaken in accordance with conventionally accepted standards.

1–17 Chapter 13 discusses essential study skills. Aimed specifically at the undergraduate law student, it considers how to gain maximum benefit from attendance at lectures, tutorials and seminars. It advises on deep reading techniques, how to rank secondary sources and then how to succinctly record and collate research findings in a coherent and meaningful way to enable the researcher when revisiting their research after a lapse of time to quickly isolate salient features. This Chapter concludes by outlining universal referencing conventions and illustrates how to construct a bibliography of sources consulted—an essential requirement for any piece of academic work.

1–18 Chapter 14 expands on the essential skills-base discussed in Ch.13 and advises further on how to produce work of a high standard when writing essays, solving legal problems or when preparing to deliver an oral presentation. How to summatively evaluate the research experience by means of personal reflection is also dissected. Finally, revision strategies and exam technique are discussed.

> **NB** In the following Chapters the undernoted symbols have been used to denote:
> 📖—a paper information source;
> 🖱—an electronic information source.

The Essence of the Book

1–19 *Legal Research Skills for Scots Lawyers* is not intended to be read from cover to cover. It is envisaged that it will be referred to as and when appropriate, throughout the undergraduate, post-graduate and professional career, as a manual of first resort when a research project is to be undertaken. Diagrams and screen shots have been included where applicable to aid explanation and illustrate the stages or processes to be followed when using certain sources. Worked examples are also given to show the methodology or stages to be followed when using specific materials. Any examples given reflect the position at the time of writing.

Legal Research Skills for Scots Lawyers has a firm focus on mainstream sources of law and legal **1–20** information which are widely available to students and practitioners in Scotland. As such, neither this book nor indeed any other can hope to provide an exhaustive exposition of all possible sources of information. Neither does the text purport to provide an exhaustive commentary on or analysis of the Scottish legal system. There are many excellent works which already do this. Accordingly, references and hyperlinks are provided, where appropriate, to guide the reader to selected texts or websites which deal with specific aspects of the Scottish legal system in greater depth.

All website addresses cited in this book are correct at the time of writing.

DEFINING LEGAL RESEARCH

The requirement to undertake legal research is an unavoidable consequence of studying law. J. **1–21** M. Jacobstein and R. M. Mersky define this task as "the process of identifying and retrieving information necessary to support legal decision-making (*Fundamentals of Legal Research*, 8th edn (Foundation Press, 2002) p.1). M.J. Lynch, on the other hand, takes a more philosophical approach, stating that legal research " . . . is not merely a search for information; it is primarily a struggle for understanding" ("*An Impossible Task but Everybody has to do it—Teaching Legal Research in Law Schools*", L. Libr. J. 1997, Vol. 89, Pt 3, p.415). C. Cook, et al, opine that the purpose of legal research is "the need to find law which applies to a set of facts" (*Laying Down the Law*, 8th edn (Ethos ACT Law Society, 2012) available as a free download at *http://www.e-bookspdf.org/* [accessed May 20, 2014]). Whilst these definitions vary, it is a universal truth that legal research skills do not just consist of learning how to use a law library or how to look up the law.

Research skills and the undergraduate student

Scottish universities offering the Bachelor of Laws degree (LLB) are accredited by the Law **1–22** Society of Scotland, see *http://www.lawscot.org.uk/* [accessed May 20, 2014] and the Faculty of Advocates, *http://www.advocates.org.uk/* [accessed May 20, 2014], which are the professional bodies for Scots lawyers. Both bodies prescribe core subjects to be taught at undergraduate level, although how these are to be taught is a matter for each individual institution. On a UK wide basis, the Quality Assurance Agency for Higher Education, an independent body which scrutinises the quality, standards and performance of universities and certain colleges, prescribes skills standards (known as benchmark statements) for specific undergraduate degrees. The benchmark statements for law detail general expectations of skills standards to be attained, in addition to a body of legal knowledge, at each stage of study, with the expectation increasing as the student migrates between stages of study. Prime amongst these requirements is the ability to competently undertake legal research:

> ➢ "A student should demonstrate a basic ability to identify accurately the issue(s) which require researching, identify and retrieve up-to-date legal information, using paper and electronic sources and use primary and secondary legal sources relevant to the topic under study."
> ➢ "A student should demonstrate a basic ability to recognise and rank items and issues in terms of relevance and importance, bring together information and materials from a variety of different sources . . . and be able to undertake independent research in areas of law which they have not previously studied starting from standard legal information sources."

See *http://www.qaa.ac.uk/Publications/InformationAndGuidance/Pages/Subject-benchmark-satatement-Law-2007.aspx* [accessed May 20, 2014] for further information.

1–23 No matter the stage of study or professional practice attained, legal research is best initiated and advanced by considering the nature of the task at hand. The preparation of a case note (see paras 3–49—3–51) requires a different approach and methodology from a task involving giving legal advice to a hypothetical client in an examination setting or in professional situation where analysis of the applicable law is required prior to explaining it to a client and/or lay person. The commonality between the multifarious tasks undertaken by legal practitioners, however, is the ability to locate, read and digest relevant information and then formulate a valid legal opinion based on the evidence yielded by such research.

1–24 Accordingly, finding information is a very important, but small, part in the research process, e.g. finding the leading case on the definition of s.3 of the Dangerous Dogs Act does not in itself advance legal research or reasoning. It is only the first step in a methodical process employed to determine whether, on the facts of a pending untried case, the dog in question was, as a matter of law, dangerously out of control in a public place or not. To form a legal opinion the following research steps must also be taken:

> ➢ Reading and analysing any previous case(s) (if there are any) where s.3 was the subject of judicial consideration;
> ➢ Reading any earlier cases referred to by legal counsel in such previous cases;
> ➢ Reading cases which have subsequently referred to any prior case(s);
> ➢ Thinking about the competing legal arguments made in the prior case(s);
> ➢ Applying the legal rules laid down by the court in the prior case(s) to the set of circumstances which present in the untried case;
> ➢ Reading academic articles (if there are any) which have commented on the leading case(s) where s.3 has been interpreted;
> ➢ Formulating then advancing a legal argument/opinion based on the summation of the research undertaken.

THE NATURE OF LAW AND LEGAL RESOURCES

1–25 "Psychiatrists have suggested that a student who enters upon the study of law is in search of the security provided by certainty. He expects to find a fixed unchanging body of unambiguous rules which, once absorbed, will furnish a clear solution to any legal problem which arises in a professional lifetime. It is not like that at all." (W.A. Wilson, *Introductory Essays on Scots Law*, 2nd edn (1984), p.1). Accordingly, basic research skills will facilitate "learning the law" as it stands at a given point in time. However:

> "What a student ought to be able to do at the end of any law degree is find the law by proper research and apply it to a given set of facts. A lawyer who simply regurgitates notes, lengthy passages from which may have little or no application to the problem in question and which may in any event be three or four years out of date, is of little value to a modern firm of solicitors." (R. Rennie, "What sort of lawyers do we want?" 2007 S.L.T. (News) 1.)

It is a rounded understanding of what holistic legal research entails and how to undertake it that will outlive time-limited knowledge. Thus the ability to locate, analyse and construct a legal argument, whether written or oral, by marshalling legal rules, principles and authority, is not subject to a use-by date. Rather, with the passage of time such skills become accentuated and honed.

In summation, *all* legal researchers are required to carry out research in a way that is precise, **1–26** accurate, current and comprehensive. This book is designed to teach and develop those skills.

Primary and secondary materials

In order to evaluate the material retrieved, the researcher must be aware of the strengths and **1–27** limitations of the various information sources available. Legal materials can be divided into primary and secondary sources of law. Primary materials comprise formal sources of law and include legislation and case law. The ability to read and interpret primary sources is a core activity that will be undertaken on a daily basis. Secondary sources comprise commentaries on the law. Examples of secondary sources are text books, journal articles and increasingly, blogs or internet groups with an interest in a specific area of law, e.g. IPKAT at *http://ipkitten.-blogspot.co.uk/* [accessed May 20, 2014], which publishes contributions from practitioners and academics with an interest in intellectual property law. However, the role and validity of secondary sources when constructing a legal opinion or argument, unlike primary sources, are dependent on the expertise and standing of their author in the legal community. For that reason such materials, abundant and freely available on the internet as they are, must be approached with caution, e.g. Wikipedia is an interesting experiment in online information dissemination, but it is a totally inappropriate source for consideration when undertaking legal research. Rather, recourse to respected legal journals, either in paper or electronic form, is required. Recreational use of the internet must therefore be distinguished from its use when undertaking bona fide legal research.

Authority of legal materials

Early awareness and understanding of the legal authority the above sources yield are key to **1–28** undertaking successful legal research. Primary sources take precedence over secondary sources; only primary sources can be relied upon when constructing legal argument. However, primary sources of legal information can be sub-divided into official and unofficial publications. This is an important distinction to draw because reliance can only be placed on official information, e.g. the official publication detailing EU legislation is the Official Journal of the European Union. (O.J.), available at *http://eur-lex.europa.eu/oj/direct-access.html* [accessed 24 June, 2014]. However, there are many other sources for and versions of EU legislation which have been produced commercially. They may be easier to access when carrying out research online, but the content is not considered authoritative because it has not come from an official source. Unofficial sources which appear to reprint the official text verbatim may have been edited and it is important to be fully aware that any editorial comment given alongside an unofficial publication is not a statement of the law, rather it is a statement of opinion. As such it can, at best, only be considered a secondary source.

The need for accuracy and precision when giving legal advice

The importance of finding up-to-date information is stressed repeatedly throughout this book. **1–29** Basing legal advice on outdated law would make the advice given completely wrong. From the student's perspective, citing sources that are no longer good law would lead to a poor grade being awarded but for a practitioner doing so the outcome would be far more serious as s/he would have acted negligently. Jonathan Rayner's 2008 article in the Law Society Gazette "Net-surfing Lawyers warned of Compliance Risk", *http://www.lawgazette.co.uk/47152.article* [accessed May 20, 2014] lays bare the calamity that lies ahead for practitioners (and their clients) if they resort to the imprecise and often downright wrong legal information freely and easily accessible on the internet instead of conducting methodical and appropriate legal research to define the current law with precision and accuracy.

1–30 Law students have to quickly come to terms with the fact that the study of law is a precise discipline. Language is used in a precise way. Lawyers use words such as "aforesaid", not to be particularly obscure, but in order to make the meaning beyond doubt. Documents drafted by practitioners (such as contracts and wills) may give rise to significant consequences and will likely be read some years after they are written. It is therefore vital that the document accurately reflects the original intention(s) of the party or parties concerned.

1–31 Precision is also required in the way documents are read. The study of law involves paying attention to detail, e.g. the difference between the use of the words "may" and "shall" in a piece of legislation can be crucial when advising a client on the likely outcome of litigation. Legal research has also to be carried out in a precise way. It is not sufficient to have a vague or hazy knowledge of the law. The requirement for precision can even be discerned in the nature and construction of law text books. These tend to contain more precise indexing systems and references to sources than books used by many other disciplines.

The distinctive nature of a law library

1–32 Law libraries too tend to be different from other libraries. They will generally contain a greater volume of reference materials than other subject-specific libraries, e.g. collections of legislation and case law are published in chronological order due to: (a) the vast number being produced; (b) the need for prompt publication; and (c) tradition. In order to facilitate searching these primary sources various textual aids have been developed. These include Citators, current law year books, digests and indexes which are also to be found in paper form in a law library. How to use such aids is discussed in Ch.3 and beyond.

1–33 Most libraries will have online catalogues which allow ease of access to information about the resources available to researchers both within the library itself and from selected external sources. It is presumed that all law students will be given information about their own university law library and instruction on how to search the catalogue(s). Accordingly, generic information on how to do so is not included in this book.

1–34 Law librarians are a vital part of any legal team and seem to have (almost) magical powers to conjure up obscure case reports or texts from a variety of external sources or networks. Making full use of the skill and expertise of a law librarian to locate primary and secondary sources required for a research project is not "cheating", but just common sense if the researcher has been unable to locate the required information after a thorough search of the sources available to them.

Chapter 2
Using Electronic Resources for Legal Research

Significant abbreviations used in this chapter

- BAILLI—British and Irish Legal Information Institute
- CoE—Council of Europe
- ECHR—European Convention on Human Rights
- GTLD—Generic Top Level Domain
- GLIN—Global Legal Information Network
- S.L.T.—Scots Law Times
- HUDOC—Human Rights Documentation
- ICANN—Internet Corporation for Assigned Names and Numbers
- ICLR—Incorporated Council of Law Reporting for England and Wales
- ILAS—Institute of Advanced Legal Studies
- ILO—International Labour Organisation
- IT—Information Technology
- LJI—Legal Journals Index (Westlaw)
- LLI—Legal Information Institute
- SLC—Scottish Law Commission
- SI—Statutory Instrument
- Spice—Scottish Parliament Research Briefings and Fact Sheets
- TLD—Top Level Domain
- URL—Uniform Resource Locator
- WIPO—World Intellectual Property Organisation

As detailed in Ch.1, using the internet to undertake legal research presents challenges for the **2–01** legal researcher as well as solutions. Although the increase in the provision of electronic open source and subscription legal information over the past 10 years has greatly aided accessibility to legal materials—and is to be welcomed by and large—the sheer amount of information which can be retrieved has a tendency to overwhelm even the most experienced researcher and make it more difficult to efficiently identify *relevant and authoritative* sources. Inappropriate use of the internet as a research tool will prove inefficient and counter-productive in terms of the time devoted to gathering information which may prove, upon closer inspection, to be irrelevant and/ or of limited value. Further, given the complete lack of quality control on the internet, many websites accessed will contain inaccurate and often downright wrong information. Likewise, even if a website provides information that was accurate at the time of writing, the passage of time will likely ensure that such information becomes out of date. It is also likely that the inexperienced researcher may reach the mistaken conclusion that the ease with which vast amounts of electronic material can be accessed means that they can by-pass paper-based sources when undertaking a research project.

2–02   Whilst it is true that many older case reports, statutes and journal articles have been reproduced in digital form, it is still not yet the case that all materials essential for the study of Scots law are available electronically—hence the Quality Assurance Agency for Higher Education's (see para.1–22) requirement for law students to be able also to locate sources in paper form. Accordingly, and for the foreseeable future, legal research will encompass both paper and electronic sources. These should not be regarded as opposing ways of presenting information, nor should one source be considered superior to the other.

AVAILABILITY OF ELECTRONIC RESOURCES: OPEN SOURCE AND SUBSCRIPTION SOURCES COMPARED AND CONTRASTED

2–03   Open source and subscription electronic resources are to be distinguished for a variety of reasons. First, open source internet resources are available to anyone free of charge, although registration may be required in some instances. Subscription resources must be paid for. Second, open source resources may or may not comprise or contain reference to formal sources of law, official documents or academic articles of merit whose contents can be studied and quoted with confidence, whereas subscription resources will generally contain official information and afford access to quality journals. Further, open source materials will often be out of date (and must be approached with caution) whilst subscription resources will constantly be updated. Subscription databases also have the advantage of offering qualitative legal information in a structured environment that can be searched in an efficient way. Both open source and subscription legal resources are discussed in this chapter. Guidance is given on appropriate open source resources and search strategies to be adopted when seeking legal information on the internet. How to navigate and search Westlaw, see *http://legalresearch.westlaw.co.uk/* [accessed May 20, 2014], and LexisNexis, *https://www.lexisnexis.co.uk/en-uk/home.page* [accessed May 20, 2014], the subscription databases most commonly offered by Scottish universities, is also illustrated. Researchers will be able to find out which subscription services (including legal journals) their institution provides by consulting its library's web pages or contacting the law librarian.

Open source primary sources: legislation and case reports

2–04   Most jurisdictions, Scotland being no exception, make many official government legal resources freely available on the internet. Whilst contemporary primary sources can be found with comparative ease, older statutes and cases may only be available in paper form in a law library or from a subscription database.

Locating Legislation

2–05   ➢ *Legislation.gov.uk* is the generic address through which much legislation applying within all UK jurisdictions (Scotland, England, Wales and Northern Ireland) can be found. A researcher of Scots law will have to consult legislation enacted by the Westminster parliament to discover if a specific piece of primary or secondary legislation emanating from this parliament extends to Scotland, i.e. has legal effect in Scotland;

       ➢ UK (Westminster) public general Acts from 1801 to the present date are available here, *http://www.legislation.gov.uk/ukpga* [accessed May 20, 2014]. The data held between 1801 and 1987 is incomplete. However, all acts from 1988 to the present day are available with amendments to certain acts also shown in a revised document. Both data sets can be accessed here, *http://www.legislation.gov.uk/uksi* [accessed May 20, 2014];

➢ All acts of the Scottish (Holyrood) Parliament, since its inception in 1999, can be accessed here, *http://www.legislation.gov.uk/asp* [accessed May 20, 2014];

➢ All SSIs enacted at Holyrood can be found here, *http://www.legislation.gov.uk/ssi* [accessed May 20, 2014];

➢ Per all of the above, a search can be undertaken by year of enactment or by using the search facility provided;

➢ Acts of the old Scottish Parliament (1424–1707) can be found here, *http://www.legislation.gov.uk/aosp* [accessed May 20, 2014], although most, if not all, are of historical rather than contemporary interest.

NB Legislation of whatever type enacted by the Scottish Parliament (old and new) extends to Scotland only, i.e. it has no legal affect whatsoever in any other jurisdiction.

Locating case law

The internet has dramatically enhanced the ability of legal researchers to locate case law in most **2–06** jurisdictions throughout the world. Although not every case heard before a court is reported, i.e. the subject of a formal report of the proceedings, the legal issues under discussion and the judgment reached by the judge or judges hearing the important cases will be. These may be cases heard at first instance—cases before a court for an initial hearing—or appeal cases where the prior decision(s) are challenged by the unsuccessful party or parties to the litigation.

Scottish cases

The Scottish Courts website, at *http://www.scotcourts.gov.uk/* [accessed May 20, 2014], is an **2–07** excellent resource that contains, in addition to court judgments from 1998 onwards (generally those where a significant point of law is under consideration), much information about the different courts operating in Scotland and their specific jurisdiction, i.e. what types of cases they are empowered to hear. At the outset, it is important to draw a distinction between civil and criminal courts. The following diagram shows the hierarchy of Scottish courts in both the civil and criminal sphere and whether a court is a court of first instance or an appeal court.

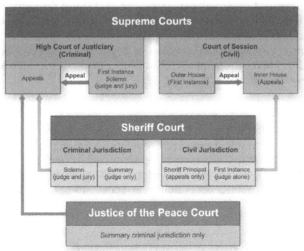

The UK Supreme Court is the final court of appeal for Scottish civil cases and it also has jurisdiction to hear Scottish criminal cases in which a devolution issue has been raised under the Human Rights Act 1998, which enshrines the Convention for the Protection of Human Rights and Fundamental Freedoms, generally referred to as the European Convention on Human Rights ("ECHR").

2–08 An overview of the Supreme Court can be gained by accessing its home webpage at, *http:// supremecourt.uk/* [accessed May 20, 2014], with the following link doing likewise per the role of the Supreme Court in Scottish appeals. *http://www.supremecourt.gov.uk/docs/jurisdiction-of-the-supreme-court-in-scottish-appeals.pdf* [accessed May 20, 2014].

NB The British and Irish Legal Information Institute ("BAILII"), although not an official source provides all Court of Session opinions from September 1998 onwards and selected decisions from 1879 to August 1998. See *http://www.bailii.org/* [accessed May 20, 2014].

English Case Law

2–09 The Incorporated Council of Law Reporting for England and Wales ("ICLR"), *http:// www.iclr.co.uk/* [accessed May 20, 2014], publishes the official law reports from superior and appellate courts in these jurisdictions. Whilst ICLR is not open source, since October 2012, summaries of selected judgments published by ICLR can be accessed via BAILII.

Selected open source secondary sources

E-books

2–10 Non-subscription access to e-books pertaining to Scots law is a fairly recent innovation. Some publishers will provide limited access on their own webpage to a new text, presumably in the hope that the viewer will purchase the same either in electronic or paper form. Google Books search engine, *http://books.google.com/* [accessed May 20, 2014], can locate texts from any jurisdiction where a publisher has given permission for a preview of a book to be viewed, or, in rarer cases, permission to download the entire text. As ever, older texts should be approached with caution given they will likely not reflect the current law. Project Gutenburg, *http:// www.gutenberg.org/* [accessed May 27, 2014], currently offers over 40,000 e-books which can be downloaded for free, but only a small percentage of these pertain to law and a smaller percentage still pertain to Scots law. That said, Project Gutenburg may hold, either now or in the future, an obscure or out of print text of interest to the legal researcher engaged in historic research. Legal 500, *http://www.legal500.com/assets/pages/ebooks/index.html* [accessed May 20, 2014] also offers free legal texts covering a multitude of jurisdictions as does Ebookee, at *http:// ebookee.org/law.html* [accessed May 20, 2014].

Encyclopaedias

2–11 Legal encyclopaedias provide the researcher with a broad brush overview of a defined area of law. Most encyclopaedias available online are provided by American universities and will assist the researcher engaged in perhaps a comparative analysis of domestic and American law in a particular field. In general, legal encyclopaedias are only available via subscription. Westlaw publishes an encyclopaedia of UK law (including Scots law), as well as encyclopaedias on specific subject matter.

International Organisations and Bodies Responsible for Administering Treaties and Conventions

These are specialised agencies dealing with law and policy in defined areas, e.g. the United **2–12** Nation's Internal Labour Organisation ("ILO") publishes NORMLEX, a database on international labour standards which details national employment and social security laws. See *http://www.ilo.org/dyn/normlex/en/f?p = NORMLEXPUB:1:0::NO* [accessed May 20, 2014]. Likewise, the Council of Europe ("CoE") administers the ECHR and operates the European Court of Human Rights ("ECtHR"). See *http://www.echr.coe.int/Pages/home.aspx?p = home&c =* [accessed May 27, 2014].

Journals

Most authoritative legal journals are available only through subscription, either on a pay-as- **2–13** you-go basis or through payment of an annual fee to the database provider. However, high quality open source journals can still be found online, e.g. *SCRIPTed A Journal of Law, Technology and Society* is published quarterly by Edinburgh University, see *http://script-ed.org/* [accessed May 20, 2014], and contains peer reviewed articles from 2004 to the present day. From a qualitative perspective, only articles which have been subjected to peer review can be consulted with confidence. Peer review ensures that prior to publication an article has been evaluated for merit by at least two leading academics publishing in the same field as its author. Non-peer reviewed journals and stand alone articles online should therefore, as a rule of thumb, be approached with caution.

Blogs

Likewise, blogs and social networking sites where legal issues are raised are generally little more **2–14** than discussion boards or a forum for their author(s) to promote a particular point of view by commenting on high profile legal issues or areas of specific interest. Twitter, for example, is awash with commentary on legal issues which range from Tweets posted by practicing lawyers to those from lay persons involved with a single issue campaign group. Although such communications may prove informative, they will often comprise the subjective opinion of the author and others. Accordingly, such fora should never be considered a valid source of legal information.

However, many bona fide blogs dealing with specific areas of law, e.g. IPKat, *http://ipkitten.* **2–15** *blogspot.co.uk/* [accessed May 20, 2014], a site developed and contributed to by academics and practitioners in the field of intellectual property law, is an excellent resource which provides contemporary information and objective comment on recently decided cases or proposed legislative initiatives. Although a secondary source of law (once any subjective "blog" comment by subscribers has been disregarded), this site can provide a firm foundation for further research and the location of primary materials. Likewise, *Inforrm Blog*, (also known as the International Forum for Responsible Media), *http://inforrm.wordpress.com/* [accessed May 20, 2014], invites interaction with subscribers on a range of legal issues posed by the influence of mass media on everyday life. This site, where contributions from legal practitioners and academics feature prominently, also provides an archive of material on past and pending cases before the courts in the UK, EU and beyond.

That said, blogs should always be approached with caution. Rarely can such resources be **2–16** quoted with confidence and they are, by and large, not on a par with the law as stated or author comment given in journal articles and textbooks. However, they can prove to be a useful resource from which to form an overview on a specific legal issue and also provide information about current legal developments which can then be followed up and verified, or otherwise, by recourse to an official or peer-reviewed source.

NB Websites hosted by law firms may also provide commentary on current legal issues and offer an analysis of the reason(s) for the decision in a recently decided case of legal significance. Whilst these sources are secondary sources, they too can provide a legitimate starting point for further research and, on occasion, may be quoted and referenced in a research project if the author is recognised as being a leading practitioner/published author in the area of law concerned.

Newspapers

2–17 The majority of UK newspapers, both national and local, publish an online edition, however few have a dedicated team of legally qualified journalists reporting on current legal issues. The Times, at *http://www.thetimes.co.uk/tto/public/article2873691.ece* [accessed May 20, 2014], can be relied upon for accurate and objective discussion. However, at the time of writing a subscription must be paid to access the electronic version which is published each Thursday. The Guardian's law page, *http://www.theguardian.com/law* [accessed May 20, 2014], is, at the time of writing, an open source and offers a free weekly legal newsletter, "The Bundle", which is delivered to subscribers via email. See *http://www.theguardian.com/law/series/the-bundle* [accessed May 20, 2014].

Official Government publications

2–18 Scottish Government publications can be viewed at *http://www.scotland.gov.uk/Publications/Recent* [accessed May 20, 2014]. Westminster Government publications presented to Parliament and certain departmental papers from May 2005 onwards are to be found on the Government's Official Documents website at *http://www.official-documents.gov.uk/* [accessed May 20, 2014]. The UK Official Documents archive, *http://www.archive.official-documents.co.uk/* [accessed May 20, 2014], contains selected papers from 1994 to April 2005.

Official publications from statutory bodies

2–19 Statutory bodies are created by government and are required to publish papers and reports within their terms of reference, e.g. the Law Commissions Act 1965 established the Scottish Law Commission ("SLC") whose remit includes the provision of independent advice on law reform to the government of the day with. For general information about the work of the SLC access, *http://www.scotlawcom.gov.uk/* [accessed May 20, 2014].

2–20 Certain SLC publications, including reports detailing necessary changes in the law and how this ought to be achieved—an extremely valuable research resource—can be accessed here, *http://www.scotlawcom.gov.uk/publications/* [accessed May 20, 2014].

Locating legal abbreviations online

2–21 In addition to providing access to primary and secondary sources of law the internet can yield various open source resources that will, if used properly, enhance knowledge, understanding and the presentation of research:

> ➢ The Cardiff Index to Legal Abbreviations database provides a search facility to establish or check the meaning of abbreviations used in legal publications and by courts in the English speaking world and beyond. See *http://www.legalabbrevs.cardiff.ac.uk/* [accessed May 20, 2014];

➢ The Institute of Advanced Legal Studies ("ILAS") publishes a useful list of abbreviations for UK and international legal journals. See *http://ials.sas.ac.uk/library/guides/docs/guide7_abbreviations.pdf* [accessed May 20, 2014];

➢ Commonly used Latin abbreviations can be found here, *http://latin-phrases.co.uk/abbreviations/* [accessed May 20, 2014].

Further open source resources: gateways and subject directories

Below is a selection of web addresses which provide links to further useful websites where legal 2–22 materials can be accessed. Many are provided or hosted by academics, law schools or legal practitioners. Thus materials retrieved from or by initially consulting such repositories can generally be held to be of appropriate quality for consideration for inclusion in a research project. Such sites—which may classify sources according to subject—are variously referred to as legal gateways or subject directories. For the sake of consistency they are referred to below as legal gateways.

3 Reasons to Use Legal Gateways: 2–23

➢ To identify relevant online resources in an area of law that is unfamiliar;
➢ To check an important source has not been overlooked; and
➢ They provide an easily accessible alternative to bookmarking important sites individually.

The gateways listed below are divided into three categories: Scottish; English and International although they have tendency to overlap.

Scottish Materials Gateways 2–24

⟁ Delia Venables' Portal to Legal Resources in the UK and Ireland. This gateway contains an up-to-date list of Scottish legal sites and resources including links to databases and legal updates published by some of the leading firms of solicitors in Scotland. See *http://www.venables.co.uk/scotland.htm* [accessed May 28, 2014].

⟁ The Journal of the Law Society of Scotland. This publication's archive goes back to December 1998. See *http://www.journalonline.co.uk* [accessed May 28, 2014].

⟁ Scottish Council of Law Reporting (edited by Sheriff Derek O'Carroll). This site gathers together under subject headings hyperlinks to websites of relevance to the Scots lawyer. A brief description of each site is also given. See *http://www.scottishlawreports.org.uk/resources/links/links.html* [accessed May 28, 2014].

⟁ Scottish Law Online describes itself as a "web portal for lawyers, solicitors or advocates, academics, students or the public who are interested in Scots Law." It is an independent and long established web resource (1997) and includes: an A to Z of Scots law; a resources section which has links to key Scottish sites; Scots Law Student Zone which provides career advice, academic links and an opportunity to share views; an archive for the Scots Law Student Journal; Corporate Zone which contains business related links and a news section. See *http://www.scottishlaw.org.uk/* [accessed May 28, 2014].

⟁ Scottish Parliament Research Briefings and Fact Sheets [SPICe] are organised by and year and by subject. See *http://www.scottish.parliament.uk/parliamentarybusiness/Research.aspx* [accessed May 28, 2014].

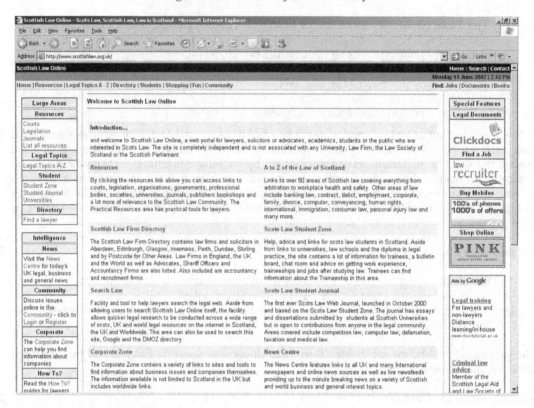

2–25 UK Materials Gateways

> ➤ *GOV.UK* is searchable database where Westminster reports, policy documents and much more can be accessed. See *https://www.gov.uk/* [accessed May 28, 2014].
>
> ➤ The House of Commons Library Research Papers are an occasional series of papers, numbered by year and sequence of publication. See *http://www.parliament.uk/about/how/publications/research/* [accessed May 28, 2014].
>
> ➤ Lawlinks is hosted by the Templeman Library, University of Kent. It contains annotated lists of websites which have been categorised by subject which makes it easy to use. It covers UK and worldwide resources. See *http://www.kent.ac.uk/library/subjects/lawlinks/* [accessed May 28, 2014].
>
> ➤ The Inner Temple Library is primarily a source of English law however it offers a current awareness newsletter containing information about a wide range of domestic and international legal issues. See *http://www.innertemplelibrary.org.uk/* [accessed May 28, 2014]. This site also publishes articles by practicing barristers, at *http://www.innertemplelibrary.com/* [accessed May 28, 2014], and provides links to further legal gateways, at *http://www.innertemplelibrary.com/legal-links/* [accessed May 28, 2014].
>
> ➤ Legal Resources in the UK and Ireland, Delia Venables contains links to the UK and the world. This site also offers access to legal "apps" and links to newsletters and provides a useful narrative about each resource listed. See *http://www.venables.co.uk/* [accessed May 28, 2014].

> ➢ WorldLII is maintained by the World Legal Institute. It contains (at the time of writing) 1246 databases of legal information from 123 countries. In addition there is a particularly useful subject category of links under each country which gives an indication of which materials are available in English. See *www.worldlii.org* [accessed May 28, 2014].

> ➢ ILAS offers Eagle-i a database containing UK, European, and International law. See *http://ials.sas.ac.uk/eaglei/project/eiproject.htm* [accessed May 28, 2014].

> ➢ Findlaw.com is a US based site which allows access to a range of legal resources including articles by legal practitioners. See *http://www.findlaw.com/* [accessed May 28, 2014].

> ➢ Flare Index to Treaties ("ILAS") Global Law Library contains over 2000 bi-lateral and multi-lateral treaties from 1353 to the present day. See *http://193.62.18.232/dbtw-wpd/textbase/treatysearch.htm* [accessed May 28, 2014].

> ➢ Jean Monnet Center for International and Regional Economic Law & Justice is hosted by New York University School of Law and contains access to a large range of documents pertaining to international and EU law. See *http://centers.law.nyu.edu/jeanmonnet/* [accessed May 28, 2014].

> ➢ Human Rights Documentation ("HUDOC") is a searchable database containing full decisions of the ECtHR and various other human rights related documents. A monthly bulletin entitled "Case Law Information Note" is, in particular, a useful resource that gives summaries of recently decided and pending cases. See *http://hudoc.echr.coe.int/sites/eng/Pages/search.aspx#* [accessed May 28, 2014].

> ➢ Law Library of Congress is part of the Global Legal Information Network [GLIN]. GLIN is a public database of official texts of laws, regulations, judicial decisions, and other legal sources contributed by governmental agencies and international organisations. Each document is accompanied by a summary in English. See *http://www.loc.gov/law/find/databases.php*. The GLIN global journal database can be accessed here. *http://www.loc.gov/law/news/glin/* [accessed May 28, 2014].

> ➢ Legal Information Institute ("LII") at Cornell Law School LII holds a collection of US and world legal materials which can be searched country by country. It includes the online sources of constitutions, statutes, judicial opinions, and related legal material from around the world. See *http://www.law.cornell.edu/* [accessed May 28, 2014].

The commonality between all legal gateways accessed is that they will refer the researcher to a variety of further resources which will, in turn, refer him or her to others.

As detailed above, the main difference between open source and subscription resources is that **2–27** paid for services can be relied upon to be accurate and up-to-date. If it were otherwise, such services would suffer reputational damage and not survive in what has become a highly competitive marketplace. Researchers who are fortunate to have access to subscription databases should therefore, where possible, check the accuracy of any information harvested from non-official sites on the internet in that environment or by consulting the paper sources in a law library. "Non-official" describes any source which is not published by a Governmental source or international body governed by treaty or convention.

A further important difference is that, although open source materials tend to allow fast access **2–28** to a range of primary and secondary sources, subscription resources will offer additional features and information which can, if used properly, enhance the quality and currency of a research project, e.g. case summaries detailing the salient points of law for determination will often feature as will detailed information about the treatment of a decided case by a subsequent court, i.e. whether a particular case has been overruled meaning that it no longer reflects the law on a particular point.

2–29   Every subscription legal database, or more accurately, every subscription legal database service will usually comprise of individual databases which can be searched methodically using sophisticated search tools to locate legislation, cases, journal articles and other materials. However, each database will require the user to adopt different search techniques by using the bespoke search tools provided. For those used to searching for information on the internet by simply typing words or phrases into a search engine this will seem, initially, a rather labour intensive method of locating information. The benefit, however, of undertaking a structured search within a database is that in most instances relevant, rather than random, results will emerge, thereby saving the researcher from sifting through masses of information, much of which will ultimately prove irrelevant.

2–30   Whether searching on the internet for open source resources or within the closed confines of a subscription database it is vital to develop search strategies and techniques appropriate for that particular source. However, devising an appropriate search strategy is only the first step. Thereafter, the legal researcher is required to evaluate the information retrieved and then reference it appropriately in a piece of work.

SEARCH STRATEGY FOR ELECTRONIC RESOURCES

Searching on the internet for open source material: avoiding information overload

2–31   "Web search engines are built for people who do not know how to search. It's as simple as that! They are designed so that the researcher relinquishes control of the search, with the expectation that the researcher doesn't really know how to construct a sophisticated search, and therefore doesn't really want control. Thus, the researcher types in a question and the search engine steps in and takes over, retrieving the answer to the question, if it's out there, and three million other sites, most of which are totally irrelevant". (D. Botluk, *Strategies for Online Legal Research: Determining the Best Way to Get What You Need* (2000) available at *http://www.llrx.com/features/strategy.htm* [accessed May 20, 2014].)

2–32   At the time of writing, the number of websites indexed by the search engines, Google, Bing and Yahoo, totals 1.94 billion pages. Although no figures are available for the number of indexed pages containing legal information, a conservative estimate would run into millions rather than hundreds of thousands. In any event, without devising a search strategy prior to undertaking a specific project the researcher will not only waste precious time (all projects have a deadline) but run the risk of locating out-of-date and/or inaccurate materials, e.g. obsolete or significantly amended pieces of legislation will still be available on the internet in original form and will remain so until removed or replaced. Typing "The Scotland Act 1998" into a search engine yields 5,100,000 hits. The first hit is for the *legislation.gov.uk* website. As this is an official UK government source it can be presumed that the information it contains was accurate when posted. However, it is not up-to-date, as such. The following words appear at the start of the webpage: "There are outstanding changes not yet made by the legislation.gov.uk editorial team . . . ". This is followed by a hyperlink "View outstanding changes" which directs the reader to further hyperlinks where the outstanding changes can be viewed via the relevant SI. Thus, the Scotland Act 1998 on this page is technically up-to-date, but not at first glance as further research is required to locate the amending provisions. For this reason alone, adopting a search strategy is vital when undertaking legal research and should never be considered an optional extra or unnecessary step in the process.

Every research project is unique. However, by asking oneself at the outset the simple question, **2–33** "What information is being sought?" the researcher will focus more quickly on the materials they are seeking and, just as importantly, where and how best to locate them, e.g. if the purpose of a research project is to evaluate the Data Protection Act 1998, following initial guidance given by a tutor, the researcher would turn their attention to the following materials:

> ➤ Primary Scottish/UK legal materials such as cases or Acts of Parliament—the Data Protection Act 1998 is an Act of the Westminster Parliament which applies throughout the UK and can be located on the official *legislation.gov.uk* website here, *http://www.legislation.gov.uk/ukpga/1998/29/contents* [accessed May 20, 2014].
> ➤ Primary EU legal materials—the 1998 Act was enacted to "transpose" (see para.10–11) EU Directive 95/46/EC thus reference to this document is required. The Directive can be accessed here, *http://eur-lex.europa.eu/LexUriServ/LexUriServ.do?uri=CELEX:31995L0046:en:HTML* [accessed May 20, 2014].
> ➤ International Conventions—the Council of Europe Convention for the Protection of Individuals with regard to Automatic Processing of Personal Data 1981 preceded the EU Directive and the 1998 Act. It is therefore an important source of information. See para.2–12 and *http://conventions.coe.int/Treaty/en/Treaties/Html/108.htm* [accessed May 20, 2014].
> ➤ UK Government reports/background papers, etc., e.g. *www.parliament.uk* [accessed May 20, 2014] is a gateway to an abundance of official reports/research papers/library notes from the House of Lords etc.
> ➤ Journal articles—Westlaw and LexisNexis et al hold a variety of academic papers in selected journal volumes which discuss the 1998 Act.

A particular research project may require the researcher to locate some or all of the above **2–34** materials and also further resources, therefore it is impossible to list all potential elements necessary in each instance. However, all projects will require the location of primary and generally secondary sources of law and it is the best use of time to identify them with clarity and precision before a word is typed into a search engine.

Search engines

Search engines such as Bing, Firefox, Google (Chrome) and Yahoo make use of programs that **2–35** locate web pages across the internet. They automatically create enormous free-form databases which can then be searched. This process is mechanistic and based on word matching in the same way that mobile devices harness predictive text. Search engines employing word matching do not incorporate any form of quality control or objective judgment. That said, the process(es) employed by such search engines provide a platform for tracing vast amounts of information and will present results obtained in order of relevancy to the search term(s) entered. However, the order of presentation can be skewed by advertising links paid for by businesses keen to appear at the top of search engine lists. However, if required this can be remedied in most cases, e.g. Google currently displays links to adverts on the right hand side of the first page of results, but allows users to opt out of seeing such links by controlling their "ad settings" by accessing the following link, *https://www.google.co.uk/settings/ads/preferences* [accessed May 20, 2014]. Google also provides a "GoogleGuide" webpage where a more detailed explanation of how this search engine operates can be consulted. See *http://www.googleguide.com/google_works.html* [accessed May 20, 2014].

When searching by subject, the more specific the search term, the more accurate the results **2–36** achieved will be. However, forethought as to the terms entered is required. If search terms are too general, e.g. "EU law" is entered in a search engine when seeking information on forthcoming EU legislation, the results achieved will most likely be of no relevance. Therefore, it is advisable to make use of advanced search facilities and not to limit a search to one search engine or legal gateway as no single search tool will index all the possible resources available on the internet, e.g. the Google Scholar toolbar provides an advanced scholar search function with various sub-search fields where academic articles may be sought with either partial or complete information. Yahoo Search provides a similar service. It is further advisable to make use of any "help" function offered by a given search engine as this service may contain further helpful advice on how to construct a directed search. Experience will of course enable the researcher to collate their own e-library of frequently used resources and these can be bookmarked. Some search engines also offer this facility if an account is opened.

2–37   Per the example given above, a researcher in this area will soon discover that the European Law Monitor, *http://www.europeanlawmonitor.org/* [accessed May 20, 2014], is an excellent website for locating then tracking EU legislative proposals and their progression, or otherwise, through the EU legislative process, (which is detailed in Ch.10).

Using appropriate search terms

2–38   At the outset, the researcher must think carefully about the nature of the research project. Is the topic under consideration narrow or wide? For example, if the topic is about art.8 of the ECHR and cases heard by the ECtHR concerning cases brought by Turkish citizens, it would be superfluous to begin a search by seeking information on the ECHR or art.8, other than to provide background information on the origin and development of the Convention and the terms of art.8, as the following example illustrates:

   ↳   Search term: ECHR—**1,190,000 results**
   ↳   Search term: ECHR Article 8—**312,000 results**
   ↳   Search term: ECHR Article 8 case law—**197,000 results**
   ↳   Search term: ECHR Article 8 case law since 2009—**1,210,000 results**
   ↳   Search term: ECHR Article 8 case law 2013—**848,000 results**
   ↳   Search term: ECHR Article 8 case law since 2009—**906,000 results**
   ↳   Search term: ECHR Article 8 case law Turkey—**798,000 results**
   ↳   Search term: ECHR Article 8 case law Turkey 2009—**277,000 results**

The above example illustrates that using an appropriate search term or terms is crucial but not definitive. A broad search must continue to be refined until a consistently reducing number of hits within which to search for relevant material is achieved. This is not an example of the law of diminishing returns where continuing application of effort declines in effectiveness after a certain level of result has been achieved. Rather, fewer (relevant) results are what the researcher is aiming for as a properly conducted search is narrowed.

2–39   Students are required to conduct research in order to submit a piece of work that answers the question or topic as detailed in the title given by the tutor or, if a project is to be generated by the researcher themselves, e.g. a final year dissertation proposal, it will be important to consider carefully the core aspects of the general subject under scrutiny to ensure that the completed project reflects the actual title.

Example of a tutor generated title:

2–40   "Discuss the doctrine of stare decisis and its application in Scotland." (This doctrine is explained and discussed in Ch.3.)

♺   Search term: Doctrine of stare decisis—**266,000 results**;

♺   Search term: Doctrine of stare decisis in Scotland—**7,340,000 results**—curiously this search term yields more results;

♺   Search term: The doctrine of stare decisis and its application in Scotland—**7,340,000 results**—thus changing the previous search terms slightly has no effect on the number of results achieved;

♺   Search term: Scotland and stare decisis—**688,000 results**—a narrower range of results than produced by the prior two searches, but still significantly more than the original search term yielded.

The above is instructive and underscores the fact that even close adherence to a given title does not necessarily or magically produce a narrow range of relevant responses and that further research within these responses will be required. Further, quantity, even when diminishing, does not equate with quality. The most likely first "hit" when entering even a carefully thought out term or terms into a search engine will be Wikipedia, which is not to be considered a reliable secondary source of law under any circumstances. This resource styles itself as a "free encyclopedia that anyone can edit". Accordingly, although it is tempting to view this site, or similar, even for the limited purpose of locating hyperlinks to further electronic sources referred to in a specific page, it should be borne in mind that these links may lead the researcher to outdated materials of dubious provenance that will compromise the quality of the research project.

Choosing the "best" search method

As shown in para.2–38, even search terms that precisely capture the essence of the topic will **2–41** produce more hits than any researcher could possibly consult in a lifetime. To expedite the process of gathering open source materials of appropriate quality most universities will provide students with initial training and then on-going support in a range of academic skills under the broad heading of information literacy. Such training will likely be provided by an academic librarian who, as detailed in Ch.1, is one of the most valuable resources a researcher can consult to provide guidance and assistance with a wide range of research-related issues and queries.

Many universities will also provide a gateway to open source databases designed to assist the **2–42** researcher with instructions on how put such tools to best advantage, also being given by the subject librarian. NoodleTools, see *http://www.noodletools.com/tools/index.php* [accessed May 20, 2014] is one such resource. (NB NoodleTools publishes a user's guide "Smart Tools, Smart Research" at *http://www.noodletools.com/tools/noodletools_users_guide.pdf* [accessed May 20, 2014] and provides a platform from which the researcher can initially, define the scope of a topic by using one of the search engines provided.)

Other tools include Infomine which offers a focussed and structure search with which to browse **2–43** open source resource collections. The results achieved can then be refined or enhanced by using further bespoke open source resources, such as Surfwax and iSEEKeducation, to create the researcher's own bookmarked, web-based repository or library of the information gathered.

Whilst such platforms offer a structured and supported environment, it is vital for researchers to **2–44** become familiar with the use of keywords. Keywords are words or short phrases that appear with greater frequency than the norm in a body of text located on the internet. Research undertaken by a team of academics at the University of Louvain, in Belgium, led to the publication in 2010 of an "Academic Keyword List" that lists 930 high frequency keywords that, statistically, will feature more often in academic papers, etc. than other types of publications. The full list, which is divided into high frequency nouns, verbs and adjectives can be viewed here, *http://www.uclouvain.be/en-372126.html* [accessed May 20, 2014].

2–45 Taking, as examples from the Louvain list, the words "interpretation" and "wholly", when added to the search terms in para.2–40, "Scotland and stare decisis", (which yielded 688,000 results), and structured thus—"Interpretation of stare decisis wholly in Scotland" using the Google Researcher search function at *http://www.mygooglest.com/* [accessed July 28, 2014] the number of results achieved is 125,000.

2–46 The example given above shows the value, in terms of time and relevance to a given topic, in choosing the most appropriate search term(s). Whether using a commercial search engine, a legal gateway or perusing an official government website, key words can significantly reduce the number of results initially achieved and, of course, if a search term produces too few results it can be expanded by adding in further keywords to achieve a broader band of responses.

2–47 Internet for Law offers free online tutorials designed to assist student researchers when searching open source resources. These can be accessed here, *http://www.vtstutorials.co.uk/ws// tracking/launchcontent.aspx?cv=44F5E07D-4809-4851-93F2-A436C626AE7E&e=A0000&c= 8EF8563D-BC82-41D3-8521-045C1F4C830C&SID=bc1afaf0-b200-4c45-afaf-91a36335e691* [accessed May 28, 2014].

Searching subscription databases; Westlaw and LexisNexis; avoiding information overload

2–48 The benefits derived from consulting subscription databases are as follows:

> ➤ Such resources contain the revised form of legislation and provide up-to-date information about the status of cases;
> ➤ They offer a comprehensive range of materials which can be searched from a single point;
> ➤ The ease with which the researcher can link between and bookmark different documents; and
> ➤ The variety of search tools at the disposal of the researcher.

2–49 The two subscription databases most widely used by law students and practitioners in Scotland are Westlaw and LexisNexis. Both are part of large global publishing organisations (respectively, Thomson Reuters and Reed Elsevier) and provide full text access to various UK, Scottish and EU primary legal materials, including revised versions of legislation and case reports and secondary sources such as journal articles. Both also offer alert services per current awareness and news and the ability to download, print or email materials to oneself. The majority of Scottish universities will offer students access to one or both of these subscription services with instruction on how to navigate them being given by the in-house academic librarian or IT trainer. All users will be provided with unique log in credentials and a password to enable them to access any database subscribed to either via their institution's library homepage or directly through the database provider's publicly available webpage.

2–50 The legislation, case law and secondary sources these databases provide overlap to a certain extent. However, each (at the time of writing) offers unique features.

A particular strength of Westlaw is that it includes a Legal Journals Index ("LJI") containing over half a million abstracts of journal articles from English language journals published in the United Kingdom and Europe. The index also allows the user to search all law journals published in the UK back to 1986. An additional subscription service which may be provided by a specific institution allows PDF versions of 32 Sweet & Maxwell full text journals back to 2003 to be downloaded. Whilst a more limited number of journal articles are available in full-text, both full-text articles and article abstracts are indexed and categorised with Sweet & Maxwell's Legal Taxonomy. Full-text and abstracted articles can also be searched for separately with the LJI abstract service providing access to publisher details for each journal referred to.

Westlaw holds the following legal journals which are dedicated to and provide excellent cov- **2–51** erage of Scots law and procedure:

> ➢ Edinburgh Law Review; selected coverage from 1996 onwards.
> ➢ Scots Law Times Articles; selected coverage from 1997 onwards.
> ➢ Scottish Planning Law & Practice; selected coverage from 1986 to 1993.
> ➢ Scottish Planning & Environmental Law; selected coverage from 1993 onwards.
> ➢ Scottish Criminal Law Journal; selected coverage from 2008 onwards.

LexisNexis is particularly useful for accessing materials pertaining to tax law and includes the *Stair Memorial Encyclopaedia* (an important information source for Scots lawyers which is discussed in Ch.8). It also offers free iPhone apps for selected cases.

The content of Westlaw and LexisNexis is regularly updated, with additional features being **2–52** provided or new resources being added to offer users further services. Westlaw's current awareness service is updated daily (excepting weekends) and provides information on "cases, legislation, and legal developments derived from official publications, press releases and legal news relating to the United Kingdom". LexisNexis provides a comparable service in this respect.

Users will, if they enjoy access to both Westlaw and LexisNexis, develop a preference for one, **2–53** generally on the basis that it is more "user friendly" in terms of the ease with which it can be navigated to locate materials of relevance to the researcher's requirements. However, as no single legal database is ever likely to prove totally comprehensive for a researcher's needs, multiple sources of information will need to be consulted. In the context in subscription databases it is extremely useful for the researcher to develop and maintain awareness of the contemporary resources offered by all of the databases they enjoy access to. How to navigate both Westlaw and LexisNexis is discussed is some detail throughout Chs 4–7 and, where applicable, in subsequent chapters.

NB A further subscription database, HeinOnline which focuses mainly on North American jurisdictions, is subscribed to by some Scottish universities. At the time of writing, it does not offer access to Scottish primary sources. However, certain English case reports (1220–1873) are available and as of December 2013 links to these have been added to another subscription database JustCite which also provides links to Westlaw and LexisNexis. See *http://home.heinonline.org/* [accessed May 28, 2014].

How legal databases work

2–54 Legal databases do not work by thinking about the data they contain to retrieve results by concept or legal significance. Instead, they operate by matching the words and phrases entered with words and phrases present in the database. It is important to take this into consideration when undertaking a search.

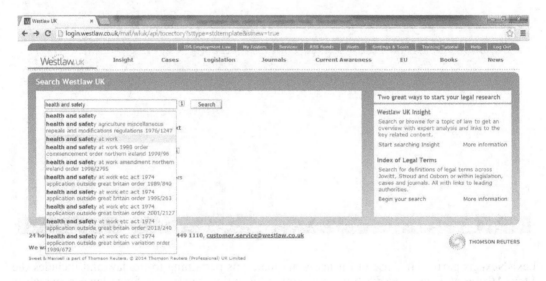

For example, if materials on "health and safety" are being sought and the words "health and safety" are entered in the Westlaw general search terms box, a drop down menu will appear listing various health and safety statutory provisions. If any of these are of relevance, by clicking on same and hitting the search button the required provision will be located. However, if none of the provisions offered are selected and the search proceeds on the basis of the words "health and safety" the system will retrieve all mentions of these words in any resources the user has ticked as it will not automatically know that materials concerning a certain aspect of the law of health and safety are required and will find all materials which contain these words—many of which will be pertinent to another area of law, e.g. employment law.

This feature of databases means that searches using basic free text (simply inputting English **2–55** words or phrases) must be carefully constructed in order to efficiently retrieve meaningful results. Fortunately the majority of legal databases make it easy for a basic free text search to be edited or narrowed once the results of an original search have been evaluated. However, it is far more efficient to construct the appropriate search terms in the first place.

Search techniques for legal databases

At this point it is presumed that the researcher has already considered the fundamental ques- **2–56** tions posed in para.2–33, "What is the purpose of the search?" and "What information is being sought?" The next step is to appreciate, as detailed above, that a database will merely match the terms used with words within it.

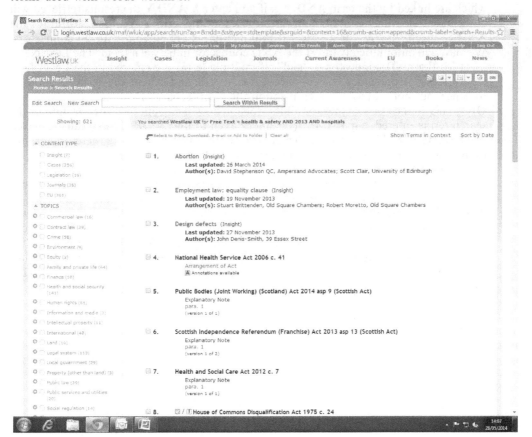

2–57 In the example given above, if the purpose of the search is to find recent legislation on health and safety by typing in "health and safety 2013" to "Search Westlaw" the most recent 2013 provisions are presented in date order. Arguably, the phrase "health and safety 2013" will, in any event, be too general. If the purpose is to locate legislative provisions dealing with health and safety in hospitals, expanding the general search term will restrict the number of results retrieved to a more manageable level and to ones which are more likely to be relevant.

The above illustrates that even a more precise search will yield results prior to 2013 and that further enquiry within the results achieved will be required. However, a search term should not be too specific otherwise relevant materials may well be overlooked. Likewise, if too many terms are used the database will struggle to find exact matches for your search. The search term "health and safety 2013 hospitals Inverness", e.g. yields no matches.

Using Boolean search techniques

2–58 Most databases use "Boolean" search techniques to limit or widen a given search. Boolean searching (named in honour of George Boole, a 19th century English mathematician) means that some words have special roles and they are called Boolean "operators" or "connectors". As the names suggest they affect the way that search terms "connect" to each other.

2–59 The main connectors are:

  ✇ **AND**—This connector searches for material which contains all the search terms entered which are linked by the term **AND**, e.g. if you enter **X AND Y** the results retrieved will all be materials which contain **both** the term **X** and the term **Y**. Westlaw's form for the **AND** connector is "**&**" or a space. If multiple terms are entered with no connectors, Westlaw will automatically insert the AND connector in between them. The LexisNexis form for the **AND** connector is "**and**". If multiple terms are entered in the LexisNexis environment it presumes it is a phrase, i.e. it will find where the terms are found together, but not materials which mention the terms separately.

  ✇ **OR**—This connector searches for all the documents which contain either or both of the search terms entered, e.g. if a search is undertaken to find **X OR Y** the results retrieved will be materials which contain either **X**, **Y**, or both **X OR Y**. This will therefore retrieve more results than using the **AND** connector as it does not limit the results to material where both terms occur. This can be useful where there are alternative names or spellings for a particular subject. In both databases, the **OR** connector (which in both cases is "**or**") searches for either or both search terms within the same materials.

  ✇ **NOT**—This connector searches for material where one search term occurs and the other search term does not occur, e.g. if the search terms is for **X NOT Y**, this connector will only retrieve materials which contain the term **X** and do not contain the term **Y**. The issue here is that if materials containing Y are excluded certain materials which contain both **X** and **Y** will also be excluded. Per LexisNexis, the form for **NOT** is "**and not**". In Westlaw the form is "**%**".

2–60 In addition to the above, both Westlaw and LexisNexis offer further forms of proximity searching. The connectors and symbols available are listed below with selected grammatical and numerical connectors.

Westlaw

Connector	Symbol	Retrieves
AND	& (or a space)	Search terms in the same document: **trade & mark & registration**
OR	or	Either search term or both: **photo** or **photograph**
Phrase	" "	Search terms appearing in the same order as in the quotation marks: **"actus reus"**
Grammatical Connectors	/s	Search terms in the same sentence: **fireraising** /s **wilful**
	/p	Search terms in the same paragraph: **hearsay** /p **admissibility**
	+s	The first term preceding the second within the same sentence: **burden** +s **proof**
	+p	The first term preceding the second within the same paragraph: **right** +p **duty**
Numerical Connectors	/n	Search terms within "n" terms of each other (where "n" is a number): **accused** /3 **jurisdiction**
	+n	The first term preceding the second by "n" terms (where "n" is a number): **capital** +3 **punishment**
BUT NOT	%	Documents not containing the term or terms following the % symbol: **taxation** % **income** Use the % connector with caution; it may cause relevant documents to be excluded from your search result.

Root expander

To search for terms with multiple endings use the "!" character, e.g. "object!", will retrieve object, objects, objected, objection, objecting, objectionable, objective.

To search for words with variable characters, use the * character. When you place the universal **2–61** character within a term, it requires that a character appear in that position, e.g. withdr*w will retrieve withdraw and withdrew.

Westlaw will automatically retrieve irregular plurals, i.e. plurals which are not created by **2–62** adding, as is generally the case, an "s" or "es" to the end of the singular word, e.g. entering "child" will also retrieve "children" and if "forum" is entered "fora" will also be retrieved.

Turn off plurals of a particular term by placing the # symbol in front of the term. For example **2–63** to retrieve "damage", but not "damages", type #damage. Placing the # symbol in front of a term also turns off the automatic retrieval of equivalencies. To retrieve "knife" but not "knives" enter #knife.

2–64 Typing "good-will" will retrieve "good-will", "goodwill" and "good will".

LexisNexis

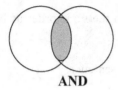 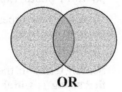 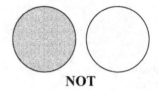

AND   **OR**   **NOT**

AND

2–65 Use AND when all the terms must appear and may be far apart from each other, e.g. "full moon AND wolf".

If searching for a phrase that contains the word "and", omit the word AND from your search, e.g. "up down" would find the phrase "up and down"

AND NOT

2–66 Use AND NOT to exclude specific terms, e.g. the following search would be undertaken if the results sought should not include information about white terriers: "terrarius OR terrier AND NOT white".

> **NB** Because this connector excludes all terms following it, it must be used at the end of a search string.

OR

2–67 Use OR when at least one of the terms must appear (such as synonyms, alternate spellings, or abbreviations), e.g.: angel OR seraphim

W/n

2–68 Use W/n to specify the proximity between the terms. The W/n connector does not specify the word order—either word may appear first, e.g. "delictual liability W/15 nuisance".

To determine the value to use for "n", consider the following as a rule of thumb:

If Seeking...	Use...
Find terms in the same phrase	W/3, W/4, or W/5
Find terms in the same sentence	W/15
Find terms in the same paragraph	W/50

W/s (within sentence), W/p (within paragraph), or W/SEG (within segment) can also be used.

PRE/n

Use PRE/n to find two words when the first word must precede the second word by a specified **2–69** number of words, e.g. the following search, "culpable PRE/3 homicide", would find articles in which "culpable" precedes "homicide" by three or fewer words:

NOT W/n

Use NOT W/n when the first word is required to appear in the document and the second word **2–70** may also appear, but not within "n" words of the first word, e.g. "new NOT W/5 york" would retrieve instances where the word "new" appears separated from the word "york". However, the two words may appear alongside one another viz. "New York" elsewhere in the document.

Further useful search points include: **2–71**

- ➤ When searching for terms with multiple endings use the "!" character.
- ➤ To search for words with variable characters, use the * character.
- ➤ Lexisnexis will automatically retrieve irregular plurals.
- ➤ Turn off plurals for a particular term by placing the w/5 command after the search term and # symbol in front of the term.
- ➤ A hyphen will be read as a space, thus hyphenated words will be understood as two separate words.

Natural language/free text

As shown above, Westlaw and LexisNexis allow a search to be undertaken via natural language **2–72** or free text searching. This means that Boolean searching is not used. The databases will, however, effectively turn the terms input into a Boolean search. Whilst this may seem an easier option for the user, Holland and Webb underscore the fact that "the selection mechanism tends to be relatively crude, so a natural language search can actually throw up more irrelevant material than a well-constructed Boolean search" (*Learning Legal Rules*, 8th edn (Oxford: OUP, 2013)). The example given in para.2–40 is a case in point.

Basic and advanced search options

Whilst the option of a free text search will yield, with time and patience, relevant results and a **2–73** Boolean search will generally provide accurate results more rapidly, advanced search options which allow searching by different fields can well prove to be more productive. Fields might be the title of a legislative provision, the citation of a case, the name of one of both of the parties to litigation and the name of the author of a journal article. Field searching is possible because part of the publishing process has involved words being tagged according to their function within a document. Thus when details of a case are being entered into a database by a publisher, legislation titles, party names, etc., are treated in a different way from the normal text of a document. This ensures that they will be recognised as being a member of a certain class of data, e.g. legislation title data. Field searching allows the researcher to search more efficiently and narrow their search to a much greater extent than either the free text or Boolean method.

Keyword/subject categories

In addition to parts of the document being identified as fields, publishers also classify documents **2–74** into categories by assigning appropriate keywords or subject categories to them. An illustration of this is the case of *Bett v Hamilton*, 1998 J.C. 1 (which also features in Ch.3). In Westlaw this case has been given the subject classification of "criminal law" and two keywords have been assigned to it: "offences against property" and "Scotland". Thus if the researcher accesses Westlaw and uses the advanced search option (located at the top right hand of the cases search page), and enters "offences against property" and "Scotland" into the subject/keyword field they will retrieve this case in the generated list of search results.

2–75 Keyword searches, as discussed earlier in this chapter with reference to open source resources, can be extremely fruitful. However, outcomes, particularly in subscription sources will depend on whether the publisher of a database has classified material in the same way that the user would classify it. Clearly, there will sometimes be a mismatch and a free text and/or Boolean search may still be required.

Expanding or reducing results retrieved

2–76 As previously stated, databases per se allow the researcher to narrow an initial search by searching further or to drill down within the original search results. However, this may not be helpful if the initial search proceeded on the basis of an inappropriate term or phrase.

2–77 If a large number of results are retrieved the following methodology should be adopted:

    ↳ Revisit and rethink the search terms used and consider alternatives.
    ↳ Use the advanced search option as opposed to the basic search and make use of the field options offered by the database. This will limit your search and make it more specific.
    ↳ Make use of basic Boolean techniques, e.g. use the **AND** connector to add additional search terms.

If no or fewer results are achieved and further materials are sought:

    ↳ Check the spelling of the search terms used. Mis-typing is often the culprit in a failed search.
    ↳ Think of alternative words for the initial search terms.
    ↳ Use the **OR** connector to combine search terms.
    ↳ Use the root expander technique "!" suggested in para.2–61 when searching for terms with multiple endings.

Snowballing

2–78 This is a technique which allows a researcher to migrate from a specific to a more general search. If the initial search retrieves useful materials, close attention ought to be paid to the way the database has classified them. This is achieved by locating the subject heading or keywords which have been used to describe them. These terms can then be used to search for further relevant results. References and any relevant links to other documents that are contained in the results can then be followed up. A further search to locate any other materials published by the same author or organisation can then be undertaken as many authors will publish prolifically in the same field.

Summary of when different types of electronic sources should be consulted

2–79 It is not terribly useful to lay down specific guidelines as the sources to be used will vary depending on the nature of the research project and, of course, authorisation or otherwise to access subscription databases. However, some general guidance can be provided:

When to use a search engine:

2–80   ↳ To conduct an initial survey if unfamiliar with the topic;

- ✎ To consult a free source of primary information, such as the Scottish Courts website at *http://www.scotcourts.gov.uk/* [accessed May 28, 2014] or the UK official legislation database at *legislation.gov.uk*;
- ✎ When fast access to a very recent case or piece of legislation is required;
- ✎ When looking for a case which has not been reported; and
- ✎ When seeking access to the original as opposed to the revised version of legislation.

When to consult a gateway:

- ✎ To identify relevant online resources in an area of law that is unfamiliar;   **2–81**
- ✎ To check that an important online source has not been overlooked; and
- ➢ To find links to key materials in one environment—this will save a researcher time as they will not have to bookmark (store each webpage's unique Uniform Resource Identifier ("URI")) for retrieval at a later date.

When to consult a subscription database:

- ➢ When searching for primary legal materials as they will provide revised full text leg-   **2–82** islation and up-to-date information on the status of a case. Subscription databases also contain materials which aid the researcher's appreciation of the significance of primary materials, such as summaries and links to relevant materials which have discussed the case or statute; and
- ➢ When seeking secondary sources, such as full-text journal articles contained in the database where primary sources are analysed or citations for journal articles to be found elsewhere.

HOW TO EVALUATE OPEN SOURCE RESOURCES

The golden rule when undertaking any research project is that the materials found (in electronic **2–83** and paper form) should not be accepted at face value. Clearly, the date of publication of a text book or a journal article will provide a directory digit as to its currency, but it is always worth remembering that some materials in even the most recent editions or volumes will be out-of-date in some respects given the lead in time between their construction and the subsequent date of publication. Likewise, a reported case may have been appealed to a higher court in the interim and awareness of this is vital if a researcher it to generate accurate and up-to-date work. How to categorise and evaluate the validity of legal materials in general is discussed in greater detail throughout Ch.13. However, there are particular issues pertaining to open source resources and these are summarised below:

- ➢ Anyone can post material on the internet and it is highly unlikely that the majority of web pages have been subjected to a quality control process in the way that text books and journal articles are subject to rigorous stages of quality control as they have to be accepted for publication by publishers or an editorial board and then edited by subject-specialists before publication;
- ➢ Essential quality indicators may not be obvious on internet resources, i.e. the source of the material, the date it was written and/or posted, even the country where it originated may not be discernible. In a law library or a subscription database, on the other hand, it is clearly stated who wrote a book, and when, and the legal jurisdiction to which it relates;

> ➢ A search engine, as detailed above, can retrieve thousands or even millions of results. A further downside of this broad brush method of searching is that results are presented in a list ranked by relevancy to search terms used meaning that authoritative sources, such as official sites, e.g. the UK Parliament's *legislation.gov.uk* website, may appear alongside links to utterly inappropriate materials on, e.g. a blog or a chat room. This can lead to the inexperienced researcher consulting such sources in the mistaken belief that because they appear next to an official source of legal information they will contain authoritative materials. This cannot happen in a library which will offer a selection of books or periodicals that have been selected by an academic librarian or law lecturer for their currency and worth.

Criteria for the Evaluation of Online Resources

2–84
- Who wrote the material? Is the author an expert in the field or someone standing on a virtual soapbox?
- Who published it? Is it an individual or an organisation?
- Is it an official site?

Ways of finding answers to these questions include looking for the author's name or the name of whoever has published the site. This may not be obvious from the homepage. If not, enter the author's name into a search engine, such as Bing, and follow up on the results. Is s/he a member of staff at an academic institution? If so, which one? Most university websites list the publications of staff members or research teams as do not for profit legal organisations, e.g. the World Intellectual Property Organization ("WIPO") whose bi-monthly magazine with contributions from experts in the field can be accessed at *http://www.wipo.int/wipo_magazine/en/pdf/2013/* [accessed May 28, 2014]. Such information may also be contained in an "about us" section of a web page which can be accessed from a tab on the site's menu bar. If there is a "contact option" that may give an email or physical address at which to contact the body concerned. There should also be a link at the foot of the homepage of a website to the organisation that sponsors or hosts the site. Investigate the host organisation's website by following any such links.

2–85 If the website is hosted by an academic institution, drill down within the site to find out whether the content has been produced by a single academic department, a researcher or by a team of researchers based in different institutions or organisations located throughout the world. If the author is a person, find out what else they have published. If they are based in the United Kingdom and write about UK legal issues check this by entering their name as an author in the Legal Journals Index which is available as part of the journals section of Westlaw.

2–86 The Uniform Resource Locator ("URL") should also be consulted. This is the web address for the webpage and will be located at the top of the browser, e.g. information about the publisher of this text can be accessed on the W. Green homepage at *http://www.sweetandmaxwell.co.uk/wgreen/* [accessed May 28, 2014]. The URL can also provide further information about the source of the site.

URL Breakdown

- ✎ The server name is the host computer or server for the web page. Sometimes, but not always, it identifies the name of the organisation concerned.
- ✎ The Top Level Domain ("TLD") can be very useful as it provides an indication of the type of organisation that is hosting the site. Here the TLD is .co. which (like .com) means that the organisation is a company or commercial organisation. From this piece

of information alone it can be discerned that the site is of a commercial, rather than an academic nature. Other TLDs include:

> ➤ **.ac* means the organisation is a university, college or school. (The US equivalent is .edu).
> ➤ **.gov* is used by government servers.
> ➤ **.org* is used by non-profit making organisations or charities. The country part of the URL identifies the country where the site is hosted, domestically this is styled *.uk*. Other examples frequently encountered would be:

> - **.au* Australia.
> - **.ca* Canada
> - **.cn* China.
> - **.ie* Ireland.
> - **.in* India.
> - **.nz* New Zealand.
> - **.za* South Africa.

NB In the US many sites do not use their TLD which is *.us*.
.eu identifies official documents and communications emanating from the EU.

Generic TLDs

In 2013, the Internet Corporation for Assigned Names and Numbers ("ICANN"), the orga- **2–87** nisation that assigns TLDs (through the Internet Assigned Numbers Authority), announced that it will be issuing in the region of a 1,400 new generic TLDs (known as gTLDs). At the time of writing, they are exclusively in the sphere of business and commerce, e.g. *.christmas* and *.movie*. However, it is possible that ICANN will release further TLDs in the foreseeable future which may be of assistance to those engaged in legal research. The home page of ICANN which provides regular updates on this organisation's activities can be accessed here, *http://www.icann.org/* [accessed May 20, 2014].

The guiding principle when consulting non-official internet sources is simply that if in doubt **2–88** about the provenance of a site any materials located there should not be included in a research project.

Once the author (or authors) and publisher has been identified, the following questions ought to **2–89** be posed. Whilst not an exhaustive list, it provides initial guidance on how to evaluate open source resources and will enable the inexperienced researcher to begin the process of evaluating the materials located:

1. What is the date of the publication? Although older publications may contain valid information and/or critical comment, the issues under discussion may have been overtaken by, for example, legislative changes or a case being successfully appealed to a higher court. If no date is given, conduct another search including the original search terms and the numerals for the current year and/or the current month and/or the date on which the search is being conducted. This approach can yield recent developments within days, hours or even minutes of the same being published on both official and unofficial sources.

2. Which jurisdiction(s) is the work purporting to cover? Is it referring to Scots law or UK law or that of another jurisdiction? Is it an area of law where UK-wide provisions apply or is it an area where the Holyrood Parliament also has competence to legislate? For a Scots

lawyer determining the extent of a legislative provision is vital. If a provision does not extend to Scotland, i.e. it has no legal effect there, then it has no relevance or applicability to the Scottish legal system.

3. Is any bias declared, for example membership of a particular political party or pressure group? Is the resource trying to sell something and/or is it trying to persuade you to join an organisation? By determining the rationale for and the intended audience of a particular web-based resource the researcher will gain an insight into possible bias in the materials made available. Many lobby groups, political parties and individuals have websites whose primary purpose is to persuade others to follow a particular line of thinking on a specific matter. The objectivity of such a resource will therefore be in doubt. The fact that material contains bias does not, however, automatically render it unreliable. By locating an authoritative source providing a differing viewpoint the researcher can balance the competing arguments and reach a reasoned conclusion, e.g. the Labour Research Department, *http://www.lrd.org.uk/* [accessed May 29, 2014] (founded in 1912), provides UK trade unions et al with information on areas of interest, such as health and safety and various aspects pertaining to employment law. Research emanating from this organisation can be compared and contrasted with official Government publications on these topics to enable the researcher to reach a balanced and rounded conclusion on the issue under scrutiny.

4. How was the research conducted? (Chapter 12 discusses differing research methodologies.) If a source or document presents results of, e.g. a survey of users of a service underpinned by legislation (such as care home residents) seeking information about their experience of the service, the primary question is how much information is given about the research process and the methodology employed? The ultimate question is: can the methodology selected be justified? To answer this, a researcher has to consider whether the methodology has been used appropriately which entails posing further questions. Has it been used according to convention, i.e. followed current academic guidelines in the field concerned? Is it an established methodology or is it considered by the legal establishment to be experimental?

5. Further relevant questions would depend on isolating the methodology employed, but might include: is a copy of the questionnaire used to elicit responses in the public domain? Are details given of sample size and/or is the response rate from the originally selected sample provided? Such questions must be posed to enable the researcher to evaluate whether the published results allow the reader to assess their validity, e.g. if percentages are used, is there sufficient information to allow the reader to convert them to real numbers? (See para.12–22.)

6. How well has the document found been researched? Footnotes/references will provide an indication of the breadth and quality of the sources referred to in a work. If these contain references to previous researchers in the field the next question ought to be: does the document present an argument? If so, how is this presented? Is it supported and convincing in light of the prior sources referred to? Are any conclusions which have been reached based on the evidence presented? It is also worth considering how the document relates to other works. Does it follow on from arguments made or does the conclusion reached disagree with or contradict the findings reached by prior authors? In any event, what do other sources in subsequent documents have to say about it? Has it received critical reviews? If it has, who has been critical? Experts in the field or rivals?

Accuracy

In order to evaluate the accuracy of open source resources, where possible, benchmark research **2–90** findings against official or subscription sources, both electronic and paper. This approach allows the researcher to use their (developing) powers of analysis to evaluate both the quality and accuracy of the information gathered, e.g. compare the information on a website with information in a legal text. If there is a conflict it may mean that the internet resource contains more up-to-date material or it could mean that the internet resource is untrustworthy and should not be used.

Scotland is a small and (almost) unique jurisdiction on the world stage and, although there are **2–91** many valid internet sources of relevance for Scots lawyers, the internet has a strong US bias and many of the materials found through a general search will be relevant only to that legal system. Many domestic websites will also fail to take account of the fact that Scots law is different and distinct from that of the rest of the United Kingdom in many areas thus the margin for error or confusion is great, e.g. The Occupiers' Liability Act 1957 states the law for England and Wales whereas the Occupiers' Liability (Scotland) Act 1960 contains comparable but different provisions in respect of Scotland. Whilst the word "Scotland" might seem logically to differentiate the two, a general internet search using the terms "occupiers liability act" yields page upon page of links to the 1957 provision where links to other jurisdictions, e.g. US, Canada and South Africa, also feature heavily. Searching in this way, the inexperienced researcher, unaware of the separate Scottish equivalent, will likely fall into error. If in doubt about the provenance of a UK statutory provision, search again using the full title of the act and consult an official source and then locate the "extent" section towards the end of the act. Details are given there as to which parts of the United Kingdom a specific act operates in.

Currency

The importance of ensuring that research is up-to-date is stressed throughout this book. Web **2–92** pages, unlike printed publications, can be updated or altered by the author at any time, even on a daily basis. On the other hand, many websites will not have not been updated for months or even years. In dynamic areas of law, web resources, both official and unofficial, may be the best source of information. The example given in para.2–37 per the European Law Monitor's efficacy in tracking prospective EU legislation, see *http://www.europeanlawmonitor.org/* [accessed May 20, 2104] can be consulted then compared with the EU's official website, *http://eur-lex. europa.eu/en/index.htm* [accessed May 29, 2014].

A website may contain a publication date or the date of the last update may be displayed, **2–93** usually at the foot of a page. The "about us" section, if there is one, may also contain details of how frequently the site is refreshed. If a website provides dates for when the website was created and last modified this is a good indicator of currency. If unsure or unclear as to the vintage of a web page click on a selection of the hyperlinks given there—if the links are broken or yield elderly sources this will strongly suggest that the parent site has not been updated recently. Elderly sources have their uses, however, and can still be consulted by way of gathering historical background information for a project looking at, e.g. the genesis and the trajectory of a piece of legislation that has been subsequently amended, perhaps several times or even repealed in its entirety.

The presentation of material on the internet can be an indicator of the quality of the content. **2–94** Obvious grammatical and spelling errors imply that the text has not been carefully reviewed or edited prior to publication, whereas the clear and logical arrangement of a website can suggest that the content was carefully compiled and structured. However, beware—good presentation can also mask poor content. The best indicator of quality is the presence of objectively presented information supported by valid authority.

CITATION OF ELECTRONIC SOURCES

2–95 Where legal material is available in both electronic and paper formats the paper source ought to be cited. This means that if a case, e.g. from Westlaw or an article from HeinOnline is used there is no need to state that it was accessed via the particular database. Instead, it should be referenced as if the paper version had been consulted (see para.13–62). Likewise, databases such as LexisNexis or Westlaw should not be included in a bibliography. When referring to URLs these should be enclosed with < > symbols as this helps to differentiate them from other punctuation, e.g. < *http://www.wgreen.co.uk/* > .

2–96 This system has not been used in *Legal Research Skills for Scots Lawyers* due to the requirement to conform to the publisher's house style. The URL should be split at the end of a line only after the forward slashes in the address. Hyphens or other punctuation should not be added. The case of the characters in the address should not be altered.

2–97 Cases obtained from electronic sources (e.g. the Scottish Courts website) and not otherwise reported should use the neutral citation from its date of introduction. This was introduced in to the senior courts in Scotland from January 1, 2005 (see para.3–36) and into the Privy Council, House of Lords (Supreme Court), Court of Appeal and High Court in England from January 11, 2001 (see para.9–24). This means that judgments from these courts have been issued with unique judgment numbers and case references and are completely independent of published reports. The reason it was adopted was to make it easier to cite and trace unreported judgments.

2–98 Journals that are only published on the internet should be cited with the usual reference details for articles along with the URL for the website and details of the date accessed, e.g. R. Ong, "Regulating Spam in Hong Kong and Malaysia: Lessons from Other Jurisdictions" [2005] 1 JILT, < *http://www2.warwick.ac.uk/fac/soc/law/elj/jilt/2005_1/ong/* > accessed March 29, 2014.

2–99 Web pages should be cited as follows: author or institution, title, (type of document, if relevant), date of issue (if available), <URL> and date accessed, e.g.:

> ➢ The Network of Heads of European Environment Protection Agencies *The Contribution of Good Environmental Regulation to Competitiveness* 2005 < *http://org.eea.europa.eu/ documents/prague_statement/prague_statement-en.pdf* > accessed January 6, 2014;
> ➢ Department of the Environment, Transport and the Regions, *The Government's Response to the Environment, Transport and Regional Affairs Committee's Report,* October 2000 < *http://www.odpm.gov.uk/index.asp?id=1143711* > accessed December 14, 2013;
> ➢ W. Tinning, "Hotel smoking area has legal Lord fuming", *The Herald* (Glasgow April 6, 2007) < *http://www.theherald.co.uk/news/news/display.var.1313196.0.0.php* > accessed April 6, 2014.

Material on CD Rom

As with the internet, if the CD Rom is replicating an existing paper source, reference the paper **2–100** source. Otherwise, include the following details: author/editor, "title" publisher CD Rom, edition or date, e.g. A. Smith, "A Load of Rubbish", Awful Publishing Ltd CD Rom Autumn 2006.

> **NB** CD Rom material is rarely used in practice or at undergraduate/post-graduate level nowadays given the proliferation of electronic databases.

Emails

Email communications should be cited in the following manner: author (type of statement and **2–101** date), e.g.:

> ➢ Statement by Magenta Brown (Personal email correspondence, February 10, 2014).

Chapter 3
An Introduction to Cases

Significant abbreviations used in this chapter

- CSIH—Court of Session Inner House
- CSOH—Court of Session Outer House
- G.W.D.—Greens Weekly Digest
- HCJ—High Court of Justiciary
- HCJAC—High Court of Justiciary Appeal
- H.L.—House of Lords
- JCPC—Judicial Committee Privy Council
- S.L.T.—Scots Law Times
- S.C.—Session Cases
- S.C. (P.C.)—Session Cases Privy Council
- UKHL—UK House of Lords
- UKSC—UK Supreme Court

THE IMPORTANCE OF CASE LAW AND THE DOCTRINE OF JUDICIAL PRECEDENT

3–01 Case law is used to define a legal principle when expressing or arguing a point of law. Before the ability to construct a legal argument can be attained it is essential that familiarity with and a deep understanding of different series of law reports, the various ways in which cases can be located and the layout and content of a reported case are achieved. This chapter will explain the nature of law reporting, provide an introduction to the principal series of law reports of relevance to Scots lawyers and show how the vital skills of reading and analysing cases are developed. Chapter 4 will complement and deepen this knowledge by advising how to locate cases with incomplete information by adopting different search strategies. EU case law is discussed in Ch.10 and cases concerning international law are briefly covered in Ch.11.

3–02 A thorough understanding of the importance of case law is essential as it is one of the primary sources of Scots law, second only to legislation in terms of legal authority. The doctrine of judicial precedent, often referred to in its alternative form, the doctrine of stare decisis (Latin for "let the decision stand") allows judgments in previous cases to influence decisions in later cases. The strict version of this doctrine means that: "[a] single decision from a qualifying court will bind all future courts dealing with the same point of law" (M.C. Meston, et al, *The Scottish Legal Tradition*, new enl. edn (1991), p.11). Meston's definition encompasses two important concepts surrounding the decision reached in an earlier (prior) case. For the doctrine to operate the case concerned has to be: (a) "in point", meaning that it concerns the same point of law; and (b) come from a "qualifying" court. If both of these elements are in place the prior case is binding, requiring a subsequent court to follow the earlier decision.

This is the theory, but, in practice, there are techniques which the judiciary can employ to avoid **3-03** following a binding precedent, e.g. a contemporary qualifying court can, as shown below, convene a larger court to overrule a binding precedent, i.e. the contemporary court sits with a greater number of judges than that of the court creating the case precedent. Further discussion of the doctrine of judicial precedent is to be found in *The Laws of Scotland: Stair Memorial Encyclopaedia*, Vol. 22 paras 334–345 and R.M. White and I.D. Willock, *The Scottish Legal System*, 5th edn (Haywards Heath: Bloomsbury, 2013) pp.297–316.

Prior cases can be binding or persuasive in a current case. The status of the previous case will **3-04** depend on the position in the court hierarchy of the court which heard it. In general, decisions from a court higher in the hierarchy will bind a lower court which must apply the prior decision whereas decisions of a lower court in the same hierarchy can persuade a higher court to follow the legal reasoning therein but the higher court is never bound to do so.

The status of the court: is it a qualifying court?

Civil Courts: hierarchy   **3-05**

Sheriff Court	***bound*** by decisions of	Inner House of the Court of Session, UK Supreme Court* (previously the House of Lords) and the Court of Justice of the European Union**
	usually follows (but not bound to)	Decisions of own Sheriff Principal
	not bound by decisions of	Other Sheriffs, Sheriffs Principal in other Sheriffdoms or Lords Ordinary sitting in the Outer House of the Court of Session
Sheriff Principal	***bound*** by decisions of	Inner House of the Court of Session, UK Supreme Court,* and the Court of Justice of the European Union**
	not bound by decisions of	Sheriffs, other Sheriffs Principal or Lords Ordinary
Lord Ordinary	***bound*** by decisions of	Inner House of the Court of Session, UK Supreme Court,* and the Court of Justice of the European Union**
	not bound by decisions of	Sheriffs, Sheriffs Principal or other Lords Ordinary
Inner House	**bound** by decisions of	Either of its Divisions, UK Supreme Court,* and the Court of Justice of the European Union**
	has power to overrule a previous Inner House decision by convening a larger court	
	not bound by decisions of	Sheriffs, Sheriffs Principal or Lords Ordinary
UK Supreme Court	***bound by*** decisions of	Court of Justice of the European Union; can however overrule its own previous decision (See Practice Statement [1966] 3 All E.R. 77, [1966] 1 W.L.R. 1234, HL)

* Decisions in Scottish appeals are binding. (Criminal Proceedings etc. (Reform) (Scotland) Act 2007.) Decisions in non-Scottish cases concerning statutory provisions which are applicable in both jurisdictions are probably binding.

Decisions in non-Scottish cases on areas of law which are different are not binding, but can be persuasive if they concern matters of general jurisprudence. This is discussed in greater depth in *The Laws of Scotland: Stair Memorial Encyclopaedia*, Vol. 22, paras. 270–285. See para.8–04 for further information about this publication.

** Only if the decision requires consideration of the meaning or effect of any EU treaty or secondary legislative provision (See Ch.10 and s.3 of the European Communities Act 1972).

3–06 *Criminal courts: hierarchy*

Justice of the Peace Court (JP) (formerly the District Court)	**bound** by decisions of	"A magistrate sitting in the district (now JP) court is *probably bound* by rulings of any superior criminal court or of a single judge or sheriff", D.M. Walker, *The Scottish Legal System*, 8th edn (Edinburgh: W. Green, 2001) p.447.
Sheriff Court	**bound** by decisions of	High Court of Justiciary (Appeal)
	not bound by decisions of	Other Sheriffs, will consider and treat the rulings of single judges in the High Court of Justiciary (trial) with the greatest of respect
High Court of Justiciary (Trial)	**bound by** decisions of	High Court of Justiciary (Appeal)
	not bound by decisions of	Single judges in the High Court of Justiciary (Trial) but will likely follow such prior decisions
High Court of Justiciary (Appeal)	has power to *overrule*	A previous High Court appeal decision by convening a larger court
	not bound by decisions of	UK Supreme Court unless a **Devolution issue** (discussed in Ch.5) is under consideration.

Which part of the previous decision is binding?

3–07 To the non-lawyer the most interesting part of a case is the outcome, but to those studying law it is almost an irrelevance. The prime point of interest is the legal reasoning adopted by the court in order to reach its decision. However, not all of the previous case (precedent) under scrutiny is binding. Only the part which deals with the "reasoning on the same point of law" is held to be "in point". This element of the prior case is referred to as the ratio decidendi.

3–08 There is no agreed definition of the ratio decidendi and little clear guidance exists on how to identify it. Indeed, lawyers will often disagree about the content of a particular ratio decidendi which will then give rise to both legal argument and debate before a court to allow a judge(s) to provide a definitive answer. The situation is further complicated by the fact that some cases may have no ratio decidendi at all, while others may have more than one and, pivotally, that even the agreed ratio decidendi of a particular case may not remain static. Later cases may re-interpret it and it is possible for a rule which emerged from the original case to be expanded or contracted by a court over a period of time. In any event, discerning the ratio decidendi of a case requires skills of analysis and interpretation.

One way of developing these skills is to read as many cases as possible and construct a case note **3–09** for leading cases (initially as directed by tutors) that will include a brief explanation of the reason(s) for the decision reached by the court in each instance. Before this can be achieved familiarity with the major series of case reports and with the general format and form of judgments is required. These vital pre-requisites to authoring a case note which isolates the ratio decidendi of a case are explored below.

NB Per curiam, meaning "by the court", are explicit statements of the law made by the court (one with multiple judgments) to clarify a point of law. There may be one judgment given by one judge on behalf of the whole court, or the other judges may make comment.

The per curiam statement will probably not form part of the ratio decidendi of the case, but is nevertheless intended to be an authoritative statement of the law. Statements per curiam may be found near the end of case report or they may be in the head note (rubric), e.g. *MacGillivray v Johnston*, 1994 S.L.T. 1012.

Importance of the current status of a case

Not only is it important to know the outcome of a case it is also essential to be aware of the **3–10** current status of that case as a decision from a lower court may be appealed to a higher court or courts, which may overturn or ultimately reinstate the original decision. Even when a final decision is reached a case may be overruled by a later case and thereafter have no value or affect whatsoever as a case precedent.

There are various things that can happen to a case during its lifetime. These are referred to in the **3–11** following terms:

> ➢ *Affirmed*: The present court agrees with the decision of a lower court concerning the same case.
> ➢ *Applied*: The present court accepts that it is bound by the ratio decidendi of a previous case and applies the same reasoning in the present case.
> ➢ *Approved*: The present court agrees that a decision made by a previous lower court was correctly decided.
> ➢ *Considered/Discussed/Commented on*: These terms all mean that the present court has entertained discussion or debate on the earlier case.
> ➢ *Distinguished*: The present court decides that an apparently binding precedent is not in point as it has found material differences between the two cases. It, therefore, does not have to follow the previous case. However, the previous case still remains as authority for future cases which are in point.
> ➢ *Overruled*: The present court rejects a previous decision of a lower court. The earlier decision is struck out and can no longer be used as authority on the legal point under consideration there.
> ➢ *Reversed*: The present court disagrees with the decision of a lower court concerning the same case.

THE REPORTING OF CASES

Reported cases

3–12 Vast numbers of cases are heard by Scottish courts every year, but only a small percentage of these are reported in law reports. A case report is a very different creature from that of the report of a case appearing in the media. Whereas the latter seeks to inform and/or entertain, cases which are reported in the law reports are those which carry legal significance, i.e. cases (generally appellate decisions) which clarify or perhaps define a new principle of law or those which interpret a particular part of legislation for the first time. A permanent record of proceedings is not automatically kept for all cases heard in court. In criminal cases no transcript is kept of summary trials and the same is true in the civil sphere for small claims and summary cause cases in the sheriff court.

3–13 Editors of the various law reports decide which cases are to be reported and this may result in the same case appearing in several different series of law reports. If this occurs, a case will have more than one citation, both or all of which can be consulted with confidence.

3–14 The selection criteria used by the editorial team of Scots Law Times (S.L.T.) one of the leading case report series published in Scotland (by Thomson Reuters) are as follows:

> ➢ Cases which make new law, either because they deal with novel situations or extend the application of existing rules.
> ➢ Cases where the judges restate old principles of law in modern terms or which are examples of modern applications of old principles.
> ➢ Cases where the law is clarified by an appellate court when inferior courts have reached conflicting decisions; also non-appellate decisions discussing issues regularly litigated, e.g. the distinction between murder and culpable homicide.
> ➢ Cases which interpret legislation, unless the matter is of little general application beyond the parties involved.
> ➢ Cases which interpret clauses in, e.g. contracts and wills, which are likely to be of wider application.
> ➢ Cases where the courts clarify points of practice or procedure.
> ➢ Cases which, while turning on their facts, may be of guidance in comparable cases, e.g. decisions of damages and the balance of convenience when considering an application for an interim interdict.

Cases which turn purely on questions of fact, trite law (a commonly known and undisputed, principle of law) bad pleading or which generally contain nothing which has not already been laid down in prior reported cases will not be reported.

Unreported cases

3–15 The fact that a case has not been formally reported in a law report series has no effect whatsoever on its weight as a precedent. Even in the recent past it was relatively difficult to obtain transcripts of unreported cases. This has become somewhat easier with the advent of courts in most jurisdictions publishing their decisions on their own websites and the fact that both open source and subscription databases will generally include selected unreported cases. In Scotland, transcripts of unreported cases may also be obtained (for research purposes) by contacting the Operations and Policy Unit at the Scottish Court Service (*enquiries@scotcourts.gov.uk*). The increased availability and use of unreported cases has resulted in a new citation system for cases and this is detailed in para.3–36.

Definition of a law report

A law report is not a verbatim account of the whole court proceedings. Therefore it will not **3–16** (generally) contain an account of the evidence led or the names of witnesses etc. The only facts to be included in a law report are those relevant to the legal issue under determination. Thus fact and law are separate component parts of a reported case. Once facts have been established to the required legal standard, a judicial decision is then reached on the point (or points) of law.

HOW CASES ARE PUBLISHED

The development of law reporting in Scotland

Early Scottish law reports were known as "Practicks". These date from the 15th century to the **3–17** early 17th century and are hardly recognisable as a law report as we understand them today. They have been described as embryo law reports (*Stair Society, An Introductory Survey of the Sources and Literature of Scots Law* (Edinburgh, 1936), p.27) as they tended to be notes compiled by judges for their own use where publication for the benefit of a wider audience was not envisaged. They were brief in the extreme consisting of little more than details of the parties' names and the legal principle(s) involved.

Examples of published collections of Practicks are: **3–18**

- ➢ Balfour's Practicks (1469–1579)
- ➢ Spotiswoode's Practicks (1541–1637)
- ➢ Hope's Minor Practicks (1608–1633)
- ➢ Hope's Major Practicks (1608–1633)

Further information about the Practicks can be found in the Stair Society publication, *An Introductory Survey of the Sources and Literature of Scots Law* (Edinburgh, 1936), Ch.3.

In the 17th century many different individuals published private collections of case reports **3–19** which were then circulated amongst legal practitioners. Gradually, law reporting became more formalised. A significant step forward occurred at the beginning of the 19th century with the restructuring of the Court of Session. From 1821, cases from the Court of Session were reported in the Session Cases (S.C.) volume of case reports and it was with this innovation that the modern system of law reporting was born.

Modern law reporting

Some introductory points: **3–20**

- ➢ As detailed above, some cases are reported in different series of law reports. If this occurs, the most authoritative law report for that jurisdiction should be cited. In Scotland, the most authoritative series of law reports is S.C. followed by the S.L.T.;
- ➢ Some series of law reports are full text and others are digests/summaries, e.g. S.C. is a full text series, whilst Green's Weekly Digest (G.W.D.), for example, contains short summaries of cases;
- ➢ Some series are general and others are specific to one area of law. The main series of law reports are general, they report cases across the legal spectrum, whereas specialist

series publish according to subject matter, e.g. Fleet Street Reports only includes cases concerning intellectual property matters;

➤ Law reports are published by year in chronological order and most series are bound in annual volumes. The current year's issues appear as slim paper booklets prior to being bound into annual volumes and are usually located beside the annual volumes in a law library;

➤ Many, but not all, series of law reports are now available electronically and can be found in several of the major subscription legal databases.

3–21 The principal modern series of law reports

Title	**Session Cases**
Abbreviation	S.C.
Citation	Since 1907 (apart from the addition of Privy Council decisions from 2001—2009 and UK Supreme Court decisions from 2009 onwards) the citation has been as follows.

Each annual volume consists of four parts which are paginated separately:

(a) Scottish cases decided by the Judicial Committee of the Privy Council referred to as S.C. (P.C.), e.g. *Robertson v Higson*, 2006 S.C. (P.C.) 22;

(b) Scottish cases decided by the House of Lords, referred to as S.C. (H.L.), e.g. *Martinez v Grampian Health Board*, 1996 S.C. (H.L.) 1;

Scottish cases decided by the UK Supreme Court 2009 onwards (civil and devolution issues) referred to as S.C. (U.K.S.C.), e.g. *Cadder v HMA*, 2011 S.C. (U.K.S.C.) 13;

(d) Cases decided by the High Court of Justiciary, referred to as J.C., e.g. *Smart v HM Advocate*, 2006 J.C. 119;

(e) Cases decided by the Court of Session, referred to as S.C., e.g. *Brown v Brown*, 1972 S.C. 123.

The series of Session Cases which appeared between 1821 and 1906 are referred to by the names of the five respective editors:

First Series	Shaw S.	16 Vols 1821–1838
Second Series	Dunlop D.	24 Vols 1838–1862
Third Series	MacPherson M.	11 Vols 1862–1873
Fourth Series	Rettie R.	25 Vols 1873–1898
Fifth Series	Fraser F.	8 Vols 1898–1906

These are cited by the volume number, the initial of the editor and the page number, e.g. *M'Calman v M'Arthur* (1864) 2 M. 678. This indicates that you will find the report in Session Cases, third series, Vol.2, edited by MacPherson, at p.678.

The series began by covering decisions in the Court of Session. The House of Lords (Scottish appeals) was covered from 1850 and was separately paginated, e.g. (year) 3 M. (H.L.) page no. The High Court of Justiciary was included from 1874 and was paginated separately, e.g. (year) 2 F. (J.) page number.

Period covered	1821 to present
Publisher and Editor	The Scottish Council of Law Reporting, A.F. Stewart.
Comments	In Scotland the Session Cases series of law reports is the most authoritative.
	The judgments are revised by the judge prior to publication.
	Be wary of separate pagination.
Courts covered	Court of Session, High Court of Justiciary, Lands Valuation Appeal Court and all decisions on Scottish appeals to the UK Supreme Court (House of Lords and the Judicial Committee of the Privy Council).
Format	These reports are arranged as follows:
	(a) List of judges in the courts covered;
	(b) Index of case names—accessible by either party's name. These are arranged in sections under the relevant court:

> **NB** Court of Session (includes Lands Valuation Appeal Court).

	At the back of each volume is the following information:
	(a) Index of Matters—a subject index. It includes "Words and Phrases" as a heading.
	(b) Cases referred to judicially in that volume in alphabetical order of the first party.
	(c) Cases affirmed, reversed, commented on, etc. in that volume, in alphabetical order of first party's names.
Updated	six times a year.
Title	**Scots Law Times**
Abbreviation	S.L.T.
Citation	
Full report from superior court	*Kapri v Lord Advocate*, 2013 S.L.T 743
Notes of a report	*F. MacGregor v MacNeill*, 1975 S.L.T. (Notes) 54
Sheriff Court report	*Gardner v Edinburgh City Council*, 2006 S.L.T. (Sh. Ct) 166
Land Court report	*Crofters Commission v Mackay*, 1997 S.L.T. (Land Ct) 2
Lands Tribunal of Scotland report	*DSM Nutritional Products v Assessor for Ayrshire Valuation Joint Board*, 2014 S.L.T. (Lands Tr) 7
Lyon Court report	*Douglas-Hamilton, Petitioner*, 1996 S.L.T. (Lyon Ct) 8
Previous citation convention between 1893–1908	Citation was by volume, e.g. *Thomson v Landale*, (1897) 5 S.L.T. 204
Period covered	1893 to present
Publisher and Editor	W. Green, B. Dragotta, S. Hyslop.

Comments	Be wary of the separate pagination.
	Publishes law reports and articles and practitioner orientated information. Contains cases from 1893. Forty paper issues per year.
Courts covered	UK Supreme Court, (Privy Council, House of Lords), Court of Session, High Court of Justiciary, sheriff courts, Scottish Land Court, Lands Valuation Appeal Court, Lands Tribunal for Scotland and Court of the Lord Lyon.
Format	The annual volumes consist of the following information:
	(a) List of judges in the Court of Session.
	(b) The law reports are arranged in sections relating to the court which heard the case. The sections are separately paginated and contain separate indexes of cases, case reports and indexes of cases according to subject matter. The sections are:
	Superior courts, sheriff courts, Scottish Land Court, Lands Tribunal for Scotland, Lyon Court.
	News section. This includes:
	Articles, Acts of Adjournal/Sederunt, appointments, book reviews, business changes, case commentaries, coming events, general information, letters to the editor, parliamentary news, obituaries/ appreciations, subject index and taxation.
	Since 1989 two annual volumes have been produced.
	Volume one contains:
	List of judges in Court of Session
	Superior court cases and indexes
	Volume two contains:
	Index of all cases in the two volumes in one index, but organised in separate sections
	News section
	Cases and indexes for cases in sheriff court, Scottish Land Court, the Lands Tribunal of Scotland and the Lyon Court
Details of updates	Published weekly. Cumulative indexes are published after every ten issues.
	1961–90 and 1991–2002 cover cases reported in the SLT during these years.
Title	**Scottish Civil Law Reports**
Abbreviation	S.C.L.R.
Citation	e.g. *M v State Hospitals Board for Scotland* (OH) 2013 S.C.L.R. 745 *Johnstone v Finneran* (Sh. Ct) 2003 S.C.L.R. 157 (Notes)
Period covered	1987 to present
Publisher and Editor	The Law Society of Scotland, Sheriff M.J. Fletcher.
Comments	Commentaries are included for selected cases.
Courts covered	UK Supreme Court (Privy Council, House of Lords), Court of Session, sheriff court.

Format	Annual volumes contain the following information:
	(a) Index of cases reported by name—accessible by both parties' name.
	(b) Digest of cases—arranged by subject matter. "Words" is included as a heading.
	(c) Statutes, Statutory Instruments and Court Rules judicially considered.
	(d) Cases judicially considered.
	(e) Case reports. The cases are arranged in two sections: full reports and notes which are paginated as one. Some of the cases are accompanied by commentaries by experts in the area of law concerned.
Updated	Paper and online six times a year.
Consolidated indexes	Index 1987–1996. This consolidates the information contained in the first four tables above for the period.
Title	**Scottish Criminal Case Reports**
Abbreviation	S.C.C.R.
Citation	e.g. *Bennett v HM Advocate*, 2006 S.C.C.R. 62
Period covered	1981 to present
Publisher and Editor	The Law Society of Scotland, Sheriff G.H. Gordon, Q.C.
Comments	Commentaries are by the editor
Courts covered	UK Supreme Court per devolution issues (previously the Privy Council) High Court of Justiciary, sheriff court
Format	The annual volumes contain the following information:
	(a) List of judges in the High Court of Justiciary
	(b) Index of reported cases—accessible by both parties' names
	(c) Digest of cases according to the subject matter which includes "Words" as a heading
	(d) Statutes and Statutory Instruments judicially considered
	(e) Cases judicially considered
	(f) Case reports. Selected cases are followed by commentaries.
Updated	Paper and online six times a year.
	Cases reported
	Digest of cases
	Statutes and Statutory Instruments judicially considered
	Cases judicially considered
	The Indexes include cases reported in Justiciary Cases, S.L.T. and the 1981–1990 index includes cases reported in the S.C.C.R. Supplement 1950–80.
	The Scottish Criminal Case Reports Supplement (1950–1980). This addition to the series contains a selection of cases decided by the High Court between 1950–80 which had not been previously reported.
	It contains the following information:
	(a) Index of cases reported—accessible by both parties' names
	(b) Digest of cases according to subject matter

(c) Statutes and Statutory Instruments judicially considered between 1950– 80

(d) Cases judicially considered between 1950–80

(e) Case reports

Title	**Greens Weekly Digest**
Abbreviation	G.W.D.
Citation	Within G.W.D. the cases are referred to by issue number and paragraph number, e.g. 2014 *Donaldson v Scottish Legal Aid Board*, G.W.D. 12–218. This case will be found in the 2014 folder in Issue 12 at para.218.
Period covered	1986 to present
Publisher and Editor	W. Green, B. Dragotta, S. Hyslop
Comments	It reports all decisions of the Scottish courts received by W. Green. Reports of significance are subsequently reported more fully elsewhere. Arranged by subject
Courts covered	UK Supreme Court (previously Privy Council, House of Lords), Court of Session, High Court of Justiciary, sheriff court, Scottish Land Court.
Format	Annual Service Files contain:
	(a) Index of cases digested (alphabetical by first party's name)
	(b) Index of subject matter
	(c) Table of statutes considered
	(d) Table of quantum of damages
	(e) Case digests
Updated	40 times a year. Cumulative indexes are published three times a year. Index 1986–1995—consolidates all four indexes for that period.

3–22 *Specialist Series of Scottish Law Reports*

Title	**Greens Reparation Law Reports**
Abbreviation	Rep.L.R.
Citation	*Forbes v City of Dundee District Council*, 1997 Rep.L.R. 48
Period covered	1996 to present
Publisher and Editor	W. Green, D. Kinloch
Comments	Includes commentaries
Available in	&
Courts covered	UK Supreme Court (previously House of Lords), Court of Session, Sheriff court
Format	Editorial and case reports with a separate quantum cases section. Some cases are in note form.
Updated	six times a year.
Consolidated indexes	Annual consolidated index containing an alphabetical list of first named parties and an index of subject matter.
Title	**Greens Housing Law Reports**
Abbreviation	Hous.L.R.

Citation	*Johnston v Dundee City Council*, 2006 Hous.L.R. 68
Period covered	1996 to present
Publisher and Editor	W. Green, M. Dailly
Comments	Includes commentaries on the cases.
Courts covered	UK Supreme Court (House of Lords), Court of Session, Sheriff court, Lands Tribunal for Scotland, Decisions of Local Government Ombudsmen, Housing Association Ombudsmen.
Format	Editorial
	Case reports
Update	four issues a year.
Title	**Greens Family Law Reports**
Abbreviation	Fam.L.R.
Citation	*Treasure v McGrath*, 2006 Fam.L.R. 100
Period covered	1997 to present
Publisher and Editor	W. Green, R.P. Macfarlane and J.M.L. Scott
Comments	Commentaries are provided
Courts covered	European Court of Human Rights, UK Supreme Court (House of Lords), Court of Session, sheriff court
Format	Editorial
	Subject index
	Case reports
Update	six issues a year.
Title	**Scottish Land Court Reports**
Abbreviation	S.L.C.R.
Citation	e.g. *Cawdor Trustees v Mackay*, 2005 S.L.C.R. 76
Period covered	1913 to present
Courts covered	Scottish Land Court
Format	Index of cases (alphabetical order of first party)
	Case reports
	Digest of cases via subject headings
	Free digests of cases since 1982 are available online (*http:// www.scottish-land-court.org.uk/digest.html*) as are recent unreported decisions (*http:// www.scottish-land-court.org.uk/recent.html*)

Reporting of Scottish Cases in England

Some Scottish cases appear in the following series of English law reports: **3–23**

> ➤ Appeal Cases;
> ➤ Weekly Law Reports; and
> ➤ All England Law Reports

The English law report series and other legal resources are discussed in Ch.9.

Specialist series of law reports covering the United Kingdom

3–24 There is an increasing range and number of specialist series of law reports. Examples include: British Company Cases ("B.C.C."), Environmental Law Reports ("Env.L.R."), Family Law Reports ("F.L.R."), Industrial Cases Reports ("I.C.R."), Industrial Relations Law Reports "(I.R.L.R."), Medical Law Reports ("Med.L.R.") and Reports of Tax Cases ("T.C.").

3–25 *Older Series of Scottish Law Reports*

Title	**The Scottish Law Reporter** &
Abbreviation	S.L.R. or Sc.L.R.
Period covered	1865–1924 (Vols 1–61)
Courts covered	House of Lords, Court of Session, Court of Justiciary, Court of Teinds
Format	Index of cases (either party's surname)
	Index of statutes
	Index of subjects
	Case reports
	(all paginated together)
Title	**Sheriff Court Reports** (Sh. Ct. Rep.) (usually to be found bound as Scottish Law Review and Sheriff Court Reporter) &
Abbreviation	S.L.R. or S.L.Rev. or Sc.L.R.
Period covered	1885–1963 (Vols 1–79)
Courts covered	Sheriff Court
Format	First part contains collections of the Scottish Law Review. These contain articles and professional news/information.
	Second part (all in the one volume) is Sheriff Court Reports:
	Contents
	Index of cases (either party)
	Digest of cases accessible via subject headings
	Scottish Land Court Reports
	Index of cases
	Case reports
	Digest of cases accessible via subject headings
Title	**Scottish Jurist**
Abbreviation	S.J. or Sc. Jur.
Period covered	1829–1873
Courts covered	House of Lords, Court of Session, Court of Justiciary, Court of Teinds
Format	Index of Matters (subject index)
	Index of case names
	Court of Session (pursuer and defender)
	Court of Session (defender and pursuer)
	House of Lords
	High Court of Justiciary
	English decisions generally applicable to Scots law
	Scottish cases

Title	**Morison's Dictionary of Decisions**
Abbreviation	M. or Mor.
Period covered	1540–1808
Format	This collection of cases consists of twenty two volumes. There are 19 volumes of cases. Volumes 20 and 21 contain a digest of cases from the main volumes. Volume 22 contains supplementary material. There is an Appendix which includes cases which were reported while the Dictionary was being published.

The work is paginated continuously throughout all the volumes. It is not referred to by volume number but by year and page number, e.g. *Johnston v Napier* (1708) M. 16511.

Other works are frequently kept with *Morison's Dictionary*:

Morison's Synopsis (1808–1816)

Tait's Index. This contains an index of the cases in *Morison's Dictionary* in alphabetical order of pursuer.

Brown's Supplement (1628–1794) (B.S.). This covers cases which were not included in *Morison's Dictionary*.

Old reports which covered House of Lords decisions in Scottish appeals

Brown's Synopsis of Decisions (1540–1827) Robertson (1707–27); Craigie, Stewart and Paton **3–26** (1726–1821); Dow (1813–1818); Bligh (1819–1821); Shaw; (1821–1824); Wilson & Shaw (1825–1835); Shaw & Maclean (1835–1838); Maclean & Robinson (1839); Robinson (1840–41); Bell (1842–1850); MacQueen (1851–1865); Paterson (1851–73)

NB From 1850 Scottish appeals to the House of Lords were reported in S.C.

Old reports which covered Court of Session decisions

Morison's Dictionary of Decisions (1540–1808); Brown's Synopsis of Decisions ; (1540–1827); **3–27** Durie (1621–1642); Brown's Supplement (1622–1794); English Judges; (1655–1661); Stair (1661–1681); Gilmour and Falconer (1665–1677); Dirleton (1665–1677); Fountainhall (1678–1712); Harcarse (1681–1691); Dalrymple (1698–1718); Forbes (1705–1713); Bruce (1714–1715); Kames (Remarkable Decisions) (1716–1752); Edgar (1724–1725); Elchies (1733–1754); Clerk Home (1735–1744); Kilkerran (1738–1752); Falconer (1744–1751); Kames (Select Decisions) (1752–1768); Hailes (1766–1791); Bell (1790–1792); Bell (1794–1795); Hume (1781–1822); Deas and Anderson (1829–1833); Scottish Jurist (1829–1873); Scottish Law Reporter (1865–1924); Faculty Collection/Faculty Decisions (Old Series) (1752–1808); Faculty Collection/Faculty Decisions (New Series) (1808–1825); Faculty Collection/Faculty Decisions (Octavo Series) (1825–1841); Bell's Dictionary of Decisions (1808–1832).

NB From 1821 Court of Session cases were reported in S.C.

Old reports which covered High Court of Justiciary decisions

3–28 Shaw (1819–1831); Syme (1826–1830); Swinton (1835–1841); Broun (1842–1845); Arkley (1846–1848); Shaw (1848–1851); Irvine (1851–1868); Couper (1868–1885); White (1885–1893); Adam (1893–1916).

NB From 1874 decisions of the High Court of Justiciary were reported in Session Cases.

Old reports covering decisions of other courts

3–29 Fergusson (1811–1817)—Consistorial Court; Murray (1815–1830)—Jury Court; McFarlane (1838–1839)—Jury Court; Shaw (1821–1831)—Teind Court.

Old reports of sheriff court decisions

3–30 Guthrie's Select Sheriff Court Decisions (1854–1892); Scottish Law Review (1885–1963).

NB Sheriff court decisions have been reported in Scots Law Times since 1893. More detailed information on old sheriff court records can be found in the Stair Society publication, *An Introductory Survey of the Sources and Literature of Scots Law* (Edinburgh, 1936) Ch.10. Many of the old collections of reports were reprinted at the beginning of this century in a series called Scots Revised Reports, which contains selected cases from *Morison's Dictionary*, part of the Faculty Collection/Faculty Decisions, House of Lords Appeals, *Shaw, Dunlop, Macpherson* and cases reported only in the Scottish Jurist between 1829–65.

3–31 More detailed information on the old series of law reports can be found in *Stair Society, An Introductory Survey of the Sources and Literature of Scots Law* (1936), Ch.4.

Citation conventions

3–32 In order to locate cases in the various law reports it is necessary to become familiar with the referencing system for cases. The reference for a case is called its "citation". The citation of a case is made up of five elements:

> ➤ The name of the case—this will usually be the names of the parties involved;
> ➤ The year in which the decision was reported;
> ➤ The volume number of the relevant report, if applicable;
> ➤ The abbreviation used to denote a particular law report—a table of abbreviations appears at the start of the book;
> ➤ The page number of the volume at which the case report begins.

In order to locate a case, follow the citation, for example:

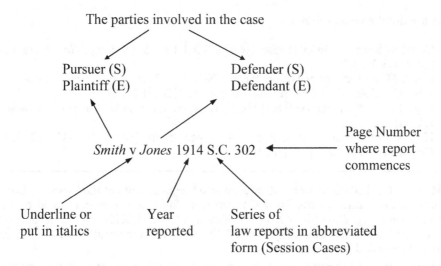

Civil cases

The parties are usually referred to by the pursuer's name followed by defender's name, e.g. **3–33** *White v Green*. If the case is appealed the order is reversed, i.e. *Green v White*.

Criminal cases

In cases where solemn procedure is used (where the judge sits with a jury of 15 people), the **3–34** Crown is referred to as Her Majesty's Advocate (HM Advocate/HMA). If the case is prosecuted under summary procedure (without a jury), the surname of the Procurator Fiscal is used to represent the Crown. In certain cases where anonymity is to be preserved the parties are referred to by initials, e.g. *A v B*.

> **NB** In England and Wales, criminal cases are cited thus; *R v Smith*. "R" stands for Rex or Regina depending on whether there is a King or Queen on the throne at the relevant time.

Others

Since 2001 law reports published by Sweet & Maxwell (e.g. Criminal Appeal Reports, etc.) have **3–35** used a case number as opposed to a page number as their citation, e.g. *Dyson Ltd v Registrar of Trade Marks* [2007] 2 C.M.L.R. 14 refers to case number 14 of the second volume of the 2007 Common Market Law Reports.

Media neutral citations

A system of media neutral citation was introduced into some Scottish courts from January 1, **3–36** 2005. This means that opinions from the Court of Session, High Court of Justiciary and High Court of Justiciary sitting as an appeal court have been issued with unique judgment numbers. This system means that case references are completely independent of published reports. The reason it has been adopted is to make it easier to cite and trace unreported judgments.

3–37 Opinions are numbered as follows:

> ➤ Court of Session, Outer House: [year] CSOH 1 (2, 3, etc.), e.g. *Hawthorne v Anderson* [2014] CSOH 65;
> ➤ Court of Session, Inner House: [year] CSIH 1 (2, 3, etc.), e.g. *The Assessor for Lothian Valuation Joint Board v Over the Counter Ltd* [2014] CSIH 28;
> ➤ High Court of Justiciary: [year] HCJ 1 (2, 3, etc.), e.g. *HM Advocate v Voudouri* [2006] HCJ 4;
> ➤ High Court of Justiciary sitting as an appeal court: [year] HCJAC 1 (2, 3, etc.), e.g. *Chalmers v HM Advocate* [2014] HCJAC 24.

NB Media neutral citations were introduced into the judgments of the House of Lords and the Judicial Committee of the Privy Council from 2001 and were continued by the UK Supreme Court, e.g. *Davidson v Scottish Ministers* [2005] UKHL 74; *North and others v Dumfries and Galloway Council* [2013] UKSC 45. Media neutral citations for English courts are discussed further in Ch.9.

Paragraph numbering

3–38 With effect from January 1, 2005, all Scottish opinions are issued with paragraph numbering but no page numbers. Any particular paragraph of the case to be referred to is cited in square brackets at the end of the neutral citation, e.g. *Allan v HMA* [2014] HCJA 60 [12]. This means that the reference is to para.12 of *Allan v HMA* which was the first opinion of the High Court of Justiciary issued in 2005.

Unreported cases

3–39 Unreported cases with no neutral citation are cited as follows: party names (court and the date of judgement in brackets), e.g. *Pink v Purple* (Anywhere Sheriff Court, November 2, 2013).

NB If a case is published in a printed format and also available electronically, it is good practice to reference the printed source for the case only.

Use of brackets in Scottish case reports

3–40 Where the date is an essential part of the reference to the volume, the convention is that the year is not put in brackets. If the date is not essential, it is put in round brackets or it may not be given at all. The five series of Session Cases between 1821 and 1906 are referred to by citing the first letter of the surname of the editor or chief reporter, e.g. *Goldston v Young* (1868) 7 M.188. This indicates that it was the 7th year of Macpherson's editorship. After 1906 the year was essential in citations and brackets are not used, e.g. *Errol v Walker*, 1966 S.C. 93.

3–41 The earliest volumes of Scots Law Times (1893–1908) are cited by volume number using brackets, e.g. *Peden v Graham* (1907) 15 S.L.T. 143.

3–42 After 1908, the year alone is used and is therefore essential. No brackets are used, e.g. *Dunfermline D.C. v Blyth & Blyth Associates*, 1985 S.L.T. 345.

3–43 Thus, no brackets are used by the modern Scottish law reports. Prior to the introduction of neutral citation, square brackets were never used in Scottish case citations. Now they are only used in neutral citations. In contrast, square brackets are used by most modern English law reports, e.g. The Law Reports, the All England Law Reports and the Weekly Law Reports.

Summary—using citation details to locate a case report   **3–44**

name and citation

↓

identify the series of law reports
from the abbreviated form in the citation,
if necessary check one of information sources
on abbreviations listed below

↓

locate appropriate volume
of series of law reports

↓

turn to the page number
and the case should commence on that page

NB Take particular care when consulting law reports which have separate paginations, e.g. S.L.T.

Abbreviations for unfamiliar case reports

If an unfamiliar abbreviation is encountered the best source for identifying it is the Cardiff **3–45** Index to Legal Abbreviations, available at *http://www.legalabbrevs.cardiff.ac.uk* [accessed May 20, 2014]. This resource can be searched either from abbreviation to title or from title to abbreviation. It contains abbreviations from nearly 300 jurisdictions.

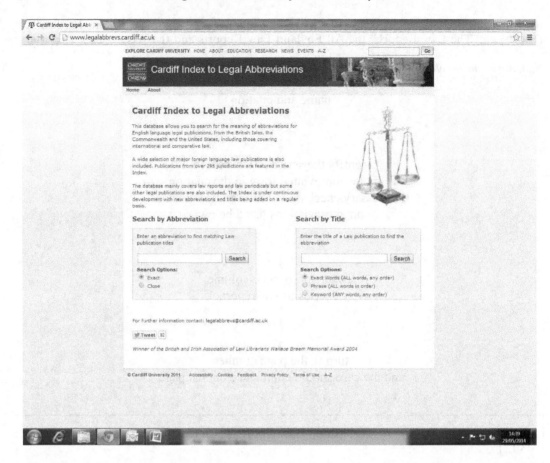

The following publications also assist in finding the meaning of abbreviated forms of case reports:

> ➢ D. Raistrick, *Index to Legal Citations and Abbreviations*, 3rd edn (London: Thomson/ Sweet & Maxwell, 2008);
> ➢ *The Laws of Scotland: Stair Memorial Encyclopaedia*. There is a table of abbreviations at the beginning of each volume in the series;
> ➢ Current Law–Monthly Digest, Yearbooks and Case Citators (see Ch.4).

READING CASES

Anatomy of a case

3–46 Reading cases is a skill that develops through practice. At the outset, a clear understanding of the anatomy of a case, i.e. how it is conventionally laid out, is vital. However, even when this is grasped it will take time to become familiar with their overall structure and the forms of expression used by the judiciary. The case below appeared in the Session Cases. Case reports in other series of law reports will be similar, but not identical. Different features of the law report are marked with numbers which correspond to the following list:

[1] The names of the parties.

[2] The date when the case was heard in court. The opinion of the court is usually delivered some time after the actual hearing. There is then a further lapse of time before the case will appear in the law reports. In this instance, the case was heard in July 1997 and appeared in the first issue of Session Cases for 1998.

[3] The names of the judge(s) who heard the case.

[4] In criminal cases the first named party is usually the Crown and the accused (the panel) would be the second party. However, here the panel has appealed the original decision and he has become the first named party; he is referred to as the "appellant". The Crown is referred to as the "respondent".

This case has been initiated under summary procedure and the Crown is therefore referred to as the surname of the Procurator Fiscal in whose jurisdiction the case is being tried. Here the Crown appears as Robert T. Hamilton who was the Procurator Fiscal in Dunfermline at the relevant time. In cases taken under solemn procedure the Crown is referred to as HM Advocate/HMA.

The names in italics opposite the parties' names are those of their representatives in court. The representative for the Crown is referred to as "QC, A-D". The Q.C. stands for Queen's Counsel and means that he is a senior advocate. The A-D stands for Advocate Depute.

[5] The section in italics is written by the editor of the law report. It gives an indication of the subject matter of the case and the legal issue involved. The first words indicate the heading under which this case is classed in the subject index for the law reports. This case will appear twice—once under Crime—Malicious Mischief and again under Words & Phrases—"Detriment".

[6] This is the headnote or rubric. It is a summary of the case and is not part of the law report proper. The temptation to read only the headnote of a case should be resisted. It should not be relied upon as accurate. It is written by the editor of the law reports and not the judge. Another reason not to rely solely on the headnote is that the significance and interpretation of a case can change over a period of time. The headnote remains frozen at one point in time and is not altered.

The headnote will give a summary of:

(a) The material facts
(b) The legal issues involved
(c) The decision of the court

[7] This section outlines the judicial history of the case.

[8] The entries in italics are the prior authorities referred to in the case. Here, there is a list of cases (including an unreported case) and an authoritative writing by Alison, (see Chapter 8). In the past, only books by such long dead and revered authors would be referred to in court. This convention has been relaxed in recent years and modern authorities do now appear although they are not formal sources of law.

[9] This section gives details of the court, the judge(s) and the date of the hearing. In Scotland presenting the judgment of the court is referred to as delivering the opinion of the court.

[10] The opinion of the court is the most important part of the case report. In *Bett v Hamilton* there is only one opinion/judgment. Cases can have a single judgment or multiple judgments. The presence of multiple judgments makes it more difficult to isolate and understand the reasoning behind the court's decision; e.g. all judges may agree with the decision but adopt completely different reasoning in doing so and a case can have no discernable ratio decidendi as a result. In recent years the courts have tended to provide one judgment, with the other judges stating that they have read it and

that they agree with it. However, if they wish, judges who concur with the leading judgment can still present their own reasoning separately. If a judge dissents (does not agree with the majority view), their full judgment will published.

There is no one style that judges use to write a judgment. Accordingly, judgments tend to be individualistic pieces of legal prose. Some are clear and easy to comprehend whereas others will be less so. In general, judgments have become more reader-friendly in recent years with the introduction of paragraphs, headings and concluding remarks.

The capital letters which appear down the side of the page allow a precise reference to be given to part of the opinion, e.g. Lord Sutherland starts to discuss the case presented for the appellant at 1998 J.C. 2 D.

[11] The outcome of the case.

[12] The agents acting in the case. Here More & Co. is the firm of solicitors representing the pannel. The Crown Agent is the term used for those acting on behalf of the Crown.

JC   1
[1]   BETT v HAMILTON   A
No 1   Lord Sutherland, Lord Johnston
[2]   23 July 1997   and Lord Dawson   [3]
[4]   ROBERT JOHN BETT, Appellant — *M E Scott*
            ROBERT T HAMILTON (Procurator fiscal, Dunfermline), Respondent —
                              Campbell, QC, A-D

[5]   *Crime—Malicious mischief—Whether material patrimonial loss required—Pannel charged with*
        maliciously moving video surveillance camera resulting in detriment to the benefit which a bank
        had attempted to secure by having camera—Whether loss of benefit to be obtained from use of   B
        camera constituted malicious mischief—Whether "detriment" meant simply "implied dis-
        advantage"—Whether crime constituted

        Words and phrases — "Detriment"   C

[6]   A pannel was charged on a libel, the terms of which narrated that he had maliciously moved a
        video surveillance camera with a pole or similar instrument so as to point the camera in such a
        direction that it did not show or record activity in an area which it had been set to cover,
        whereby the running costs associated with the camera were wasted and the building was
        exposed to increased risk of housebreaking, theft and vandalism. The pannel tabled a plea to
        the relevancy of the charge in that it did not set forth a competent charge of malicious   D
        mischief. The sheriff held that the acts of the pannel had resulted in detriment to the benefit
        which the bank had attempted to secure by having a surveillance camera. He considered that
        the bank suffered a financial loss in that the running costs of the camera were incurred without   E
        any benefit and also the bank was exposed to the unnecessary risk of vandalism or house-
        breaking being committed at its premises. The pannel appealed.

        Held (1) that what was required for a charge of malicious mischief was that there should be a
        wilful intent to cause injury to the owner or possessor of the property, which injury might be
        either in the form of physical damage or in the form of patrimonial loss; (2) that the running
        costs of the camera would have been incurred in any event even if it had been pointing in the   F
        right direction, so that what had been lost to the bank was such benefit as they might have
        obtained from the fact that the camera was pointing in the correct direction and possibly
        deterring vandals or thieves; and (3) that to describe such loss of benefit as patrimonial loss
        extended the latter concept too far and was altogether too speculative; and appeal allowed.

[7]   ROBERT JOHN BETT was charged in the sheriffdom of Tayside Central and Fife at Dunfermline
        at the instance of Robert T Hamilton, procurator fiscal there, with a contravention of the
        Criminal Law (Consolidation) (Scotland) Act 1995, sec 52(1) and a charge of malicious
        mischief. The panel tabled a plea to the relevancy in respect of the charge of malicious   G
        mischief. After hearing parties, the sheriff made certain deletions to the charge and held that

the charge set forth a relevant charge of malicious mischief. The terms of the charge are as set forth in the opinion of the court.

The pannel appealed to the High Court of Justiciary.

[8]   *Cases referred to*:
Advocate (HM) v Wilson, 1983 S.C.C.R. 420
Monro (George), July 17, 1831 (unreported)   H

Textbook referred to:
Alison, *Criminal Law*, ii, 451

[9]   The cause called before the High Court of Justiciary, comprising Lord Sutherland, Lord Johnston and Lord Dawson for a hearing on 23 July 1997.*Eo die* the opinion of the court was   I delivered by Lord Sutherland.

2   BETT v HAMILTON   1997

[10]   OPINION OF THE COURT — The appellant was charged on summary complaint with a con-   A travention of the Criminal Law (Consolidation) (Scotland) Act 1995, sec 52(1), the relevancy of which is not challenged, and a further charge purporting to set out an offence of malicious mischief. The appellant tabled a plea to the relevancy of the second charge. The sheriff made certain deletions to the charge (which the Crown did not argue before this court should be restored) and thereafter held that the remainder constituted a relevant offence of malicious mischief. The terms of the charge, as they now remain, are as follows: "The Royal Bank of Scotland, having at their own expense, placed and operated a surveillance camera so as to show and record activity at the front of the building occupied by them in East Port, Dun-   B fermline, for the purpose of enhancing the security of said building by deterring persons from acts of housebreaking, theft and vandalism at said building and making it possible to identify those who carry out such acts, you did on 7 December 1996 in said East Port, Dunfermline, maliciously move said camera with a pole or similar instrument so as to point said camera in such a direction that it did not show or record activity in the area which it had been set to cover whereby the running costs associated with said camera were wasted and said building was exposed to increased risk of housebreaking, theft and vandalism." The view taken by the sheriff was that the acts of the appellant resulted in detriment to the benefit which the bank   C had attempted to secure by having a surveillance camera. He considered that the bank suffered a financial loss in that the running costs of the camera were incurred without any benefit and also the bank was exposed to the unnecessary risk of vandalism or housebreaking being committed at its premises.

Counsel for the appellant before this court submitted that actual injury or harm, damage or   D patrimonial loss had to occur before mischief could be established. Neither wasted running costs nor the increased risk of housebreaking or theft or vandalism could constitute mischief. In *HM Advocate v Wilson* it was held that physical injury or damage was not necessary provided that there was an element of patrimonial loss. The accused in that case had activated an emergency stop button wilfully, recklessly and maliciously and brought a power station generator to a halt, causing a loss of production of electricity which had to be replaced at a cost of £147,000. Lord Justice-Clerk Wheatley, having set out Hume's definition of malicious mischief, said that the basic constituents involved in the crime of malicious mischief were that   E it had to be a deliberate and malicious act to damage another's property or to interfere with it to the detriment of the owner or lawful possessor. He went on to say: "It is clear from the words used in the libel that the Crown seek to establish that the act of the respondent founded upon was deliberate and malicious. The Crown further seeks to prove that this act resulted in a generating turbine being brought to a halt for an extended period of time with a consequential loss of generated electricity. In terms of Hume's second ground *supra* this would be an interference with the employer's property and the wording of the libel is such as to be habile to carry the inference that the initial positive wilful, reckless and malicious act was intended to   F harm the employer by causing patrimonial injury ... To interfere deliberately with the plant so as to sterilise its functioning with resultant financial loss such as is libelled here is in my view a clear case of interference with another's property which falls within Hume's classification of malicious mischief, and consists with the words in the phrase." Counsel therefore accepted that it is not necessary to prove physical damage but argued that there must at least be some material patrimonial loss before the crime of malicious mischief can be established. In the present case, as far as the running costs of the camera were concerned, these costs would have been expended anyway and there was no additional cost. What was lost, if anything, was the benefit to be obtained from the use of the camera. The same argument applied to the other part of the complaint which narrated that the bank lost the benefit of the security of the surveillance camera. That was not something which constituted patrimonial loss. It is clear from what the Lord Justice-Clerk said in *Wilson* that when he used the word detriment he was referring to patrimonial loss. The only other case involving detriment to an owner which was held to constitute malicious mischief, apart from *Wilson*, was an unreported case referred to in Alison, *Criminal Law*, ii, 451 (*George Monro*, July 17, 1831) where an accused was convicted of opening a barrel, thus allowing the contents to escape, causing loss to the owner of the contents. Accordingly it was submitted that loss of benefit was not the same as patrimonial loss and was insufficient to warrant the charge of malicious mischief.

G

H

I

JC   BETT v HAMILTON   3

In reply the Advocate-depute founded on the words of Lord Justice-Clerk Wheatley that to interfere with the property of another to the detriment of the owner would be sufficient. The word "detriment" in his submission simply implied disadvantage. The bank in the present case had installed this camera for a particular purpose and incurred costs in the running of that security device. If the purpose was destroyed or interfered with then the running costs were wasted and thus became a patrimonial loss. He submitted that where outlay is incurred to maintain a benefit, if the benefit is destroyed then the continuing costs constitute patrimonial loss. Furthermore loss of protection from vandalism or theft is a serious matter. The camera was installed to protect the bank against the risk of serious crime and this risk could be quantified in financial terms. For these reasons he submitted that there was an ascertainable patrimonial loss in this case and that accordingly the charge was relevant.

A

B

C

D

In our opinion the Crown have not averred sufficient in this case to constitute a relevant charge of malicious mischief. What is required in such a charge is that there should be a wilful intent to cause injury to the owner or possessor of the property. This injury may be either in the form of physical damage or in the form of patrimonial loss. We do not consider that the matters referred to by the Advocate-depute properly constitute patrimonial loss. The running costs of the camera would have been incurred in any event, even if it had been pointing in the right direction, and accordingly what has been lost to the bank is such benefit as they might have obtained from the fact that the camera was pointing in the correct direction and possibly deterring vandals or thieves. The same can be said of the loss of security which they might have sustained through the absence of this camera performing its proper function. In our opinion to describe such loss of benefit as patrimonial loss extends the latter concept too far and is altogether too speculative. The bank on these averments suffered no financial loss whatsoever and therefore there is no patrimonial loss. We shall therefore allow the appeal and sustain the appellant's plea to the relevancy of the second charge on the complaint.

E

F

G

H

[11]   The Court allowed the appeal.

[12]   *More & Co — The Crown Agent*   I

Analysis of cases

3–47   The major point of interest to the legal scholar is the reasoning which the court adopted in order to reach its conclusion, i.e. the ratio decidendi, the legal reason for the decision. As detailed above, lawyers will often disagree about the content of a particular ratio decidendi and the situation may be further complicated by the fact that some cases have no ratio decidendi at all, while others may have more than one. Accordingly, there is no easy way of learning how to identify the ratio decidendi. It requires skills of analysis and interpretation. One way of developing these skills, in addition to reading as many cases as possible, is to consult law reports which provide commentaries where the reader's understanding of the case can be benchmarked against that of the commentator.

Initial guidance for reading cases

An introduction to case law will feature in early instruction given at all undergraduate law **3–48** students, as to the nature and sources of Scots law. How to read a case, i.e. which elements require detailed scrutiny and why this is so, follows a methodical and logical process of "abstraction" which can be defined as, "reducing the information content . . . in order to retain only information which is relevant for a particular purpose". See *http://www.newworldencyclo pedia.org/entry/Abstraction* [accessed May 20, 2014].

> ➢ Concentrate on cases which are the first to define a principle or interpret a statute. Cases which are illustrative of a rule are not as important as those which expounded the rule in the first place.
> ➢ Do not consider cases that have subsequently been overruled unless specifically interested in a historical perspective of an area of law.
> ➢ Concentrate on the "leading" judgment in each case if there is more than one in agreement with the decision reached. Students will initially be guided in this respect by their tutors and text book references to a specific judge in a specific case.
> ➢ Do not spend time (which could be far better spent) reading dissenting judgments unless seeking persuasive authority to construct a novel legal argument.

Preparation of a student case note: abstracting the law

A student case note is essentially a structured summary of all the important information in a **3–49** case report. Ideally, a case note should not generally exceed 300 words (excluding the parties names/citations and court). However, the length will be dictated by the complexity and/or importance of the case. In any event, it is never acceptable or indeed necessary to copy out copious passages detailing the facts of the case. Mere facts fail to capture any legal reasoning. Rather, a court will determine the facts and then apply the law to them—thus the body of a case note must do likewise and have as its focus:

> ➢ Material (relevant) facts (in brief);
> ➢ The decision;
> ➢ The reason for the decision (ratio decidendi). This is the most important part of the case note which defines the court's reasoning).

A good case note thus enables its author to:

> ➢ Find the case again;
> ➢ Understand the points of law discussed;
> ➢ Appreciate why the case is a case precedent or leading case;
> ➢ Use the case effectively in a research project or an exam.

A case note should contain the following information: **3–50**

> ➢ The names of the parties;
> ➢ Citation(s). Listing all citations, providing alternatives for future reference if, e.g. subscription databases are not available or one required law report is missing from the library;

- ➤ The court which heard the case and the names of the judge(s). The court is vital because of the doctrine of stare decisis and the binding or otherwise nature of case law;
- ➤ The decision. This means whether the appeal was allowed or whether the defender was liable, etc. Note whether the decision was unanimous or whether a judge or judges dissented;
- ➤ A précis of the material facts. Material facts are those facts that are legally relevant to the court's decision. These aid understanding and appreciation of the application of the law in the specific circumstances of the case, illustrating the operation of legal principle in practice;
- ➤ The issue(s) of law raised in the case;
- ➤ The decision made by the court on the legal issues raised;
- ➤ The reason(s) for the decision made by the court. This is the most important part of the case report and should comprise the majority of the word count;
- ➤ Any additional comments, e.g. a quotation for use in an exam or research project if a judge has expressed a point of law in a clear and succinct way. However, any quotation should be short and can be reduced in length by using "..." between non-essential words (as shown below). Here you would also note if the court has done something significant, such as overrule another case or interpreted a piece of legislation for the first time.

Case notes should either be collated in paper or electronic form or both by (i) subject, (ii) topic and (iii) alphabetical order.

3–51   *Example of a student case note*

Bett v Hamilton, 1998 J.C. 1
Lord Sutherland, Lord Johnston and Lord Dawson
High Court of Justiciary (sitting as an appellate court)

Facts
A bank installed a surveillance camera situated to record movement at the front of its premises. B was charged with the offence of malicious mischief being accused of moving the camera so that it no longer covered the area at the front of the bank. The bank continued to pay the running costs of operating the camera while it was out of position and thus not protecting their premises.
Hume defined MM as a crime requiring a deliberate and malicious act to damage another's property or to interfere with it to the "detriment" of the owner or lawful possessor. The specific issue was whether "detriment" required patrimonial loss or whether some other form of disadvantage would be sufficient.

Decision
Appeal allowed.
Reason(s) for the decision:
The offence was defined as requiring "... wilful intent to cause injury to the owner or possessor of the property ... injury may be either in the form of physical damage or in the form of patrimonial loss". The running costs of the cameras would have been incurred even if the camera had been pointing in the correct direction. There had been no loss, merely a loss of benefit. Loss of benefit did not constitute patrimonial loss. Thus malicious mischief requires patrimonial loss.

Word count (excluding parties' names/citation/court/judges) 209 words.

In the above example, the case note is well below the upper suggested word count limit of 300 **3–52** words. However, the case report is relatively short and there is only one legal issue under discussion. In a lengthier and more complex case where perhaps multiple points of law are to be determined or there is a dissenting judgment of some significance it may prove more challenging to keep the contents of the note within manageable bounds.

Chapter 4
Search Strategies for Finding Cases

Significant abbreviations used in this chapter

- A.C.—Appeal Cases
- BAILLI—British and Irish Legal Information Institute
- G.W.D.—Greens Weekly Digest
- I.C.L.R.—Incorporated Council of Law Reporting for England and Wales
- SCOLAG—Scottish Legal Action Group
- S.C.—Session Cases
- S.C.C.R.—Scottish Criminal Case Reports
- S.C.L.R.—Scottish Civil Law Reports
- S.L.T.—Scots Law Times

AIDS TO TRACING CASES

4-01 Cases can be traced using the following resources:

> ➤ Full text subscription electronic databases (paras 2–48—2–82);
> ➤ Full text open source electronic databases (paras 2–04—2–47);
> ➤ Collections of case digests (para.4–25);
> ➤ Using case citators (paras 4–26—4–31);
> ➤ Consulting commentaries on case law and indexes of such commentaries (para.4–25);
> ➤ Consulting one or more series of law reports and their various indexes (para.4–87).

These are discussed in turn in this chapter.

Full text subscription electronic databases

4-02 As detailed in Ch.2, Westlaw and LexisNexis are the most likely subscription resources that will be available to undergraduate and postgraduate researchers. Both allow access to a large volume of case law, although many older case reports are still unlikely to be routinely included. In addition to providing full text access to domestic, EU and some comparative cases, additional features, as initially discussed in Ch.2, also appear and are designed to aid the user. Researchers can search by party name, citation or free text. The provision of information about the status of a case, e.g. whether it has been overruled, then allows the researcher to fully chart the judicial history of a case. Further features enable scholarly articles and commentary about cases to be located with relative ease.

4-03 Westlaw contains circa 400,000 full text case reports with an estimated 5,000 cases added on an annual basis. Series peculiar to Scotland, unsurprisingly, contain the word "Scotland" in the title. Whilst many of the series listed below contain reports confined exclusively to the English jurisdiction, a proportion of non-Scottish volumes are relevant to the Scots lawyer researching a topic where the law is the same throughout the United Kingdom, e.g. Fleet Street Reports contain certain intellectual property law cases and these can be cited in confidence given the uniformity of legislation throughout the UK.

NB The full list of case report series available on Westlaw can be accessed from the search cases home page by linking through the Law Reports and Transcripts tab located at the bottom of the page.

Westlaw

Main Case volumes

Administrative Court Digest	2001–Present
Admiralty and Ecclesiastical Cases	1865–1875
Appeal Cases	1875–1890
Appeal Cases	1891–Present
British Company Cases	1983–Present
Business Law Reports	2007–Present
Chancery Appeals	1865–1875
Chancery Division	1875–1890
Chancery Division	1891–Present
Civil Procedure Law Reports	2000–Present
Commercial Law Cases	1994–Present
Common Market Law Reports	1962–Present
Common Pleas	1865–1875
Common Pleas Division	1875–1880
Costs Law Reports	1910–Present
Criminal Appeal Reports	1908–Present
Criminal Appeal Reports (Sentencing)	1979–Present
Crown Cases Reserved	1865–1875
English Reports	1220–1865
English and Irish Appeals	1866–1875
Entertainment and Media Law Reports	1993–Present
Environmental Law Reports	1993–Present
Equity Cases	1865–1875
European Commercial Cases	1978–Present
European Copyright and Design Reports	2000–Present
European Human Rights Reports	1979–Present
European Human Rights Reports, Commission Decisions	1983–2004
European Human Rights Reports, Summaries and Extracts	2004–Present
European National Patent Reports	2000–2003
European Patent Office Reports	1979–Present
European Patent Office Reports A (1979-85, J decisions)	1979–1985
European Patent Office Reports B (1979-85, T decisions)	1979–1985
European Patent Office Reports C (1979-85, T decisions)	1979–1985
European Trade Mark Reports	1996–Present
Exchequer	1865–1875
Exchequer Division	1875–1880
Exchequer Reports (Welsby, Hurlstone and Gordon)	1854

Family Law Reports (Scotland)	1998–Present
Family Division	1972–Present
Fleet Street Reports	1966–Present
Fraser's Session Cases, 5th Series (House of Lords, Scotland)	1899–1906
Fraser's Session Cases, 5th Series (Justiciary cases, Scotland)	1899–1906
Fraser's Session Cases, 5th Series (Scotland)	1899–1906
Housing Law Reports	1981–Present
Housing Law Reports (Scottish)	1996–Present
Human Rights Law Reports (UK)	2000–Present
Industrial Cases Reports	1972–Present
International Litigation Procedure	1990–Present
Justiciary Cases (Scotland)	1930–Present
King's Bench	1901–1952
Landlord and Tenant Reports	1998–Present
Personal Injury and Quantum Reports	1992–Present
Planning Appeal Decisions	1986–Present
Privy Council	1865–1875
Probate	1891–1971
Probate Division	1875–1890
Probate and Divorce	1865–1875
Professional Negligence and Liability Reports	1955–Present
Property and Compensation Reports Digest Pages	1994–2000
Property, Planning and Compensation Reports	1949–Present
Property, Planning and Compensation Reports Digest Pages	2001–Present
Public And Third Sector Reports	2009–Present
Queen's Bench	1865–1875
Queen's Bench Division	1875–1890
Queen's Bench	1891–Present
Reparation Law Reports (Scottish)	1996–Present
Reports of Patent Cases	1977–Present
Road Traffic Reports	1970–Present
Scotch and Divorce Appeals	1866–1875
Scots Law Times	1893–Present
Scots Law Times (Land Ct)	1964–1992
Scots Law Times (Land Court Reports)	1993–2005
Scots Law Times (Lands Tribunal Reports)	1971–1992
Scots Law Times (Lands Tribunal Reports)	1993–Present
Scots Law Times (Lyon Court Reports)	1996–2004
Scots Law Times (Lyon Ct)	1950–1986
Scots Law Times (Notes)	1946–1981
Scots Law Times (Poor Law Reports)	1932–1941
Scots Law Times (Sheriff Court)	1922–1992
Scots Law Times (Sheriff Court Reports)	1993–Present
Scottish Criminal Law	2007–Present
Session Cases	1898–Present
Session Cases (House of Lords Cases, Scotland)	1930–Present
Session Cases (Justiciary 1907-16, Scotland)	1907–1916
Session Cases (Privy Council/Supreme Court Cases, Scotland)	2001–Present
Weekly Law Reports	1953–Present

Westlaw offers the following search options; basic search with free text, advanced search or browse.

The basic Westlaw search

From the welcome page, select the cases tab from the navigation bar at the top of the screen. This will link to the cases basic search page, where cases can be searched for by entering:

➢ Party name—just enter the names, there is no need to insert "and" or "v";
➢ Citation—the exact citation format in terms of brackets and spaces is not required as Westlaw will match it to the nearest citation, e.g. [2014] A.C. 1 can be simplified to "2014 ac 1" for search purposes;
➢ Free text—allows terms or phrases relating to the subject matter of the case to be located. Westlaw searches for these within the text of all case analyses and the judgments. Searching can be improved if "terms and connectors", detailed in Ch.2 are employed;
➢ Subject/keyword—e.g. divorce, murder, deeds, etc.;
➢ Terms defined—e.g. treaty, convention, protocol, etc.

NB The list of "connectors" tab (see paras 2–58—2–59), is located at the top of the search section on the right hand side. Note also that the search boxes are not case sensitive. If the Terms in context box, which is located beneath the aforementioned search options, is ticked extracts containing the search terms will be displayed in the results list.

Advanced Westlaw search

4–05 Select advanced search on the cases basic search page.

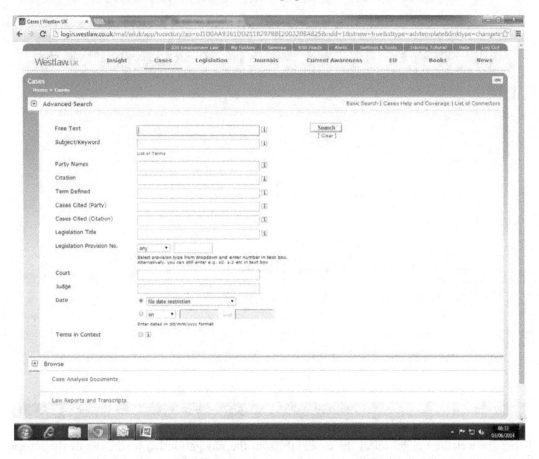

This function allows a greater amount of information to be entered to further refine a search. Advanced search modes include:

> Search by free text and subject headings and keywords. The list of terms link beneath these options links in turn to a listing of legal subjects and keywords as derived from Thomson Reuter's Legal Taxonomy. Cut and paste the relevant word into the subject/keyword field;

> Search for any cases interpreting a specific section, regulation, rule or article of legislation by entering the legislation title or statutory instrument name and number, e.g. Freedom of Information (Scotland) Act 2002, in the legislation title or legislation provision number field;

> Search for any cases citing specific cases. Enter the party name(s) in the cases cited (party) field or the citation in the cases cited (citation) field;

> Search by the name of the court in which the case was heard;

> Search by the name of a judge;

➢ A search can be restricted by date by selecting one of the periods from the date restriction drop-down list or a date can be specified by entering it in DD/MM/YYYY format.

The default order of documents retrieved is reverse chronological, thus the most recent judg- **4–06** ment will appear at the top of the list of results. If relevancy is the key issue, or how often the entered search terms appear within the documents, click on terms in context.

The cases result list includes: **4–07**

➢ Party name;
➢ Subject/keywords used to index the case using the Thomson Reuter's Legal Taxonomy, e.g. Causation; Prosecutions; Water Pollution;
➢ Where reported—a list of all citations where the case has been reported;
➢ Links to case analysis (see para.4–15) and each of the full text case reports;
➢ Some results might show status icons next to the title of the case indicating that either the case has been judicially considered elsewhere (indicated **C**) or that the case has been overruled or reversed on appeal (indicated by **◼**).

A search can be edited or deleted or a new one undertaken by selecting edit search or new **4–08** search. To refine a long list of results even further, a search can include additional terms by entering the new search term(s) in the field at the top of the page and clicking search within results. This can be a useful way of increasing the relevancy of the initial results.

Browsing for cases

From the welcome page, select the cases heading from the navigation bar at the top of the **4–09** screen. This will link to the cases basic search page. As an alternative to the basic search, a browsing option can be selected. Browsing can be undertaken by choosing either the case analysis documents or the full text reports and transcripts for the desired cases. The former will include more cases than the latter.

When selecting case analysis documents, an alphabetical list of all case reports offered by **4–10** Westlaw is displayed with the title of the report on the left hand side of the screen and the citation format (the abbreviated form for the series concerned) on the right. Once a case report series has been selected the search will continue to a list of years or volume numbers for that report. A list of cases in alphabetical order will be displayed for that year.

If a case report series for which Westlaw do not hold any full text judgments is selected only a **4–11** link to the case analysis document will be available. If the full text judgment is available in another report series held by Westlaw, the full text citation will appear with a hyperlink so that the judgment can be accessed directly without the need for a new search.

The law reports and transcripts link will display all case reports held on Westlaw in full text. The **4–12** name of the series appears on the left with the corresponding citation format on the right of the screen. Accessing one of the report series will take the user to a list of years or volume numbers for that case report series. Within that list of years, an alphabetical list of cases is displayed. If a case is held in full text in more than one report series, links to all full text reports will be given.

The browse feature allows the scope of a search to be limited to individual publications or years. **4–13** e.g. if the user only wishes to search Session Cases (S.C.), this series of law reports should be selected and the search terms entered in the fields at the top of the screen.

4-14 Browsing also allows for the speedy location of a case if only partial information is known, e.g. the researcher might recall that a case was reported in 2012 in S.L.T. but cannot recall the complex spelling of a party's name. The browse feature removes this impediment by allowing him/her to go to the law report for a specific year and browse the contents.

4-15 The case analysis function is a useful feature in that it provides a summary of information about a case with links to materials held elsewhere within Westlaw. The various fields used are:

where reported	This lists all case report series that have reported the case. The list runs in order of persuasive authority of a particular law report series (e.g. S.C., S.L.T., Scottish Civil Law Reports, S.C.L.R.).
case digest	This consists of: ➢ **Subject**—the legal subject as assigned by Westlaw, e.g. Criminal Law; ➢ **Keyword**—terms contained in the Thomson Reuter's Legal Taxonomy describing issues involved in the case, e.g. intention; murder; culpable homicide; defences; ➢ **Summary**—contains key phrases, e.g. provocation; self-defence; intention or recklessness; and ➢ **Abstract**—the facts of the case and a summary of the decision.
appellate history	The direct, reported progress of the decision through to appeal, in chronological order.
significant cases citing	This provides a list of selected cases cited within the case. Click the case name and citation to access it (if it is available in Westlaw).
cases citing this case	Lists the cases that have cited the case currently being viewed.
legislation cited	This provides links to legislation cited in the case. If legislation is not available on Westlaw or is no longer in force no links will be available.
journal articles	A list of citations to articles about the case which have appeared in legal journals. Links will go to the full text (if available on Westlaw).

Westlaw case analysis

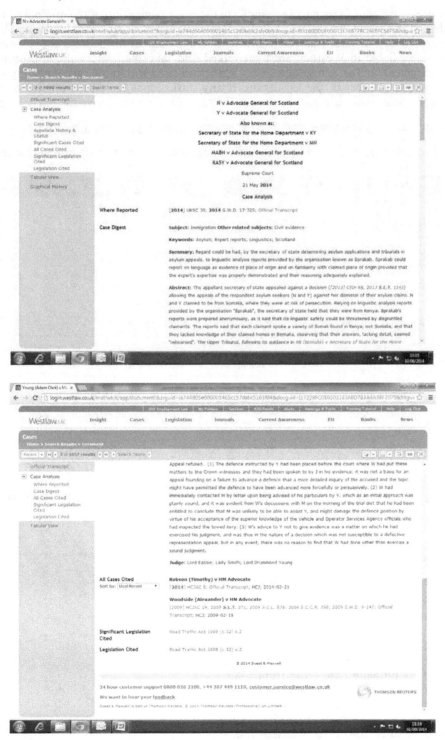

Full text case reports

4-16 Westlaw uses a system of star paging to indicate the exact pagination of the original printed law report that is being read. To ensure accurate referencing when citing a case in a research project find the preceding star page number to locate the page number in the hard copy. Citations to law reports available in Westlaw are hyperlinked and take the user to the appropriate case analysis document. In force, i.e. still current legislation cited within the case is also hyperlinked and links to the full text of the legislation. If any status icons have been applied to the case analysis document, these will also remain at the top of the screen above the party name.

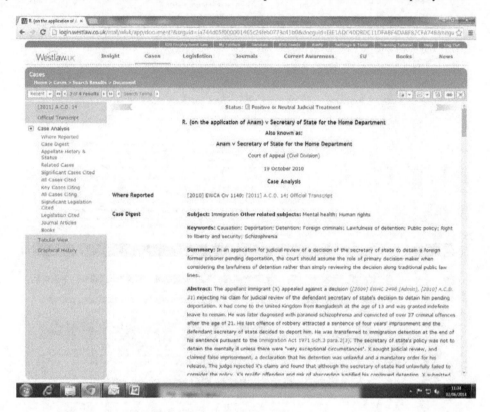

LexisNexis

Main Case volumes

The Law Reports from 1865
All England Law Reports from 1936
All England Commercial cases from 1999
All England European Cases from 1995
Bankruptcy and Personal Insolvency Reports from 1996
Butterworths Company Law Cases from 1983
Butterworths Human Rights Cases from 1996
Butterworths Medico-Legal Reports from 1986
Construction Law Reports from 1985
Costs Law Reports from 1910 (selected volumes)

Education Law Reports from 1995
Estates Gazette Law Reports from 1985
Family Court Reports from 1987
Industrial Relations Law Reports from 1972
International Tax Reports from 1997
International Trust and Estate Law Reports from 1998
Justice of the Peace Law Reports from 1945
Licensing Law Reports from 2001
Local Government Reports from 1999
Lloyd's Law Reports from 1951
Occupational Pension Law Reports from 1992
Offshore Financial Law Reports from 1996
Reports of Patent Cases from 1947–1997
Scottish Criminal Case Reports from 1981
Scottish Civil Law Reports from 1987
Session Cases from 1930
Simon's Tax Cases from 1973
Tax Cases from 1875
Times Law Reports from 1988
West Indian Reports from 1958

Searching LexisNexis for case Law

Choose the cases tab from the homepage. This opens up the cases search field. The Select **4–18** Sources drop-down list will list the sources that each institution or body subscribes to. The user should select whichever series they wish to search. If the citation is known it should be entered it into the citation field. Ignore brackets or other punctuation. It is possible to specify a particular page or paragraph if the detail is entered into the box below the citation field.

If the parties' names only are known these can be entered (one or both names) in the case name **4–19** field. If both parties' names are entered insert "and" between them, i.e. "Pink and Yellow", do not enter "Pink v Yellow". If the names are unknown, enter words or phrases in the search terms box using Boolean connectors (see detailed paras 2–58—2–59), to indicate the desired relationship of the terms. It is also possible to narrow a search to documents published on a particular date or date range. This is most useful if the user is searching for recent transcripts of cases as opposed to cases which have been published in the law reports. There is a summary field which allows terms to be entered to search various fields (such as catchwords, headnotes, decisions and facts) within the case summary. The cases search form also allows a search to be undertaken by court, judge(s), counsel and case type, i.e. either a full transcript, summary or digest of the case.

Results can be retrieved by clicking on search. Search results can then be refined by sorting the **4–20** results according to relevance, date etc. and narrowed by selecting a specific case report series. Once the case report has been accessed further options can be selected to locate related cases or commentary.

SELECTED FULL TEXT OPEN SOURCE DATABASES

4–21 As discussed throughout Ch.2, open source databases afford free and often speedy access to electronic collections of case reports. However, such resources are often restricted to more recent judgments of specific courts and, unlike subscription databases, will offer few additional search fields or features with fewer still providing headnotes or summaries of cases, although the UK Supreme Court is a notable exception in respect of the latter. See *http://www.supreme-court.gov.uk/decided-cases/index.html* [accessed May 30, 2014].

Scottish Courts

4–22 The Scottish Courts website, *http://www.scotcourts.gov.uk/* [accessed June 2, 2014] (updated daily at 2pm), is a well structured and useful resource especially for researchers seeking recent cases determining significant point of Scots law., In addition to offering full text opinions (the Scottish term for judgment), see *http://www.scotcourts.gov.uk/search-judgments/about-judgments* [accessed May 30, 2014], where links to further resources are provided, including:

> ➢ General information about the different Scottish courts, details about judges and sheriffs and a virtual tour of the Court of Session;
> ➢ Printable information about the jurisdiction of sheriff courts and their locations;
> ➢ Details of the bodies involved in the administration of the courts;
> ➢ Information on the Rolls of Court (court business on a daily basis) and court fees;
> ➢ Rules of the Court of Session, Sheriff Court Ordinary Cause Rules and all Rules of Court made after 2002;
> ➢ Practice notes, various court forms, guidance notes for small claims and summary cause procedure, and other information for court users; and
> ➢ A glossary of legal terms.

Case coverage   Court of Session and the High Court of Justiciary, including opinions in some sentence appeals from September 1998 onwards.

Sheriff Court cases from September 1998 where there is a significant point of law or particular public interest.

Comments   The site allows a search for opinions by keyword, citation or by a structured search. The keyword search searches all opinions on the site whereas the structured search allows the researcher to restrict their search to either the higher courts or the sheriff courts. The structured search allows a search to be undertaken by: type of opinion, date, judge, pursuer (appellant), defender (respondent) and type of action. The results can be restricted to the first hundred results. The site also lists the fifty most recent opinions (based on the date these were uploaded as opposed to the actual date of the opinion).

British and Irish Legal Information Institute ("BAILLI")

BAILII is a full text searchable database. It is updated on a daily basis and holds domestic, **4–23** European and international case law in addition to an abundance of further legal information. The most significant UK resources are detailed below. See *http://www.bailii.org* [accessed May 30, 2014].

Case coverage	UK courts.
	House of Lords decisions November 14, 1996–July 31, 2009.
	UK Supreme Court decisions from 29 October, 2009 onwards.
	Privy Council judgments 1996 onwards and selected earlier judgments.
	Court of Appeal (Civil Division) and High Court (Administrative Court and Crown Office List), all cases from 1996 to August 1999, all significant handed down decisions September 1999 to December 2002, and all substantive judgments January 2003 onwards.
	Court of Appeal (Criminal Division), all decisions from 1996 to August 1999 and some significant handed down decisions August 1999 onwards.
	Tribunals including;
	Employment Appeal Tribunal, selected decisions from 1976.

Special Immigrations Appeals Commission decisions from 2003 onwards.

UK Competition Appeals Tribunal decisions from 2002 onwards.

UK Asylum and Immigration Tribunal (successor to the Immigration Appellate Authority and the Immigration Appeals Tribunal) selected decisions from 1994

UK Special Commissioners of Income Tax Decisions from 1999.

UK Social Security and Child Support Commissioners' Decisions selected decision from 1972.

UK VAT and Duties Tribunals Decisions selected decisions from 1989.

Nominet UK Dispute Resolution Service.

The full list can be accessed here, *http://www.bailii.org/form/search_multidatabase.html* [accessed May 30, 2014].

Scottish material

Scottish Courts.

House of Lords decisions November 14, 1996–July 31, 2009.

Supreme Court decisions from 29 October, 2009 onwards.

Privy Council decisions 1996–29 October, 2009.

Decisions available on the Scottish Courts website.

Comments

All of the data have been converted into a consistent format and a generalised set of search and hypertext facilities added. This means that it is possible to search across all its databases and jurisdictions.

➢ The results appear in order of relevance. It is possible to reorder the results in order of title, jurisdiction or date. Recent decisions can be accessed via the latest cases links on the front page. Cases can be browsed in alphabetical order listed by jurisdiction. Significant cases can be browsed by subject category. The results appear in order of relevance. It is possible to reorder the results in order of title, jurisdiction or date.

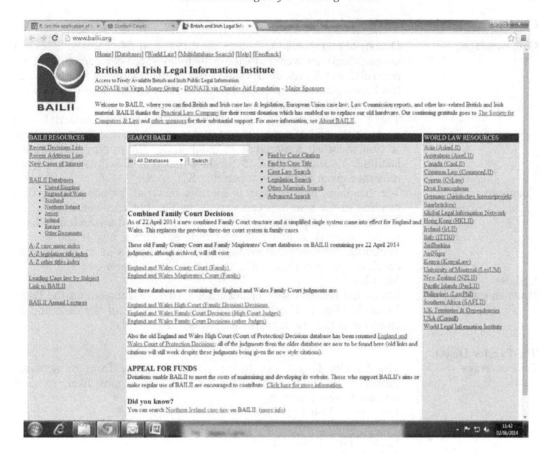

Scottish Land Court *http://www.scottish-land-court.org.uk/*	The Scottish Land Court is a court of special jurisdiction (limited to **4–24** specific subject matter) which has jurisdiction to hear cases dealing with disputes between agricultural tenants and landlords.
Case coverage	Headnotes for reported cases from 1982 to date are accessed via the Digest of Cases link at *http://www.scottish-land-court.org.uk/ digest.html* [accessed May, 2014]. From 1964 to date, decisions have also been published in S.L.T.

COLLECTIONS OF CASE DIGESTS

Digests contain brief summaries of cases and outline in précis form the contents of a case. **4–25** However, a fuller understanding of a case will only be achieved by consulting a source which offers the full text.

Current Law Yearbooks and Monthly Digests

Case coverage	Digests of all reported UK cases since 1947 and references to cases (no matter when they were reported) which have been considered, applied, overruled, etc. by the courts since 1947. Full coverage of Scottish cases has been achieved from 1991 onwards. Prior to that year digests were available in the Scottish Current Law Series.

The Yearbooks have a separate section for Scottish material. The index at the end of each Yearbook does not have a separate Scottish section. Scottish material is indexed under the appropriate subject heading. You are alerted to the fact that it is a Scottish case if the reference given ends with a capital "S".

Comments   The headings only appear if there is material included under that heading so the headings can vary from Yearbook to Yearbook.

The choice of subject category is not foolproof and a search may have to be undertaken under several different terms, e.g. if the user is searching for cases concerning water pollution, s/he might have to check under "environment", "pollution" and "water".

Updates   Monthly.

Hints on use   Check the relevant subject headings in the Yearbooks and the latest Monthly Digest. These will lead you to a digest of the case and to citations in the law reports. See paras 8–23—8–31.

The Faculty Digest

Case coverage   The Faculty Digest can be purchased in paper form or accessed through a subscription database. This resource is most likely to be of interest to practitioners.

1868–1922, Vols 1–5.

Vol.6—Indexes covering 1868–1922.

Faculty Digest Supplements.

1922–30, 1930–40, 1940–50, 1951–60, 1961–70, 1971–80, 1981–90.

Information is organised in the Supplements as follows:

> ➢ Cases digested by subject matter
> ➢ Cases judicially referred to (including English cases referred to in the Scottish courts but not Scottish cases referred to in English courts).
> ➢ Statutes, Acts of Sederunt, Statutory Orders, etc. judicially commented on—arranged by year.
> ➢ Words judicially defined.
> ➢ Index of cases in the digest—alphabetical order (both parties listed).

Scottish material

Comments   Courts covered: Court of Justice of the EU, UK Supreme Court (House of Lords), Court of Session, High Court of Justiciary, Lands Tribunal, Land Court and selected (in a supplement) sheriff court cases, Scottish Criminal Case Reports and Scottish Civil Law Reports. Useful for tracing older Scottish cases.

It allows searches to be made by subject, names of both parties, legislation, cases judicially referred to and words judicially defined.

The Digest (formerly the English & Empire Digest)

Case coverage	This is a large paper collection of case summaries from 1500 onwards. Further information about this resource can be found here, *http://www.law.ox.ac.uk/lrsp/print/case_law_indexes5.php*
Comments	The Digest comprises 52 main volumes which are collated by subject. A brief summary of cases and their subsequent judicial treatment are offered. An annual cumulative supplement updates this body of work. A consolidated Table of Cases (currently in three volumes) contains an alphabetical index of all cases cited in England (and Wales), Scotland, Australia and other Commonwealth countries The jurisprudence of the Court of Justice of the EU and the European Court of Human Rights (ECtHR) is also available.

The Digest is probably the most widely available paper source of information about the treatment of Scottish cases in English courts. Further details on this resource can be found in para.9–42.

Shaw's Digest

Case coverage

Comments   This Digest does not always appear in the same format with different editions being bound differently. Cases are arranged by subject and there are indices of pursuers' and defenders' names at the end of a volume or, if produced in several volumes, in the final volume.

House of Lords decisions 1726–1868 and Scottish superior courts 1800–1868.

Scots Digest

Case coverage   The Faculty Digest was a continuation of Shaw's Digest.

Comments   This digest also appears in different formats. Cases are arranged by subject and the volumes contain a table of cases and a table of cases judicially considered. There is a Digest of Sheriff Court Cases reported in the S.L.T between1893–1943. Digests of old Scottish cases are listed in paras 3–17—3–19.

House of Lords cases 1707–1947 and cases from Scottish superior courts 1800–1947.

This Digest was superseded by Scottish Current Law.

Case Citators

Case citators provide an efficient and methodical way of tracking information about the current **4–26** status of a decided case.

Current Law Case Citators do not contain the full text or even summaries of a case. Rather, **4–27** they are a tool for tracing decided cases and their subsequent judicial treatment. Thus a case Citator can best be described as a volume that lists information about cases.

> **NB** Current Law is published by Sweet & Maxwell and comprises three series: Case Citators, Legislation Citators and Yearbooks. How to use these resources is discussed primarily in Chs 4,5,6,7 and 10.

Current Law Case Citators	These volumes list cases in alphabetical order and list information about each one. The Current Law Case Citators are published in several parts (see below) with updates published in the form of Digests which are published in cumulative form each month.
Case coverage	All reported English cases since 1947 and references to cases (no matter when they were reported) which have been considered, applied, overruled, etc. by the courts since 1947. If a case has been reported more than once, each alternative citation is given. Scottish cases were incorporated in Citator form in 1948 (rather than 1947), and prior to 1991 they were only to be found in the Scottish Current Law Series. Since 1991 Scottish cases have featured in the parent Current Law Case Citator volumes and are listed separately at the back of each volume (following on from the listing of English cases).
Comments	Current Law Case Citators are a useful starting point unless the case concerned is very recent (within the last month) or old (pre-1947 and not commented on by the courts since 1947).
	Whilst the Current Law Case Citators are an extremely efficient way of tracing cases, they do require the user to have an appreciation of how they are structured and it is essential to adopt a systematic and consistent approach to using them to search for cases.

4–28 The Current Law Case Citators are published in four consolidated volumes: 1948–1976, 1977–1997, 1998–2001 and 2002–2004, with annual volumes being published from 2005 onwards reflecting the ever increasing number of reported cases. Each volume is divided into three parts:

> ➤ Index of cases in the digest—alphabetical order (both parties)⇨English, Welsh and Northern Irish cases;
> ➤ Index of cases in the digest—alphabetical order (both parties)⇨Scottish cases;
> ➤ Index of cases in the digest—alphabetical order (both parties)⇨Ships' Names Index (from 1977 onwards)

The Scottish section of the Case Citator contains the following information:

> ➤ Index of cases in the digest—alphabetical order (both parties). Details of cases decided or judicially considered in the Scottish courts for the period covered by the volume of the case Citator;
> ➤ Index of cases in the digest—alphabetical order (both parties);
> ➤ References to English cases judicially considered in Scotland during the period covered by the volume of the Case Citator.

NB Scottish cases which have been published in English law reports are included in both the Scottish and English sections of the Case Citator.

4–29 The Case Citators contain:

> ➤ An index of cases in the digest—alphabetical order (both parties);
> ➤ The full name of any case reported between 1947 and the current year. Cases are listed alphabetically by the first party's name;
> ➤ Lists of citations in law reports and journals where the case may have been digested;

> ➤ References to the Current Law Yearbook where the case is digested. Most references have a year before the paragraph number, e.g. 05/5032. This refers you to the 2005 Yearbook, para.5032;
> ➤ The history of any case (irrespective of date) which has been judicially considered from 1947 to date. The reference given is to the digest of the case which considered the case listed.

NB Each volume starts with a list of abbreviations of the various series of law reports and journals and the Monthly Digest contains an updated Case Citator (referred to as the Table of Cases) each month.

Annotated Excerpt from a Case Citator

[1] *Grosvenor Developments (Scotland) v Argyll Stores*, 1987 S.L.T. 738 (Ex. Div.): **4–30**
affirming **[2]** 1987 S.L.T. (Sh. Ct.) 134 .... **[3]** *Digested, 87/**4846**:*
Followed, 92/5944, 95/6204: **[4]** *Approved, 94/5971: Distinguished, 94/5970*
Grosvenor Metal Co., *Re* [1950] Ch. 63; (1950) 93 S.J. 774; [1949] 2 All E.R. 948; 65T.L.R. 755;
[67 L.Q.R. 25] .... *Digested, 50/**1395**: Approved and followed,*
93/4826
Group 4 *Total Security v Jaymarke Developments*, 1995 S.C.L.R. 303
.... *Digested, 95/**6365***
Group 4 *Total Security v Ferrier*, 1985 S.L.T. 287; 1985 S.C. 70
.... *Digested, 85/**4092**: Applied, 86/4023*
Grugen v HM Advocate, 1991 S.C.C.R. 526 .... *Digested, 91/**4644***
Grummer v HM Advocate, 1991 S.C.C.R. 194 .... *Digested, 91/*
4815: *Commented on, 92/5570: Applied, 95/5620*

Key:

[1] Name.
[2] Citation.
[3] References **in bold** indicate where the case has been digested, e.g. this case is digested in the 1987 Yearbook, para.4846.
[4] References in normal type show where the case has been considered, e.g. this case was approved in a case listed in the 1994 Yearbook, para.5971.

Searching the Case Citators

Scottish cases are listed at the end of each volume and a common error for the new researcher to **4–31** make is to consult the English section when seeking a Scottish case. If the approximate year of the case is known a search should begin by consulting the appropriate volume. Once the case has been located all the citators subsequent to the date of the case must be consulted prior to checking the Table of Cases in the latest Monthly Digest to bring a search up to date as possible. If the approximate year of the case is not known a search must begin by consulting the first, i.e. the earliest volume and then all subsequent volumes/latest Monthly Digest to ensure a complete history of the case is collated.

JustCite

4–32 JustCite is an online subscription legal citator that provides a cross-referenced index to a collection of domestic and international legal information which allows the user to identify materials across open source databases (such as BAILII) and across subscription databases (such as Westlaw and LexisNexis). It provides links to full text material which can then be accessed if, (i) the materials are freely available in a law library or (ii) the researcher has access to the relevant The JustCite home page allows a search to be undertaken by case name, citation or subject. Alternatively, the index tab can be used to browse through a title index of cases listed in alphabetical order nested under various headings (including Scottish cases). It also allows browsing by subject (Scotland is a subject and there are various subcategories), words and phrases, ships' names or by year (Scottish cases can be searched for separately).subscription database. See *http://www.JustCite.com/* [accessed June 2, 2014].

4–33 The information retrieved can include:

> ➤ Alternative citations;
> ➤ A brief summary of the case;
> ➤ Subject matter categorisation;
> ➤ Cases, statutes and statutory instruments judicially considered;
> ➤ Subsequent cases with details of their effect, if any, on the earlier case;
> ➤ Academic Journal Articles/Case Comment. The numbers of these secondary sources available is meagre when compared to an identical search using, e.g. Westlaw.

Scottish cases can be searched separately. However, if a search is undertaken to locate Scottish cases which have been reported in England the vast majority of the reference details will be found in the UK entry only (the Scottish entry being very brief). Therefore it is better to search under both categories.

Updates:	Material is added on a daily basis.
	JustCite does not support Boolean operators. If more than one word is typed in the subject box on the search screen, JustCite will look for documents that contain all of those words. A phrase can be searched for by putting it into parenthesis, e.g. "duty of care".

NB Accompanying commentaries on case law and indexes of these commentaries can be particularly useful if searching for cases by subject matter.

JOURNALS AND CASEBOOKS

Legal Journals Index

4–34 This is an index which covers over hundreds of journals from the UK and English language European journals. It contains abstracts of journal articles. It was originally published in paper form, but is now more usually encountered in its electronic existence which can be accessed via Westlaw.

Case coverage	Commenced in 1986. References to case notes and articles which discuss cases.
	This index covers all journals published in the UK which are devoted to law or frequently contain articles on legal topics.
Scottish material	Scottish journals currently covered: Edinburgh Law Review, Journal of the Law Society of Scotland, Juridical Review, Scottish Legal Action Group (SCOLAG), S.L.T., Scottish Construction Law, Scottish Human Rights Journal, Scottish Licensing Law and Practice.
Updates	Daily.

Tables of cases in textbooks

Case coverage	This will depend on the text. The table of cases will usually contain the citation and page reference to where it is discussed in the text. Tables of cases in textbooks are usually found at the beginning of the book after the contents page. The cases are listed in alphabetical order of the first named party.
Comments	Ensure that the most recent edition of a textbook is consulted.
Updates	In general textbooks are not updated annually. However many publishers offer online updates.

The Laws of Scotland: Stair Memorial Encyclopaedia

	This encyclopaedia gives a commentary on Scots law only. It is arranged alphabetically in broad areas of the law and contains articles on each area.
	Cases are referred to throughout the encyclopaedia.
Updates	Paper—Annual Cumulative Supplements and table of cases. In addition the Service Binder is updated twice a year.
	Online (The Laws of Scotland Online) is provided by LexisNexis and is updated bi-monthly.

NB Search the paper version by subject or by the first party's name. The online version can be searched by using free text.

Casebooks

	Casebooks (sometimes called Cases and Materials texts) contain excerpts from legal materials on a particular subject accompanied by commentary which discusses the excerpts and puts them in context, e.g. C.H.W. Gane, C.N.S. Stoddart and J. Chalmers, *Casebook on Scottish Criminal Law* (Edinburgh: W. Green, 2009).
Case coverage	Depends on the text.
Comments	Casebooks can provide a fast and efficient way of getting information about key cases in a subject area. However, they should not be regarded as a substitute for reading the cases themselves. Casebooks only contain short excerpts from the materials and do not allow the reader to appreciate the complete nature of the legal reasoning in the context of the case.

Law reports

Case coverage

This will vary according to the series of law reports. The subject categories adopted are also variable. The Scottish law report series are discussed in Ch.3. Details of the main English series are given in Ch.9.

Comments

Not all series contain the same indexes, e.g. some series have separate tables of words and phrases judicially considered. Other series include the information in a subject index under "W" for word. Where possible, consult cumulative versions of the indexes. This will save having to check the annual volumes. The consolidated indexes are usually published separately but are generally located next to the appropriate series of law reports in a law library.

Updates

Varies according to the series of law reports.

The Consolidated Index

Published by the Incorporated Council of Law Reporting for England and Wales ("ICLR") this index (known as the Red Book) provides a continuous indexing system to the principal English law reports from 1951 to date. Bound volumes of the Consolidated Index are available as follows:
1951–60, 1961–70, 1971–80, 1981–90, 1991–2000, 2001–2005 and 2006–2010.
Decisions after 2010 are published (three times each year) in supplements known as the Pink Book. Recent updates can be found at the beginning of each issue of the Weekly Law Reports and the Consolidated Indexes can be accessed by subscribing to the ICLR's Citator+ online facility.
The Consolidated Index contains:
All cases reported in The Law Reports, the Weekly Law Reports and the Industrial Cases Reports.
References to cases reported in:
All England Commercial Cases, All England European Cases, All England Law Reports, Criminal Appeal Reports, Lloyd's Law Reports, Local Government Reports, Road Traffic Reports, and Simon's Tax Cases.
The index contains nine different tables.

NB Only important Scottish cases are covered.

Check the table of cases reported and table of cases judicially considered. To ensure that you are up to date, check through: (i) Red Index; (ii) Pink Index; (iii) the Weekly Law Reports.

SEARCH STRATEGIES FOR LOCATING CASES

This section outlines different methods and starting points which can be used to locate cases if, **4–35** e.g. knowledge of the case(s) sought is incomplete or when undertaking research in a completely new (to the researcher) area of law.

Given there are numerous and alternative ways of finding legal information, comments as to the **4–36** respective strengths and weaknesses of the most comprehensive sources are given prior to considering the merits of more limited sources. However, it is not a simple matter of listing the best and worst sources. Much will depend on the facilities available to the researcher who may or may not be fortunate enough to have access to a well-resourced law library that also offers access to subscription databases. Electronic and paper alternatives are denoted thus: ⏦ and 📖 respectively.

The following search strategies are considered: **4–37**

- ➢ Finding cases by name only where a citation is incomplete or unknown.
- ➢ See paras 4–43—4–45.
- ➢ Finding cases by subject. This allow for an efficient search when interested in a specific subject area with limited or no knowledge of the relevant case law. See paras 4–58—4–65.
- ➢ Finding cases which contain precise words or phrases that have been interpreted by the judiciary. See paras 4–72—4–81.
- ➢ Finding cases interpreting legislation. This covers the situation where the specific legislative provision is known but the researcher has no knowledge of any cases which have considered it. See paras 4–81—4–91.
- ➢ Finding journal articles which discuss a case. Identifying such articles and sourcing them aids understanding of the reasoning adopted by the judiciary in a case. See paras 4–92—4–99.
- ➢ Determining the current status of a case. This is vital to find out whether a case is still binding law, whether it has been commented on or overruled. See paras 4–100—4–109.
- ➢ Finding out about a very recently decided case. It is very important to be aware of current developments in the law. New cases are reported daily and the sources for very recent cases tend to be different from those for older cases. See paras 4–110—4–117.
- ➢ Finding cases from other courts of special jurisdiction, e.g. The Court of the Lord Lyon or the Employment Tribunal. See paras 4–118—4–125.

Finding cases by name only—citation unknown

The best method of locating a Scottish case when only the parties' names are known is to use **4–38** a subscription database unless an older case is sought. If so, follow the advice given in paras 4–53—4–57.

Westlaw ⏦ subscription database
From the welcome page, select the cases heading from the navigation bar at the top of the **4–39** screen. This link leads to the cases basic search page, where a search for cases is undertaken by entering either or both parties' names in the party names field. The template is not case sensitive and there is no need to insert the "v" or "and" connectors detailed in paras 2–58—2–59. This field will link to details about the case and the full text if it is available in Westlaw.

LexisNexis ⌁ subscription database

4–40 Choose the cases tab from the homepage. This opens up the cases search form. If only the parties' names are known enter one or both names in the case name field. If both parties' names are used insert "and" between them, i.e. "Green and Brown", do not enter "Green v Brown".

Justis UK and Irish Primary Case Law/Specialist Case Law ⌁ subscription database

4–41 The "Search In Cases" screen allows for the selection of a specific series of case reports or multiple case report series to be searched in addition to a series of field categories, e.g. names of parties, citation, court etc. Select the required case reports and then select the field category for "parties". Further information about this service can be found at *http://www.justis.com/* [accessed May 30, 2014].

Current Law Case Citator 📖

4–42 This is the best paper resource to utilise unless the case is very recent (within the last month) or old (pre-1947 and not commented on by the courts since 1947). Current Law includes all reported cases since 1947 and references to cases (no matter when they were reported) which have been considered, applied, overruled, etc., by the courts since 1947. The case citators are arranged alphabetically by the name of the first party. The citator will provide the citation for the case which can then be located in the relevant series of law reports.

Using Current Law to find a citation for a case by name only

4–43 ⌁ **Step 1**: Check through the Case Citators in chronological order. If a Scottish case is being sought consult the Scottish section at the back of the volume. If unsure whether the case is Scottish or English check both the English and Scottish sections. Cases are listed in alphabetical order of the first named party. If the case is listed, its full citation(s) will be given next to it;

⌁ **Step 2**: Check the table of cases in the most recent Monthly Digest (an updating service).

By way of example, how to find the citation for *Lockhart v Robb* when all that is known is the names of the parties and that it is a Scottish case:

⌁ **Step 1**: Check the Scottish Current Law Case Citator volume 1948–1976.
⌁ There is no entry.
⌁ **Step 2**: Check the Case Citator volume 1977–1997. Make sure that it is the Scottish section (Pt II) which is consulted.
Here there is an entry for the case and one citation is given: 1988 S.C.C.R. 381.

Using Current Law to find a citation if the case name and the year is known but not the citation or jurisdiction

4–44 In this example the name of the case is *A, Petitioner* and the year is 2011, but the month the opinion was handed down is not known.

⌁ Check the appropriate Current Law Yearbook and consult the Table of Cases at the beginning of the volume. All cases included in the Yearbook are listed alphabetically;
⌁ Next to the case name all the citations for the case will be listed. In this example, two citations are given in the 2012 volume: [2011] CSOH 215 and 2012 S.L.T. 370. (NB The opinion was handed down December 23, 2011—hence the citations given detailing separate years);
⌁ Select a report then locate the full text case report either in paper or electronic format.

> **NB** A summary (or digest) of a case can also be accessed within the paper Current Law series.

Opposite the entry for a case in the relevant Current Law Case Citator a reference is given for a paragraph number where the case is digested in a Current Law Yearbook. The reference is made up of the year/paragraph number. The paragraph number of the case digest is shown in **bold**.

Using *Galt v Goodsir*, 1982 J.C. 4; 1982 S.L.T. 94; 1981 S.C.C.R. 225 as an example: **4–45**

    ✍ Locate the case in the relevant Case Citator (here volume 1977–1997). Opposite the entry for the case is a reference that states "Digested 82/**4292**";

    ✍ Locate the Yearbook for 1982 and then paragraph number **4292**. The entry contains the following information:

       • "Identification of driver [Road Traffic Act 1972 (c. 20) ss.6(1) and 168(2)]. *Held*, that an admission by the owner of a car made under s.168(2) of the Road Traffic Act 1972 that he had been the driver two days before was admissible evidence against him on a charge under s.6(1), although the result of the laboratory test was not known to the police when the request under s.168(2) was made: *Galt v Goodsir*, 1982 S.L.T. 94."

Further Case Citators subscription ⌐⌐
The JustCite Citator service, provided by Justis, and *The Laws of Scotland: Stair Memorial* **4–46** *Encyclopaedia* and The Laws of Scotland Online (Stair Memorial Encyclopaedia) from Lex-isNexis can also be searched using the methodology detailed above.

Tables of cases in legal textbooks 📖
Tables of Cases in textbooks are usually found at the beginning of the book after the contents **4–47** page. The cases are conventionally listed in alphabetical order of the first named party. It should be noted that criminal cases where the prosecution is undertaken by the Crown in the shape of Her Majesty's Advocate (HMA), will generally appear in text book Tables of Case under the letter A as follows; *Advocate (HM) v Aitken*, 1975 S.L.T. (Notes) 86.

Indexes in the law reports 📖
Most series of law reports include indexes of cases for a specific volume and may have cumu- **4–48** lative updates covering many years. The indexes are usually accessible from either party's name. In order to use the paper volumes of the various series of law reports efficiently, the most likely series of law reports and the approximate date should be discerned at the outset.

If the case is recent then the Scottish Courts website ⌐⌐ free and or BAILII ⌐⌐ free can be **4–49** consulted.

Sources for UK cases, but not for Scottish cases

The Consolidated Law Reports Index 📖
This index provides a continuous indexing system to the principal English law reports from 1951 **4–50** to date, with only selected Scottish cases given coverage.

Casetrack ⌐⌐ subscription
Casetrack provides full text judgements from the Court of Appeal (Civil and Criminal Divi- **4–51** sions) and the High Court in England and Wales.

Lawtel ⟡ subscription legal current awareness digest service

4–52 This online digest service is updated every 24 hours and contains summaries (not full text) of reports from the main English courts. The coverage starts from January 1, 1980. Only Scottish cases which are followed in England are available.

Indexes helpful for locating older cases

The Index to Morison's Dictionary 📖

4–53 This publication covers cases from 1540–1820.

Scots Digest 📖

4–54 House of Lords cases from 1707–1947 and cases from Scottish superior courts from 1800–1947.

The Faculty Digest 📖

4–55 This covers cases from 1868–1990.

The Digest 📖

4–56 This is predominantly an English reference work. Scottish cases are referred to after English counterparts. Check the consolidated table of cases to find the correct volume number. The case table in the appropriate volume refers to the requisite paragraph number.

Finding an older case

4–57 Find the Scottish case of *Branford's Trustees v Powell*:

> ✤ This case does not appear in Westlaw, JustCite or Current Law. This would suggest that it is an older case, i.e. pre-1947;
> ✤ Check the Faculty Digest;
> ✤ Volume 6 is an indices volume covering 1868–1922. Check in the Cases in Digest Table.
> ✤ There is no entry for this case.
> ✤ The Supplement volumes now need to be checked on a volume by volume basis. Volume 1922–1930 does contain a reference to this case and refers the reader to p.29. The entry there gives a summary of the case and alternative citations: 1924, S.C. 439; 61 S.L.R. 306 and 1924, S.L.T. 334;
> ✤ Reference to this case could also be found by checking the Consolidated Table of Cases in the Stair Memorial Encyclopaedia.

Finding cases by subject

4–58 Encyclopaedias, reference works or textbooks are ideal starting points for research by subject. Unlike an electronic database, they will not just identify a case, they will place it in context. This means that such resources explain the background of the case, its impact on the area of law concerned, how it has been interpreted by the courts in addition to offering critical and/or analytical comment on it. Encyclopaedias or reference works can also provide the researcher with the information necessary to refine search terms which will make searching the full text databases a more efficient and manageable experience. When consulting an encyclopaedia or reference work look at the Table of Cases which will be located at the beginning of the work. This will list cases in alphabetical order.

The Laws of Scotland: Stair Memorial Encyclopaedia 📖

4–59 Search by subject by checking:

> ➢ The Consolidated Index;
> ➢ The relevant volume or reissued title which contains a Table of Cases;
> ➢ Update a search firstly by checking the Annual Cumulative Supplement;
> ➢ Then update by checking the Service Binder.

The Laws of Scotland Online (*Stair Memorial Encyclopaedia*) ⌐⌐ subscription from LexisNexis
The online version can be searched by free text. **4–60**

General reference texts 📖
These tend to have been updated over the years and run to several editions thus the primary task **4–61**
is to ensure that the most up-to-date edition is consulted. An example is Gloag and Henderson,
The Law of Scotland, 13th edn (Edinburgh: W. Green, 2012). General reference works tend not
to provide much detail about cases but should provide the reader with a citation. If a fuller
discussion of the case is required consult a dedicated textbook in the relevant area.

Westlaw ⌐⌐ subscription database
From the landing page, select the cases heading from the navigation bar at the top of the screen. **4–62**
This will link to the cases basic search page, where cases can be searched for by entering subject
terms into free text. Westlaw will search for these within the text of all case analyses and
judgments. If a search by phrase is preferred put same inside quotation marks. Searching can be
improved if connectors are used.

LexisNexis ⌐⌐ subscription database
Choose the cases tab from the homepage. This opens up the cases search form. Enter words or **4–63**
phrases in the enter search terms box. Connectors can be used to show the relation of the terms
selected. See paras 2–58—2–59.

Justis UK and Irish Primary Case Law/Specialist Case Law ⌐⌐ subscription
See para.4–41. **4–64**

JustCite ⌐⌐ subscription legal citator
See para.4–46. **4–65**

Current Law Yearbooks 📖
Check the relevant subject headings in the Yearbooks and the latest Monthly Digest. These will **4–66**
lead you to a digest of the case and to citations in the law reports. The Yearbooks have a
separate section for Scottish material. The index at the end of each Yearbook, however, does
not have a separate Scottish section. Scottish material is indexed under the appropriate subject
heading. The reader is alerted to the fact that it is a Scottish reference if the reference given ends
with a capital "S".

Check the appropriate subject heading in the index at the back of the Yearbook. The headings **4–67**
only appear if there is material included under that heading so the headings can vary from
Yearbook to Yearbook. The subject categorisation can sometimes leave a lot to be desired thus
it is prudent to search under related terms.

Subject Indexes in Various Series of Law Reports

Session Cases (S.C.), the paper version of the S.L.T., S.C.C.R, S.C.L.R. and G.W.D all have **4–68**
subject indexes. The ease of use will depend on whether the approximate dates and/or the
frequency of consolidation volumes of the subject indexes are known. If the date is unknown
and there are no consolidated indexes, a search must be conducted volume by volume.

4–69 Recent cases will appear on the Scottish Courts website and BAILII shortly after the judgement has been issued.

Sources useful for UK cases but not for Scottish cases

Halsbury's Laws of England 📖 and ⌁ subscription
4–70 See Ch.9.

Lawtel ⌁ *subscription* legal current awareness digest service
4–71 Lawtel only covers Scottish cases which are followed in England. It can be searched by free text or a structured search.

Finding cases containing certain words or phrases

4–72 Most electronic databases, both subscription and open source, allow a search to be undertaken for particular words and phrases. However, as detailed at several points in Ch.3, when searching a database in this way the researcher will retrieve all results where a selected word or phrase occurs in a case. It is therefore preferable to check sources which have selected relevant cases for you and contain specific indexes of words and phrases judicially considered.

Judicial dictionaries 📖
4–73 These are publications specifically dealing with the interpretation of words and phrases. Scottish publications include: W.J. Stewart, *Scottish Contemporary Judicial Dictionary* (Edinburgh: W. Green, 1995), and A.W. Dalrymple and Gibb, *Dictionary of Words and Phrases* (Edinburgh: W. Green, 1946).

4–74 A recent UK publication that provides judicial definitions of words and phrases in decided cases or statutory provisions is D. Greenberg, *Stroud's Judicial Dictionary of words and Phrases*, 8th edn (First Supplement) (London: Sweet and Maxwell, 2013).

Current Law Yearbooks ⌁
4–75 Consult the "Words and Phrases Judicially Considered Tables" in the appropriate Yearbook and the latest Monthly Digest. The Table lists words and phrases alphabetically. Beside a particular word or phrase will be the paragraph number for where the case is digested.

Subject indexes of law reports 📖 and ⌁ subscription
4–76 The subject indexes of many law reports include "Words and Phrases" as a subject heading. Law reports which do include: S.C., S.C.L.R., S.C.C.R, the Faculty Digest and The Law Reports Index.

4–77 The Consolidated Indexes to the All England Law Reports (see para.9–13), contain a "Words and phrases judicially considered" table.

Halsbury's Laws of England 📖 and ⌁ subscription
4–78 *The Consolidated Index to Halsbury's Laws of England* has a Words and Phrases Table. This includes words which are defined or explained in Halsbury's Laws. The Consolidated Index can be accessed in paper form in a law library and also in the LexisNexis subscription database. This publication is discussed at various points in Ch.9.

The Law Reports Index 📖
4–79 This index which covers a large number of English law reports contains a table indexing subject matter which includes "Words and Phrases" as a heading.

Westlaw ✍ subscription database

From the landing page, select the cases tab from the navigation bar at the top of the screen. This **4–80** will link to the cases basic search page, where cases can be searched for by entering inter alia key subject terms into the free text search box. This allows the researcher to look for terms or phrases relating to the subject matter of the cases sought. In order to search for a phrase, quotation marks should be used to enable Westlaw to search for the search terms within the entire text of all case analyses, official judgments and transcripts.

LexisNexis ✍ subscription database

Choose the cases tab from the homepage. This opens up the cases search form. Enter words or **4–81** phrases in the enter search terms box. Connectors can be used to show the relationship of the terms. See paras 2–58—2–59.

Finding cases and interpreting legislation

The easiest method of locating this information online is using Westlaw or LexisNexis with **4–82** Citators representing the best paper-based alternative.

Westlaw ✍ subscription database

From the home page, select the cases tab from the navigation bar at the top of the screen. This **4–83** will link to the cases basic search page where advanced search (in the top right of the screen) should be selected. Enter the short title in the legislation title field and the provision in the legislation provision field. This will retrieve cases which have interpreted the specific provision.

To find out if any cases have concerned s.20 of the Freedom of Information (Scotland) Act **4–84** 2002:

- ✍ Go to the cases section and click on advanced search;
- ✍ Enter Freedom of Information (Scotland) Act 2002 into the legislation title field and click on the section option for the legislative provision and enter "20" into the box alongside. Click search.

View the results, which show three entries:

- ➤ *South Lanarkshire Council v Scottish Information Commissioner*, 2013 S.L.T. 799;
- ➤ *Glasgow City Council v Scottish Information Commissioner*, 2010 S.C. 125;
- ➤ *Common Services Agency v Scottish Information Commissioner*, 2007 S.C. 231.

If a summary of one or all of these cases is required, click on case analysis. If the full judgment is sought, click on the citation. The above cases also have alternative citations listed.

Current Law Legislation Citators 📖

The Legislation citator volumes list cases opposite the entry for the Act concerned. To find out if **4–85** any cases have concerned a particular statutory provision:

- ✍ Check through the legislation citators in chronological order. Look under the piece of legislation. If a case has taken place, it will appear opposite the statute or section thereof.
- ✍ Check the most recent update for the citator in the Statutes Service File.

Using Current Law Legislation Citators to locate cases

4–86 To find out if any cases have concerned s.9 of the Gender Recognition Act 2004 the following steps have to be taken.

> ↳ **Step 1**: Consult the Statute Citator in the Legislation Citators volume 2002 -2004 in order to locate the chapter number of this Act. This is achieved by checking the alphabetical list of Acts at the beginning of the volume. The chapter number is seven (c.7). Once armed with the chapter number turn to the Citator itself. Look for the heading for 2004 and within that year for any entry for c.7. When the entry for the Act has been located look for section 9 (s.9) in the list underneath the heading. There are no entries for s.9.
>
> ↳ **Step 2**: Check the Statute Citator in the Legislation Citators volume 2005. There are no entries for s.9.
>
> ↳ **Step 3**: Check the Statute Citator in the Legislation Citators volume 2006. There are no entries for s.9.
>
> ↳ **Step 4**: Check the Statute Citator in the Legislation Citators volume 2007. There are no entries for s.9.
>
> ↳ **Step 5**: Check the Statute Citator in the Legislation Citators volume 2008. There are no entries for s.9.
>
> ↳ **Step 6**: Check the Statute Citator in the Legislation Citators volume 2009. A case is listed per s.9: *R (on the Application of B) v Secretary of State for Justice* [2009] EWHC 2220 (Admin.); [2009] H.R.L.R. 35 (Q.B.D (Admin).
>
> ↳ **Step 7**: Check the Statute Citator in the Legislation Citators volume 2010. A case is listed per s.9: *M v Revenue and Customs Commissioners* [2010] UKFTT 36 (TC); [2010] SFTD 1141 (FTT (Tax)).
>
> ↳ **Step 8**: Check the Statute Citator in the Legislation Citators volume 2011. There are no entries for s.9.
>
> ↳ **Step 9**: Check the Statute Citator in the Legislation Citators volume 2012. There are no entries for s.9.
>
> ↳ **Step 10**: Check the Statute Citator in the Legislation Citators volume 2013. There are no entries for s.9.

To bring the search as up-to-date as possible check the latest edition of the Statute Citator in the Statutes Service File in the library.

By following these steps the researcher can be almost certain that (up to the last month) only the two cases detailed above have concerned s.9 of the Gender Recognition Act 2004.

Law Reports Indexes 📖

4–87 ➢ S.L.T. has an alphabetical subject index and under the words "statutes and orders" legislation judicially considered is listed in alphabetical order.
➢ S.C.L.R. has a Table in each volume of "Statutes, SI and Court Rules Judicially Considered".
➢ Each volume of S.C.C.R. has a "Statutes and SI Judicially Considered" table. These are consolidated in the 1950–1980 supplement and the 1981–1990 and 1991–2000 indexes. The 1950–1980 index contains reference to High Court of Justiciary cases heard before this series of law reports came into existence and previously unreported.
➢ The Faculty Digest contains indexes of "Statutes, Acts of Sederunt, Statutory Orders etc. judicially commented on". Volume 6 contains an index for Vols 1–5; thereafter each volume of the Supplement has its own index.

➢ The Consolidated Indexes to the All England Law Reports contain a table of "Statutes Judicially Considered".

Tables of Statutes in textbooks 📖
Tables of statutes in textbooks are usually found at the beginning of the book, after the contents **4–88** page and next to the table of cases. The entries will refer to passages in the text that discuss the legislation. Relevant cases may also be discussed at the same point in the text.

Sources useful for UK cases but not for Scottish cases

Halsbury's Statutes of England 📖 and ⊕ subscription
A comprehensive and regularly updated source with which to locate English and Welsh case **4–89** law.

The Law Reports Index (Red Books) 📖
Published since 1951 by the Incorporated Council of Law Reporting, reported Appeal Cases, **4–90** Queen's Bench, Chancery and Family court cases are indexed separately in the English Law Reports series. Each main volume covers a decade, with supplements to update the main volume being published on a regular basis throughout a calendar year.

Lawtel ⊕ subscription legal current awareness digest service
On the Lawtel UK homepage click on browse legislation. This option lists legislation cited in **4–91** case law and the list can be viewed alphabetically or chronologically. Click on the name of an Act. This opens up lists which can be expanded. There is a list of cases citing specific sections of an Act and also for a list of cases citing the Act itself. Lawtel only lists cases which appear in its database of case summaries and all of the cases cited link to the Lawtel case digests. However, Lawtel does not include Scottish cases unless they have been followed in England.

Finding journal articles or case notes about a case

Westlaw ⊕ subscription database
Westlaw has a Legal Journals Index within its journals section. This search tool indexes legal **4–92** articles and case summaries from hundreds of journals and dates back to 1986. There are two different ways in which information about journal articles or case notes can be obtained in Westlaw. One is to search the journals section with the alternative being to search the case analysis for a specific case. To search the journals section access it by selecting the Journals tab from the navigation bar at the top of the screen on the home page. This will link to the journals basic search page, select advanced search facility. Enter either the party names in the cases cited (party) field or the citation in the cases cited (citation) field. Then click search.

Westlaw will also identify articles which have discussed cases in the case analysis for the case **4–93** concerned. When a case is sought in Westlaw the results retrieved will offer a link to the case analysis and the full text. Click on case analysis and scroll down to the final section of the case analysis where a list of citations to articles about the case which have appeared in legal journals is detailed. Links will go to the full text (if available on Westlaw) or to an abstract of the article.

LexisNexis ⊕ subscription database
This is not as useful for tracing journal articles as it does not have the same coverage as the **4–94** Legal Journals Index on Westlaw. Choose the journals tab from the homepage. This opens up the journals search form. Enter the case details separated by "and" in the enter search terms box.

HeinOnline ⌁ subscription database of legal journals

4–95 This database holds a number of UK law journals in its Law Journal Library. The journals are in full text which can be searched for articles about cases. However, its Scots law related holdings are currently limited.

Current Law Yearbooks 📖

4–96 Search under the appropriate subject headings in the Yearbooks and the latest Monthly Digest.

Journals 📖

4–97 If the date of the case is known check relevant journal indexes. S.L.T. often contains articles on recent cases. Specialist journals may contain commentaries on recent relevant case law, e.g. Greens Business Law Bulletin, Greens Civil Practice Bulletin, Greens Criminal Law Bulletin, Greens Employment Law Bulletin, Greens Family Law Bulletin and Greens Property Law Bulletin. They are published bi-monthly and contain commentaries about recent cases.

Lawtel ⌁ subscription legal current awareness digest service

4–98 Lawtel indexes fewer journals than the Legal Journals Index and the majority of its coverage of journals dates from 1998. To locate articles about a case, select the articles index on the home page, then choose the focused search option. Use the case law cited box to enter the name of the case. Lawtel currently has limited coverage of Scottish cases.

JustCite ⌁ subscription legal citator

4–99 JustCite currently indexes and provides links to documents from over 90 legal publishers.

Current status of a case (i.e. whether the case has been considered by the court on a subsequent occasion)

Westlaw ⌁ subscription database

4–100 It is vital for the researcher to ensure that any research undertaken about a decided case is as up-to-date as possible. If a case has been overruled by a higher court it no longer represents the law on a specific point and cannot be cited as authority for a particular proposition. There are two different ways to obtain current information about a decided case in Westlaw.

4–101 From the welcome page, select the cases heading from the navigation bar at the top of the screen to link to the cases basic search page, then select advanced search in the top right of the screen. Enter the party name(s) in the cases cited (party) field or the citation in the cases cited (citation) field. This will retrieve details of the cases which have considered the particular case. When a case search is undertaken in Westlaw the results retrieved will also offer a link to the case analysis and the full text case report. To search in this way, click on case analysis and then click on the Cases citing this case link in the left hand side of the screen. This will then link to a section of the case analysis which identifies a list of citations to cases which have cited the case. Links will go to the full text of the cases if they are available in Westlaw.

4–102 To find out if *Galt v Goodsir*, 1982 J.C.4 has subsequently been judicially considered:

    ↳   Go to the cases basic search page.
    ↳   Select advanced search in the top right of the screen.
    ↳   Enter the party name(s) in the cases cited (party) field: *Galt v Goodsir*. This retrieves two results: *Hingston v Pollock* 1990 J.C. 138 and *McMahon v Cardle* 1988 S.C.C.R. 556. Then click through to their respective case analysis and the full text judgment, (if available).

Alternatively:

> ✎ Go into the cases basic search page and enter "Galt & Goodsir" in the party names box and click search.

Westlaw has retrieved one case.

> ✎ Click on the case analysis. This shows that the case has been judicially considered by two cases. It has been applied by *McMahon v Cardle*, 1988 S.C.C.R. 556 and followed by *Hingston v Pollock*, 1990 J.C. 138. Clicking on the citations for these cases will take the researcher to the respective case analysis section which can then be clicked on to link to the full text judgment (if available).

If a case in Westlaw has been judicially considered, overruled or reversed or on appeal an alerting icon will appear in the results list—🅲, ▭ and 🅰 respectively.

LexisNexis ⌐ subscription database
LexisNexis will retrieve details of all occasions on which a case has been referred to by another **4–103** case. Go to the cases search field. In the enter search terms box enter the party names connecting them with w/8. This connector (see para.2–58) will look for the party names within eight words of each other in any case.

JustCite ⌐ subscription legal Citator
Once a case has been located in JustCite a link will be provided to show its current status via **4–104** subsequent judicial discussion (if any).

Current Law Case Citators 📖
To find out if a case has been commented on by the courts, distinguished or overruled: **4–105**

> ✎ **Step 1**: Check through the Current Law Case Citators in chronological order. Remember that if it is a Scottish case to check in the Scottish section at the back of the volume. Cases are listed in alphabetical order of the first named party. Opposite the entry for the case will be details of whether the case has been judicially considered. It will state whether the case was applied, distinguished, followed, referred to, etc.
> ✎ **Step 2**: Check the Table of Cases in the most recent Monthly Digest.

Find out if *Galt v Goodsir* 1982 J.C. 4 been judicially considered.

> ✎ **Step 1**: *Galt v Goodsir* first appears in the Case Citator volume covering the year 1982, i.e. 1977–1997. Opposite the entry for the case are two references to judicial consideration: "applied 89/**4924** and followed 90/**5753**."
>   These references are to digests of cases which respectively "applied" and "followed" *Galt v Goodsir*. See para.4–30.
>   The digests as they appear in the Current Law Yearbooks may be sufficient for the researcher's purposes. If not, they will contain the citations for the full text case reports which can then be accessed.
>   To bring the search up-to-date the following steps must also be undertaken:
> ✎ **Step 2**: Check the Case Citator volume 1998–2001.
>   There are no entries.
> ✎ **Step 3**: Check the Case Citator volume 2002–2004.
>   There are no entries.

⁋ **Step 4**: Check the Case Citator volume 2005 and then every subsequent annual volume year up to the current year.
There are no entries.

⁋ **Step 5**: Check the Table of Cases in the latest Monthly Digest. Again, there is no entry.

It can be concluded that (unless there has been a development in the last month) *Galt v Goodsir* has been judicially considered on two occasions.

The Law Reports Index 📖

4–106 Check the section on cases judicially considered.

Checking the Status of Old Scottish Cases

Faculty Digest 📖

4–107 This covers cases from 1868–1990. Check Tables of "Cases Judicially Referred to".

Scots Digest 📖

4–108 Check tables of "Cases judicially commented on" in relation to the Scottish superior courts from 1800–1947.

How to find out if an older case has been commented on by the courts, distinguished or overruled

4–109 Has *Crombie v M'Ewan*, 1871 23 D. 333 been judicially considered?

⁋ **Step 1**: Check the Faculty Digest. Volume 6, indices volume, contains a Table of Cases Judicially Referred To. This contains an entry for the above case. It was applied in *Gray v Smart*, 1892 19 R. 692; 29 S.L.R. 589.

⁋ **Step 2**: The Supplement volumes need to be checked one by one:

- 1922–1930—no entry;
- 1930–1940—no entry;
- 1940–1950—it was followed in *Brady v Napier & Son*, 1944 S.C. 18, 1943 S.N. 71, 1944 S.L.T. 187;
- 1951–1960—no entry;
- 1961–1970—no entry;
- 1971–1980—no entry;
- 1981–1990—no entry;
- 1990 to present day—no entries.

⁋ **Step 3**: Bring the search up to date by checking the Current Law Case Citator (which does not show any entries).

Finding recent cases

Open source

4–110 The quickest way of locating very recent judgments is to access the website of the court concerned—the utility of official open sources such as the Scottish Courts website, BAILLI and the UK Supreme Court's website et al having been discussed in Ch.2. However, only certain courts select cases for online publication based on an assessment of their legal significance. The Scottish Courts website is one such example with another being the Incorporated Council of Law Reporting ("ICLR") open source case summary service/latest published cases database which can be accessed via the ICLR home page. See *http://www.iclr.co.uk/* [accessed May 30, 2014]. The courts covered by ICLR include: the UK Supreme Court; the Privy Council; the

Court of Appeal, all divisions of the High Court and the Court of Justice of the EU. Applications for permission to appeal to the UK Supreme Court during a given year are also listed on the landing page. The selected cases are in most circumstance summarised and published within twenty four hours of the judgment being handed down.

Law reports are published in newspapers but these are only short summaries of a case. English **4–111** daily newspapers which publish law reports are: *The Daily Telegraph* (which has law reports from Westlaw updated every Thursday), *The Financial Times*, *The Guardian*, *The Independent* and *The Times*.

Subscription

Cases initially appear on Westlaw and LexisNexis in the current awareness section on the day **4–112** the judgement is issued and then will generally appear in full text in the cases section within twenty four hours. Westlaw's sister service Lawtel offers a same day reporting service. See *http://www.lawtel.com/Login?ReturnUrl=%2fLogin.aspx* [accessed May 30, 2014].

Case Notes is a service offered by ICLR. It provides digests of significant judgments of all senior **4–113** English courts that ICLR will not subsequently publish in full. The service is updated most working days with digests appearing within forty eight hours of the judgement being handed down.

S.L.T. and G.W.D., the All England Law Reports and the Weekly Law Reports are all pub- **4–114** lished weekly. However, given the time delay between a judgment being handed down and the case being reported in these formal series of law reports (even the weekly series of law reports) one or two months may elapse before a case report is available in this form. The first law report series in Scotland to publish a case will be G.W.D. However, this will contain a brief summary of the case only.

The Current Law Monthly Digest also provides information on recent cases. **4–115**

The varying importance of reported cases

As detailed in Ch.2 and above, there are many different sources which make reports of cases **4–116** available very quickly after judgment has been given by a court. While it is vital for legal scholars to be as up-to-date as possible, the widespread availability online of recent judgments from both official and unofficial sources poses some specific and, for the unwary, unforeseen problems. When cases initially appear online they are not categorised or "flagged" in any way to define their importance, although the status (seniority) of the court handing down the judgment may give an indication of the same with cases from appellate courts generally proving of greater interest to the researcher. However, not all reported cases are of equal significance; some will merely concur with the interpretation of a legal rule or principle yielded by a prior case whilst others may effect a change in the law, e.g. *Grant v Australian Knitting Mills Ltd* [1936] A.C. 562 applied the "neighbour" principle as originally defined by the House of Lords in *Donoghue v Stevenson* [1932] A.C. 562 with the caveat that the principle can be applied in personal injury claims only where the defect in a product "is hidden and unknown to the customer or consumer". Thus *Grant v Australian Knitting Mills Ltd* did not create a new legal principle or rule of law. Rather, it expanded upon the legal reasoning underpinning the decision in *Donoghue v Stevenson*.

A further issue is that of the lapse of time between the date of a judgment and the publication of **4–117** professional commentaries (bona fide secondary sources) which interpret the case. Such contextualised and objective comment on the legal significance of a case assists the researcher in their evaluation of its merits and ultimately whether it is worthy of inclusion in a research project. However, certain blogs or open source websites authored and hosted by legal academics or practitioners may provide valid comment—sometimes within hours of the publication of a significant judgment—and such sources can be consulted with confidence. The obvious difficulty is discerning, at least in the early stages of a research career, such valid sources from those published by non-legal commentators. Undergraduate law students should seek the guidance of their tutor if in doubt about the provenance of specific open source resources offering opinion on the interpretation and/or the merits of a recently decided case.

Finding cases from courts of special jurisdiction

4–118 Source of cases from other courts include:

(i) *Lands Tribunal for Scotland.* The website for the Lands Tribunal contains details of decisions made in recent cases that the tribunal considers to be important or significant. There are examples under the jurisdictions relating to disputed compensation, valuation for rating, tenants' rights to buy, discharge of land obligations, Land Register appeals and title conditions. There is a free text search facility and the decisions can be browsed by subject. The results retrieved will link to a summary of the case from where the full text of the decision can be accessed. See *http://www.lands-tribunalscotland.org.uk/records.html* [accessed June 25, 2014]. Selected cases have been reported in the S.L.T.1971.

(ii) *Lands Valuation Appeal Court.* Decisions are published in Session Cases (since 1907) and the S.L.T. (since 1893). Casecheck (a subscription database), see *http://www.casecheck.co.uk/CaseLaw.aspx?BlogID=700* [accessed May 30, 2014], publishes Lands Valuation Appeal Court decisions from all UK jurisdictions and selected European judgments.

(iii) *Scottish Land Court.* Decisions are published as the Scottish Land Court Reports from 1982 to the present day. Digests of cases since 1982 are available online at *http://www.scottish-land-court.org.uk/digest.html* [accessed May 30, 2014], as are recent unreported decisions, see *http://www.scottish-land-court.org.uk/recent.html* [accessed May 30, 2014]. From 1964 onwards selected cases have been published in the S.L.T.

(iv) *Court of the Lord Lyon.* See *http://www.lyoncourt.com/lordlyon/CCC_FirstPage.jsp* [accessed May 30, 2014]. Since 1950 selected cases from the Court of the Lord Lyon have been reported in S.L.T.

Finding decisions from administrative tribunals

4–119 Decisions from administrative tribunals are generally published online, although significant decisions (generally appeal cases) will appear in the law reports.

Decisions of the Scottish Information Commissioner

4–120 The Scottish Information Commissioner "is responsible for enforcing and promoting Scotland's freedom of information laws", which comprise:

➢ The Freedom of Information (Scotland) Act 2002;
➢ The Environmental Information (Scotland) Regulations 2004; and
➢ The INSPIRE (Scotland) Regulations 2009 (pertaining to environmental datasets).

Decisions can be accessed here:
http://www.itspublicknowledge.info/ApplicationsandDecisions/Decisions/decisions.php [accessed May 30, 2014].

Decisions of the Information Commissioner's Office (England and Wales)

The Information Commissioner "uphold[s] information rights in the public interest [and], data **4–121** privacy for individuals". Decision notices issued per the Freedom of Information Act 2000, the Environmental Information Regulations 2004 or the Inspire Regulations 2009, (see *http://search.ico.org.uk/ico/search/decisionnotice* [accessed May 30, 2014]), can be appealed to the First-tier Tribunal (Information Rights), see *http://www.justice.gov.uk/tribunals/general-regulatory-chamber/hearings-and-decisions* [accessed May 30, 2014].

The Information Commissioner's office can also levy fines of up to £500,000 for "serious **4–122** breaches" of the Data Protection Act 1998 and Privacy and Electronic Communications Regulations 2003 (see *http://www.ico.org.uk/enforcement/fines* [accessed May 30, 2014]), with appeals against a notice also being heard by the First-tier Tribunal (Information Rights).

Decisions of the Upper Tribunal Administrative Appeals Chamber

This body consider appeals from inter alia the following First-tier Tribunals and certain stat- **4–123** utory bodies:

> ➤ General Regulatory;
> ➤ Health, Education and Social Care;
> ➤ Mental Health Review Tribunal for Wales;
> ➤ Pensions Appeal Tribunal Scotland;
> ➤ Pensions Appeal Tribunal in Northern Ireland (assessment appeals under the War Pensions Scheme only);
> ➤ Social Entitlement;
> ➤ Special Educational Needs Tribunal for Wales;
> ➤ The Disclosure and Barring Service (formerly the Independent Safeguarding Authority) (England and Wales);
> ➤ Traffic Commissioners (England, Wales and Scotland); and
> ➤ War Pensions and Armed Forces Compensation (UK).

Further information about First-tier tribunals is available by accessing the following links, *http://www.justice.gov.uk/tribunals/aa* and *http://www.justice.gov.uk/about/hmcts/tribunals* [accessed May 30, 2014].

Decisions of the Employment Appeal Tribunal

The Employment Appeal Tribunal hears appeals from the decisions of UK employment tri- **4–124** bunals. Published full decisions from 1999 onwards can be accessed at *http://www.justice.gov.uk/tribunals/employment-appeals/judgments* [accessed May 30, 2014]. The database can be searched by topic, case number, judge, party and date. Decisions are also published in the Industrial Cases Reports and the Industrial Relations Law Reports.

Decisions of the Tax and Chancery (Upper Tribunal)

This body enjoys UK wide jurisdiction in tax cases appealed from the First-tier Tribunal in Tax **4–125** and references against decisions of inter alia:

> ➤ The Financial Conduct Authority;
> ➤ The Pensions Regulator;
> ➤ The Property Chamber (First-tier) as of July 2013 per land registration cases previously dealt with by The Adjudicator to HM Land Registry;
> ➤ The Prudential Regulation Authority.

See *http://www.justice.gov.uk/tribunals/tax-and-chancery-upper-tribunal* [accessed May 30, 2014].

NB Many tribunal decisions are also available via BAILII.

PUTTING CASES INTO CONTEXT

4–126 In order to put a case, recently decided or otherwise, into context an appreciation of its impact on the prevailing law is essential. As detailed in this chapter, there are numerous open and subscription resources available to the researcher to aid: (i) the location of case law; and (ii) understanding of the impact (thus relevance) of a recently decided case via authoritative secondary sources. Whilst individual comprehension and understanding of the ratio of a case must be achieved, undergraduate students, in particular, can facilitate this outcome more readily by adopting the following approach when evaluating the materials consulted.

> ✺ Re-examine any lecture/tutorial/seminar notes. What prominence (if any) was given by the tutor to cases discussed in class meetings? Isolate the "leading" cases and plot the trajectory (timeline) of the law in the specified area. Consider (if relevant) where an existing rule of law was applied, modified or ignored, e.g. the current law on non-contractual liability for negligent misstatement can be charted from the House of Lords decision in *Hedley Byrne & Co Ltd v Heller & Partners Ltd* [1964] A.C. 465, where it was accepted that one party may owe another a duty of care for the utterance of negligent statements if s/he assumed responsibility for the statement(s) and it was reasonably foreseeable that the party receiving the information contained in the statement would place reliance on same (in doing so the court approved the dissenting judgment of Denning LJ in *Candler v Crane, Christmas & Co* [1951] 2 K.B. 164).
>
> Thereafter, in an attempt to ensure the *Hedley Byrne* decision did not *open the floodgates* to an abundance of claims, the House of Lords, in *Caparo Industries plc v Dickman* [1990] 2 A.C. 605, required "proximity" between the parties concerned be shown and further that it must be "fair, just and reasonable" to impose a duty of care on the maker of a statement. *White v Jones* [1995] 2 A.C. 207 then extended liability to include "proximate" third parties in certain circumstance.
>
> ✺ Consult the most up-to-date recommended text book(s). Compare the information contained therein with lecture, etc., notes to confirm the trajectory of the law.
>
> ✺ Consult a major reference work such as *The Laws of Scotland: Stair Memorial Encyclopaedia* to consolidate understanding of the information gathered in class meetings and through private study.
>
> ✺ Consult academic comment or opinion on leading cases. Certain series of law reports, e.g. the S.C.C.R., S.C.L.R, Greens Family Law Reports, and Greens Housing Law Reports provide excellent coverage in their respective areas.
>
> Likewise, articles/case notes/case comments, etc., in legal journals (either in paper or electronic form) will yield an abundance of secondary materials which will: (i) aid understanding; and (ii) provide a further benchmark with which knowledge gained via class meetings and private study can be consolidated.

NB The Case Analysis section in Westlaw identifies and links to cases which have considered the case(s) of interest and relevant journal articles if available within Westlaw. The Current Law Case Citator will also provide references to any subsequent cases which have considered the case(s). The relevant case report(s) can then be examined.

Further reading

- A. Bradney, F. Cownie, J. Masson, A Neal and D. Newell, *How to Study Law*, 7th edn **4–127** (London: Sweet & Maxwell, 2014)
- J. Knowles and P. Thomas, *Effective Legal Research*, 3rd edn (London: Sweet & Maxwell, 2012)

Chapter 5
Introduction to Legislation

Significant abbreviations used in this chapter

- Asp—Act of the Scottish Parliament
- EU—European Union
- ECHR—European Convention on Human Rights
- MSP—Member of the Scottish Parliament
- Sch.—Schedule
- SI—Statutory Instrument

Author's note

At the time of writing, a referendum is due to take place on September 18, 2014 (shortly after the publication of this book) to ask the Scottish people whether Scotland should remain part of the UK or become an independent country. An affirmative majority vote in favour of the latter option will clearly impact upon the prevailing constitutional and legal regimes currently operating within the United Kingdom. However, until the outcome of the referendum is known and any subsequent changes to the status quo are made this book can only proceed by detailing the current constitutional arrangements and legislative powers of the Scottish Government, as enshrined in the Scotland Act 1998, as amended by the Scotland Act 2012.

5–01 Legislation, in all its many guises, is the prime source of Scots law. Familiarity with the concept and construction of legislation and the various forms in which it is enacted is essential to the study of law for both students and practitioners who are required to find, consult and decipher the meaning of such statutory provisions on a frequent, if not daily basis. This chapter looks (briefly) at the pre-1707 Scottish Parliament (also referred to as the Old Scots Parliament). It then focuses on the UK Parliament at Westminster and discusses the main processes by which laws are made there and details the anatomy of both an Act of Parliament and a Statutory Instrument ("SI") (respectively primary and delegated legislation).Thereafter, it discusses how to cultivate the essential skills of reading and interpreting these provisions.

5–02 The chapter then turns its attention to the Scottish Parliament at Holyrood and considers its processes for making primary and secondary legislation and the anatomy of both an Act of the Scottish Parliament and a Scottish SI ("SSI"). For the sake of consistency and clarity, the UK parliament is referred to as "Westminster", whilst the Scottish Parliament is referred to as "Holyrood" to denote, (i) their separate geographical locations and (ii) the names they are commonly known by. Chapters 6 and 7 then focus on aids to locating legislation and the different search strategies which can be adopted.

Sources of legislation for Scotland

Discussion of the sources of legislation which affect Scotland primarily requires developing an **5–03** understanding of some of key events in Scottish history. Prior to 1707, Scotland was an independent country with its own sovereign Parliament which enacted legislation without interference from any other jurisdiction. Thus the earliest statutes which still affect the law of Scotland today emerged from the pre-1707 Scottish Parliament which existed prior to the Treaty of Union in 1707. Very few of the statutes of the pre-1707 Scottish Parliament are still in force, i.e. good law and, unless undertaking a study of the history of Scots law, it is unlikely that the researcher will need to consult them. The form of these statutes is very different from the layout and style of statutes today. They are usually very short and are obviously written in the language of the time which can make them difficult for the modern reader, especially those unfamiliar with the Scots language. A partial dataset covering the period 1424–1707 can be accessed here, *http://www.legislation.gov.uk/aosp* [accessed June 3, 2014].

The Treaty of Union of 1707 dissolved both the old English and Scottish Parliaments and **5–04** created the new Parliament of Great Britain sitting at Westminster. This new Parliament was the only legislature for Scotland for nearly the next three centuries. The Treaty of Union contained safeguards for the continuation of Scots law as a separate and distinct legal tradition from that of the rest of Great Britain (and, through time, the United Kingdom). The Treaty states that no alteration is to be made in laws concerning "private right", "except for the evident utility of the subjects within Scotland" (Article XVIII) and that the Court of Session and the High Court of Justiciary were to remain within Scotland "in all time coming".

When the United Kingdom became a member state of the then European Economic Com- **5–05** munity (now European Union, referred to as the EU) in 1973 a new source of legislation was introduced into the domestic legislative landscape which prevails throughout the UK to the present day. EU law is discussed in Ch.10. Then, following a referendum in 1997 the majority of Scottish citizens voted for "devolution"—the transfer of certain legislative powers from the national Government to regional Government, i.e. from the UK Parliament at Westminster to a new Scottish Parliament at Holyrood in Edinburgh. The Westminster parliament passed the Scotland Act 1998 which details the legislative powers devolved to the Scottish Parliament and those reserved (retained) by Westminster.

The inaugural meeting of the Scottish Parliament was held on May 12, 1999. However, West- **5–06** minster remains the supreme legislator within the United Kingdom as it can enact legislation for Scotland in both reserved *and* devolved areas. (s.28(7) Scotland Act 1998). Thus, at present, legislation affecting Scotland can emerge from the Westminster Parliament, the Scottish Parliament and the EU.

Legislation enacted by Westminster

UK legislation is made by or with the authority of the Westminster Parliament and can be **5–07** divided into primary legislation, i.e. Acts of Parliament (also referred to as statutes) and delegated legislation (also referred to as secondary or subordinate legislation). Primary legislation is made by the Westminster Parliament and involves a process of parliamentary scrutiny. Delegated legislation can be made by an individual or a body who has been given the power to legislate by Westminster. The main form of delegated legislation is statutory instruments (SI) and for this reason this type of delegated legislation will feature throughout this chapter.

A key difference between the two types of legislation concerns challenges to their validity. The **5–08** validity of an Act of the Westminster Parliament can be challenged in court on the grounds that it is non-compliant with the European Communities Act 1972 and/or the Human Rights Act 1998, but cannot be struck down by a court, i.e. the provision concerned no longer has any legal effect. However, the validity of delegated legislation, if challenged, can be struck down by a court (via a judicial review) on the foregoing grounds or because the delegated provision is ultra vires, i.e. beyond the powers given in the parent Act to the individual or body empowered to make the instrument. It should be noted at this point that the validity of *all* legislation emerging from the Holyrood Parliament is open to challenge.

5–09   An Act of the Westminster Parliament can alter the general law of the United Kingdom, in which case it is called a Public General Act. However, it is also possible (although much less common) to affect only private interests by Act of Parliament. This type of Act is called a Local and Personal Act. Once an Act has become law it can be altered. The term used is "amended". An Act may be amended many times and amendments made may in turn be amended by subsequent legislation. An Act cannot be amended by something said by a judge in a case interpreting a legislative provision or by the comments of a member of the Government in the House of Commons or House of Lords (discussed below). It can only be amended by later Acts of Parliament or by an SI.

5–10   Acts of the Westminster Parliament do not cease to have the force of law just because they are old or have not been cited in court or applied for a long period of time. An Act remains part of the law until it is repealed which means that it ceases to be part of the law. Whole Acts or parts of Acts can be repealed. An Act can be repealed in one part of the UK but remain law in another area. Acts can be repealed by later Acts or by delegated legislation (providing it is within its powers, i.e. intra vires). The word "desuetude" (referring to the state of a legal provision being rendered obsolete through disuse without repeal—also known as the doctrine of implied repeal) does not apply to Westminster Acts. The doctrine of desuetude, if it applies at all within the UK now, will only apply to pre-1707 Scots Acts.

ACTS OF THE WESTMINSTER PARLIAMENT

Bills

5–11   A Bill is a provisional version of an Act before it is considered by Parliament. It is referred to as a Bill throughout its passage through Parliament and it becomes an Act after it receives the Royal Assent. A Bill may be initially published in draft form for the purpose of public consultation and be amended in light of comments received prior to its formal introduction to Parliament. There are three types of Bills: public, private and hybrid.

Public Bills

5–12   Public Bills affect the general law of the land and every member of the population. A Government Bill is a Public Bill which is presented to Parliament by a Government Minister. It will have been drafted by parliamentary draftsmen who are civil servants. Private Members Bills are Public Bills (not Private Bills) which are introduced by an individual MP (or Peer in the House of Lords) rather than by the Government. Public Bills account for the majority of Bills and, if passed, become Public General Acts.

Private Bills

5–13   Private Bills tend to be limited in effect to a certain area or organisation or even person. The process is initiated by a "promoter" instead of an MP. A promoter is someone who has an interest in the Bill. Historically there were large numbers of Private Bills, but they are much less common today. They were used to facilitate major works, such as the construction of the railways, harbours and canals. They were also used for some personal matters, such as divorce. Private Bills become Local and Personal Acts (also referred to as Private Acts). At the time of writing the Transport for London Bill is before the House of Lords and if passed by both Houses will become a Private Act in due course. The procedure relating to Private Bills is slightly different from that relating to Public Bills and is discussed below in para.5–24.

Hybrid Bills

As its name suggest, this is a Bill which affects both public and specific private interests. The **5–14** procedure used is a mixture of Public and Private Bill procedures. Such Bills are rarely enacted, but the High Speed Rail (London–West Midlands) Bill 2013–14 has been designated as a Hybrid Bill by Government and is, at the time of writing, before the House of Commons.

The procedure for a Public Bill in the UK (Westminster) Parliament

Most Bills may be introduced in Parliament in either the House of Lords or the House of **5–15** Commons. One exception is a specific provision known as a 'Money Bill' which deals with inter alia taxation. Such Bills must begin their Parliamentary passage in the House of Commons, (see s.1(2) of the Parliament Act 1911). *http://www.publications.parliament.uk/pa/ld201011/ldselect/ldconst/97/9703.htm* [accessed June 3, 2014].

A Bill must pass the stages detailed below in both Houses before it can be submitted for Royal **5–16** Assent.

House of Commons procedure

First Reading: This is the formal presentation of the Bill to Parliament. The name of the Bill is **5–17** read out and a date set for the second reading. An order is made for the Bill to be printed and to become publicly available.

Second Reading: This is where the House considers the principles contained in the Bill. The debate is recorded in *Hansard*, also known as the Official Report, which is an "edited verbatim report of proceedings of both the House of Commons and the House of Lords". Daily Debates from *Hansard* are published the next working day by 6am. See *http://www.parliament.uk/business/publications/hansard/* [accessed June 3, 2014].

Committee Stage: This stage involves consideration of the Bill on a clause-by-clause basis. The whole House can consider a Bill at Committee stage, but this usually only happens in exceptional circumstances, such as for Bills of constitutional importance. The norm is for a Bill to be considered by a Public Bill Committee (known as Standing Committees prior to the 2006–2007 session). See *http://www.parliament.uk/mps-lords-and-offices/offices/commons/scrutinyunit/public- bill-committees/* [accessed June 3, 2014].

Report Stage: This consists of the whole House considering the amendments made in Committee. If the Bill was previously dealt with by a Committee of the Whole House and no amendments were made it by-passes this stage and goes straight to the third reading stage.

Third Reading: This is where the House takes an overview of the amended Bill. When a Bill has completed this stage it then goes to the House of Lords where it has to progress through similar stages. When both Houses reach agreement the Bill goes forward for Royal Assent. This is the final stage of the Bill's passage through Parliament.

Royal assent is achieved when the Monarch of the day (currently HM Queen Elizabeth II) **5–18** expresses approval and the Bill becomes an Act of Parliament, which may come into force, i.e. has legal effect from:

> ➤ A date as stated in the Act;
> ➤ After a commencement order has been signed by the relevant government minister (a commencement order may bring the whole or part of an Act into force); or
> ➤ Midnight at the beginning of the day of the Royal Assent if neither of the above applies.

For further insight into the Constitutional convention that is Royal Assent, see N.W. Barber, *Can Royal Assent Be Refused on the Advice of the Prime Minister?* UK Const. L. Blog (September 25, 2013), available at *http://ukconstitutionallaw.org/2013/09/25/nick-barber-can-royal-assent-be-refused-on-the-advice-of-the-prime-minster/* [accessed June 3, 2014]. To track the progress of Bills currently before Parliament access the following link, *http://services.parliament.uk/bills/* [accessed June 3, 2014].

Citation of Bills

5–19 Each Bill is given a unique number, e.g. the Alan Turing (Statutory Pardon) Bill before Parliament in session 2013–14 was allocated the number "(9)" within round brackets for that session when it was introduced in the House of Lords. When it was introduced in the House of Commons thereafter it was allocated the number "(124)" to reflect the fact that it was the 124th Bill introduced in that House in session 2013–14. A session of Parliament generally runs for 12 months at which point it will be "prorogued" (discontinued) until the start of the next session. If a general election is called during a session this was also lead to the prorogation of Parliament.

5–20 To denote the fact that the Alan Turning Bill was introduced in the House of Lords the letters "[HL]" are included in the Bill's general title within square brackets. If a Bill is amended at any stage by either House it is reprinted. This will be denoted by the inclusion of the letter "R" in the Bill's designation. It will also be given a new number if this occurs. Given Bills may be amended many times as they progress through the various stages outlined above, it is, therefore, vital that the researcher is aware of which version of the Bill they are reading.

NB The number(s) of a Bill has no connection with the chapter number that will be allocated when the Bill becomes an Act. The divisions of a Bill are referred to as clauses and not as sections as in an Act of Parliament (see para.5–21 below).

The general title given to the Bill detailed above is: Alan Turing (Statutory Pardon) Bill [HL] 2013–14 and the elements of the citation of the Bill are:

> ➤ When introduced in the House of Lords; Alan Turing (Statutory Pardon) Bill (HL Bill 9) 2013–2014.
> ➤ When introduced in the House of Commons; Alan Turing (Statutory Pardon) Bill (HC Bill 124) 2013–2014.

Citation of Statutes

5–21 Acts of Parliament are normally referred to by their short title, e.g. Financial Services (Banking Reform) Act 2013. A complete citation would include the chapter number, e.g. Financial Services (Banking Reform) Act 2013 c.33. An Act can also be cited by referring to the year in which it was passed and the chapter number, e.g. 2013 c.33. Since 1963, the chapter number has been related to the sequence in which the Acts received Royal Assent during a calendar year. The above Act was the 33rd Act to receive the Royal Assent in 2013. Prior to 1963, the system was not as straightforward. Each Act was given a chapter number which related to its chronological place within the parliamentary session.

Each parliamentary session was numbered according to the Regnal year. This means the years **5–22** during which the Sovereign concerned had reigned. This was calculated from the month of accession to the throne. The Regnal year system means that Acts passed in the same calendar year can be in different Regnal years and/or in different parliamentary sessions. This means that care has to be taken when checking the older volumes of statutes. This cumbersome system was brought to an end by the Acts of Parliament Numbering and Citation Act 1962. Section 1 stated that chapter numbers were to be assigned by reference to the calendar year and not to the parliamentary session.

Thus, parliamentary sessions have never coincided with calendar years. Since 2010, they have **5–23** usually run from May to May (previously November to November).

> **NB** A table of the Regnal years appears at the front of this book. Scottish monarchs are included in the list and the citation conventions for pre-1707 Scots Acts are detailed in para.7–06.

The Procedure for a Private Bill

The normal procedure involves the presentation of a petition to Parliament by the person or **5–24** organisation "promoting" the Bill. Information about the contents of the Bill has to be widely circulated and the petitioner has to appear before an examiner. Private Bills then go through the same stages as Public Bills. Post-devolution, Scottish Private Bills which concern reserved matters are dealt with by the Westminster Parliament. They are subject to a streamlined procedure laid down in the Private Legislation Procedure (Scotland) Act 1936. Application has to be made to the Secretary of State for Scotland for a Provisional Order. If an inquiry is deemed appropriate, it is undertaken by Commissioners and sits in Scotland. The Commissioners make a report to the Secretary of State. If the Order has been approved, the Secretary of State will issue the Order. This does not become law until it has been confirmed by Parliament. The mechanism for this is an Order Confirmation Bill (which is a Public Bill) with the text of the Order appearing as the schedule to the Bill. If the Bill proceeds through a shortened parliamentary procedure, it emerges as a Local and Personal Act.

Local and Personal Acts

Citation

Private Bills become Local and Personal Acts. Historically, these Acts, introduced in 1798, were **5–25** subject to inconsistent numeration. However, they are now are cited in the same way as Public General Acts, except that, in order to differentiate them, the chapter number is printed differently:

> ➢ The chapter numbers of Local Acts appear in lower case roman numerals, e.g. Peterhead Harbours Order Confirmation Act 1992 c xii.
> ➢ The chapter numbers of Personal Acts appear in italicised Arabic figures, e.g. John Francis Dare and Gillian Loder Dare (Marriage Enabling) Act 1982 *c.1*.

As with Public Acts, the use of Regnal years was discontinued in 1963.

Anatomy of a Statute

Below is an example of a Public General Act. It has been chosen because of its atypical brevity. **5–26** Most Acts will run to several if not dozens of pages. All Acts adopt a uniform format with the majority, but not necessarily all features, appearing in all Acts. Each anatomical feature is annotated with a number which correspond to the explanation which follows:

Local Government (Gaelic Names) (Scotland) Act 1997

1997 Ch.6

Local Government (Gaelic Names) (Scotland) Act 1997　[1]

1997 Ch.6　[2]

An Act to enable local authorities in Scotland to take　[3] Gaelic names; and for connected purposes.

[27th February 1997]　[4]

BE IT ENACTED by the Queen's most Excellent　[5] Majesty, by and with the advice and consent of the Lords Spiritual and Temporal, and Commons, in this present Parliament assembled, and by the authority of the same, as follows:—

Power of council to change name into Gaelic and vice-versa.　[7]

1. In section 23 of the Local Government (Scotland) Act　[6] 1973 (change of name of local government area), there shall be inserted, after subsection (1), the following subsections—

"(1A) Where a council so change the name of their area into Gaelic, they may also, by a resolution passed in accordance with subsection (1) above and notwithstanding sections 2(3) and 3(1)(a) of the Local Government etc. (Scotland) Act 1994, decide that their name shall be "Comhairle" with the addition of the name of their area.

(1B) A council which have so changed their name into Gaelic may, by a resolution passed in accordance with subsection (1) above, change it back into English".

Short title, commencement and extent.

2.—(1) This Act may be cited as the Local Government　[8] (Gaelic Names) (Scotland) Act 1997.

(2) This Act shall come into force on the expiry of the period of two months beginning with the day on which it is passed.

(3) This Act extends to Scotland only.

Key: **5–27**

[1] The short title of the Act. This is the usual way to refer to the Act. The Short Titles Act 1896 and the Statute Law Revision Act 1948 gave short titles to many of the older Acts. Sch.2 of the Statute Law Revision (Scotland) Act 1962 gave short titles to many of the Acts of the pre-1707 Scottish Parliament.

[2] This is another way of referring to Acts—by their year and chapter number. The modern system of assigning chapter numbers dates from 1963. For the position before 1963, see para.5–21. A chapter number is assigned to each Act in chronological order throughout a calendar year. This means that this was the sixth Act of 1997.

[3] This is the long title. It sets out the purpose of the Act in very general terms. It will be more detailed than the short title. However, it is *not* a detailed narrative of the background of the Act. It is no longer the practice for modern Acts to include a preamble, but older Acts do contain an explanation of the reasons for the Act. Preambles could be quite detailed—far more so than the brief statement of purpose given in contemporary long titles.

[4] The date which appears at the end of the long title in square brackets is the date of Royal Assent. This *may or may not be* the date that the Act comes into force. See section [8] below regarding commencement generally.

[5] This is the standard enacting formula. These words indicate that the Act has the full authority of Parliament.

[6] Acts are divided up into parts called sections. Sections are numbered consecutively throughout an Act. Sections can be sub-divided into sub-sections. Sub-sections can be divided into paragraphs and further divided into sub-paragraphs.

If the Act is long or deals with a variety of quite distinct matters, it may be divided into parts **5–28** and chapters (not to be confused with chapter numbers), e.g. the Environment Act 1995 c.25 is divided into five parts:

➤ Part I The Environment Agency and The Scottish Environment Protection Agency;
➤ Part II Contaminated Land and Abandoned Mines;
➤ Part III National Parks;
➤ Part IV Air Quality; and
➤ Part V Miscellaneous, General and Supplemental Provisions.

Part I is then sub-divided into three chapters:

➤ Chapter I The Environment Agency;
➤ Chapter II The Scottish Environment Agency;
➤ Chapter III Miscellaneous, General and Supplemental Provisions Relating to the New Agencies.

Chapter II contains sections 20–36 of the Act (denoted thus "ss."). Taking s.34 below as an example, the reference to SEPA's duty to "promote the cleanliness of tidal waters" is contained in the Environment Act 1995, s.34(1)(a)(ii). This means sub-paragraph (ii) of paragraph (a) of subsection (1) of section 34 of the Act.

"**section 34. General duties with respect to water**
    (1) It shall be the duty of SEPA—
        (a) to promote the cleanliness of—
            (i) rivers, other inland waters and ground waters in Scotland; and
            (ii) the tidal waters of Scotland; and
        (b) to conserve so far as practicable the water resources of Scotland."

[7] Marginal notes are *not* technically part of the Act. They describe the content of the section in very brief terms.

[8] This section of an Act usually provides for citation of the short title, commencement and geographic extent. Per commencement, the whole or part of an Act may come into effect immediately, or after a set period of time or only after a commencement order has been signed by the relevant government minister or his/her nominee. If there is no provision for a commencement order or orders, the Act will come into force from midnight at the start of the day of Royal Assent. Per extent, it is only safe to conclude that an Act automatically applies to Scotland if the word "Scotland" is included in the short title. If this is not the case, the extent section *must* be consulted. See further guidance below.

> **NB** An interpretation section is usually, but not always, to be found towards the end of an Act. It sets out definitions of certain words which have been used in the Act. Words can be given a particular meaning for the whole of an Act or for a part of it. This Act does not have an interpretation section.

Short title

5–29 This is a re-statement of the short title as it appears at the start of the Act. See comments above in [1].

Commencement

5–30 If the Act does not contain a commencement provision there is a presumption that it comes into force at midnight at the start of the day of Royal Assent. The commencement provision in an Act can provide for it coming into force in one of three ways:

  (a) The Act can specify a particular date;
  (b) The Act can specify a period after the passing of the Act when the Act will come into force. This was the case with this Act. It came into force two months after it was passed, i.e. April 27, 1997; or
  (c) The Act can state that it is to come into force on a date to be set by a person, usually the relevant Government Minister. It would be brought into force by a type of SI called a Commencement Order.

As detailed above, the whole of an Act can be brought into force at once, or sections or parts of it can become law at different times. This means that the researcher must read the commencement section carefully and also consult the *legislation.gov.uk* website SI page at *http://www.legislation.gov.uk/uksi* [accessed June 3, 2014] if an Act is brought into force in stages. There can be considerable time delay between an Act receiving the Royal Assent and becoming law. In rare circumstance some Acts never become law.

5–31 Some terminology used in connection with an Act being brought into force can cause confusion. If an Act is referred to as "becoming law" or "coming into force" it has come into operation. If an Act has been "passed" or is referred to as "being on the statute books", it means that it has received Royal Assent but has *not* necessarily become law.

Geographic extent

If an Act applies exclusively to Scotland the word "(Scotland)" will be placed in round brackets **5–32** and appear in the short title. However, finding Westminster Acts that extend to Scotland is not as straightforward as looking for Acts with "(Scotland)" in the short title as it is possible for legislation without "(Scotland)" in the short title to apply in whole or part to Scotland. There is a presumption that Acts of the Westminster Parliament apply to the whole of the United Kingdom so if the Act is silent on this point then it is taken to apply throughout the UK. If an Act applies only to part of the UK it will state this expressly in the extent section. A Scots lawyer must therefore read the extent section of the Act prior to undertaking any further research. If the Act does not extend to Scotland it is an irrelevance.

> **NB** Schedules (Sch.) may appear at the end of an Act. A large Act may contain numerous schedules. For instance, the Environment Act 1995 above contains 24 schedules. Schedules are not divided into sections. Rather, they are divided into paragraphs and sub-paragraphs. Schedules are part of the Act and their contents are legally binding. Material is usually put into a Schedule because it is very detailed or technical and/or it is easier to present it there in tabular or list form. A common inclusion in Schedules is a list of previous legislative provisions which has been amended or repealed by the Act.

Acts of the Westminster Parliament: a summary

It cannot be presumed that because an Act of Parliament has been located online or in a law **5–33** library that it constitutes the current law. Firstly, it cannot be assumed that an Act is in force. As detailed above in the preceding paragraph, all or part of it may, or may not, have been brought into force. Further, it cannot be assumed that the Act is as originally enacted, i.e. it may have been amended or repealed in whole or part. To confirm whether any amendments/repeals have occurred follow the guidance given in the next chapter in paras 6–03—6–103.

Another dangerous assumption to make is that an Act automatically applies to Scotland. It is **5–34** only safe to do so if the word "Scotland" is included in the short title. If this is not the case, the extent section at the end of the Act *must* be consulted. See para.5–32 above. On the other hand, it can never be assumed that Acts without "Scotland" in the title do not apply to Scotland in whole or part.

Nor can it be assumed that a word used in an Act will have the same meaning as it does in **5–35** everyday usage. A word in a statutory setting can have a special meaning for a specific section or for the whole Act. Checking if any special meaning has been given to certain words of the Act involves consulting the interpretation section—if there is one it will be located near the end of an Act. A definition given for a specific word in one Act does not necessarily apply in other Acts; only definitions in Acts which are in "pari material" (i.e concern similar subject matter) can be consulted for guidance.

How to read a statute

Do not read an Act from beginning to end (unless a research project is solely concerned with a **5–36** singular Act). They are not intended to be read in that way. Instead, locate the section(s), etc. of interest if known, and if not, consult the Table of Contents page(s) preceding the Act itself to locate a relevant section, etc. This is now a relatively straightforward and speedy process if the Act concerned is fairly recent and can be located via the official *legislation.gov.uk* website.

There, the Table of Contents page for the vast majority of Acts listed provide hyperlinks to each section, etc.

5–37   At first sight statutes bear little resemblance to normal English prose. They are set out in a very formal way and the language used can be difficult to comprehend. The most important piece of advice is to read statutes carefully. The exact wording is very important as every word has been deliberately chosen for its legal effect with even the smallest of words being crucial, e.g., there is a significant difference between the word "may" which suggests that something can be done and the word "shall" which means something must be done.

5–38   Particular attention is to be paid to words at the beginning of a section, e.g. "subject to the provisions of section 10". This means that the current section is subordinate to the provisions of s.10. If there is any conflict between the two sections, s.10 will prevail.

5–39   To aid understanding of a statutory provision the following resources ought to be consulted:

> ➤ Lecture notes, if relevant;
> ➤ A textbook on the subject area. Check the Table of Statutes at the beginning of the textbook to see if any reference has been made to the Act in question. The Table should give page references detailing where the Act has been discussed in the text;
> ➤ "Annotations" to the Act. Some versions of Acts contain annotations, e.g. Current Law Statutes. These are written by experts in the relevant area of law. There is usually a long introductory note at the beginning of the Act which explains its significance and places it in context. It will also refer the reader to the parliamentary debates on the Bill. Throughout the Act there will be shorter annotations which are designed to explain the various sections and the effect they have on the existing law. Annotations can be very helpful but they are not authoritative as they only contain informed academic opinion. Only a court can provide a binding interpretation of a statutory provision.

Commentaries on legislation

5–40   These can be located by searching:

  (i)   The Legal Journals Index is an index of articles which have appeared in UK legal journals since 1986. It is available via Westlaw and the advanced search function enables searching for legislation cited in articles, see para.8–69.
  (ii) Current Law. Check under the appropriate subject in latest Monthly Digest and headings in the Current Law Yearbooks. See paras 8–19—8–33.
  (iii) The Scots Law Times and the Journal of the Law Society of Scotland often contain articles on recent legislation.
  (iv) Specialist journals, e.g. the European Journal of Law and Technology, (available at *http://www2.warwick.ac.uk/fac/soc/law/elj/jilt/* [accessed June 3, 2014]), may contain commentaries on recent relevant legislation.
  (v)   Cases which have considered/interpreted a specific piece of legislation provide references to any subsequent cases which have considered the legislation. See paras 4–82—4–91. The relevant case reports can then be examined.

How to interpret a statute

5–41   When trying to interpret the words of a statute lawyers do not have a free hand. There are rules and conventions governing how to interpret statutory provisions. Below is a diagram of possible approaches. The fine detail of statutory interpretation is outwith the scope of this work, but see suggested further reading below for discussion of this topic.

Problem word/phrase: Has it been legally defined?

—definitions section (located within Act itself)

—Interpretation Act 1978

Have any cases interpreted this word/phrase as it occurred in this Act?

—Westlaw/Current Law Legislation Citators/ Judicial Dictionary/ updated by Words and Phrases Table in Current Law Yearbooks and Monthly Digests—see paras 4–72—4–81.

Has it been defined in any statute that is in pari materia?

—Locate Acts which concern similar subject matter

NB Some or all of this information may all be contained in an annotated version of the Act.

If these initial steps do not reveal relevant information consult an English dictionary. A dictionary can provide guidance on the ordinary meaning of a word. What it cannot provide is a definitive answer. Language is a very imprecise medium and a dictionary is likely to give several different definitions of the word which are equally valid. Accordingly, dictionaries are instructive, but rarely by themselves solve legal problems. **5–42**

Linguistic presumptions

There are three "linguistic presumptions", or "rules" of statutory interpretation, which a court **5–43** may use if a word in a statute is ambiguous or unclear. However, there is no hierarchy and it is up to the individual court or judge to determine which rule(s) ought to be applied in specific cases.

> ➢ *Ejusdem Generis* ("of the same kind"). This rule suggests that when the word to be interpreted is a general word but it is accompanied by more specific words, then that word must be interpreted in light of the specific words, e.g. in *Powell v Kempton Park Race Course Co. Ltd* (1899) A.C. 143 the question for the court was whether an open air enclosure was a "*place opened, kept or used*" for gambling, contrary to the Betting Act 1853. The decision hinged on whether the open enclosure was to be included in the list of places mentioned in the Act, which listed "*house, office room or other place*". In other words, did "*other place*" include an open enclosure, which was a field. The court held that as the list of places in the act referred to indoor locations and the field was outdoors, then it was not *ejusdem generis* with the listed places, that is to say, it was not of the same type, and so was not covered by the prohibition in the 1853 Act.
> ➢ *Noscitur a sociis Noscitur a sociis* ("a thing is known by its associates"). This rule states that where a specific word is used, yet its exact meaning is unclear, it is deemed to be in accord with words it is grouped with. In *Pengelly v Bell Punch Co* [1964] 1 W.L.R. 1055 the court had to decide whether a floor used for storage came under the Factories Act 1961, whereby "*floors, steps, stairs, passageways and gangways*" had to be kept free from all obstructions. The court looked at the words surrounding "floors" and decided that the intention of Parliament was to cover areas that were passageways, and therefore a floor used for storage only was not included.
> ➢ *Expressio unius est exclusio alterius Expressio Unius Est Exclusio Alterius* ("if you don't say it you don't mean it"). This rule is used when specific types of a thing are mentioned in an Act. If this is so, it is assumed that by mentioning a specific type, then other types of similar things are not included in the Act, e.g. s.1 of the Breastfeeding etc. Scotland

Act 2005 details that it is an offence to "deliberately to prevent or stop a person in charge of a child from feeding milk to that child in a public place or on licensed premises". This section also states that "milk" for the purposes of the Act is "breastmilk, cow's milk or infant formula". Applying the *Epressio unius est exclusio alterius Expressio Unius Est Exclusio Alterius* rule, it would be highly arguable that it is not an offence to deliberately prevent or stop someone feeding a child goat's milk in a public place or on licensed premises.

Interpretation Act 1978

5-44 This is not as helpful as the name would suggest. Whilst it provides definitions of commonly used words and phrases and guidance on matters such as reading words in the singular to include the plural and vice versa, it does not apply if a specific provision defines these words and phrases differently.

Further reading

5-45 Further reading on statutory interpretation:

> ➢ J.A. Holland and J.S. Webb, *Learning Legal Rules*, 8th edn (Oxford: OUP, 2013)
> ➢ R.M. White and I.D. Willock, *The Scottish Legal System*, 5th edn (Haywards Heath: Tottel, 2013)
> ➢ W.A. Wilson, *Introductory Essays on Scots Law*, 2nd edn (Edinburgh: W. Green, 1984), "Interpreting Statutes"

DELEGATED LEGISLATION

5-46 The Westminster Parliament is the supreme law-making body within the UK but it is able to delegate its law-making powers to others. Delegated (also called secondary or subordinate) legislation is legislation made by individuals or bodies other than Parliament, but with the authority of Parliament. Authority is given by the inclusion of a provision (known as an enabling provision) in an Act of Parliament. An example is s.10(1)(8) of the Finance Act 2013: "The Treasury may by order amend the definition of 'caring responsibilities' in subsection (7)".

5-47 Delegated legislation was used increasingly throughout the 20th century and more so in the 21st century and is an important and abundant source of law. Acts of Parliament tend to provide only a broad framework stating aims and objectives or results to be achieved with delegated legislation then employed to provide the detail. Delegated legislation is used particularly in areas of law that require frequently updating and/or for detailed or technical matters. It is also used to implement the vast majority of EU legislation. Figures obtained from the *legislation.gov.uk* website illustrate the year on year growth of these legislative provisions at Westminster: in 2008, 1,481 UK SIs were made. In 2010 the figure achieved was 2,801 and in 2013 the figure reached 2,947.

5-48 Whilst there are different species of delegated legislation, SIs are the most numerous as they also comprise "rules, regulations and orders". This chapter will concentrate on SIs given they are the form of delegated legislation most frequently encountered by students and practitioners alike. Other types of delegated legislation include by-laws and orders of the Privy Council.

> **NB** Before the enactment of the Statutory Instruments Act 1946, the equivalent to modern SI were known as "statutory rules and orders".
>   Two peculiarly Scottish types of SI are "Acts of Sederunt" and "Acts of Adjournal". They are pieces of legislation enacted by the Court of Session and the High Court of Justiciary respectively. Acts of Sederunt are rules which govern procedure in the civil courts while Acts of Adjournal concern procedure in Scotland's criminal courts. Both were issued as SIs prior to devolution but are now issued as Scottish SIs. See paras 7–119—121.

An SI has exactly the same force of law as a statute. However, there is a key difference between **5–49** the two. Unlike an Act of Parliament, a statutory instrument can be challenged in court. It is only valid if the person making the legislation has been duly authorised by the "enabling" Act of Parliament and has acted within the limits of the powers laid down in that Act. If this is not the case the SI could be successfully challenged on the grounds that it was ultra vires. Other than this distinguishing feature, there are many similarities between these two legal provisions.

Acts and SI compared

 ➤ An SI can be general or local. All SIs which have general application are required to be **5–50** published. Local SIs may not be published.
 ➤ An SI can be amended or revoked (this means the same as repealed in respect of statutes). SIs remain in force until revoked or until the Act they were made under is repealed.

Further reading

Greater discussion of delegated legislation will be found in a specialist text such as A.W. Bradley **5–51** and K.D. Ewing, *Constitutional and Administrative Law*, 15th edn (Harlow: Longman, 2010).

Citation of SI

SIs are cited either by title, year and number or, alternatively, by year and running number, e.g. **5–52** Control of Pollution (Silage, Slurry and Agricultural Fuel Oil) Regulations 1991/324 or SI 1991/ 324 (alternatively SI 1991 No.324). The SIs themselves frequently stipulate the citation by which they should be referred, e.g. reg.1 of the above regulations states, "These Regulations may be cited as the Control of Pollution (Silage, Slurry and Agricultural Fuel Oil) Regulations 1991".

The 1991 regulations, which applied throughout the UK, were revoked by the Water Resources **5–53** (Control of Pollution) (Silage, Slurry and Agricultural Fuel Oil) (England) Regulations 2010 (2010/639) which only extend to England. Likewise, if the number of a SI is followed by an "S" in brackets and another number this shows that this SI applies only to Scotland, e.g. The Restriction of Liberty Order (Scotland) Amendment Regulations 1999 or SI 1999 No.144 (S.6). If trying to find a Scottish SI, ignore the Scottish number (here S.6) because the indexes for SIs only use the main number for the reference.

If the number is followed by a "C" it means that it is a Commencement Order. This is a **5–54** particular type of SI which is used to bring an Act or part thereof into operation. Commencement Orders provide additional information in their citation, e.g. the Environment Act 1995 (Commencement No.12 and Transitional Provisions) (Scotland) Order 1998 or SI 1998 No.781 (s.40) (c.16). If the number is followed by "NI" it applies only to Northern Ireland.

Anatomy of an SI

5–55 Different features are annotated with numbers which correspond to the list below.

STATUTORY INSTRUMENTS

2012 No. 2855 (S.1) **[1]**
Constitutional Law, Devolution, Scotland Forestry [2]

The Forestry Commissioners (Climate Change Functions) (Scotland) Order 2012 (Consequential Modifications) Order 2012 [3]

Made **[4]**: 7 November 2012
Coming into force in accordance with article 1(2)

The Secretary of State makes the following Order in exercise of the powers conferred by sections 104, 112(1) and 113(2), (4), (5) and (7) of the Scotland Act 1998.

In accordance with section 88(2) of that Act, the Secretary of State has consulted the Scottish Ministers.

In accordance with section 115(1) of, and paragraphs 1, 2 and 3 of Schedule 7 to, that Act, a draft of this Order has been laid before, and approved by a resolution of, each House of Parliament.

Citation, commencement and extent [5]

1.—(1) This Order may be cited as the Forestry Commissioners (Climate Change Functions) (Scotland) Order 2012 (Consequential Modifications) Order 2012.

(2) This Order comes into force on the day after the day on which it is made.

(3) This Order extends to Scotland only.

Modification of functions of the Forestry Commissioners in relation to land in Scotland

2. The Forestry Act 1967 is amended as follows—

(a) after section 7A[1] (incidental powers of Commissioners) insert—

"**7AA.—Renewable energy installations**

(1) The Commissioners may, for the purpose of complying with their general duty under section 1(2A)[2]—**[6]**

(a) promote, develop, construct and operate installations for or in connection with the generation, transmission, distribution and supply of electricity produced from renewable sources, and

(b) use electricity produced by virtue of the powers conferred by paragraph (a).

(2) In subsection (1), *"renewable sources"* means sources other than—

(a) fossil fuel,

(b) energy derived from fossil fuel, and

(c) nuclear fuel.

(3) In subsection (2), *"fossil fuel"* means—

(a) coal,

(b) lignite,

(c) peat,

(d) natural gas (within the meaning of the Energy Act 1976),

(e) crude liquid petroleum,

(f) petroleum products (within the meaning of that Act),

(g) any substance produced directly or indirectly from a substance mentioned in paragraphs (a) to (f).

(4) Nothing in this section is to be construed as exempting the Forestry Commissioners from the requirements of Part 1 of the Electricity Act 1989."

; and

(b) in section 7B(1)[3] (delegation of functions of Commissioners: Scotland), after "(3)" insert "and section 7AA".

NOTES
[1] Section 7A was inserted by the Regulatory Reform (Forestry) Order 2006 (SI 2006/780), article 2 and amended by the Public Services Reform (Scotland) Act 2010 (asp 8), section 12(1).
[2] Subsection (2A) was inserted by the Forestry Commissioners (Climate Change Functions) (Scotland) Order 2012 (SSI 2012/77), article 2.
[3] Section 7B was inserted by the Public Services Reform (Scotland) Act 2010 (asp 8), section 11.

Signed by authority of the Secretary of State [7]
David Mundell
Parliamentary Under Secretary of State Scotland Office
Dover House, London
7th November 2012

EXPLANATORY NOTE   [8]

This Order modifies the Forestry Act 1967 in consequence of provision made by the Forestry Commissioners (Climate Change Functions) (Scotland) Order 2012 (S.S.I. 2012/77) ("the 2012 Order").

The 2012 Order (which was made under section 59 of the Climate Change (Scotland) Act 2009 (asp 12)) modified the functions of the Forestry Commissioners so that they can use land at their disposal in Scotland to help the Scottish Ministers in achieving their climate change targets.

This Order modifies the functions of the Commissioners further to allow them to generate, transmit, distribute, supply and use electricity produced from renewable sources where that helps achieve those targets.

A full impact assessment has not been produced for this instrument as it has no impact on the private sector or civil society organisations.

Key: **5–56**

[1] The citation consists of the year and number. The number refers to the number issued in a calendar year, e.g. this is number 2855 for 2012. The fact that the number is followed by an "S" in brackets and another number shows that this SI applies only to Scotland. It is the first SI to apply to Scotland made in 2012.

[2] This is not part of the name of the provision—it is a subject heading used in official editions of SI.

[3] This is the short title of the SI.

[4] This part comprises relevant information relating to the parliamentary process involved in creating a SI. This is a requirement under s.4(2) of the Statutory Instruments Act 1946, which states that every SI should include details of when it is to come into force. SIs also usually include details of the date on which they were made. This part also includes a recital of the statutory authority and powers that enable the maker of the SI to issue the SI. Here the Secretary of State has exercised powers under the provisions of the Scotland Act 1998.

[5] This part will specify the correct citation to be adopted and give the date on which the SI will come into force. This part will also state if particular meanings are to be given to specific words used in the SI.

[6] SIs are divided into parts but these are not referred to as sections as in an Act of Parliament. The name given to the divisions depends on the type of SI. In this case, the SI is an Order and the divisions are called articles, with further subdivisions called

paragraphs and sub-paragraphs. If the SI is a regulation the divisions are called regulations, with further subdivisions called paragraphs and sub-paragraphs. If the SI is a rule, the divisions are called rules but further subdivisions are called paragraphs and sub-paragraphs.

[7] The signature of the person making the SI is given in this part, along with their title and the date on which the SI was made.

[8] In official editions of SI there is usually an explanatory note at the end of the SI but these tend to be brief and do not aid interpretation of the provision to any great extent. An explanatory note is not technically part of the SI.

NB This SI does not have any schedules but many will, e.g. the Children's Home Regulations 2001 has six. As with statutes, material in the schedule will tend to be technical and/or very detailed.

5–57 Although SIs are generally signed by the relevant Government Minister to bring them into force, this is not always the case. Parliament may provide for the relevant minister to authorise another person to sign an instrument on his or her behalf. This is often the case, as illustrated below, with technical, geographically limited or routine matters.

STATUTORY INSTRUMENTS

2014 No.969
ROAD TRAFFIC

The A30 Trunk Road (Fingle Glen to Alphington, Devon) (Temporary Prohibition of Traffic) Order 2014

Made 18th March 2014
Coming into force 24th March 2014

WHEREAS the Secretary of State for Transport, being the traffic authority for the A30 Trunk Road ("the A30") and connecting roads, is satisfied that traffic on a length of that road and one of those connecting roads near Exeter in the County of Devon should be prohibited because works are proposed to be executed thereon:

NOW, THEREFORE, the Secretary of State, in exercise of the powers conferred by section 14(1) (a) of the Road Traffic Regulation Act 1984, hereby makes the following Order:—

1. This Order may be cited as the A30 Trunk Road (Fingle Glen to Alphington, Devon) (Temporary Prohibition of Traffic) Order 2014 and shall come into force on 24th March 2014.

2. In this Order—

"the slip road" means the eastbound entry slip road at the A30 Fingle Glen Junction;

"the A30" means the eastbound carriageway of the A30 from the tip of the nosing of the eastbound exit slip road at the Fingle Glen Junction to the tip of the nosing of the eastbound entry slip road at the Alphington Junction;

"tip of the nosing" means the first point where an entry slip road joins the carriageway of a trunk road or the last point where an exit slip road leaves the carriageway of a trunk road;

"the works" mean resurfacing;

"a works period" means a period of 11 hours starting at 19.00 hours on Wednesday 26th March 2014 or on any subsequent day and ending when the said works have been completed;

and a reference to an article followed by a number is a reference to the article in this Order which bears that number.

3. Subject as mentioned in article 4, no person shall, during a works period, cause or permit any vehicle to enter or proceed in the A30 and the slip road.

4. The provisions of article 3 shall apply only during such times and to such extent as shall from time to time be indicated by traffic signs and shall not apply to:

   (a) a vehicle being used for police, traffic officer, fire and rescue authority or ambulance purposes;

   (b) anything done at the direction of, or with the permission of, a constable or traffic officer in uniform;

   (c) a vehicle being used in connection with the said works.

Signed by authority of the Secretary of State
Ian Parsons
A Service Delivery Team Leader
18th March 2014 in the Highways Agency

Reading an SI

Reading an SI generally raises the same issues as when reading statutes, (see paras 5–41—5–44 **5–58** above). It is often useful to read the enabling Act in conjunction with the SI as the Act, (and any annotations to it), may aid understanding of the broader context of which the SI is part.

The Scottish Parliament (Holyrood) (1999–)

Introduction

The Scottish Parliament was created by the Scotland Act 1998. It had its first meeting on May **5–59** 12, 1999 and took up its legislative powers from July 1, 1999. Holyrood consists of 129 members of the Scottish Parliament who are referred to as MSPs. Seventy-three are returned from constituencies elected by the "first past the post" system and 56 are returned under a system of proportional representation (eight regions return seven members). A Parliamentary session is for a fixed period of four years. This is different from the Westminster system where the maximum length of a parliament is five years. The Scottish Parliament has only one chamber (i.e. it is a "unicameral" Parliament, unlike Westminster which is "bicameral", i.e. comprises two chambers). Legislation is scrutinised by the Scottish Parliament as a whole and by its various committees.

Committees play a key role in the work of the Holyrood Parliament. The Parliament may **5–60** establish committees to deal with specific subject areas (known as subject committees) in addition to the mandatory committees. The mandatory committees are:

> ➢ Standards, Procedures and Public Appointments Committee;
> ➢ Finance Committee;
> ➢ Audit Committee;
> ➢ European and External Relations Committee;
> ➢ Equal Opportunities Committee;
> ➢ Public Petitions Committee;
> ➢ Subordinate Legislation Committee.

Committees must have at least five but not more than 15 members. The composition of the **5–61** committees reflects the balance of the political parties in the Parliament. The committees can examine matters within their remit or matters referred to them by the Parliament. They may:

> Consider the policy and administration of the Scottish Government (s.44 et al of the Scotland Act 1998 refers to a Scottish "Executive" rather than a Scottish "Government". However, s.12 of the Scotland Act 2012 amends s.44 as follows: "The Scottish Executive is renamed the Scottish Government");
> Consider proposals for legislation in the Holyrood and Westminster Parliaments;
> Consider EU legislation and international Conventions;
> Consider the need for law reform;
> Initiate Bills;
> Consider the financial proposals and financial administration of the Scottish Government.

5–62 The role of the Presiding Officer (an elected office and the equivalent of the Speaker in the House of Commons) is to:

> Preside over meetings of the Parliament and exercise a casting vote in the event of a tie;
> Convene and chair meetings of the Parliamentary Bureau and exercise a casting vote in the event of a tie. The Parliamentary Bureau consists of representatives of the various parties who organise the business of the Parliament;
> Determine any question as to the interpretation or application of the rules governing parliamentary procedure; and
> Represent the Parliament in discussions and exchanges with any parliamentary, governmental, administrative or other body.

Responsibility for all devolved matters was passed to the Scottish Government from the Scottish Office and other UK Government departments in 1999. The Scottish Government comprises: the First Minister; Ministers appointed by the First Minister; the Lord Advocate; and the Solicitor General for Scotland. The First Minister is head of the Scottish Government. S/he is nominated by the Scottish Parliament and formally appointed by the HM the Queen. Members of the Scottish Government are known collectively as "the Scottish Ministers" (see the Scotland Act 1998 s.44(2)). When a power or duty relating to a devolved function is conferred by an Act of Parliament it is exercisable by the "Scottish Ministers" (i.e. any member of the Scottish Government). Prior to devolution, the power would have been exercisable by a specific Minister. Any legal challenges against the Scottish Government are also brought against the "Scottish Ministers" as opposed to a specific Minister.

5–63 At Holyrood, the term "session" refers to the period between the first meeting of the Parliament after a general election and the dissolution of the Parliament before the next election. The equivalent term at Westminster is a "Parliament".

Legislative competence

5–64 Any Act of the Scottish Parliament is not law if it is outside the legislative competence of the Parliament (Scotland Act 1998, s.29). A provision would be outside the Parliament's legislative competence if it related to the "reserved" matters, i.e. areas of law making retained by Westminster. The reserved matters are listed in Sch.5 of the Scotland Act 1998. General reservations include: the constitution, foreign affairs, defence, public service, political parties and treason. There are also a range of specific reservations under the following headings: financial and economic affairs, home affairs, trade and industry, social security and media and culture.

5–65 The matters which Holyrood can consider are not listed in the 1998 Act. They are to be implied by exception. They include: criminal justice and prosecution, civil and criminal courts, legal aid, judicial appointments, the police and fire services, prisons, health services, education, local government, the environment, agriculture, forestry, fisheries, social work services, liquor licensing, housing, tourism, sport and the arts.

Acts of the Holyrood Parliament can amend or repeal pre-devolution legislation from the **5–66** Westminster Parliament but only if the subject matter of the legislation is within the legislative competence of the Scottish Parliament, i.e. it is not reserved.

Schedule 6 of the Scotland Act 1998 deals with "devolution issues". These are defined as **5–67** questions of whether:

   (i)   The Act (or any of its provisions) is within the Parliament's legislative competence;
 (ii)   Any function being exercised is a function of the Scottish Ministers, First Minister or Lord Advocate;
(iii)   A function being exercised by a member of the Scottish Government is within the devolved competence;
(iv)   The exercise of a function (or failure to act) by a member of the Scottish Government would be incompatible with the rights conferred on citizens under EU law or the European Convention on Human Rights (ECHR), (which are discussed, respectively, in Ch.10 and Ch.11).

Devolution issues which arise in Scotland may be referred by a court to the Inner House of the Court of Session (in respect of civil cases) or to the High Court of Justiciary (in relation to criminal proceedings). The issue may be further referred or appealed to the UK Supreme Court (previously this role was undertaken by the Judicial Committee of the Privy Council).

Legislation

Bills

As in the UK Parliament, proposed legislation in the Scottish Parliament begins life as a Bill. **5–68** When a Bill is passed it becomes an Act of the Scottish Parliament ("asp"). A Bill can be introduced by a:

➢   Member of the Scottish Government, in which case it is referred to as a Government Bill;
➢   Parliamentary Committee, in which case it is referred to as a Committee Bill; or
➢   Member of Scottish Parliament, in which case it is referred to as a Member's Bill.

The layout, structure and legislative drafting conventions adopted for Bills at Holyrood are very similar to Bills in the Westminster Parliament. The reason is that Acts of the Scottish Parliament form part of the UK "statute book".

Holyrood legislation may be either general or private. The majority of the section below relates **5–69** to Public General Bills.

Introducing a Bill

On introduction, a Bill must be accompanied by certain documents: **5–70**

➢   A statement by the Presiding Officer indicating whether the provisions are within the legislative competence of the Parliament. Any provisions which are viewed as outside its competence have to be identified.

> ➤ A Financial Memorandum. This sets out an estimate of the administrative, compliance and other costs arising from the provisions of the Bill. It must distinguish how such costs would fall on the Scottish Government, local authorities and other bodies, individuals and businesses.

Most Government Bills must also be accompanied by:

(i) A statement by the Minister in charge of the Bill that, in his view, the provisions are within the legislative competence of the Parliament;
(ii) Explanatory notes which summarise objectively each provision of the Bill;
(iii) A Policy Memorandum which sets out:

    (a) Policy objectives of the Bill;
    (b) Consideration of alternative methods of achieving these objectives and justification of the approach taken in the Bill;
    (c) Details of any consultation on the objectives;
    (d) Assessment of the effects, if any, of the Bill on: equality issues, human rights, island communities, local government, sustainable development and any other matter which the Scottish Government considers relevant.

If a Bill contains any provision charging expenditure on the Scottish Consolidated Fund, (a financial provision made available to Holyrood by the Westminster Government's Consolidated Fund), a report from the Auditor General must accompany the Bill. This report sets out whether the Auditor General views the charge as appropriate.

5–71 The majority of Bills dealt with by Holyrood are Government Bills. The procedure outlined below will generally apply to all Government Bills.

5–72 *Stage 1—Consideration of the general principles of a Bill*: Once a Bill has been printed it is referred to the committee within whose remit it falls. This committee is known as "the lead committee". This committee considers the general principles and prepares a report for Parliament. Parliament then considers the general principles of the Bill in the light of this report. It can:

> ➤ Refer the Bill back to the lead committee for a further report;
> ➤ Fail to agree the general principles of the Bill (in which case the Bill falls); or
> ➤ Agree to the Bill.

If the Bill is agreed, it can proceed to stage 2. There must be at least two weeks between the completion of stage 1 and the start of stage 2.

5–73 *Stage 2—Consideration of the details of the Bill*: This stage is either considered by the lead committee, another committee or a committee of the whole Parliament. Each section and schedule is considered separately. A Bill may be amended at this stage. If the Bill has been amended, it will be reprinted. If it is amended in such a way as to affect powers to make subordinate legislation, the amended Bill must be referred to the Subordinate Legislation Committee for consideration.

5–74 If the Bill is amended at stage 2 there must be at least two weeks between completion of stage 2 and the start of stage 3.

Stage 3—Final consideration: The amended Bill is considered by the whole and can be further **5–75** amended at this stage. It is possible for up to half of the sections of the Bill to be referred back to committee for further stage 2 consideration. If this occurs, on resumption of stage 3 proceedings, amendments can only be made to the provisions which were referred back to committee.

If there is a final vote on the Bill, at least a quarter of all MSPs must vote or abstain. If this **5–76** condition is not met, the Bill will be treated as rejected.

Royal Assent: If the Bill is passed, it will be submitted for Royal Assent by the Presiding Officer. **5–77** Within four weeks of the passing of the Bill the Advocate General, Lord Advocate or Attorney General can refer the question of whether the Bill is within the Parliament's legislative competence to the UK Supreme Court, (previously, i.e. prior to 2009, reference was made to the Judicial Committee of the Privy Council) for a decision per s.33 of the Scotland Act 1998. The Secretary of State for Scotland has the power to intervene and prohibit the Presiding Officer from submitting the Bill for Royal Assent. S/he may do this if there exist reasonable grounds to believe inter alia that the Bill is incompatible with devolved competence, EU law or any international obligation. See the Scotland Act 1998, s.35. Once the Bill receives Royal Assent, it becomes an Act of the Scottish Parliament. This does not necessarily mean that it becomes law. See paras 5–28 and 5–84 at annotation [7].

Citation of Bills

Bills should be referenced by Scottish Parliament (SP) Bill number, title, [printing], Session, **5–78** (year), e.g. SP Bill 27 Children and Young People (Scotland) Bill [as introduced] Session 4 (2013).

Holyrood Bills, unlike those of Westminster, keep their original numbering. Subsequent revi- **5–79** sions are indicated as follows:

> ➢ SP Bill 1   Bill as introduced
> ➢ SP Bill 1A   Bill as amended at Stage

Accompanying documentation and lists of amendments are given references which are linked to the citation of the Bill:

> ➢ SP Bill 1-PM   Policy memorandum;
> ➢ SP Bill 1-EN   Explanatory notes and other accompanying documents;
> ➢ SP Bill 1-ML   Marshalled list of amendments to the Bill as introduced—if there are several marshalled lists of amendments then they are numbered SP Bill 1- ML1, SP Bill 1-ML2, etc.;
> ➢ SP Bill 1A-ML   Marshalled list of amendments to the Bill as amended at Stage 2;
> ➢ SP Bill 1A-EN   Supplementary explanatory notes for the Bill as amended at Stage 2;
> ➢ SP Bill 1A-FM   Supplementary financial memorandum for the Bill as amended at Stage 2;
> ➢ SP Bill 1-G   Groupings of amendments—if there are several groupings then they are numbered SP Bill 1-G1, SP Bill 1-G2, etc.;
> ➢ SP Bill 1-DPM   Delegated powers memorandum;
> ➢ SP Bill 1B   Bill as passed.

Citation of statutes

5–80 Acts of the Holyrood Parliament are normally referred to by their short title, e.g. Forth Road Bridge Act 2013. A complete citation would also include the asp number—Forth Road Bridge Act 2013 asp 8.

Private legislation

5–81 In addition to public general legislation, the Holyrood can also enact private legislation which deals with devolved issues. A private Bill "is a Bill introduced for the purpose of obtaining for an individual person, body corporate or unincorporated association of persons ('the promoter') particular powers or benefits in excess of, or in conflict with, the general law, and includes a Bill relating to the estate, property, status or style, or otherwise relating to the personal affairs, of the promoter" (Rule 9A.1.1 of the Standing Orders of the Scottish Parliament). At the time of writing, SP Bill 29-EN City of Edinburgh Council (Portobello Park) Bill Session 4 (2013) is at consideration stage. Private Bills are subject to substantially different procedures from public Bills. When enacted, private Bills become Acts of the Scottish Parliament and are cited in the same way as public general Acts. Private Bills generally relate to use of land, or the property or status of the promoter.

5–82 An example of a private Act is the Stirling-Alloa-Kincardine Railway and Linked Improvements Act 2004 asp 10.

Further information on Private Bills is to be found here: *http://www.scottish.parliament.uk/ parliamentarybusiness/Bills/15709.aspx.*

Anatomy of an Act of the Holyrood Parliament

5–83 This is an excerpt from a Public General Act. While all Acts adopt the same format some, but not necessarily all, features will appear in all Acts. Different features are marked with numbers which correspond to the list below.

[1] *Tourist Boards (Scotland) Act 2006 (asp 15)*

[2] Tourist Boards (Scotland) Act 2006

[3] 2006 asp 15

[4] The Bill for this Act of the Scottish Parliament was passed by the Parliament on 24th October 2006 and received Royal Assent on 30th November 2006

[5] An Act of the Scottish Parliament to rename the Scottish Tourist Board, to increase the maximum number of members of that body and to abolish area tourist boards.

[6] 1. Scottish Tourist Board: change of name

(1) The Scottish Tourist Board is renamed VisitScotland.

(2) Accordingly, in the Development of Tourism Act 1969 (c.51), for "the Scottish Tourist Board", wherever that expression occurs, there is substituted "VisitScotland".

2. Scottish Tourist Board: increase in maximum number of members

In section 1(3) of the Development of Tourism Act 1969 (which provides for the maximum number of members of the national tourist boards), for "six" where it secondly occurs, there is substituted "eleven".

3. Abolition of area tourist boards

(1) Sections 172 to 175 of the Local Government etc. (Scotland) Act 1994 (c.39) (which make provision for area tourist boards) are repealed.

(2) The following bodies are dissolved—

    (a) the Scottish Network 1 Tourist Board, and

    (b) the Scottish Network 2 Tourist Board.

(3) Schedule 1 makes provision in connection with the dissolution of those bodies.

4. Consequential modifications

Schedule 2 makes modifications of enactments in consequence of the preceding provisions.

5. Commencement and short title

[7] (1) The preceding provisions come into force on such day as the Scottish Ministers may by order made by statutory instrument appoint.

[8] (2) This Act may be cited as the Tourist Boards (Scotland) Act 2006.

5–84 *Key:*

[1] This is referred to as the running header. It tells you where in the Act you are and is useful if you are reading a long asp. Note that the coat of arms is different from a UK Parliament Act. Scottish Acts bear the Coat of Arms of the Scottish Crown.

[2] The short title of the Act. This is the normal way to refer to the Act. Acts of the Scottish Parliament normally (but not always) have Scotland in round brackets as part of the short title. The Act itself will usually provide details of the short title in a section at the end of the Act. In this Act this appears in s.5(2).

[3] This is another way of referring to Acts—by their year and asp number. The asp number is assigned to each Act in chronological order throughout a calendar year. This means that this was the 15th Act of 2006. This is the equivalent of the chapter number in an Act of the Westminster Parliament.

[4] This is the standard enacting formula. These words indicate that the Act has the full authority of the Scottish Parliament. It appears in bold and gives details of when the asp was passed and when it received the royal assent.

[5] This is the long title. It sets out the purpose of the Act in very general terms. It will be more detailed than the short title.

[6] Acts are divided up into parts called sections. Sections are numbered consecutively throughout an Act. Sections can be subdivided into subsections. Subsections can be divided into paragraphs and further divided into sub-paragraphs. The section number and section title appear in bold. There are no marginal notes.

[7] The last section of an Act usually provides for commencement. If the Act contains no commencement provision there is a presumption that it comes into force at the beginning of the day on which it receives the Royal Assent.

The commencement provisions in an Act can provide for it coming into force in one of three ways:

(a) The Act can specify a particular date;
(b) The Act can specify a period after the passing of the Act when the Act will come into force.
(c) The Act can state that it is to come into force on a date to be set by a person or persons, usually the Scottish Ministers. This means that the commencement of the legislation has been delegated to the Scottish Government. This is the case with this Act. It would be brought into force by a type of SI called a Commencement Order. A search of sources which identify when Acts are brought into force, (see paras 7–51—7–60) will show that this Act was brought into force on January 31, 2007 by the Tourist Boards (Scotland) Act 2006 (Commencement) Order 2007.

NB The whole of an Act can be brought into force at once or sections of it can become law at different times.

---

[8] The last section of an Act usually provides for citation of the short title. This is the formal statement of the short title. The short title also appears at the start of the Act. See comments above in section [2].

NB Schedules may appear at the end of an Act. Schedules are divided into paragraphs and sub-paragraphs. Schedules have equal force in law as the rest of the Act.

Delegated legislation

Following devolution, a new type of delegated legislation was created: Scottish Statutory **5–85** Instruments. The power to make delegated legislation on a devolved matter may be contained in a pre-devolution Act of the Westminster Parliament (where the power has been transferred to the Scottish Ministers) or in an asp. Since devolution, Acts of Sederunt and Acts of Adjournal have been created as Scottish SI. This is because their subject matter is devolved, namely procedure in the Scottish civil courts and criminal courts respectively. As with SIs made at Westminster, Scottish SIs can be general or local. The vast majority of the latter are related to roads, bridges, road traffic and rights of way.

The Scottish Parliament scrutinises delegated legislation. The procedure adopted will depend on **5–86** the enabling Act. Some instruments are subject to affirmative procedure. This means that the approval of Parliament is required to allow the provisions to come into force. Alternatively, an instrument could be subject to the negative procedure which means that its provisions could be annulled by the Parliament. In this case the instrument is laid before Parliament and will come into force after a period of 40 days unless Parliament annuls it. It is also possible for instruments to be subject to a "super-affirmative" procedure where the Parliament has an initial opportunity to comment on a draft before the final version is laid for approval. Some instruments are not subject to any parliamentary scrutiny and may not even be laid before Parliament. However, the majority of Scottish SI are considered by the Subordinate Legislation Committee and at least one other Parliamentary committee.

As with its UK counterpart, the number of delegated legislative instruments passed each year **5–87** significantly outstrips the number of Acts enacted. In 1999, the first year of operation for the Holyrood Parliament one hundred and 24 Scottish SI were placed on the statute book. In 2013, 364 such instruments were produced.

Citation of Scottish SIs

Scottish SIs are cited either by title, year and number or, alternatively, by year and running **5–88** number, e.g. the Number of Inner House Judges (Variation) Order 2007 (SSI 2007/258) or SSI 2007/258 (alternatively SSI 2007 No.258). The instruments themselves frequently stipulate the citation by which they should be referred, e.g. art.1 of the above order states, "This Order may be cited as the Number of Inner House Judges (Variation) Order 2007".

Anatomy of Scottish SI

This is an example of an SSI. Different features are marked with numbers which correspond to **5–89** the list below:

SCOTTISH STATUTORY INSTRUMENTS

[1] 2007 No.258

[2] COURT OF SESSION

[3] The Number of Inner House Judges (Variation) Order 2007

[4]   *Made 21st March 2007*

Coming into force in accordance with article 1

[5] The Scottish Ministers, in exercise of the powers conferred by section 2(2A) and (2B) of the Court of Session Act 1988[1], hereby make the following Order, a draft of which has, in accordance with section 2(2D) of that Act, been laid before and approved by resolution of the Scottish Parliament:

[6] **Citation and commencement**
[7] **1.** This Order may be cited as the Number of Inner House Judges (Variation) Order 2007 and shall come into force on the day after the day on which it is made.

Variation of number of Inner House judges
2. Section 2(2) of the Court of Session Act 1988 (composition of court)[2] is amended by substituting for the word "four" where it second appears the word "five".

[8] *JOHANN M LAMONT*
Authorised to sign by the Scottish Ministers
St Andrew's House, Edinburgh
21st March 2007

[9] EXPLANATORY NOTE

(This note is not part of the Order)

This Order amends section 2(2) of the Court of Session Act 1988 to increase the number of senior judges in the Second Division of the Inner House of the Court of Session from four to five. The total number of judges in the Inner House, including the Lord President and the Lord Justice Clerk, will therefore be increased from ten to eleven.

Notes:

  [1] 1988 c.36; subsections (2A) to (2D) were inserted into section 2 by the Bail, Judicial Appointments etc. (Scotland) Act 2000 (asp 9), section 5(a).
  [2] The number of senior judges in each of the two Divisions of the Inner House of the Court of Session was increased from three to four by SSI 2001/41.

Key:

[1] The citation consists of the year and number. The number refers to the number issued in a calendar year, e.g. this is number 258 for 2007.

[2] This is not part of the name—it is a subject heading used in official editions of Scottish SI.

[3] This is the short title of the Scottish SI.

[4] This is a list of dates relating to the Parliamentary process involved in creating a Scottish SI. The details will vary depending on the procedure to which it was subject. This order contains few details but others may have additional information such as the date on which the instrument was laid before Parliament.

[5] This paragraph is a recital of the statutory authority and powers that enable the maker of the Scottish SI to issue it. Here the Minister exercised powers under the provisions of the Court of Session Act 1988, s.2(2A) and (2B).

[6] Scottish SI are divided up into parts but these are not referred to as sections as in an Act of Parliament. The name given to the divisions depends on the type of the instrument. In this case the instrument is an order and the divisions are called articles, with further subdivisions called paragraphs and sub-paragraphs. If the instrument is a regulation the divisions are called regulations, but further subdivisions are called paragraphs and sub-paragraphs. If the instrument is a rule, the divisions are called rules but further subdivisions are called paragraphs and sub-paragraphs.

[7] There are several types of article (regulation or rule) which tend to appear in most but not all instruments:
Citation and commencement. This will specify the correct citation to be adopted and give the date on which the instrument will come into force.
Interpretation. This states if particular meanings are to be given to words used in the instrument. There is no interpretation article in this order.

[8] The signature of the person making the instrument, along with their title and the date on which the statutory instrument was made. This will usually, as here, be a member of the Scottish Government.
It is possible for instruments to have schedules. As with Statutes, material in the schedule will tend to be technical and/or very detailed. This order does not have any schedules.

[9] In official editions of Scottish SI there is usually an explanatory note at the end. It is not technically part of the instrument.

NB The techniques for reading legislation enacted by Holyrood and the principles of statutory interpretation used are broadly similar to those employed when scrutinising Westminster provisions. These should be considered in conjunction with the relevant sections of the Interpretation and Legislative Reform (Scotland) Act 2010 asp 10.

Chapter 6
Search Strategies for Locating UK (Westminster) Parliament Legislation

---

Significant abbreviations used in this chapter

- asp—Act of the Scottish Parliament
- BAILLI—British and Irish Legal Institute
- EU—European Union
- ECHR—European Convention on Human Rights
- LJI—Legal Journals Index (Westlaw)
- MSP—Member of the Scottish Parliament
- Sch.—Schedule
- SI—Statutory Instrument
- S.L.T.—Scots Law Times
- TSO—The Stationery Office

INTRODUCTION

6–01 This chapter discusses search strategies for locating legislation made by or with the authority of the Westminster Parliament. It includes searching for pre-legislative documents, Bills, Acts of Parliament and the main form of delegated legislation, SIs. As detailed throughout Ch.2, the possible sources of such information has increased dramatically since the internet became all pervasive in both everyday and academic life. The increased range and sophistication of online databases also means that it is now far easier to locate some older materials and track legislative changes more quickly than in the past. However, the greater availability of a range of electronic versions of legislation means that it is vital that the researcher is aware of the quality of the information sources consulted and has the ability to evaluate the information retrieved.

6–02 Search strategies for Scottish Parliament legislation are discussed in Ch.7. To avoid repetition, the UK sources which have incorporated Holyrood generated materials will be discussed in this chapter. Chapter 7 will focus solely on how to search for materials unique to the Scottish Parliament.

UK PARLIAMENT BILLS

6–03 As discussed in para.5–17, Bills may be amended to various degrees as they proceed through the different parliamentary stages. It is therefore essential to ensure that the most current version of the Bill is consulted.

Sources of the Text of a Recent Public Bill

Public Bills before Parliament website 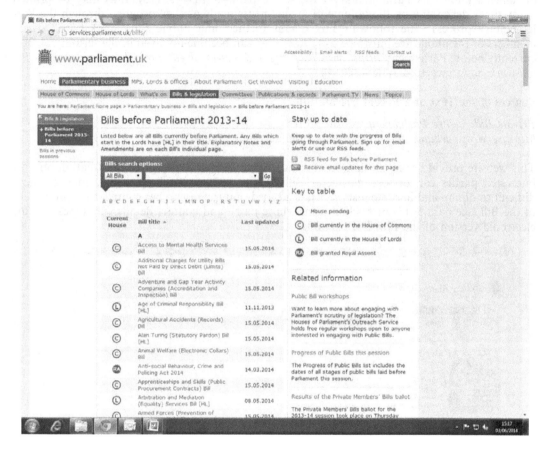 free
See *http://services.parliament.uk/bills/* [accessed June 3, 2014].

This website contains an alphabetical list of all Public General Bills currently before Parliament. **6–04** The list indicates whether the Bill is currently in the House of Commons, House of Lords or whether it has been given the Royal Assent. There is a hypertext link to the homepage of the Bill. This provides the following information:

> ➢ Whether it is a Government or a Private Members' Bill and who introduced it;
> ➢ Details of the dates of the stages the Bill has completed;
> ➢ Links to debates on the Bill accessible by date;
> ➢ Links to marshalled lists of amendments;
> ➢ Links to full text versions of the Bill at the various stages at which it has been reprinted. These are produced in both pdf and html forms;
> ➢ A short summary of the content of the Bill;
> ➢ Links to any Explanatory Notes;
> ➢ Links to any related research material.

It is possible to sign up for email alerts for the Bill homepage.

6–05 Individual Public Bills are published by the Stationery Office ("TSO"), part of the National Archives, see *http://www.nationalarchives.gov.uk/* [accessed June 4, 2014], which is an invaluable source of research materials for a variety of disciplines. Public Bills form part of a group of documents known as Parliamentary Papers. See paras 8–109—8–115). Bills may be printed many times depending on the volume of amendments made as they progress through the Parliamentary process. The following link details forthcoming Public Bill "workshops" where members of the public are informed as to how they can become involved in the scrutiny of Bills currently before Parliament, *http://www.parliament.uk/get-involved/outreach-and-training/public-bill-workshops/* [accessed June 4, 2014].

Sources of the Text of a Recent Private Bill

Private Bills before Parliament website ✋ free
http://services.parliament.uk/bills/private.html [accessed June 4, 2014]

6–06 This website provides information on current Private Bills and also gives information on how interested parties can oppose particular Bills. Paper versions of Private Bills may be more difficult to obtain and in some instances it is advised that the researcher contact the "promoter" of the Bill (see para.5–13) or his/her agent whose name and contact details will appear on the electronic version of the Bill. For example:

Buckinghamshire County Council (Filming on Highways) Bill 2013–14

Type of Bill: Private Bill
Parliamentary agents: Sharpe Pritchard
Promoted by: *http://services.parliament.uk/bills/2013-14/buckinghamshirecountycouncil %20filming%20on%20highways.html*

Finding out which stage a Bill has reached

House of Commons Weekly Information Bulletin 📖 and ⁀ free
This is published weekly when the House of Commons is in session. The full text of the House of **6–07** Commons Weekly Information Bulletin (which includes some House of Lords business) has been available online since October 1996 with weekly bulletins available in site's archive. The online version is published on a Saturday and covers the previous week's events and is available .pdf and .html format. The website is also a gateway to many other Parliamentary resources, e.g. the National Archives Official Documents home page *http://www.official-documents.gov.uk/* [accessed June 4, 2014] where Parliamentary Green Papers and White Papers (pre-legislative discussion and policy documents published by Government departments) can be viewed. At the time of writing, the homepage for this resource advises that the future of the Bulletin is under review on the grounds that the information it contains is readily available elsewhere on the UK Parliament website. The current webpage can be accessed here, *http://www.publications.parliament. uk/pa/cm/cmwib.htm* [accessed June 4, 2014].

Lawtel ⁀ subscription legal current awareness digest service
This service contains a search facility which allows a search for Bills using keywords. In the UK **6–08** Search section, enter a search term and tick the Parliamentary Bills box or go to Legislation, enter a search term and tick the Parliamentary Bills box. Both routes link to information about the Bill, including include Parliamentary stage it has reached. A link to the full text of the Bill will be provided if the Bill is available on the Parliament website.

Justis Parliament ⁀ subscription service
This service is an index to the proceedings and publications of both Houses of Parliament in **6–09** Westminster since 1979. It also provides access to proceedings of the Welsh and Northern Irish Assemblies since their inception. The Bills before Parliament section is updated daily and provides a detailed history of the Bill from its introduction to when it either receives Royal Assent or fails.

Current Law Monthly Digest 📖
This publication gives information about the stages of a Bill in the Progress of Bills Table. To **6–10** find out the stage a Bill has reached in the parliamentary process:

- ↳ **Step 1**: Check the most recent Monthly Digest;
- ↳ **Step 2**: Turn to the Progress of Bills Table. Bills are arranged in alphabetical order. Opposite the name of the Bill will be details of the stage it has reached.

The Daily List 📖 and ⁀ free
This service is provided by TSO and is available at, *http://www.tso.co.uk/daily_list/issues.htm* **6–11** [accessed June 4, 2014]. Information about a Bill that can be found in the Daily List includes the number allocated to a Bill, its publication details and whether there have been any amendments moved and when.

Scots Law Times subscription

6–12 In each issue of S.L.T. there is a news section which contains Parliamentary news. This lists new Bills and provides a brief summary of the subject matter. There is also a Progress of Bills section.

Newspapers 📖 and ⌖ free

6–13 Many newspapers and their online versions contain information about Bills and events in Parliament but unless a Bill is particularly controversial few procedural details will be given. As detailed in para.2–17 publications such as *The Guardian* offer subscribers a free weekly email bulletin containing legal news and developments.

Finding out about older Bills

6–14 It is probably unlikely that information about older Bills will be sought unless the researcher is carrying out historical research. Public Bills before Parliament in previous sessions beginning in session 2002–2003 are available at, *http://www.publications.parliament.uk/pa/pubmenu.htm* [accessed June 4, 2014]. Private Bills before Parliament in previous sessions beginning in session 2001–2002 are available at, *http://www.publications.parliament.uk/pa/privmenu.htm* [accessed June 4, 2014].

The Sessional Information Digest 📖 and ⌖ free

6–15 This Digest is the cumulative form of the Weekly Information Bulletin (see para.6–07), and provides details of Bills from 1995 to the most recent past session of Parliament. It can be accessed via this link, *http://www. publications.parliament.uk/pa/cm/cmsid.htm* [accessed June 4, 2014].

TSO website ⌖ free

6–16 This site, *http://www.tsoshop.co.uk/* [accessed June 4, 2014], can be searched using the advanced search function for the publication details of previous Bills from 1980 onwards. Details of some Bills from the late 1970s may also be accessed.

Finding out about Parliamentary debates on a Bill

The House of Commons Weekly Information Bulletin 📖 and ⌖ free

6–17 This service details the dates of Parliamentary debates.

Current Law Statutes 📖

6–18 If the Bill has since become an Act, the annual volumes of Current Law Statutes should contain details of the Parliamentary debates relevant to each Act. Look for such information in the first annotation inserted after the long title.

Explanatory Notes 📖 and ⌖ free

6–19 As of 1999, Explanatory Notes have been published for the majority of Public General Acts which result from Bills introduced into either House of Parliament. At the end of the Explanatory Note is a section entitled "Hansard References" which contains a table setting out the dates and *Hansard* references (an edited verbatim account of proceedings in Parliament, see para.5–17) for each stage of the Bill's passage through Parliament. Explanatory Notes are generally also now available for Bills in both paper and electronic form. The e-version can be accessed by selecting the relevant Bill on the "Bills Before Parliament" landing page and following the link to "Bill Documents". *http://services.parliament.uk/bills/* [accessed June 3, 2014].

Parliamentary Debates: Official Report (commonly referred to as *Hansard*) 📖 and 🖰 free and
CD Rom

The House of Commons Hansard covers proceedings in the Commons Chamber, Westminster **6–20**
Hall and General and Public Bill Committees. The House of Lords Hansard covers proceedings
in the Lords Chamber and its Grand Committees. Both contain Written Ministerial Statements
and Written Answers. The web version, *http://www.parliament.uk/business/publications/hansard/*
[accessed June 4, 2014], provides Commons debates from November 1998 onwards with coverage of debates in the Lords beginning in session 1995–96. Debates appear on the relevant
webpage at 6am on the day following the sitting. "Historic" *Hansard*, see *http://hansard.mill-
banksystems.com/* [accessed June 3, 2014], holds digitised Commons and Lords debates from
1803–2005.

Same-day access to speeches in both Chambers and Westminster Hall is also available live via **6–21**
the *Hansard* home page and from a multitude of media outlets on the internet, e.g. the BBC at
http://www.bbc.co.uk/news/politics/ [accessed June 3, 2014].

NB From the beginning of the 2006–2007 session Standing Committees have been known
as General Committees and Standing Committees on Bills are to be known as Public Bill
Committees.

Hansard is published daily while Parliament is sitting. It is also published weekly and in bound **6–22**
volumes by Parliamentary session. The material appears in columns (like newspapers) and the
columns are numbered. Each page contains two columns. References to *Hansard* are by column
number not page number. Written answers to parliamentary questions are located in a separate
section at the end of the bound volumes. Cumulative indexes are produced throughout a session
and there is a sessional index in the last bound volume for a given session. The CD Rom version
comprises the bound volumes of House of Commons debates from 1988–1989.

The way *Hansard* ought to be searched will depend on the particular part consulted: **6–23**

➢ The daily versions of Commons debates contain a table of contents which lists column
numbers, headings, time lines and the names of members. Commons debates which
have been put into bound volumes can be searched online by date. However, if the date
is unknown, use the advanced search facility to which there is a link from each bound
volume. This is an excellent search facility and can be used as an alternative to
searching the specific sections of Hansard;
➢ House of Lords debates can be searched by date, member, category or by subject;
➢ General Committee debates for each session are listed by committee. Information on
the membership of the committee and reports of proceedings of its sittings is
available;
➢ Public Bill Committee debates within each session are listed by the title of the Bill being
considered. Click on the title of the Bill to access details of the relevant Public Bill
Committee, its membership, reports of proceedings of the various sittings and the
latest version of the Bill.

COLLECTIONS OF UK PARLIAMENT ACTS APPLYING TO SCOTLAND 1707–1948

6–24 There are several collections of statutes which applied to Scotland between 1707 and 1948:

Scots Statutes

6–25 Scots Statutes Revised (Vols 1–10) covers the period 1707–1900. It includes only Acts applicable to Scotland. Volume 10 includes a subject index to the whole collection. It was superseded by Scots Statutes which covers the period 1901–1948. This, in turn, was superseded from 1949 by Scottish Current Law Statutes, see below.

Blackwood's Acts

6–26 Public General Statutes affecting Scotland (1848–1947), known as "Blackwood's Acts", was an annual publication. It included Acts with provisions which related to Scotland. In 1876 legislation from 1707–1847 which was still in force was published in three complementary volumes.

SOURCES OF MODERN UK PARLIAMENT ACTS

6–27 Acts of Parliament are published both electronically and in paper form in many different databases and series. The official electronic versions of Acts of Parliament are available online at *legislation.gov.uk* and the official paper versions are published by TSO. Printed Acts (often referred to as the Queen's Printer copies) are published singly as they receive Royal Assent and subsequently appear in annual volumes called Public General Acts and Measures (see below).

6–28 The fact that different databases and series produce versions of Acts means that different versions may include additional information such as explanatory details called annotations and/or different search facilities for accessing legislation, e.g. some publications gather together all legislation relating to a particular subject whereas others cover specific periods in time. However, it is vital that the reader is aware which version they are consulting, i.e. whether it is the original version of the Act (the Act as passed by Parliament) or whether it is a revised version which includes any amendments which have been made to it. Thus, unless the Act is newly minted the researcher must ensure they check that they are consulting the most recent version.

Official versions

Public General Acts and Measures 📖
6–29 As soon as a Bill receives Royal Assent it is published as an Act of Parliament by TSO. Each Act is printed singly and these are known as Queen's Printer copies. Since the start of 1999 a separate book of Explanatory Notes has been published with Public General Acts which result from Bills introduced into either House of Parliament.

6–30 At the end of each year, the single Acts are produced together in a publication called Public General Acts and Measures. This is the official version of Acts of Parliament. Acts are arranged in chronological order (i.e. by chapter number). These do not contain annotations. Alphabetical and chronological lists are contained at the front of each volume. At the end of the final volume for each year are tables of derivations and destinations of the Consolidation Acts for the year. There is also a table called Effects of Legislation. This gives details of Acts (in chronological order) which have been repealed, amended or otherwise affected by legislation passed during the year.

Legislation.gov.uk 🖰 free
The official electronic original version of Acts of Parliament is available from *legislation.gov.uk*. **6–31**
This service and TSO are part of the National Archives. All legislation is published on behalf of
the Controller of TSO. This site contains the full text of all Public General Acts and aims to
publish legislation simultaneously with their publication in printed form. Explanatory Notes are
generally published at the same time as the Act, but sometimes may appear shortly afterwards.

Acts of Parliament (and Explanatory Notes) are published in .html and as .pdfs which makes **6–32**
downloading the entire document and/or printing it straightforward. The Acts are grouped by
year and within each year they can be viewed either alphabetically or chronologically by chapter
number. The site also contains a function which links to an advanced search facility which
allows search by keyword, type of legislation (e.g. Acts, Explanatory Notes or local Acts),
jurisdiction or date. The material is published in its original and amended form.

Other sources of revised versions of Acts

Westlaw 🖰 subscription database
Westlaw contains all UK Public General Acts which were still in force in 1991, and all sub- **6–33**
sequent UK Public General Acts and Public General Acts of the Scottish Parliament. The
archive dates back to 1267.

> ➤ Westlaw includes a lot of additional information, such as details and links to the full
> text of amending legislation, secondary legislation made under an Act, cases citing an
> Act and the identification of journal articles discussing an Act, or part of it;
> ➤ Access is provided to successive versions of statutes since February 1, 1991. Different
> versions of an Act can be consulted back to Westlaw's "Table Top" date which is
> February 1, 1991. This is because a publication called Statutes in Force (published by
> TSO) contained legislation which was fully consolidated up to February 1, 1991. These
> consolidated versions provide the earliest version of legislation contained on Westlaw;
> ➤ Prospective amendments are listed in the Analysis (see para.6–45) and Overview
> Document features (see para.6–46). They are not incorporated into the full text until
> they are in force.
> ➤ Concurrent versions of statutes. If a UK statute has been amended differently in dif-
> ferent jurisdictions of the UK, the full text of the legislation will give details of the
> different forms. However, this is not the case with .pdf versions of Acts.

Searching in Westlaw for legislation

Westlaw has three alternative ways of searching for legislation: basic search, advanced search **6–34**
and browsing.

Basic search
From the welcome page, click the legislation link from the navigation bar at the top of the **6–35**
screen. This will link to the legislation basic search page where statutes can be searched for by
typing the name of the piece of legislation, the year and provision number (if required). If the
year is known, it is better to enter it as this will avoid retrieving multiple pieces of legislation.
The basic search screen searches legislation currently in force. If historic legislation is sought use
the advanced search facility.

The free text field allows terms or phrases to be entered and Westlaw searches for these within **6–36**
the text of statutes. Entering the title of a piece of legislation without quotation marks will
retrieve all pieces of legislation with those words in the title. If the title of the Act sought is

known enter it in quotation marks, e.g. "Defamation Act 2013". If the year and chapter number is known, enter those into the title field to find the full text of the Act, e.g. 2013 c.26 or 2013 c 26 (both will work). A space must be entered after the c or c. to retrieve the correct results.

6–37 If the title of a piece of legislation is entered without a provision number the whole of the legislation will be retrieved. The most efficient method of searching for a particular part of a piece of legislation is to enter, e.g. s.3 in the provision number box. If only a number is used, e.g. "3" the results retrieved will include all parts of the legislation that have a provision number matching the entry made. An alternative method is to click on the provision number menu and choose "section" as an option and then put "3" in the next box.

6–38 Searching can be improved by using search techniques which Westlaw refer to as 'Terms and Connectors' (see paras 2–58—2–59).

Advanced Search

6–39 Select advanced search in the top right of the legislation basic search page. The default setting is law in force. However, the advanced legislation search allows a search to be broadened to include legislation that is no longer in force by selecting either the law in force and historic law option or the point in time option. The latter option allows a search to be undertaken for legislation as it stood at a particular point in time. In order to do this the date in the format indicated by the date field must be included.

Search results for legislation

6–40 Primary legislation is retrieved first, followed by secondary legislation. If the search is under-taken by title only, the Arrangement of the Act for that legislation will be returned (see para.6–39). Searching for legislation using the free text function will return sections of legislation where those terms exist. The results list will show the name of the legislation as well as the title of the provision and the date when it came into force. Within a result list, status icons may display next to the title of the legislation indicating that either the provision has been repealed or superseded Ⓡ or has pending amendments ⒤. To narrow down a long list of results, search for additional terms by entering new search term(s) in the field at the top of the page and clicking search within results.

Browsing for legislation.

6–41 Acts can be browsed for by year, by title or by jurisdiction (e.g. Westminster or Holyrood). The browse by year function allows for the selection of a time period (prior to 1990) from which to select the year sought. From 1990 onwards a particular year can be selected. Within each year there is an alphabetical list of legislation that received Royal Assent in that year. Browsing by title allows a letter to be chosen from the alphabetical list of Acts. Once a title has been selected it will link to the Arrangement of Act for that piece of legislation.

6–42 Westlaw provides the following research options:

6–43 *Full text:* The full text legislation option incorporates any amendments up to the version in force date. This date can be found in the entry for a specific part of legislation, e.g. a section. It is clearly displayed above the start of the section. The text contains links to other legislation cited and to footnotes describing amendments which themselves link to the amending legislation. Within an Act the reader can navigate to the previous provision or the next provision by selecting the relevant link from above the legislation title.

If a provision has pending amendments that are not yet in force, a yellow exclamation flag ⟨!⟩ is **6–44** shown. To see the prospective change, select legislation analysis or overview document from the left-hand navigation bar. If viewing a historical version a red "no entry" flag ⟨⊖⟩ along with either superseded or repealed indicating a more recent version is available. To see the most recent version, select legislation analysis from the left-hand navigation bar and click on the date beneath current law in force.

Legislation Analysis: Legislation Analysis can be accessed from within a section of a piece of **6–45** legislation by selecting the Legislation Analysis from the left-hand navigation bar. This feature offers some or all of the following parts listed below. The relevant headings will appear in the left-hand navigation bar under Legislation Analysis.

Current law in force	This includes a link to the current, consolidated version of a provision. It also lists the date that the provision came into force and gives details of the provision bringing it into force and the scope of the amended version, e.g. if it takes effect on different days in different parts of the UK.
Commencement information	This gives details about the initial commencement of the provision, including commencement date, scope of the commencement and links to any commencing legislation.
Amendments pending	This details any prospective amendments to a provision, the date of the amendment (if known) and the legislation that will implement those changes.
Historic law	This lists all previous versions of the legislation that are available in Westlaw. By selecting any of the entries listed, the reader can access the legislation prior to its amendment to see how the law stood at a particular point in time. Each historical version also lists the date it came into force and the piece of legislation bringing it into force.
Extent	This shows the areas of the UK to which the provision extends.
SIs made under Act	This provides details of secondary legislation enacted with the authority of the legislation concerned.
Enabling Act	This details the Enabling Act or SI which gave authority for any SI to be enacted.
Modifications	This provides links to any legislation making non-textual amendments to the provision.
Related legislation	This provides links to legislation applying, dis-applying or referring to the provision.
Cases citing	This lists the cases that cite the section of legislation in alphabetical order. If Westlaw provides a case analysis for any of these cases, clicking on the case citation underneath the case name will enable this to be retrieved.
Journal articles	This lists citations to relevant materials taken from legal journals and law reviews. If Westlaw provides the full text of an article, there will be a link enabling access to it.

Westlaw Legislation Analysis

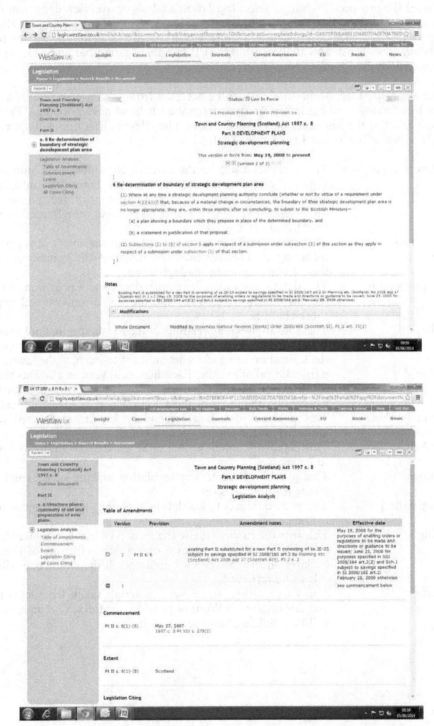

Overview document: This is a citator service which provides an extremely useful summary of **6–46** information about the whole Act. It can be accessed by clicking on Overview Document on the left-hand side of the screen. It includes:

> ➤ A list of amendments pending (i.e. those amendments not applied to the full text) and links to the amending provision where details of the amendment can be viewed.
> ➤ Commencement information pertaining to an Act (except pre-1991 commencement information). This shows when each part of the Act was brought into force and links to the commencement instrument concerned;
> ➤ Modifications. This section highlights where provisions have been modified in relation to their application to specified areas or circumstances. However, the text itself remains unchanged and links to the modifying legislation. This includes occasions when a provision may be applied differently, e.g. transitional provisions or when the interpretation of a word in a statute is altered without changing its text;
> ➤ Citator. This is a particularly useful feature. This provides links to all materials related to a provision. Legislation applying, disapplying or referring to the provision, cases citing it, journal articles referring to it, SIs made under the provision and the enabling Act or SI are all included. A Table of Amendments displays the life story of a provision with all previous (dating back to 1991 for Acts and 1948 for SIs), current and future versions presented, eliminating the need for cross-referencing. It could replace the text in the proof but the text appears to reflect the contemporary position;
> ➤ All SIs enabled under authority of an Act which are listed in alphabetical order;
> ➤ Any EU Law implemented by an Act.

Westlaw Overview

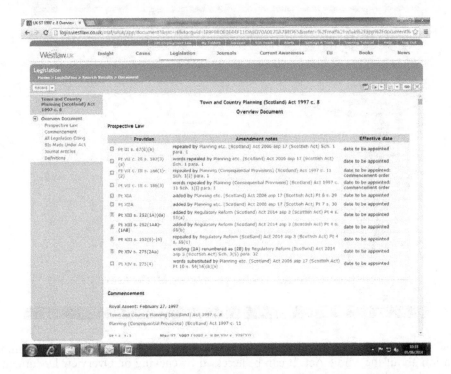

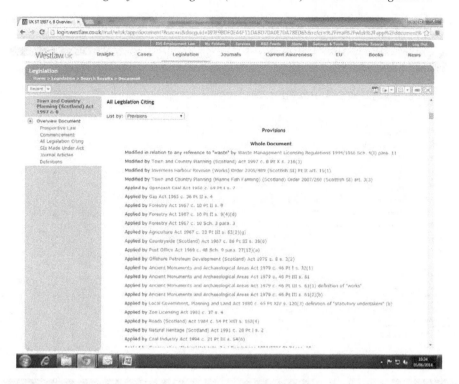

Arrangement of Act: This feature allows the reader to view the scheme of the Act and links, **6–47** either directly or via part and chapter tables, to the provisions of an Act. This replicates the official table of provisions as published with every statute by *legislation.gov.uk*. The fact that all the provisions within a piece of legislation are contained in one document means that swift navigation to or between any part or specific provision is achieved.

General Materials: The general materials section provides information relating to the Act as a **6–48** whole, as well as details about major elements such as Parts, Chapters and Schedules. It includes information about: modifications, any EU laws implemented by the enactment of the Act, related legislation, dis-applying legislation, referring legislation and cases and journal articles citing that Act or part of it.

Sources of original versions of Acts

BAILII ᕀ free
http://www.bailii.org/form/search_legis.html

6–49 The BAILII website offers inter alia UK primary and secondary legislation reproduced from *legislation.gov.uk*. The legislation search allows searching by keyword, dates and jurisdiction. The advanced search allows Boolean searching. Unlike *legislation.gov.uk*, it is possible to browse all the Acts in an alphabetical index. The material is published in its original form only thus amendments are not included.

Justis UK Statutes ⏃ subscription

6–50 This database contains the full text of all UK Acts from 1707 onwards and is the only statute-law database to contain a full set of repealed legislation. It also offers exact replica .pdfs of the legislation. All Acts appear in their original form, with links to amending legislation. Holyrood Acts from 1999 onwards are also available in like format.

Current Law Statutes 📖

6–51 Current Law Statutes (Scottish Current Law Statutes Annotated cover 1949–1990; Current Law Statutes cover 1991 to the present) contain the full original text of every Public General Act published since 1949. The English equivalent started one year earlier, in 1948. Private Acts have been included since 1992. Acts of Sederunt and Acts of Adjournal were included until 1990. Acts are published in annual volumes and within each volume the Acts are arranged in chronological order. Each Act is annotated by an expert in the relevant field and generally includes a lengthy introductory annotation which explains the Act's purpose. The introduction will also refer to the dates of the parliamentary debates on the Bill. The annotations throughout the Act are intended to clarify the effect of the various sections. The number of annotations depends on the length and complexity of a given provision. Acts from the current year appear singly in a loose leaf Statutes Service File. UK Public General Acts are followed by Private Acts and Acts of the

Scottish Parliament. At the end of the year the material in the Statutes Service File is reissued in a bound volume.

The volumes of Current Law Statutes include: **6–52**

> ➢ Chronological Table of Acts in the year;
> ➢ Alphabetical Index of Short Titles;
> ➢ Full text of Public General Acts passed by Westminster in chronological order with annotations;
> ➢ Full text of Private Acts passed by Westminster;
> ➢ Full text of Acts of the Holyrood Parliament with its own subject index;
> ➢ Commencement Diary—an alphabetical table of the commencement of statutes in that year;
> ➢ Commencement Diary—an alphabetical table of the commencement of statutes in that year;
> ➢ Commencement Orders (full text) in chronological order;
> ➢ Alphabetical Table of UK SI in that year; and
> ➢ Index by subject.

How to find details of an Act using Current Law

Check the volume of Statutes for the appropriate year. The full text (with annotations) will **6–53**
appear in chronological order. Alternatively, a summary of the Act will be in the relevant Current Law Yearbook or Monthly Digest.

Find the Civil Aviation Act 2012:   **6–54**

> ✎ **Step 1**: Check the Current Law Statutes volumes for 2012. If the chapter number is known (here it is c.19) check the spines of the volumes to locate the appropriate volume if there is more than one. Otherwise, start by checking the first volume.
> ✎ **Step 2**: Check the alphabetical list of short titles. Opposite the short title is the chapter number.
> ✎ **Step 3**: Turn to the page headed up with the chapter number. The chapter number appears in bold and is followed by a number corresponding to the section number of the Act which appears on that particular page.

Sources of revised UK Acts which exclude exclusively Scottish legislation

LexisNexis ✎ subscription database
LexisNexis includes all current Public General Acts for England and Wales. It provides the **6–55**
revised text of the legislation. Acts made by the UK Parliament which relate only to Scotland are not included, although provisions of Scottish Acts that apply or are relevant to England and/or Wales are included. Legislation from the Holyrood Parliament is, however, available. To search for Acts from the homepage locate "Scottish Parliament Acts" on the My Bookshelf feature on the right hand side of the screen. Acts can then be searched for by title, year, section number, part or schedule and using a search term. Acts can also be browsed for alphabetically.

Halsbury's Statutes of England 📖 and ✎ subscription
This publication provides comprehensive coverage of UK legislation but excludes statutes which **6–56**
relate only to Scotland and sections of UK statutes which relate to Scotland only. Halsbury's Statutes are available on LexisNexis and are discussed further in Ch.9.

Current Law Legislation Citators

6–57 While the Current Law Legislation Citators are an efficient way of tracing statutes, they do require the user to have an appreciation of how the citators are organised and it is essential to adopt a systematic approach to searching them.

6–58 A legislation citator is (i) a chronological list of all Acts passed within the UK since 1947 which (ii) includes information about amendments to any Act or details about any Act that has been interpreted by the courts since 1947. For Scottish legislation, 1948 is the operative year. The Current Law Legislation Citators (formerly called Statute Citators) are published in volumes, some of which span several years whereas others contain information covering a single year only. The Current Law Legislation Citators should be used in conjunction with the Current Law Statutes Service File where cumulative monthly updates of the Legislation Citator for the current year are to be found.

6–59 The legislation citators list all amendments, modifications and repeals to primary and secondary legislation made in the years covered by the specific volume. Acts and SIs passed by the Scottish Parliament since 1999 are included. Since 1993 the legislation citators are in fact a combination of two citators—a statute citator and a SI citator.

6–60 Contents of the legislation citators are arranged as follows: Table of Abbreviations; Alphabetical Tables of Statutes cited in the statute citator and SIs cited in the SI citator (this includes Scottish SIs, statute citator and SI citator).

6–61 The statute citator is listed first. It is arranged in the following order:

> ➢ Acts of the Scottish Parliament since 1999 listed in chronological order by year and asp number;
> ➢ Acts of the Northern Ireland Assembly since 2000 listed in chronological order by year and reference to number;
> ➢ Public General Acts of the UK Parliament and Welsh Legislation since 1947 listed in chronological order by year and chapter number.

The statute citator contains:

> ➢ Details of amendments and repeals since 1947 to statutes of any date, including details of the amending or repealing provisions;
> ➢ In respect of any Act, the names and citations of cases in which it has been judicially considered since 1947;
> ➢ In respect of any Act, details of SIs issued under its provisions;
> ➢ In respect of any Act, details of whether it has been consolidated by an Act passed since 1989.

The SI citator is arranged in the following order:

> ➢ Scottish SIs listed in chronological order by year and number;
> ➢ Statutory Rules issued by the UK Parliament listed in chronological order by year and number;
> ➢ SIs made by the UK Parliament listed in chronological order by year and number.

The SI citator contains:

> ➤ Details of amendments and repeals since 1993 made to SIs of any date;
> ➤ In respect of any SI, the names and citations of cases in which it has been judicially considered since 1993;
> ➤ In respect of any SI, details of the SIs issued since 1993 which have been made under its provisions.
> ➤ In respect of any SI, details of whether it has been consolidated by an Act passed since 1993.

Searching the Statute Citators

If the task is to locate any changes to an Act of Parliament, consult the citator covering the **6–62** period when the Act was passed. Once the reference to the Act in that volume has been located, check all the subsequent citators in chronological order and then the Current Law Statutes Service File. This will ensure that all subsequent developments relating to the Act in question are located. If there is no mention of the Act it has not been altered within the time period covered by the citator(s) consulted.

Terms used to describe legislative effects

Various terms are used to describe legislative effects. The following definitions are those most **6–63** frequently used:

> ➤ **added**—means that a new provision has been inserted by subsequent legislation;
> ➤ **amended**—means that the text of the legislation is modified by subsequent legislation;
> ➤ **applied**—means that it has been brought to bear or exercised by subsequent legislation;
> ➤ **consolidated**—means that previous Acts dealing with the same subject area or matter have been brought together in subsequent legislation, with or without amendments;
> ➤ **disapplied**—means that an exception has been made to the application of an earlier enactment;
> ➤ **enabling**—means giving power for the relevant SI to be made;
> ➤ **referred to**—means direction from other legislation without specific effect or application;
> ➤ **repealed**—means rescinded by subsequent legislation;
> ➤ **restored**—means that it has been reinstated by subsequent legislation;
> ➤ **substituted**—means that the text of a provision is completely replaced by subsequent legislation;
> ➤ **varied**—means provisions have been modified in relation to their application to specified areas or circumstance. However the text itself remains unchanged.

Excerpt from a statute citator

---

[1] 26. Housing (Scotland) Act 1987 [2]   **6–64**
s.2, amended: 1989, c.42, s.161.
s.5A, added: 1993, c.28, s.149. **[3]**
s.5B, added: *ibid.*, s.151.
s.17, repealed in pt.: *ibid.*, s.157, Sch.22. **[4]**
ss.17A–17C, added: *ibid.*, s.153.
s.19, amended: *ibid.*, s.155. **[5]**
s.20, amended: *ibid.*, s.154.

s.21, see *Pirie v City of Aberdeen District Council* (O.H.), 1993 S.L.T. 1155. **[6]**
s.21, amended: 1993, c.28, s.155.
s.22A, added: *ibid.*, s.152.
s.24, amended: 1990, c.40, s.65.

Key:

   [1] Chapter number.
   [2] Short title.
   [3] An addition to the Act.
   [4] Part of the Act has been repealed.
   [5] Changes to the Act.
   [6] A case concerning a section of the Act.

NB *Halsbury's Statutes Citator* (available in LexisNexis) records such information thus:

Budget (Scotland) Act 2011 (asp 4)

See "Is it in Force?" for details of initial commencement.

Section

3	am by	SSI 2011/434, art 2; SSI 2012/105, art 2
6	rep by	Budget (Scotland) Act 2012, s 8
Sch 1	am by	SSI 2011/434, art 3; SSI 2012/105, art 3
Sch 2	am by	SSI 2011/434, art 4; SSI 2012/105, art 4
Sch 3	am by	SSI 2012/105, art

JustCite ⊕ online subscription legal citator

6–65 JustCite allows a search for statutes to be undertaken by title or reference (e.g. including the section number along with the short title of an Act). Acts can be searched for separately by ticking the appropriate box on the right-hand side of the screen. Alternatively, a search can be conducted using the index tab which provides title indexes of statutes listed in alphabetical order that can then be browsed. Scottish legislation is not listed separately.

6–66 The information retrieved includes:

> ➤ The status of the provision;
> ➤ A link to the particular reference. Clicking on this link will open a new window showing various sources of the full text of the entire Act or individual sections;
> ➤ Lists of sections which have been amended and the amending legislation;
> ➤ Lists of sections which have amended other legislation and the legislation amended;
> ➤ Cases which have interpreted the section.

LOCATING STATUTES: SEARCH STRATEGIES AND SELECTED RESOURCES

There are various strategies that can be employed to locate legislation and different starting **6–67** points from which to achieve a particular research task, e.g. the task may be to research a familiar area of law where the sources required are known which makes searching relatively straightforward. On the other hand, an unfamiliar area of law where knowledge of relevant legislation is scant may present or situations may arise where some knowledge of the relevant legislation's title exists but is incomplete.

Below are selected sources which provide relevant resources for the Scottish researcher seeking **6–68** legislative provisions. These have been ranked in order of relevance, thus sources which exclude Scottish materials appear lower in the list even though they may be excellent information sources for UK (as opposed to Scottish) material. Sources which provide access to revised versions of legislation are given prominence because sources of original versions of Acts will require additional research to check for any amendments or repeals. Both electronic and paper sources are listed.

The majority of research projects where legislation is the subject of scrutiny will require the **6–69** researcher to consider the following issues as a matter of routine:

> ➢ The current status of a statute. It is vital to know whether a statute has been brought into force or whether it has been amended or repealed (see paras 6–93—6–104);
> ➢ Whether a court has interpreted the legislation (see paras 4–82—4–88).
> ➢ Whether any journal articles have discussed or analysed the legislation.

Finding statutes by subject

Major textbooks/reference works and encyclopaedias 📖
Legal encyclopaedias and reference works (see paras 4–72—4–81) are ideal starting points for **6–70** research by subject. Unlike an electronic database which may simply locate a piece of legislation, these resources will place it in context by explaining its background, how it fits (or otherwise) in to the area of law under scrutiny and how it has been interpreted. Encyclopaedia or reference works can also provide further information which may help the researcher to refine initial search terms prior to undertaking a subsequent search in a full text database. As discussed at various points in Ch.2, conducting a subject search on a database with broad subject terms sees the retrieval of hundreds or even thousands of hits—most of which have no relevance to the researcher's quest. When consulting these resources, look at the Table of Statutes which will be located at the beginning of the work. This will list statutes in chronological order.

The Laws of Scotland: Stair Memorial Encyclopaedia 📖
If using the paper version check the Consolidated Index. This will direct the reader to the **6–71** relevant volume or reissued title. Each subject area has its own Table of Statutes. This information can be updated by checking the Annual Cumulative Supplement and the Service Binder(see para.8–10).

The Laws of Scotland Online (Stair Memorial Encyclopaedia) ⏚ subscription from LexisNexis
It is possible to search the whole of Stair using free text or to limit a search to various titles. The **6–72** browse function will open up an alphabetical list of all the titles and link through to the chosen topic.

Westlaw <img> subscription database

6–73 From the welcome page, select the legislation heading from the navigation bar at the top of the screen. This will link to the legislation basic search page, where subject terms can be entered into the free text box. Westlaw will search for these within the short titles and the text of legislation. Searching can be improved by using the search techniques discussed in paras 2–58—2–59.

Legislation.gov.uk <img> free

6–74 *legislation.gov.uk* allows an advanced search to be undertaken for keywords in the title of an Act or in the content of legislation in the database. Further features enable the researcher to restrict this by type of legislation, extent and date range.

Current Law Yearbooks and Monthly Digests <img>

6–75 Check the subject headings in the consolidated indexes in the master volumes of the Yearbooks, the more recent Yearbooks and the Monthly Digest. See paras 8–23 and 8–31.

Justis UK Statutes <img> subscription

6–76 This database contains the full text of all Acts of Parliament in England, Wales and Scotland from 1235 to the present day (including repealed legislation). All Acts appear in their original form with links to amending legislation.

BAILII ⌐⊕ free
BAILII only contains Public General Acts from 1988. The legislation search allows searching by   **6–77**
keyword, dates and jurisdiction. The advanced search allows Boolean searching. Acts are
published in original form thus amendments are not included.

LexisNexis ⌐⊕ subscription database
While LexisNexis provides the revised text of legislation, Acts made by the UK Parliament   **6–78**
which relate exclusively to Scotland are not included.

Halsbury's Statutes 📖 and ⌐⊕ subscription
Information about legislation can be accessed by subject unless it is exclusively Scottish legis-   **6–79**
lation. See Ch.9 for full information about this resource.

Current status of a statute—is it in force yet?

The Act itself

As detailed in para.5–28, the date the Act comes into force may be the date of Royal Assent or it   **6–80**
may be detailed in the commencement section at the end of the Act. Thus the commencement
section of the Act must always be checked. If the Act is silent, it comes into force on the date of
the Royal Assent. If the Act stipulates a specific date or time period then that is the relevant
date. Alternatively, the Act (or part of it) may come into force at a time to be set by the relevant
government Minister. If this is the case, the researcher must check if a commencement order has
been issued and find out which part(s) of the Act have been brought into force and when.

Westlaw ⌐⊕ subscription database
To check whether a specific section of an Act has been brought into force first search for the   **6–81**
piece of legislation and section in the basic search box. This will retrieve the current version of
the section. At the start of the entry, underneath the section heading, Westlaw provides details
of commencement. The phrase "version in force" will be followed by a date. This is the commencement date. It will be followed by the words "see Commencement for further information". Clicking on the word commencement will link to the relevant commencement order. If
there is no "version in force" date the words "see Commencement for further information" will
still appear. This means that the section has not yet been brought into force. Click the word
commencement. This will link to the legislative provision governing the commencement of that
particular section.

If details about commencement for an entire Act are sought, search for the piece of legislation   **6–82**
and section in the basic search box. This will retrieve the arrangement of the Act. Click on the
overview document link. This will retrieve a list of details of commencement for all the different
parts of the Act. Commencement details will appear first unless there are any amendments
pending, in which case click on the commencement link in the navigation bar or scroll down to
the commencement details. These show when each part of the Act was brought into force and
link to the commencement instrument.

Is It in Force? 📖
This is a twice yearly publication which covers inter alia all Public General Acts in England and   **6–83**
Scotland (including Acts of the Scottish Parliament) over the previous 25 years. The years are
presented in chronological order and within each year the statutes are listed alphabetically.
Opposite the short title are details of the relevant commencement provisions. If the same Act
applies to England, Wales and Scotland but there are differences in, e.g. commencement date,

this is acknowledged by separating the Scottish information and following it with an "(S)" (see paras 7–51—7–60).

6–84   The volume also contains a section entitled "Statutes Not Yet in Force" which lists provisions of Acts for which no commencement dates have yet been appointed. An example is the Easter Act 1928 which was given the Royal Assent on August 3, 1928 but which has never been brought into force.

6–85   Note that this publication does not include full information on amendments and repeals.

Is It in Force? ⌐₿ subscription service as part of LexisNexis
6–86   The online version is updated daily and links through to the relevant commencement orders.

Lawtel ⌐₿ subscription legal current awareness digest service
6–87   Lawtel is updated daily and holds all statutes since 1984. On the Lawtel homepage click on statutory law. Enter the search terms in the box and click search. In the search results click on the link to the details of the Act. From here, click on the link to the statutory status table. This lists all the sections of the Act in a table, with entries relating to commencement, amendment and repeal.

Current Law Legislation Citators and Current Law Statutes 📖
6–88   The information in the Current Law Legislation Citators is updated by the Statutes Service File which contains a Commencement Diary. This notes, alphabetically by statute, the commencement of statutes from January of the current year as initiated by Orders and by statutory provisions. There is a Commencement Diary covering the year in the annual volumes of the Current Law Statutes. From 1992 Commencement Orders have been reprinted in the annual volumes. There is also a Dates of Commencement Table in the Monthly Digests.

6–89   To find out if a Commencement Order has been issued in relation to an Act, check the Commencement Diary in the relevant volume of Statutes Annotated and check the Dates of Commencement Table in the latest Monthly Digest or the Commencement Diary in the Statutes Service File.

legislation.gov.uk ⌐₿ free
6–90   *legislation.gov.uk* provides commencement information at the bottom of the text of a section of an Act. If a provision has been amended but no date has been set for the change to come into force the database provides a prospective version of the relevant section(s).

LexisNexis ⌐₿ subscription database
6–91   While LexisNexis provides commencement information, Acts made by the UK Parliament that relate exclusively to Scotland are not included.

TSO Daily, Weekly or Monthly Lists 📖 and ⌐₿
6–92   These publications will contain details of Commencement Orders. The free online version of the Daily List is at *http://www.tsoshop.co.uk/parliament/bookstore.asp?FO = 38797* [accessed June 5, 2014].

Current status of a statute—finding amendment and repeals

Westlaw ⚘ subscription database

The legislation contained in Westlaw has incorporated any amendments or repeals. Words **6–93** which have been inserted or substituted are contained in square brackets and a footnote provides details of and a link to the amending legislation. An *ellipsis*, denoted thus [. . .], indicates that text has been repealed and the repealing legislation is referenced and linked via a footnote.

If a section has been amended several times the footnote only references the most recent **6–94** amendment. To see details of all amendments select overview document from the left- hand navigation bar and then select citator. The citator lists all the amendments to an Act and provides links to the amending legislation.

If a section of a UK Act has been amended differently in Scotland and in England, the reader is **6–95** alerted to this when looking at the section itself. The section shown will be the most recent version of the Act with a footnote containing the version from the other jurisdiction. This means that, depending on timing, some sections may be those extant (still in existence) in Scotland and others may be those extant in England. This causes no problems when looking at the Act section by section as the footnotes will alert the reader if there are other versions of the section. However, if a .pdf version is used it will contain the most recent version of the Act, i.e. in these circumstances Westlaw will not create separate .pdfs to show a Scottish or English version of an Act. This means that extreme care must be taken in relation to UK Acts which have been amended differently in different jurisdictions and involves checking the .pdf against the information in the citator in the overview document.

Prospective amendments are not incorporated into the text. If a provision has pending **6–96** amendments that are not yet in force, a yellow exclamation flag [!] is shown. To see the prospective change, select legislation analysis or overview document from the left-hand navigation bar.

Westlaw allows historic versions of the Act to be viewed back to 1991. To do this, use the **6–97** advanced search facility. The default setting is law in force, but further options, law in force and historic law, or point in time, can be selected. The latter option allows for legislation as it stood at a particular point in time to be scrutinised. In order to do this, the date in the format indicated by the date field must be included. If viewing a historical version of legislation, a red "no entry" flag 🚫 along with the words "superseded" or "repealed" will be given indicating a more recent version is available. To view the most recent version, select legislation analysis from the left-hand navigation bar and click on the date beneath the current law in force tab.

Current Law Legislation Citator 📖

This resource is the most efficient, best paper source for locating changes to Scottish legislation. **6–98** However, citators require the user to have an appreciation of how they are organised.

Using Current Law to find out if an Act has been amended or repealed: **6–99**

✎ **Step 1**: Check the statute citators in the volumes of legislation citators in chronological order starting from the date of the Act. In order to locate the chapter number, check the alphabetical list of Acts at the beginning of the volume. Once armed with the chapter number turn to the statute citator itself. Under the entry for the Act, the citator will list any amendments that have been made.

✎ **Step 2**: In order to be aware of all amendments (up to the last month) check through all the statute citators up to the most recent update for the citator in the Statutes Service File.

Lawtel ✑ subscription legal current awareness digest service

6–100 Lawtel is updated daily and covers all statutes since 1984. On the homepage click on statutory law. Enter search terms in the box and click search. Click on the link in the search results to the details of the Act. Click on the link to the statutory status table. This lists all the sections of the Act in a table, with entries relating to commencement, amendment and repeal.

Halsbury's Statutes 📖 and ✑ subscription

6–101 Halsbury's Statutes is a valuable tool with which to locate and track UK legislation. It contains the amended text of legislation currently in force and has an effective updating service. Unfortunately it does not include exclusively Scottish legislation.

LexisNexis ✑ subscription database

6–102 LexisNexis provides the revised form of legislation which incorporates amendments and repeals. An ellipsis, denoted thus (. . .), indicates that text has been repealed. Square brackets denote text that has been inserted or substituted. Italicised text means that the content is prospectively repealed or substituted. The notes section at the end of each document indicates the changes that have been made to the text. However, Acts that were made by the UK Parliament and relate exclusively to Scotland are not included.

Chronological Table of the Statutes 📖

6–103 The Chronological Table of the Statutes [1235–2006] is published by TSO and comprises two volumes. Statutes are listed chronologically by year and chapter number. When the title of the Act appears in italics it means it has been repealed. If it appears in bold type then the Act is still, at least in part, in force. Details of amendments and repeals are given.

Finding whether the courts have considered an Act

6–104 If the specific Act is known, consult paras 4–82—4–88 for detailed information on the most efficient strategies to employ.

Finding whether any journal articles have been written about an Act

Westlaw ✑ subscription database

6–105 Westlaw is the best way of tracing this information as it contains the Legal Journals Index ("LJI") within its journals section. This indexes legal articles and case summaries from hundreds of journals and dates back to 1986. There are two different ways to obtain this information in Westlaw. One is to search the journals section and the alternative is to search the legislation analysis for the Act. To search the journals section access it by selecting Journals from the navigation bar at the top of the screen of the welcome page. This links to the journals basic search page. There, select advanced search in the top right of the screen. Enter the short title in the legislation title field and the provision details in the legislation provision no. field. Click search.

6–106 Westlaw will also identify articles which have discussed legislation in the legislation analysis for the Act concerned. Links will go to the full text (if available on Westlaw) or to an abstract of the article.

LexisNexis ⁀ subscription database
Select the journals tab from the homepage. This opens up the journals search form. Enter the **6–107**
details of the Act in the search terms box.

HeinOnline ⁀ subscription database of legal journals
This database holds a number of UK law journals in its Law Journal Library. However, its **6–108**
Scots law holdings are currently limited.

Current Law Yearbooks 📖
Check under the appropriate subject headings in the Yearbooks and the latest Monthly Digest. **6–109**

Lawtel ⁀ subscription legal current awareness digest service
Lawtel indexes fewer journals than the LJI offered in Westlaw and the majority of its coverage **6–110**
of journals dates from 1998. To locate articles about an Act, select the articles index on the
home page, then choose the focused search option. Use the statutes cited box to enter the short
title of the Act.

NB Searching for journal articles is discussed further in paras 8–61—8–70.

Finding out whether any SIs have been made under an Act

See paras 6–187—6–193. **6–111**

LOCAL AND PERSONAL ACTS

Aids to tracing Local and Personal Acts

Chronological Tables of Local Acts and of Private and Personal Acts 📖 and ⁀
The Chronological Table of Local Legislation 1797–1994 and Chronological Table of Private **6–112**
and Personal Acts 1539-1997 2000 supplement includes corrections to the first edition texts and
is published by TSO. Further information can be found here *http://www.legislation.gov.uk/
changes/chron-tables/local/intro* [accessed June 4, 2014]. An extremely useful glossary of
Chronological Table abbreviations is available here. *http://www.legislation.gov.uk/changes/
chron-tables/chron-table-abbreviations.pdf* [accessed June 4, 2014].

Public General Acts and Measures 📖
Local and Personal Acts are listed in alphabetical order in the bound volumes of Public General **6–113**
Acts and Measures. See paras 6–29—6–32.

The Daily List 📖 and ⁀ free
The Daily List and its cumulative versions list Local and Personal Acts. The online version is **6–114**
available at *http://www.tsoshop.co.uk/parliament* [accessed June 4, 2014].

Sources of Local and Personal Acts

Current Law Statutes 📖
Since 1992 the full text of Private Acts is published in the final volume of Current Law Statutes **6–115**
for the year concerned.

Legislation.gov.uk ⬚ free

6–116 The full text of Local Acts from 1991 to the present day can be found here *http://www.legislation.gov.uk/ukla* [accessed June 4, 2014]. Acts appear in their original format only.

Libraries

6–117 Whilst some Local and Personal Acts can be purchased from TSO, some older Acts can be difficult to locate. The Scottish-based researcher may be able to locate more obscure provisions (likely in paper form) in collections held by a public library in the relevant geographic area (the area covered by the Act) or by contacting one of the following bodies:

> ➢ Aberdeen University library (Local Acts and Private Acts 1797 (38 Geo.3) onwards);
> ➢ The Advocates' Library (Edinburgh) (Local Acts and Private Acts 1797 (38 Geo.3) onwards). See *http://www.advocates.org.uk/library/index.html* [accessed June 4, 2014];
> ➢ Edinburgh University library (Local Acts and Private Acts 1797 (38 Geo.3) onwards);
> ➢ Glasgow University (Local Acts and Private Acts 1797 (38 Geo.3) onwards, Scottish Acts only);
> ➢ The Mitchell library (Glasgow) (Local Acts and Private Acts 1895–1922, 1923–1956 (incomplete), 1957 onwards). See *http://www.glasgowlife.org.uk/libraries/the-mitchell-library/Pages/home.aspx* [accessed June 4, 2014];
> ➢ St Andrews University library (Local Acts 1797 (38 Geo.3) onwards and Private Acts 1815–1885);
> ➢ The Signet library (Edinburgh) (Local Acts 1801 onwards. Private Acts 1815 onwards). See *http://www.wssociety.co.uk/* [accessed June 4, 2014].

Sources of Statutory Instruments

Legislation.gov.uk

6–118 Statutory instruments, like Acts of Parliament, are published both in paper form and electronically in many different databases and series. The official paper versions are published by TSO and the official electronic versions are available on the *legislation.gov.uk* website. The website provides the full text of all published SI since the beginning of 1987. Statutory instruments of general application are always published as are more contemporary local SIs, e.g. the Vale of White Horse (Electoral Changes) Order 2014. Older instruments may, however, prove difficult to locate in both formats.

6–119 *legislation.gov.uk* does not publish SIs in conjunction with the enabling Act of Parliament Rather, SIs are grouped by year and within each year they can be viewed chronologically by number. Since June 2004, an Explanatory Memorandum has been published with all SIs and these can be easily located on the webpage for a given SI. Statutory instruments are published in .html or .pdf format—the latter option facilitating easy downloading/printing of the entire document. Explanatory Memoranda are published in .pdf format only.

6–120 From November 1, 1997, all draft SIs awaiting approval are published on the website, *http://www.legislation.gov.uk/draft/2014* [accessed June 4, 2014], and remain available even when superseded by an official version or withdrawn. They are arranged by subject within each year. They are not available in printed form.

The *legislation.gov.uk* advanced search function allows a search to be undertaken by keyword, **6–121** type of legislation (e.g. SIs or draft SIs), jurisdiction or date.

Different databases and series produce different versions of SIs (see below), therefore it is vital **6–122** that the researcher is aware whether they are reading the original version or a revised version incorporating any amendments which have been made to it. As with Acts, the original version of an SI should be treated with caution as it represents a historical document. At the time of writing, *legislation.gov.uk* only publishes SIs in their original form.

Statutory instruments made by the Westminster Parliament and relating to Scotland have a **6–123** main number and an additional number which relates to its sequence in the issue of SIs for Scotland made during that year. The Scottish number should be ignored when trying to trace an instrument. The indexes all use the main number for the reference.

Further official publications

Statutory Rules and Orders and SIs Revised 📖
Prior to the enactment of the Statutory Instrument Act 1946 (in force 1948) which repealed the **6–124** Rules Publication Act 1893, SIs were called Statutory Rules and Orders. This publication is a consolidated version of all SIs in force up to the end of 1948 and is arranged under subject headings.

SIs (1949–) 📖
This series is published by TSO and contains the full text of general SIs. General SIs are **6–125** published individually and can be purchased direct from TSO. The series is published in annual volumes, arranged in numerical order with a subject index. Prior to 1961, volumes were arranged by subject with a numerical index. Usefully, this series provides a list of local SIs (both printed and non-printed).

Further sources of original versions

Justis UK Statutory Instruments 🖱 subscription
This database contains SI for England, Scotland and Wales from 1671 to the present in full text **6–126** form.

BAILII 🖱 free
BAILII holds SIs reproduced from *legislation.gov.uk*. UK statutory instruments from 2002 **6–127** onwards are located in the UK legislation section. Statutory instruments made by the Holyrood Parliament from 1999 onwards are available in the Scottish legislation section. The legislation search function allows SIs to be searched for by keyword, date and jurisdiction. The advanced search function allows Boolean searching. The SIs held are available as continuous web pages as opposed to .pdfs.

Specialist loose-leaf encyclopaedias and collections of legislation 📖
Specialist loose-leaf encyclopaedias (see para.8–17) and collections of legislation may contain **6–128** copies of selected subject-specific SI.

Current Law Yearbooks 📖
As with Acts, SIs are digested in the Current Law Yearbooks and Monthly Digests. The full text **6–129** of Commencement Orders are printed in the Yearbooks (for each successive year since 1992) and in the loose-leaf service file (for the current year) (see para.8–31).

Sources of Revised Versions

Westlaw ⌁ subscription database

6–130 Westlaw holds a selection of UK SIs of general application published between 1948 and 1991. All UK SIs from 1992 onwards and all SIs made by the Holyrood Parliament since its inception in 1999 are available, but no draft versions are held.

Sources of revised versions excluding exclusively Scottish material

LexisNexis ⌁ subscription database

6–131 Full text, revised form of UK SIs are available, but SIs applying exclusively to Scotland are not.

Halsbury's Statutory Instruments 📖 and ⌁ subscription

6–132 This resource contains information on every current SI of general application in England and Wales. However, it does not reprint all Sis, with many merely being summarised, and it does not include exclusively Scottish SI. See "Aide to Tracing Statutory Instruments".

Searching for SIs

Westlaw ⌁ subscription database

6–133 Westlaw offers three alternative ways of searching for SIs: basic search, advanced search and browsing.

Basic search

6–134 From the welcome page, click the legislation link from the navigation bar at the top of the screen. This will migrate to the legislation basic search page, where SIs can be searched for by inputting the name of the piece of legislation, the year and provision number (if required). If the year is known, it is always prudent to enter it as this will avoid retrieving multiple pieces of legislation. Likewise, if only the title is known, enter it in quotation marks, e.g. "The Marriage (Same Sex Couples) Act 2013 (Consequential Provisions) Order". Entering the title of a SI without quotation marks will retrieve all pieces of legislation with those words in the title. If only the year and number are known, enter those into the title field, e.g. 2014/137.

6–135 The free text field allows a search to be undertaken by inputting terms or phrases which Westlaw will then search for within the text of all SIs held. Searching can be improved if search techniques referred to by Westlaw as "Terms and Connectors" are used (see paras 2–58—2–59).

> **NB** The basic search function only searches legislation currently in force. If historical legislation is sought the advanced search option ought to be selected.

6–136 *Display of search results:* If the search is undertaken by title only, the "Arrangement of SI" for that legislation will be returned. Searching for legislation using the free text function will return sections of legislation where those terms exist. The results list will show the name of the legislation, as well as the title of the provision and the date when it came into force. Within a result list status icons may display next to the title of the legislation indicating that (i) either the provision has been repealed or superseded ℝ, or (ii) has pending amendments !. To whittle down a long list of results, the original search can be narrowed by entering additional terms in the field at the top of the page and then clicking search within results.

Browsing for SIs

Browsing can be undertaken by year, title or jurisdiction for both Westminster and Holyrood **6–137**
SI. The browsing by year function allows a time period (prior to 1990) to be selected from which
the year sought can then be perused. From 1990 onwards a year can be selected. Within each
year there is an alphabetical list of legislation that received Royal Assent in that year. Browsing
by title allows a letter to be selected to yield an alphabetical list of SIs. The same legislative
materials that are available for Acts are available for SIs.

Lawtel subscription legal current awareness digest service

Lawtel's SI Database indexes SIs from 1984 onwards and allows SIs to be (i) traced, and (ii) **6–138**
checked to determine whether they have been amended or revoked. This service provides links
to the full-text, where available, and is updated daily. To carry out a search: click on statutory
instruments on the homepage; enter the search terms in the box (or select focused search which
allows for a search by title, number, enabling Act, date coming into force, and area of application); and click search. Click on the link in the search results to locate details of the SI. The
details shown will include the instrument's number, the enabling Act, date it came into force, a
list of effects it has had on other legislation, its area of application and a link to the full original
text of the instrument and the Explanatory Memorandum on the *legislation.gov.uk* website.

Current Law Legislation Citators

The Current Law Legislation Citators list all amendments, modifications and repeals to primary **6–139**
and secondary legislation made in the years covered by the specific volume. Since 1993 the
legislation citators have been a combination of two citators—a statute citator and an SI citator.
The SI citator appears after the statute citator. It is arranged in the following order:

> ➢ Scottish SIs are listed in chronological order by year and number;
> ➢ Statutory rules issued by the UK Parliament are listed in chronological order by year
> and number;
> ➢ SIs made by the UK Parliament are listed in chronological order by year and number.

The SI citator contains:

> ➢ Details of amendments and repeals since 1993 made to SIs of any date;
> ➢ In respect of any SI, cases in which it has been judicially considered since 1993;
> ➢ In respect of any SI, details of the SI issued since 1993 which have been made under its
> provisions;
> ➢ In respect of any SI, where it has been consolidated by an Act passed since 1993.

Searching Current Law SI Citators

The 1972–1988 Legislation Citator contains a "Table of SI Affected 1947–1988". It is arranged **6–140**
chronologically and within each year numerically. It lists amendments and revocations to SI
made from 1947–1988.

The 1989–1995 Legislation Citator, which includes the SI Citator1993–1995, contains a "Table **6–141**
of Statutory Instruments Affected 1989–1992". This lists amendments and revocations to SI
made between 1989–1992.

The Current Law SI Citator for the periods 1996–1999 and 2000–2001 is also contained in the **6–142**
relevant legislation citator.

6–143 Since 2001, annual combined volumes of statutes and SIs have been published. Before a particular year ending, SI citator updates can be found in the Statutes Service File.

6–144 In all volumes the materials are arranged in chronological order by reference to the year and then within the year, in numerical order according to the number of the SI. In order to locate the number, consult the alphabetical list of SI at the beginning of the volume. Details on the Statutes Service File are at para.8–34.

Excerpt from a SI Citator

6–145 **[1] 1956. Act of Sederunt (Sheriff Court Ordinary Cause Rules) 1993 [2]**
amended: SI 96/2167 r.2, Sch. **[3]**
applied: SI 97/687 Sch.1.
Ch.33 Part II, applied: SI 96/125 art.3.
Form G13, see *Stewart v Callaghan* 1996 S.L.T. 12 (Sh Ct). **[4]**
r.33.22A, applied: SI 96/2444 Reg.18.
r.33.29, applied: SI 97/687 Sch.1 Table.
r.36.14, applied: SI 96/207 Sch.8, para.43.
r.128, applied: SI 96/207 Sch.8, para.43.

1972. Advice and Assistance (Assistance by Way of Representation) (Scotland) Amendment Regulations 1993
revoked: SI 97/3070 reg.2, Sch. **[5]**

Key:

> **[1]** SI Number
> **[2]** Name of SI
> **[3]** Changes made to the SI
> **[4]** Case reference
> **[5]** This SI has been revoked

How to find out if an SI has been amended or revoked

6–146 ✥ **Step 1**: Check the SI citators in the volumes of legislation citators/stand alone annual volumes in chronological order starting from the date of the SI. In order to locate the number, check the alphabetical list of SI at the beginning of the volume.
✥ **Step 2:** Armed with the number, turn to the appropriate entry for the SI. There the xitator will list any amendments that have been made.
✥ **Step 3**: In order to find all amendments (up to the last month) check through all the SI citators up to the most recent update for the citator in the Statutes Service File.

How to find out if any cases have concerned a particular SI

6–147 ✥ **Step 1**: Check through the SI citators in chronological order. Look under the entry for the SI. If a case has concerned a particular SI it will appear opposite the entry.
✥ **Step 2**: Check the most recent update for the citator in the Statutes Service File.

How to find an SI:

↳ **Step 1**: If the year and name of the SI is known check the Alphabetical List of SI for the **6–148** year in the appropriate Yearbook. If the full citation is known but not the name of the SI, check the Numerical List of SI for the year in the appropriate Yearbook. In both instances, opposite the entry for the SI will be a reference to a paragraph number.

↳ **Step 2**: Turn to the appropriate paragraph where there will be a digest of the SI. It will provide details of its full title, a short summary of its content, details of the legislation it is made under and the date it was brought into force.

JustCite ∾ subscription legal citator
JustCite holds UK SI (from 1671) and all Holyrood SI. These can be searched for by title or **6–149** reference (which means e.g. giving the year and number of a SI). Statutory instruments can be searched separately by ticking the appropriate box. Alternatively, search using the index tab to browse through separate title indexes of SIs listed in alphabetical order. Scottish legislation is not listed separately.

The information retrieved includes: **6–150**

> The status of the provision;
> A link to the particular reference. Clicking on this link will open a new window showing various sources of the full text of the SI;
> Lists of parts which have been amended and the amending legislation;
> Lists of parts which have amended other legislation and the legislation amended.

List of Statutory Publications (London Gazette Supplement) 📖
The List of Statutory Publications is published monthly by TSO. It includes details of general **6–151** and local SIs for the UK, England and Wales and Scotland published during the previous month and any attendant Explanatory Notes. They are arranged by jurisdiction alphabetically by title and type or subject. The publication is consolidated at the end of a year and appears as an annual List of Statutory Publications.

Daily List 📖 and ∾ free
The Daily List lists SIs published by TSO. It is the first official record of the existence of a SI. **6–152**

Journals 📖 and ∾ subscription.   **6–153**

Aids that Contain the Original Version of SI

Justis UK SI ∾ subscription
Justis contains the original form of UK SI for England, Scotland and Wales from 1671 and **6–154** Scottish SI made by Holyrood from 1999.

Legislation.gov.uk ∾ free
This website contains the original form of UK SIs from 1991 and Scottish SIs made by the **6–155** Scottish Parliament from 1999.

BAILII ∾ free
BAILII contains the original form of UK SIs from 2002 and Scottish SI made by Holyrood **6–156** from 1999.

Aids that exclude exclusively Scottish material

LexisNexis ⌁ subscription database

6–157 LexisNexis has the full text revised version of SI in force in England and Wales but excludes exclusively Scottish SI. However, it does contain Scottish SIs made by the Holyrood Parliament from 1999.

Halsbury's SI ⌂ and ⌁ subscription

6–158 Halsbury's SI database does not include exclusively Scottish SIs. However, it does contain the revised form of UK SIs.

Finding SIs when only the title is known (i.e. the year and number are not known)

Westlaw ⌁ subscription database

6–159 The legislation search in Westlaw allows a search to be undertaken by title field. See paras 2–58—2–59 for guidance if using Westlaw's "terms and connectors". Statutory instruments can also be browsed by title via one of the browse options on the legislation search page.

Lawtel ⌁ subscription legal current awareness digest service

6–160 This digest service only includes legislation from 1984. On the homepage click on SI. Using the focused search allows for a search by title. Enter the search terms in the box and click search. Click on the link in the search results to the details of the desired SI.

Current Law Yearbooks and Monthly Digests ⌂

6–161 There are alphabetical lists of SIs in the Current Law Yearbooks and in the Monthly Digests. The lists will provide the year and number of the SI. The Current Law Yearbooks and Monthly Digests only provide a summary of the SI.

Current Law SI Citator ⌂

6–162 The Current Law SI Citators (1993–present) include an alphabetical list at the start of each volume. Citators enable the researcher to locate the year and number and to check if the SI has been amended or repealed.

The Laws of Scotland: Stair Memorial Encyclopaedia ⌂

6–163 Check the Consolidated Table of Statutes or, if the subject area is known, go to the individual title. Each title has a list of legislation.

The Laws of Scotland Online (*Stair Memorial Encyclopaedia*) ⌁

6–164 Enter the title of the SI as the search term in the commentary search form.

Subject Specialist Encyclopaedias and Collections of Legislation ⌂

6–165 Specialist loose-leaf encyclopaedias and collections of legislation can be searched via any Tables of SI provided or by the subject index.

Sources that contain the original versions of SIs

Justis UK SI ⌁ subscription

6–166 Justis contains the original form of UK SIs for England, Scotland and Wales from 1671 and Scottish SIs made by the Holyrood Parliament from 1999.

Legislation.gov.uk
This government website contains the original form of UK SIs from 1991 and Scottish SIs made **6–167**
by the Holyrood Parliament from 1999. A search can be undertaken by title or the site can be
browsed alphabetically.

BAILII 🖰 free
BAILII contains the original form of UK SIs from 2002 and Scottish SIs made by the Holyrood **6–168**
Parliament from 1999. The legislation search allows searching by keyword in the title of the SI.
The advanced search allows Boolean searching.

Sources that exclude exclusively Scottish material

LexisNexis 🖰 subscription database
LexisNexis has the full text revised version of SIs in force in England and Wales, but excludes **6–169**
exclusively Scottish SIs. It does contain Scottish SIs made by the Holyrood Parliament from
1999. The legislation search allows searching by keyword in the title of the SI.

Halsbury's SI 📖 and 🖰 subscription
This resource excludes exclusively Scottish SIs.   **6–170**

Finding SIs by subject

The Laws of Scotland: Stair Memorial Encyclopaedia 📖
Check the Consolidated Index where detailed subject headings are listed to locate the relevant **6–171**
volume or reissued title. To bring a search up to date consult the Annual Cumulative Supplement and the Service Binder. See para.8–07.

The Laws of Scotland Online (*Stair Memorial Encyclopaedia*) 🖰
Enter details of the subject area as the search term in the commentary search form. See para.8– **6–172**
04.

Subject Specialist Encyclopaedias and Collections of Legislation 📖
Specialist loose-leaf encyclopaedias and collections of legislation can be searched via any Tables **6–173**
of SI provided or by the subject index.

Westlaw 🖰 subscription database
The legislation search in Westlaw allows a free text search.   **6–174**

Lawtel 🖰 subscription legal current awareness digest service
On the homepage click on SI. Enter the search terms in the box and click search. Alternatively **6–175**
use the focused search to search by subject. Click on the link in the search results to the details of
the SI.

Current Law Yearbooks and Monthly Digests 📖
Check the Yearbooks under the appropriate subject heading. This will yield a reference to a **6–176**
paragraph number. The Current Law Yearbooks and Monthly Digests will only contain a
summary of the SI.

Sources that contain the original version of SI

Justis UK SI ⚲ subscription

6–177 This resource contains the original form of UK SIs for England, Scotland and Wales from 1671 and Scottish SIs made by the Holyrood Parliament from 1999. Search by subject using a keyword.

Legislation.go.v.uk ⚲ free

6–178 This official resource contains the original form of UK SIs from 1991 and Scottish SIs made by the Holyrood Parliament from 1999. Use the advanced search to search by free text.

BAILII ⚲ free

6–179 BAILII contains the original form of UK SIs from 2002 and Scottish SIs made by the Hoyrood Parliament from 1999. The legislation search allows searching by keyword *in* the title or words in the text. A search can be restricted to UK SIs and/or Scottish SIs. The advanced search allows Boolean searching.

Sources that exclude exclusively Scottish material

LexisNexis ⚲ subscription database

6–180 LexisNexis has the full text revised version of SIs in force in England and Wales, but excludes exclusively Scottish SIs. It does contain Scottish SIs made by the Holyrood Parliament from 1999. It is possible to search by keyword.

Halsbury's SIs 📖 and ⚲ subscription

6–181 This resource excludes exclusively Scottish SIs.

Current status of SIs—finding amendments and repeals

Westlaw ⚲ subscription database

6–182 Westlaw provides the amended text of SIs and provides links to the amending legislation.

Lawtel ⚲ subscription legal current awareness digest service

6–183 On the Lawtel homepage click on SI then enter the search terms in the box and click search, or alternatively use the focused search to search by title. Click on the link in the search results to the details of the SI. The entry there gives information about amendments and repeals from 1984.

Current Law SI Citators 📖

6–184 The citators list amendments and repeals from 1993 onwards.

Sources that exclude exclusively Scottish material

LexisNexis ⚲ subscription database

6–185 LexisNexis has the full text revised version of SIs in force in England and Wales but excludes exclusively Scottish SIs. It does contain Scottish SIs made by the Holyrood Parliament from 1999.

Halsbury's SIs 📖 and ⚲ subscription

6–186 The paper version is up to date to within a month and contains the amended versions of SI. The electronic version is updated daily.

Finding SIs made under an enabling Act

Westlaw ⁂ subscription database
Go to Legislation and search under the title of an Act, this will retrieve a link to the arrange- **6–187** ments of the Act. Click on overview document which appears in the left hand navigation bar. This brings up a list of information about the Act. Click on the link to SIs made under the Act. This will retrieve a list of all the SIs made under the Act which are linked so that the researcher can link thorough to view the full amended text of the SI. If SIs made under the Act does not appear as an option in the overview document this means that no SIs have been made under the Act.

Lawtel ⁂ subscription legal current awareness digest service
Lawtel only contains material after 1984. Search by title of the Act and then click on the link to **6–188** the statutory status table. This will contain a link to SIs enabled by the Act where all SI made under the Act can be located.

Current Law Statute Citator 📖
The Current Law Statute Citators provide details of SI instruments made under an Act. The **6–189** details are listed alongside the entry for the Act. Begin the search by checking from the year the Act was passed in order to locate whether any SIs have been made under it.

Sources that exclude exclusively Scottish material

LexisNexis ⁂ subscription database. **6–190**

Halsbury's Statutes of England 📖 **6–191**

Finding whether the courts have considered an SI

The techniques are very similar to tracing whether the courts have interpreted a statute. See **6–192** paras 4–82—4–86.

Finding whether any journal articles have been written about a SI

The techniques are very similar to tracing articles about a statute. See paras 6–105—6–110. **6–193**

COLLECTIONS OF LEGISLATION

Parliament House Book 📖
The Parliament House Book contains revised Westminster and Holyrood legislation covering **6–194** selected areas of Scots private law and court procedure. It includes:

➤ Primary legislation;
➤ Delegated legislation;
➤ Practice notes;
➤ Solicitors practice rules;
➤ Notes for guidance issued by public departments;
➤ Greens annotated rules of the Court of Session;
➤ Practice and procedure of the Scottish Parliament.

It is published in a loose-leaf format consisting of five volumes. The Parliament House Book is arranged in different divisions. Within each division the material is arranged chronologically. Statutes are followed by SIs and other regulations, then by tables and guidance notes. The first page of each division lists its contents. The Parliament House Book is updated five times a year. The date at the foot of each page is the date when the page was last updated. The references given throughout are to the division and page number, e.g. The Sheriff Courts (Scotland) Act 1971 is referenced as D74. This means that it is contained in Division D at p.74. As of 2013, the Parliament House Book has been made available on Westlaw.

Specialised collections of legislation

6–195   An increasing number of subject-specific collections of legislation are now being produced. They tend to be annotated. Examples include: Renton and Brown's *Criminal Procedure Legislation, Scottish Conveyancing Legislation, Scottish Family Law Legislation, Scottish Landlord and Tenant Legislation, Scottish Social Work Legislation* and *Scottish Trusts and Succession Service.*

6–196   There are numerous collections of legislation produced for the student market. They tend to contain a selection of subject-specific legislation. Some include annotations, but many do not. They are usually single-volume paperback works which are updated annually. Texts without annotations are sometimes allowed to be taken into examinations.

Further reading

6–197   ➢ P. Clinch, *Using a Law Library*, 2nd edn (London: Blackstone Press, 2001) Chs 10 and 11 cover Scottish legislation
➢ G. Holburn and G. Engle, *Butterworths Legal Research Guide* (London: Butterworths, 2001)
➢ J. Knowles and P. Thomas, *Effective Legal Research* (London: Sweet & Maxwell, 2006)
➢ P.A. Thomas and J. Knowles, *Dane & Thomas How to Use a Law Library*, 4th edn (London: Sweet & Maxwell, 2001). This contains a separate Scottish chapter.

Chapter 7
Search Strategies for Finding Scottish (Holyrood) Parliament Legislation (Pre-1707 and Post-1999)

Significant abbreviations used in this chapter

- BAILLI—British and Irish Legal Institute
- Sch.—Schedule
- SI—Statutory instrument
- S.L.T.—Scots Law Times
- SPICe—Scottish Parliament Information Centre.
- TSO—The Stationery Office

This chapter discusses search strategies for finding legislation from the pre-1707 Scottish Par- **7–01**
liaments and from the Scottish Parliament at Holyrood created in 1999. Discussion of the pre-
1707 Scottish Parliaments presages suggested search strategies for locating materials emanating
from Holyrood namely: Bills, Acts of the Scottish Parliament and Scottish only statutory
instruments.

The fact that the Holyrood Parliament assumed certain legislative powers in 1999 has impli- **7–02**
cations for the legal researcher. First, it means that the information sources for this modern
institution were created in a world where use of electronic sources was the norm. Second,
although many legislative instruments are modelled on the form and style of Westminster,
Holyrood has adopted a more modern format for such provisions. The official Scottish Parliament website, *http://www.scottish.parliament.uk* [accessed June 5, 2014], contains a vast
amount of information and is well laid out with quick search and advanced search facilities. It
contains information designed for people with different levels of interest in the Parliament
ranging from a casual visitor to an academic legal researcher. Once familiar with the site it is a
mine of useful information about the workings of the Parliament and the legislation that it
produces. In particular, the Parliamentary Business tab at the top of the page provides a
gateway to many of the resources discussed below.

The Scottish Parliament Homepage

Parliamentary Business Homepage

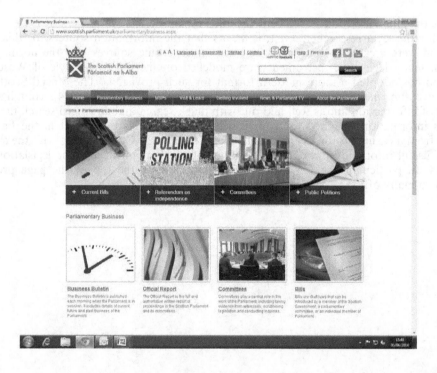

This chapter discusses information sources unique to the Holyrood Parliament. In order to **7–03** avoid repetition, the UK-wide legal information sources which have encompassed Holyrood materials as detailed in Ch.6 will be cross referenced in this chapter, as appropriate.

PRE-1707 SCOTTISH LEGISLATION

Regiam Majestatem is the work commonly regarded as containing the earliest collection of **7–04** Scottish legislation. It dates from either the late 13th or 14th century. The *Stair Memorial Encyclopaedia* (Vol.22, para.512) refers to it being "essentially a commentary on the procedures of the royal courts". It is not a completely Scottish document in that it is based on a 12th century English work (*Tractatus De Legibus et Consuetudinibus Regni Anglie*, by de Glanvill). However, it is not just a copy of the earlier work—it has adapted it to describe the legal system that was developing in Scotland. Another work of the period is the *Quoniam Attachiamenta*. It is a Scottish work and concerns procedure in the feudal courts. The two works are usually printed together. The modern edition of *Regiam Majestatem* is edited by Lord Cooper, Stair Society, Vol.11, 1947. There is a recent edition of *Quoniam Attachiamenta*, edited by T.D. Fergus, The Stair Society, Edinburgh 1996.

There is a lack of information about early Scottish legislation due to "the loss of our public **7–05** records, the most valuable of which were carried off into England, first by Edward I, and afterwards by an order of Oliver Cromwell, about the middle of the seventeenth century. Apart from six isolated rolls of 1292–3, 1368–9 and 1388–9, there are no original parliamentary records existing prior to 1466" (*An Introductory Survey of the Sources and Literature of Scots Law*, The Stair Society, Edinburgh 1936, p.4).

Sources of Legislation from the Pre-1707 Scottish Parliaments

Legislation from the pre-1707 Scottish Parliaments is usually referred to as Scots Acts. There are **7–06** two main sources of Scots Acts. *Acts of the Parliaments of Scotland 1124–1707*, edited by T. Thomson and C. Innes, was published during the 19th century. This is known as the Record edition. It has been called the "authoritative edition" (P.G.B. McNeill "Citation of Scots Statutes", 1959 S.L.T. (News) 112). The other collection is *Laws and Acts of Parliament 1424–1707* by Murray of Glendook. The author of the above article goes on to refer to this as "a collection of statutes which is neither official nor authoritative, and which is full of inaccuracies". The content of the two works does not always agree and the numbering of Acts is different. The Registration Act 1579, referred to below, could be referred to as A.P.S. III 142 in the Record edition or 1579 c.75 in Glendook's work. It is given the chapter number 13 in the Record edition, but Glendook's work refers to it as Ch.75.

Details of other early editions of Scots statutes are given in *An Introductory Survey of the* **7–07** *Sources and Literature of Scots Law*, The Stair Society, Edinburgh 1936, Ch.1. Scots Acts which were still in force in 1908 were reproduced in a single volume called Scots Statutes Revised 1424–1707. The Statute Law Revisions (Scotland) Act 1964 repealed many Acts of the old Scottish Parliament. Acts which were still in force following this Act were reprinted in The Acts of the Parliaments of Scotland 1424–1707, published in 1966.

There is now access to electronic versions of Scots Acts. Legislation.gov.uk contains the text of **7–08** more than 100 Scots Acts and Westlaw has a significant holding. A digital edition of the Acts of the Scottish Parliament from 1235 to 1707 is available on The Records of the Parliaments of

Scotland to 1707 website, *http://www.rps.ac.uk/* [accessed June 6, 2014]. This searchable database is hosted by the University of St Andrews.

Citation of Scots Acts

7–09 The correct citation of Scots Acts is by the short title or by the calendar year and chapter number or by the volume, page and chapter number of the Record edition. The Acts did not originally have short titles, but all surviving Scots Acts were given short titles by Sch.2 of the Statute Law Revision (Scotland) Act 1964. An example from Sch.2 is the Act formerly known by "For pwnishment of personis that contempnandlie remanis rebellis and at the horne". It acquired the short title The Registration Act 1579.

7–10 Prior to 1964, Scots Acts were cited by calendar year and chapter number in the Glendook edition or by the volume and page number of the Record edition. This is still the case for Scots Acts which have been repealed.

Tracing Scots Acts that are still in force

7–11 There are still a number of Scots Acts which are still in force today. *Legislation.gov.uk* allows an online search to be undertaken by legislation type here *http://www.legislation.gov.uk/aosp* [accessed June 6, 2014]. It is also possible to trace these Acts in paper form by checking the Chronological Table of Statutes where Acts of the pre-1707 Parliaments of Scotland are included in a separate table at the end of the second volume. The search can then be updated by using the volumes of the Current Law Legislation Citators and the latest edition of the citator in the Statutes Service File. The utility of Current Law as a resource is discussed throughout Ch.6.

SCOTTISH PARLIAMENT (1999–) BILLS

7–12 Given that Bills are amended to various degrees as they migrate from one parliamentary stage to the next it is essential to ensure that the most current version of the Bill is consulted. Details on the parliamentary procedures for passing a Bill in the Holyrood Parliament are discussed in paras 5–68—5–77.

Sources of the text of a current Bill (Public and Private)

Scottish Parliament website ⏚ free

7–13 On the home page of the Scottish Parliament website click on Parliamentary Business. This will link to a page entitled Bills where links to information about current and previous bills are provided.

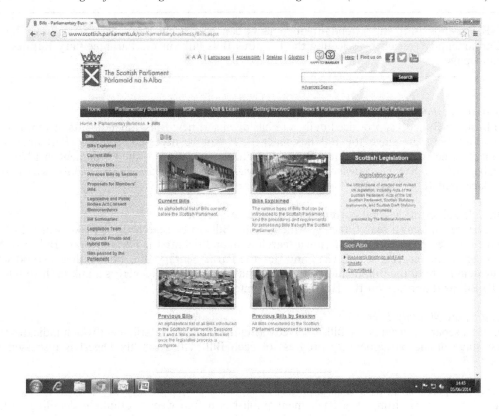

The information available on the page dedicated to current bills includes:

> ➢ The short title of the Bill;
> ➢ Details of the progress of the Bill;
> ➢ The content of the Bill at various stages, i.e. as introduced and as amended;
> ➢ The accompanying documents (see para.5–70);
> ➢ SPICe briefings (briefings written by research specialists in the Scottish Parliament Information Centre);
> ➢ Details of amendments.

Individual Bills are published by RR Donnelley and appear on purple paper. Bills may be **7–14** printed many times depending on the amount of changes made as they progress through Parliament.

Finding out which stage a current Bill has reached

Scottish Parliament website ⏻ free
On the Current Bills page all Bills before Parliament are listed in alphabetical order. Once a Bill **7–15** has been selected by clicking on the relevant link, all the stages the Bill has completed or has still yet to complete are listed in chronological order with dates given where appropriate. Proposed Private Bills and proposals for Members' Bill can also be accessed from this webpage.

> **NB** Previous Bills and attendant documents can be searched for alphabetically or by Parliamentary session by selecting the Previous Bills link on the Parliamentary Business homepage.

The Business Bulletin 📖 and 🕀 free

7–16 The Business Bulletin is produced daily and has details of new Bills, amendments or reprints of Bills along with the stage the Bill has reached. It can be accessed from the Parliamentary Business home page where Business Bulletins from the inception of the Parliament in 1999 can also be located. See *http://www.scottish.parliament.uk/parliamentarybusiness/BusinessBulletin.aspx* [accessed June 5, 2014].

Lawtel 🕀 subscription legal current awareness digest service

7–17 This service contains a search facility which allows Bills to be searched for by keyword. Either use the UK Search section by entering a search term and ticking the Parliamentary Bills box, or go to legislation, enter a search term and tick the Parliamentary Bills box. Either method will locate details about the Bill, including the stage that it has reached. There is a link to the full text of the Bill as it appears on the Holyrood Parliament website.

Current Law Monthly Digest 📖

7–18 There is a separate Progress of Bills table covering the Holyrood Parliament which indicates the latest stage in the parliamentary progress of each Bill. The Monthly Digest is discussed in para.8–23.

Scottish Parliament weekly eBulletin 🕀 free

7–19 When Holyrood is sitting, the Parliament publishes a free weekly eBulletin detailing forthcoming events and business. To subscribe to this service access the following link, *http://www.scottish.parliament.uk/parliamentarybusiness/eBulletin.aspx* [accessed June 5, 2014].

Journals 📖

7–20 Journals may contain information about the progress of Bills. The S.L.T. (available on Westlaw) has a Parliamentary News (Scotland) section which notes the introduction and progress of Bills.

Newspapers 📖 and 🕀

7–21 The Scottish broadsheets, e.g. the *Scotsman* and *Glasgow Herald*, contain information about Bills and other legislative developments at Holyrood.

SPICe Current Law Statutes 📖

7–22 Once the Bill is published in this series it will contain annotations which will contain information about the background to the Act and the passage of the Bill.

Finding out about Parliamentary debates on a Bill

The Scottish Parliament Official Report 📖 and 🕀 free

7–23 The Official Report is a substantially full account of proceedings in Parliament (it is the equivalent of *Hansard* per the Westminster Parliament). The website for this resource, *http://www.scottish.parliament.uk/parliamentarybusiness/OfficialReport.aspx* [accessed June 6, 2014], publishes debates on inter alia Bills and Committee inquiries and evidence sessions, and states that the Official Report for meetings of the Parliament will likely be available electronically and in paper form by 8am on the day following a specific meeting.

Committee meetings are published in accordance with a schedule agreed for specific meetings. **7–24**

The website can be browsed by date or searched using the Official Report search facility to **7–25**
locate specific keywords. To consult the most recent reports of committee and full parliamentary
meetings where Bills are considered access the following link, *http://www.scottish.parliament.uk/
parliamentarybusiness/24162.aspx* [accessed June 6, 2014].

The reference for the Official Report for meetings of the Parliament should include SP OR **7–26**
followed by full details of the date and column numbers, e.g. SP OR 22 January 2014, col
26841–26842. The reference for the Official Report for Committee meetings should include SP
OR followed by the appropriate committee abbreviation, the date and column numbers e.g. SP
OR ERD 24 April 2006, col 3061–3104. The reference for the Official Report for written
answers should include SP WA date, parliamentary question number, e.g. SP WA 28 March
2007, S2W-32485.

Explanatory Notes 📖 and ⏚ free
All Acts of the Holyrood Parliament which result from Bills introduced by the Scottish Min- **7–27**
isters (except for Acts which result from Budget Bills) are accompanied by Explanatory Notes.
At the end of each Explanatory Note is a section called Parliamentary History which contains a
table setting out, for each stage of the proceedings in the Scottish Parliament for the Act, the
dates on which the proceedings at that stage took place, the references to the Official Report of
those proceedings and the dates on which the Committee Reports and other papers relating to
the Act were published and the references to those Reports and other papers.

7–28 Explanatory Notes are available via the *legislation.gov.uk* website where the majority of references in Explanatory Notes are hyperlinked to the relevant Official Report. Explanatory Notes are also published in paper form by TSO. The office of the Queen's Printer for Scotland, *http://www.scotland.gov.uk/Topics/Government/queensprinterforscotland* [accessed June 6, 2014], lists all Explanatory Notes published since the inception of the Holyrood Parliament alphabetically and by year.

Current Law Statutes 📖
7–29 If the Bill has since become an Act, the annual volumes of Current Law Statutes should contain details of the Parliamentary debates relevant to each Act in the first annotation inserted after the long title.

Passage of the Bill Series 📖
7–30 This series consists of a volume for each Bill which contains all the relevant documentation from the passage of the Bill through to its enactment including: the Bill as introduced, accompanying Explanatory Notes; verbatim debates; meetings held; and the relevant parts of the Official Report. The University of Glasgow library holds a full collection of this series. For further information access *http://universityofglasgowlibrary.wordpress.com/2013/09/13/scottish-parliament-passage-of-bills-series/* [accessed June 6, 2014].

The Business Bulletin 📖 and ⌂ free
7–31 The Business Bulletin is published daily at 8am when Holyrood is in session and comprises past, current and future business of Parliament. See *http://www.scottish.parliament.uk/parliamentarybusiness/BusinessBulletin.aspx* [accessed June 6, 2014].

SOURCES OF ACTS OF THE SCOTTISH PARLIAMENT

7–32 Acts of the Scottish Parliament, like their UK counterparts, are published both electronically and in paper and in many different databases and series. For information about the layout and structure of an Act of the Scottish Parliament see para.5–83. Different versions of Acts may include additional information, such as annotations and/or different search facilities for accessing legislation. However, as with Westminster, or indeed legislation from any other jurisdiction, the researcher must be aware whether it is the original version of the Act (i.e. the Act as passed by Parliament) which is being consulted or whether it is a revised version which includes any amendments which have been made to it. In most instances, it is up-to-date revised version of legislation that will be sought, unless a research project is undertaken for the purposes of tracking specific legislative changes in a given area of law. Thus, the original version of an Act should be treated with caution in most circumstance as it represents a historical document. There may not have been any amendments since the original version was passed, but unless this is verified, consulting the original version could lead to serious error.

Official version

Acts of the Scottish Parliament 📖
7–33 After a Bill receives Royal Assent the official paper version is published by TSO under the authority of the Queen's Printer for Scotland. Each Act is printed singly and these are known as Queen's Printer copies. Explanatory Notes are published with all Acts of the Scottish Parliament which result from Bills introduced into the Parliament by the Scottish Ministers (except for Acts which result from Budget Bills). The text of the Explanatory Notes is produced by the Scottish Government Department responsible for the subject matter of the Act.

At the end of each calendar year the single Acts are produced together in a publication called **7–34** Acts of the Scottish Parliament. This is the official version of the Acts which are arranged in chronological order by asp number. These do not contain annotations. Alphabetical and chronological lists are contained at the start of each volume. At the end of each volume are tables of derivations and destinations of the Consolidation Acts for the year. There is also a table called Effects of Legislation. This is in two parts. Part 1 gives details of Acts of the Scottish Parliament (in chronological order) which have been repealed, amended or otherwise affected by Acts of the Scottish Parliament, Scottish SIs, Acts of the Westminster Parliament and SIs made during the year. Part 2 gives details of Acts of the Westminster Parliament (in chronological order) which have been repealed, amended or otherwise affected by Acts of the Scottish Parliament which received Royal Assent during the year concerned. The index to the volume is organised alphabetically by short title and then by section.

Office of the Queen's Printer for Scotland ⌧ free
The official full text original version of Acts of the Scottish Parliament, as published by the **7–35** Office of the Queen's Printer for Scotland, are accessed through the *legislation.gov.uk* website. For general enquiries about the work of the Office, email *oqps@nationalarchives.gsi.gov.uk*.

legislation.gov.uk provides links to the full original text of all Acts of the Holyrood Parliament **7–36** and also the revised version. Explanatory Notes are generally published at the same time as the Act.

Sources of revised versions of Acts

In addition to revised versions of Acts published on the *legislation.gov.uk* website the following **7–37** resources provide revised versions.

Westlaw ⌧ subscription database
Westlaw contains the full text of all Public General Acts of the Scottish Parliament in revised **7–38** form. For general information on how to efficiently search for Acts in this database, see paras 6–33—6–48. However, when searching for Acts of the Holyrood Parliament the following steps are recommended:

 ↳ From the welcome page, click the legislation link from the navigation bar at the top of the screen;
 ↳ Scroll down to the bottom of the screen and select either of the following browse options, jurisdiction or Scottish Parliament;
 ↳ Click on the preferred option to open a new search page. Then select the basic search option or click through to the advanced search option which will be restricted to legislation made at Holyrood.

NB An alternative method is to follow the instructions above, but, instead of using the search box, scroll down to the bottom of the screen to the browse options where Acts of the Scottish Parliament can be located by year or alphabetically by short title.

LexisNexis ⌧ subscription database
LexisNexis contains the full text of all Public General Acts of the Scottish Parliament in revised **7–39** form. To search for an Act:

 ↳ Select the legislation tab from the homepage. This opens up the legislation search form;

∾ Select Scottish Parliament Acts from the Select Sources drop-down list;
∾ Go to the type field and select Statute from the drop-down list;
∾ If the name of the Act is unknown, enter words or phrases in the enter search terms box.

Boolean connectors can be used to show the relation of the terms selected. See paras 2–58—2–59. If the title or part of the title is known, enter search terms in the legislation title field, giving the year if known. If only part of the title is entered, use Boolean connectors to link the search terms. If a particular section is sought, enter the number in the provision field. Retrieve the results by clicking on search.

Sources of Original Versions of Acts

BAILLI ⚘ free
http://www.bailii.org/scot/legis/num_act/ [accessed June 6, 2014]

7–40 The official full text original version of Acts of the Scottish Parliament can also be accessed on BAILLI by year or alphabetically by title. The Acts are contained in the Scottish Legislation section of the site and are reproduced courtesy of *legislation.gov.uk*. The search function allows a search to be undertaken by keyword or using the Boolean technique.

Justis UK Statutes ⚘ subscription and CD Rom
7–41 This database contains the full text of all Acts the Scottish Parliament in their original form, with links to amending legislation.

SEARCH STRATEGIES FOR FINDING ACTS OF THE SCOTTISH PARLIAMENT

This section considers how to locate Acts of the Holyrood Parliament from different starting **7–42** points, e.g. an area of law new to the researcher may be the subject of scrutiny or knowledge of the sought legislation's title may be incomplete. There are numerous ways of finding such legal information and this section contains lists of various alternative sources along with comments as to their relative strengths and weaknesses. The most comprehensive sources are listed first. Sources which provide access to revised versions of legislation are given prominence because sources of original versions of Acts will require additional research to locate any amendments or repeals.

> **NB** Although Private Bills are subject to different procedures from Public Bills, on enactment all Bills become asps and Private asps are numbered in the same single series as Public asps and can therefore be searched for in the same way.

Finding whether courts have considered the legislation is discussed in paras 4–82—4–91. This **7–43** covers the situation where you know of a specific legislative provision and you want to find out if any cases have discussed it or interpreted it in a particular way. Finding whether any articles have been written about legislation involves the same techniques as for UK Parliament legislation and is discussed in paras 6–105—6–110.

The following search strategies are considered in this chapter: **7–44**

> ➢ Finding statutes by subject. See paras 7–45—7–50;
> ➢ The current status of a statute. It is vital to know whether a statute has been brought into force or whether it has been amended or repealed. See paras 7–51—7–65.

Finding Acts of the Holyrood by subject

Major textbooks, reference works and encyclopaedias
Recommended textbooks or reference works, such as *The Stair Memorial Encyclopaedia*, (see **7–45** para.8–04), are ideal starting points for research by subject. Unlike electronic databases, they do not just identify a piece of legislation, they place it in context. Thus such resources explain how a legislative provision operates in a specific area of law, how it interacts, or otherwise, with other similar provisions (legislation in pari materia), how it has been interpreted by a court and offer further comment on it other relevant matters. Encyclopaedias or reference works can thus provide the information necessary to refine an electronic search which will make searching full text databases more manageable. As detailed throughout Ch.2, if a subject search is conducted on a database with broad subject terms hundreds or even thousands of not always relevant hits will be retrieved. Searching with more relevant terms will produce fewer but more relevant hits.

Westlaw ⌁ subscription database and LexisNexis ⌁ subscription database
Both these databases contain the revised form of Acts made at Holyrood and can be searched **7–46** using sophisticated search techniques including searching for keywords in the title or free text searching of the content of legislation.

Legislation.gov.uk 🖰 free

7–47 This official source provides the full text of all Holyrood Acts in their original and revised form. Acts can be searched for by title, year or asp number via the general search feature. Advanced search allows for a more detailed search to be undertaken and thus, for a subject search, is to be recommended.

BAILII 🖰 free

7–48 The BAILII website contains the full text of all Holyrood Acts in their original form. The legislation search allows Acts of the Scottish Parliament from 1999 onwards to be searched as detailed in para.7–40 above.

Justis UK Statutes 🖰 subscription

7–49 This database contains the full text of all Acts of the Scottish Parliament in their original form with links to amending legislation.

Current Law Yearbooks and Monthly Digests 📖

7–50 Check the subject headings in the consolidated indexes in the master volumes of the Current Law Yearbooks and then the more recent Yearbooks and Monthly Digests.

Current status of an Act of the Scottish (Holyrood) Parliament—is it in force yet?

The Act itself

7–51 As with Acts made at Westminster, the date a Holyrood Act comes into force may be the date of Royal Assent or it may be detailed in the commencement section at the end of the Act (see para.5–77). Thus the commencement section of the Act must always be consulted. If the Act is silent it comes into force on the date of Royal Assent. If the Act stipulates a specific date or time period then that is the relevant date. Alternatively, the Act (or part of it) may come into force at a time to be set by the Scottish Ministers. If this is the case, a further search must be undertaken to find out if a commencement order has or orders have been issued to determine which part(s) of the Act have been brought into force.

Westlaw 🖰 subscription database

7–52 The subject searching technique is the same as for Acts made at Westminster.

LexisNexis 🖰 subscription database

7–53 The subject searching technique is the same as for Acts made at Westminster.

Is It in Force? 📖

7–54 This twice-yearly publication includes Acts of the Scottish Parliament and covers the previous 25 years. The current edition is "Is It in Force? Spring 2014" The years are presented in chronological order and within each year the statutes are listed alphabetically (they are not separated out by jurisdiction). Opposite the short title are details of the relevant commencement provisions. The volume also contains Statutes Not Yet in Force which lists provisions of Acts for which no commencement dates have yet been appointed.

> **NB** This publication does not include full information on amendments and repeals. As it is a twice-yearly publication it is always out of date. If available, the researcher should consult the electronic version detailed in para.7–55.

Using the paper version of *Is It in Force?*

- ✤ Find out if The Criminal Cases (Punishment and Review) (Scotland) Act 2012 asp 7 has **7–55** been brought fully into force.
- ✤ Consult the latest edition of *Is It in Force?* Turn to the entries for 2012. The statutes are listed in alphabetical order, so check under the letter C. Once the title of the Act has been located view the sections or Parts in force.
- ✤ Part 3 of this Act came into force on the day of Royal Assent. The remainder of the Act was brought into force by s.3 of The Criminal Cases (Punishment and Review) (Scotland) Act 2012 (Commencement, Transitional and Savings) Order 2012 No 249 on September 24, 2012.

Is It in Force? ᪣ subscription
The online version of *Is It In Force?* is available from LexisNexis and is updated daily with links **7–56** provided to the relevant commencement orders.

Lawtel ᪣ subscription legal current awareness digest service
Lawtel is updated daily. **7–57**

Current Law Legislation Citators and Current Law Statutes 📖
The searching technique is the same as for Acts of the Westminster Parliament. See Ch.6 in **7–58** general.

Journals 📖
Many journals, e.g. S.L.T., contain information about legislation which is coming into force. **7–59**

The Daily List ᪣ free
The Daily List and its weekly and monthly consolidated forms contain details of Commence- **7–60** ment Orders.

Current status of an Act of the Scottish Parliament—finding amendments and repeals

Westlaw ᪣ subscription database
Westlaw provides the revised form of legislation which incorporates amendments and repeals. **7–61**

LexisNexis ᪣ subscription database
LexisNexis provides the revised form of legislation which incorporates amendments and repeals. **7–62** An ellipsis, denoted thus (...), indicates that text has been repealed. Square brackets denote text that has been inserted or substituted. Italicised text means that the content is prospectively repealed or substituted. The notes section at the end of each document indicates the changes that have been made to the text.

Current Law Legislation Citators 📖
This is the best paper source for locating changes to legislation. The principles of and techniques **7–63** for searching these Citators are detailed initially in paras 6–88—6–89. However, Acts of the Scottish Parliament are listed separately in the legislation Citators at the beginning of each volume.

Lawtel ᪣ subscription legal current awareness digest service
Lawtel is updated daily. **7–64**

Chronological Table of the Statutes 📖

7–65 This resource is published annually by TSO. See para.6–92.

Finding whether the courts have considered an Act of the Scottish Parliament

7–66 If the specific Act sought is known and the purpose of a search is to find out if any cases have discussed it or interpreted it in a particular way (see paras 4–82—4–91).

Finding whether any articles have been written about an Act of the Scottish Parliament

7–67 The same techniques used to locate articles about Westminster legislation are employed. See paras 6–105—6–110.

Finding whether any SIs have been made under an Act of the Scottish Parliament

7–68 The same techniques used to locate SI made at Westminster are employed. See paras 6–187—6–193.

SCOTTISH STATUTORY INSTRUMENTS

7–69 This section relates to Scottish SIs made at Holyrood. Statutory instruments made for Scotland by the UK Parliament at Westminster are discussed in Ch.6.

7–70 Scottish SIs, like Acts of the Scottish Parliament, are published both electronically and in paper and in many different databases and series. All Scottish SIs which are of general application will be published, but local SIs may not be. Information about the layout and structure of a Scottish SI is detailed in para.5–55. Since July 2005 Scottish SI laid before Holyrood have been accompanied by Explanatory Notes which provide an overview of the provision and brief commentary on each part and section, etc. The official version of SIs are published separately from their parent Act

7–71 The majority of databases used by legal researchers will contain both Acts and SIs. As with Acts, different databases and series produce different versions of SIs and it is vital that the up-to-date revised version of an SI, which includes any amendments which have been made to it, is relied upon rather than the original (historic) version.

Sources of Scottish SIs

Official versions of Scottish SI
Individual Scottish SI 📖

7–72 General Scottish SIs are published individually and can be purchased from TSO.

Annual volumes of Scottish SIs 📖
7–73 Annual volumes of Scottish SIs are published by TSO. They contain:

> ➢ A copy of all general Scottish SIs for the period arranged in number order;
> ➢ A classified list of local instruments;
> ➢ Tables showing the effect on enactments and previous statutory rules or SI (whether Scottish or not) of the Scottish SI included in the edition;
> ➢ An annual numerical and issue list of Scottish SIs;

> ➤ An index which is arranged by subject heading and then alphabetically within the subject heading.

Legislation.gov.uk ⏁ free

This site contains the full text of all published Scottish SIs. The aim is to publish Scottish SIs on **7–74** the site simultaneously or at least within 24 hours of their publication in printed form. Draft Scottish SIs can be accessed here, *http://www.legislation.gov.uk/sdsi* [accessed June 6, 2014]. These will remain on this site until they are superseded by a Scottish SI or until they are withdrawn. A search can be undertaken within a given year alphabetically or by subject heading, e.g. all SIs published are available in original form only.

Sources of revised versions of Scottish SI

Westlaw ⏁ subscription database

Westlaw contains all published Scottish SIs in revised form. Draft SIs are not included. **7–75**

LexisNexis ⏁ subscription database

The full text revised form of all published Scottish SIs are available. **7–76**

Sources of Original Versions of Scottish SI

BAILII ⏁ free

See para.7–48. **7–77**

Justis ⏁ subscription

See para.7–49. **7–78**

Specialist encyclopaedias and collections of legislation 📖

Specialist loose-leaf encyclopaedias and collections of legislation may contain copies of selected **7–79** Scottish SIs relevant to their subject area.

Current Law Yearbooks and Monthly Digests 📖

Scottish SIs are digested in the Current Law Yearbooks and Monthly Digests. The full text of **7–80** Commencement Orders is printed in the Yearbooks and in the loose-leaf service file (for the current year). See paras 8–23—8–33.

Aids to tracing Scottish SIs

Westlaw ⏁ subscription database

Westlaw holds all published Scottish SIs made by the Holyrood Parliament in revised form. **7–81** Draft SIs are not included. For information on searching for Scottish SI see Ch.6, "Search Strategies for Locating UK (Westminster) Parliament Legislation", as the majority of search techniques recommended there apply to locating Scottish provisions. However, it is possible to restrict your searching to Scottish Parliament materials. From the welcome page, click the legislation link from the navigation bar at the top of the screen. Scroll down to the bottom of the screen and one of the browse options is to browse by jurisdiction: Scottish Parliament. Click on this option to open a new search page. Here a basic search or an advanced search can be carried out.

LexisNexis ⏁ subscription database

LexisNexis contains all published Scottish SIs made by the Scottish Parliament in revised form. **7–82** Choose the legislation tab from the homepage. This opens up the legislation search form. Select Scottish Parliament SIs from the Select Sources drop-down list. Go to the type field and select

Statutory Instrument from the drop-down list. If the name of the instrument is unknown enter words or phrases in the enter search terms box. Boolean connectors can be used to show the relation of the terms (see para.2–58). If the instrument number is known, enter the year in the legislation title field and the series number in the series number field. If the title or part of the title is known, enter search terms in the legislation title field, giving the year if known. If only part of the title is entered, use Boolean connectors to link the search terms (see paras 2–58—2–59). Retrieve the results by clicking on search.

Lawtel ⌐ subscription legal current awareness digest service

7–83 Lawtel is updated daily. To search generally see para.6–160. To search for Scottish SI click on SI on the homepage. Click on the focused search tab, enter the search terms including "Scotland" in the title field, enter an "s" in the application field and then click on search. Note: if "s" only is put in the application field this will not restrict the search to Holyrood SIs, it will include all SI instruments which apply in Scotland. The next step is to click on the link in the search results to the details of the instrument. The details shown will include the instrument's number, the enabling Act, the date the instrument came into force, a list of effects it has had on other legislation and a link to the full original text of the instrument and the Explanatory Note on the *legislation.gov.uk* website.

Current Law Legislation Citators ⌐

7–84 This is the best paper source for locating Scottish SIs. The methodology for searching these volumes is outlined at various points in Ch.6. The only additional issue is to remember that Scottish SIs issued by the Holyrood Parliament are listed separately in the legislation citators at the beginning of each volume.

JustCite ⌐ subscription legal citator

7–85 JustCite includes all SIs made at Holyrood since the inception of the Parliament in 1999. Scottish legislation is not listed separately.

List of Statutory Publications ⌐

7–86 The List of Statutory Publications for all recent UK, Scottish, Welsh and Northern Ireland legislation is published monthly in the London Gazette. See *http://www.london-gazette.co.uk/issues/60448/supplements/2/page.pdf* [accessed June 6, 2014].

Daily List ⌐ and ⌐ free

7–87 The Daily List lists Scottish SIs published by TSO.

Journals ⌐ and ⌐

7–88 Information about very recent Scottish SIs will also be available in journals such as S.L.T.

Aids that contain the original versions of SIs

Leglislation.gov.uk ⌐ free

7–89 Statutory instruments on this site are held in original form, i.e. "as made" only.

BAILII ⌐ free

7–90 See para.7–40.

Justis UK SI ⌐ subscription and CD Rom database

7–91 See para.7–41.

Finding a Scottish SI when only the title is known (i.e. the year and number are not known)

Westlaw ⌐⌐ subscription database
Westlaw allows SIs to be searched for in the legislation title field. See paras 2–58—2–59 for **7–92**
guidance when using Westlaw's terms and connectors. Westlaw also allows SIs to be browsed
for by title. On the legislation search page, scroll down to the bottom of the screen and select
browse by Jurisdiction: Scottish Parliament. Click there to open a new search page. Then, scroll
down to the bottom of the screen to the browse options one of which allows Scottish SI to be
browsed for alphabetically by title.

LexisNexis ⌐⌐ subscription database
LexisNexis's Scottish Parliament SI database allows a search to be undertaken using the leg- **7–93**
islation title field. See paras 2–58—2–59 for guidance when using this database's terms and
connectors.

Lawtel ⌐⌐ subscription legal current awareness digest service
Lawtel offers a search by title using the focused search function (see para.7–108). **7–94**

Current Law Yearbooks and Monthly Digests ▭
There are alphabetical lists of SI in the Current Law Yearbooks and in the Monthly Digests. **7–95**
These lists provide the year and number of each SI but only contain a summary of each SI. In
order to trace the full text consult one of the sources detailed in the section starting at para.7–114.

Current Law SI Citator ▭
The Current Law SI Citators have an alphabetical list at the start of each volume which includes **7–96**
Scottish SI. The citators enable the researcher to locate the year and number of the desired
instrument(s) and to check if an instrument has been amended or repealed. In order to trace the
full text consult one of the sources detailed in the section starting at para.7–114.

The Laws of Scotland: Stair Memorial Encyclopaedia ▭
Check the Consolidated Table of Statutes or, if the subject area is known, go to the individual **7–97**
title. Each title has a list of legislation (see para.8–04).

The Laws of Scotland Online (*Stair Memorial Encyclopaedia*) ⌐⌐
Enter the title of the Scottish SI as the search term in the commentary search form (see para.8– **7–98**
11).

Subject specialist encyclopaedias ▭
Specialist loose-leaf encyclopaedias (see para.8–17) and collections of legislation can be searched **7–99**
by Tables of SI or by the subject index. Some works will include the full text of the particular
instrument.

Sources that contain the original versions of Scottish SIs

Legislation.gov.uk
At the time of writing, there are no proposals to include revised versions of Scottish SIs in this **7–100**
database.

BAILII ⌐⌐ free
See para.7–40. **7–101**

Justis SI [☞] subscription database.

7–102 Justis holds the official versions of Scottish SI as they appear on the *legislation.gov.uk* website.

Finding Scottish SI by subject

The Laws of Scotland: Stair Memorial Encyclopaedia 📖

7–103 Check the Consolidated Index. This lists detailed subject headings and enable the researcher to locate the relevant volume or reissued title. The information found can be updated by checking the Annual Cumulative Supplement and the Service Binder. See para.8–04.

The Laws of Scotland Online (Stair Memorial Encyclopaedia) [☞]

7–104 Enter details of the subject area as the search term in the commentary search form (see para.8–11).

Subject Specialist Encyclopaedias and Collections of Legislation 📖

7–105 Specialist loose-leaf encyclopaedias and collections of legislation can be searched by Tables of SI or by the subject index. The amount of information located will depend on whether the encyclopaedia includes the full text of the particular SI.

Westlaw [☞] subscription database

7–106 The legislation search in Westlaw allows a search to be undertaken by using the free text search function. See paras 2–58—2–59 for guidance on using Westlaw's terms and connectors. Scottish SI can also be browsed by title.

LexisNexis [☞] subscription database

7–107 For guidance on using this database's terms and connectors, see paras 2–58—2–59.

Lawtel [☞] subscription legal current awareness digest service

7–108 On the homepage click on SI. Enter the search terms in the box and click search. Alternatively use the focused search to search by title. In either case, click on the link in the search results to view details of the SI.

Scottish SIs 📖

7–109 The index to these annual bound volumes is arranged by subject (see para.7–96).

Current Law Yearbooks and Monthly Digests 📖

7–110 Check the Yearbooks under the appropriate subject heading. This will provide a reference to a paragraph number (see para.8–32). The Current Law Yearbooks and Monthly Digests will only contain a summary of the SI. In order to trace the full text consult one of the sources detailed in paras 7–81—7–88.

Current status of a Scottish SI—finding amendments and repeals

Westlaw [☞] subscription database

7–111 Westlaw provides the revised form of Scottish SIs which incorporates amendments and repeals. It shows when the current version of the instrument was brought into force and provides links to the amending legislation.

LexisNexis [☞] subscription database

7–112 LexisNexis provides the revised form of SI which incorporates amendments and repeals. An ellipsis, (...), indicates that text has been repealed. Square brackets denote text that has been inserted or substituted. Italicised text means that the content is prospectively repealed or substituted. The notes section at the end of each document indicates the changes that have been made to the text.

Lawtel ⌁ subscription legal current awareness digest service
On the homepage click on SI then enter the search terms in the box and click search. Alter- **7–113**
natively use the focused search to search by title. In either case, click on the link in the search
results to access details of the Scottish SI. The entry for the instrument contains information
about amendments and repeals.

Current Law SI Citator 📖
This forms part of the Current Law Legislation Citator volumes and is the best paper source for **7–114**
locating changes to legislation. The methodology for searching these citators is outlined in paras
6–57—6–66. The only additional issue is to remember that Scottish SIs are listed separately at
the front of each volume.

Scottish SIs ⌁
The annual volumes contain tables showing the effect on enactments and previous statutory **7–115**
rules or SIs of the Scottish SI included in the edition. However, one of the above sources would
then need to be consulted to bring a search up-to-date.

Finding Scottish SIs made under an enabling Act

The sources and search techniques are the same as for UK SIs made at Westminster (see paras **7–116**
6–93—6–102).

Finding whether the courts have considered a Scottish SI

The principles are the same as for Westminster legislation (see paras 4–82—4–91). **7–117**

Finding whether any journal articles have been written about a Scottish SI

The principles are the same as for Westminster legislation (see paras 6–105—6–110). **7–118**

ACTS OF SEDERUNT AND ACTS OF ADJOURNAL

Two types of peculiarly Scottish SIs are Acts of Sederunt and Acts of Adjournal. They are pieces **7–119**
of legislation enacted by the Court of Session and the High Court of Justiciary respectively. Acts
of Sederunt are rules which govern procedure in the civil courts while Acts of Adjournal concern
procedure in Scotland's criminal courts. Prior to the inception of the Holyrood Parliament in
1999, they were enacted as SIs by the Westminster Parliament. Since devolution they have been
created as Scottish SIs.

Given that these provisions are enacted as a species of SI, the relevant sources are the same as **7–120**
for UK SI prior to 1999 and Scottish SI from 1999 onwards. Consult Chs 6 and 7 to locate
same. In addition, an annotated version of Acts of Sederunt which are currently in force is
contained in Vol.2 of the *Parliament House Book* and an annotated version of Acts of Adjournal
currently in force is contained in Renton and Brown's *Criminal Procedure Legislation*. Acts of
Sederunt and Acts of Adjournal also appear in the S.L.T. when they are enacted.

Acts of Sederunt and Acts of Adjournal made after May 2002 can be accessed on the Scottish **7–121**
Courts website. They were previously published in Current Law Statutes Annotated, but this

ceased in1991. The cumulative indexes in Current Law Yearbooks and Monthly Digests can be searched under "Act of Sederunt" and "Act of Adjournal" where a summary of each instrument is given.

COLLECTIONS OF LEGISLATION

Parliament House Book

7–122 The *Parliament House Book*, published by Sweet and Maxwell, contains revised UK and Scottish legislation covering selected areas of private law and court procedure.

Specialised collections of legislation

7–123 An increasing number of subject-specific collections of legislation which include both UK and Scottish Parliament legislation are now being produced commercially. One such compendium, Family Law Statutes and Orders 2013/2014, is published by W. Green.

Chapter 8
Further Resources of Relevance to the Scots Lawyer

Significant abbreviations used in this chapter

- EU—European Union
- ISBN—International Standard Book Number
- LJI—Legal Journals Index (Westlaw)
- S.L.T.—Scots Law Times
- SLC—Scottish Law Commission
- SI—Statutory Instrument
- TSO—The Stationery Office

This chapter discusses further avenues of enquiry when seeking both primary and secondary **8–01** sources of Scots law. Many of the resources referred to apply in a UK-wide context. Where this is so, emphasis has been placed on the Scottish dimension.

INSTITUTIONAL WRITERS

Institutional writings comprise a "closed class of works" which are regarded as the third formal **8–02** source of Scots law, after legislation and case law. The list of Institutional Writers is described as "closed" in that no new works, however worthy, may be added to it. As detailed below, these works were authored by certain distinguished jurists between the 17th and 19th centuries and, despite the passage of time, are taken to represent the law of Scotland if there is no statute or case law "in point" in an area of law where society's norms have undergone little fundamental change in the intervening years. While it is no longer true to say that the Scots lawyer frequently turns to the works of the Institutional Writers in day to day practice, the influence of these works is still very much with us. In the past they had considerable influence on the development of case law and the doctrine of judicial precedent means that this will endure long into the future.

Whilst there is no unanimity as to the complete list of writers and works, the most widely **8–03** accepted Institutional writers and works are:

- ➢ Civil law:
  - Sir Thomas Craig, *Jus Feudale*, 1603;
  - Andrew McDouall, Lord Bankton, *An Institute of the Laws of Scotland*, 1751;
  - James Dalrymple (Viscount Stair), *The Institutions of the Law of Scotland*, 1681;
  - John Erskine, *An Institute of the Law of Scotland*, 1773;

- George Joseph Bell, *Commentaries on the Law of Scotland*, 1804 and *Principles of the Law of Scotland*, 1829;

➢ Criminal law:

- Sir George Mackenzie, *The Laws and Customs of Scotland in Matters Criminal*, 1678;
- David Hume, *Commentaries on the Law of Scotland Respecting Crimes*, 1797;
- Archibald Alison, *Principles of the Criminal Law of Scotland*, 1832 and *Practice of the Criminal Law of Scotland*, 1833.

LEGAL ENCYCLOPAEDIAS

The Laws of Scotland: Stair Memorial Encyclopaedia

8–04   Although there are several encyclopaedias on specific subject areas, *The Laws of Scotland: Stair Memorial Encyclopaedia* (usually referred to as the *Stair Memorial Encyclopaedia*) is the only modern encyclopaedia which provides a comprehensive narrative statement of the law of Scotland. It is an important source of information which includes more than 130 titles by over 300 authors. This is a modern work and has no connection with Viscount Stair other than being named in his memory.

8–05   The commentary is arranged alphabetically in broad areas of the law and consists of substantial articles (referred to as "titles") on each area. The style of the titles varies as they are written by many different contributors. Each contributor has specialist knowledge of the area of law discussed. Within each area of law, the titles are divided into numbered paragraphs. These are the basis of the referencing system for the encyclopaedia. It is important to remember that references are to the paragraph number not the page number, e.g. the EU dimension to customs and excise law is discussed in Vol.7, paras 1003–1030. Each title has an index and a consolidated index for the entire encyclopaedia is also provided.

8–06   The encyclopaedia is available in both paper form and online. The paper version of the encyclopaedia originally consisted of 25 paper volumes which were published between 1986 and 1996. Each volume contains several titles on different topics. Since 1999, titles from the original volumes have been updated and issued as separate booklets. These are stored in binders as opposed to bound volumes. The system of reissuing may cause confusion as the re-issued titles supersede the title in the original bound volume but the bound volume still remains on the library shelf until all titles within it are re-issued. This means that two versions of the same title may be available so it is vital to ensure that the most up-to-date version is consulted. The material in the reissued booklets is referred to within Stair by the abbreviated form of its title and the paragraph number, e.g. the nature of offences against the state is discussed in Crim 531. Each volume and reissued booklet consists of the following:

➢ List of Abbreviations;
➢ Table of Statutes;
➢ Table of Orders, Rules and Regulations;
➢ Table of Other Enactments;
➢ Table of Cases;
➢ Title(s). In the bound volumes the titles are in alphabetical order of the subject area with each title having its own table of contents;

➢ Index. At the back of each volume and reissued booklet there is an index. There is one index for each subject title covered.

The encyclopaedia is kept up to date by an annual Cumulative Supplement published in March. **8–07** This brings all the volumes up to date to December 31 of the previous year. The Cumulative Supplement is itself updated every four months and is published in loose-leaf form in a Service Binder. Changes are listed by volume number and then by subject within the volume followed by the reissued titles. This does not contain new commentary but notes the effects of new case law or legislation. The Service Binder also contains glossaries of Scottish and EU legal terms.

The Cumulative Supplement contains: **8–08**

➢ Table of Statutes;
➢ Table of Orders, Rules and Regulations;
➢ Table of Cases;
➢ Updates on a volume by volume basis followed by updates on the reissued titles in alphabetical order.

A Consolidated Index is also published on an annual basis. It is organised in alphabetical order of subject. References are to volume (or reissue abbreviation) and paragraph number. Volume numbers/reissue abbreviations are in bold. In addition, there are annual volumes of Consolidated Tables of Cases and Consolidated Tables of Statutes etc. The Table of Cases is listed by first party's name. This is useful for tracing Scottish cases. The Consolidated Tables of Statutes, etc. consist of consolidated tables of: Statutes, Orders, Rules and Regulations, EU legislation, Treaties and Conventions and other enactments.

The updating of the encyclopaedia has meant that the paper version is rather cumbersome in **8–09** comparison to its online form (see para.8–04).

Using the Stair Memorial Encyclopaedia
To search by subject: **8–10**

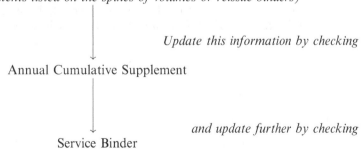

Consolidated Index

or

Reissued title or relevant volume (if not reissued)
(identified from contents listed on the spines of volumes or reissue binders)

Update this information by checking

Annual Cumulative Supplement

and update further by checking

Service Binder

➢ Remember that the reissued titles supersede the titles in the volumes and that references are always to paragraph number and not page number.

To access information from a case name:

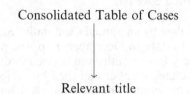

Consolidated Table of Cases

Relevant title

➤ Remember to check in the Service Binder as it may include more recent cases

To access information by title of statute:

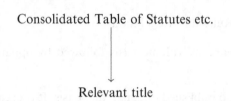

Consolidated Table of Statutes etc.

Relevant title

➤ Remember to check in the Service Binder as it may include more recent legislation.

The Laws of Scotland Online (*Stair Memorial Encyclopaedia*) ⌧ subscription

8–11 The online version is available from LexisNexis. The original volumes and reissued titles can be accessed with ease, together with the text of the most recent annual cumulative supplement which is updated bi-monthly. Updating material and original text can be viewed on screen together, the updating material appearing at the bottom of the screen. The Stair Memorial can be searched by free text or a search can be limited to specific titles using the browse function which opens up an alphabetical list of all titles.

8–12 Further hypertext links that enable the user to link between narrative, cases and legislation.

Citation of the Laws of Scotland: Stair Memorial Encyclopaedia

8–13 The style of reference to the *Stair Memorial Encyclopaedia* depends on whether the material is from one of the original volumes or a reissue:

➤ Material in a title in one of the original volumes should be styled thus: *The Laws of Scotland: Stair Memorial Encyclopaedia*, Vol.6, paras 896–922;
➤ Material in a title that has been reissued should be styled thus: *The Laws of Scotland: Stair Memorial Encyclopaedia* Criminal Procedure Re-issue, para.183.

NB There is no need to cite the date of publication given that this resource is updated on an ongoing basis.

Halsbury's Laws of England

8–14 *Halsbury's Laws of England* is the equivalent of the *Stair Memorial Encyclopaedia* in that it provides a comprehensive guide to the law of England (see Ch.9).

The Encyclopaedia of the Laws of Scotland (originally known as Green's Encyclopaedia of the Laws of Scotland)

There were three editions of *The Encyclopaedia of the Laws of Scotland.* The first edition (1896– **8–15** 1904) was published 10 years before *Halsbury's Laws of England.* This encyclopaedia drew its inspiration from *Bell's Dictionary and Digest.* The first edition was edited by J. Chisholm. According to the preface of a later edition the aim of the work was to "help the practitioner, and especially the country practitioner who has not at his hand an extensive law library, to see exactly how the law stands on any particular subject". It states that the second edition greatly augmented and enlarged the first edition, "'Noting up' is a process which is beyond all but the laborious and meticulous few. The ordinary practising lawyer has neither the heart nor the leisure for such as task".

The second edition (1909–14), also edited by J. Chisholm, ran to 12 volumes and contained **8–16** short sections on topics which ran in alphabetical order. An example of the different topics is: accounts; accretion; accumulation; accumulation of prisoners; accusation, false; acids, throwing; acknowledgement; *a coelo usque ad centrum,* etc. The third edition (1926–35) was edited by Viscount Dunedin and ran to 15 volumes. This edition gathered topics together to a greater extent, e.g. "acids, throwing" now appeared under "crime". Following its publication there were a number of supplementary volumes issued. The final updating was an appendix to the supplement published in 1949 and it brought the law up to June 30, 1952.

Loose-leaf encyclopaedias

There are now an increasing number of specialist encyclopaedias covering a variety of subjects. **8–17** They tend to contain a mixture of legislation and narrative and can be extremely useful sources of information. They also tend to be produced as loose-leaf publications which are updated regularly. They, therefore, have an advantage over text books which do not elect to provide updates via a dedicated website. Loose-leaf publications are updated by the removal of out-of-date pages and the insertion of new pages. It is not uncommon to find that pages have been misfiled. Great care should therefore be taken when consulting such publications to ensure that you are looking at the most current edition issued. To ensure the most recent update is consulted check the date given at the beginning of the work. Examples of specialist encyclopaedias include: *Armour on Valuation for Rating*; Butterworth's *Scottish Family Law Service*; *Employment Tribunal Practice in Scotland*; *Encyclopaedia of Health and Safety at Work*; Garner's *Environmental Law*; Harvey on *Industrial Relations and Employment*; McEwan and Paton on *Damages for Personal Injuries in Scotland*; Renton and Brown's *Criminal Procedure*; *Scottish Planning Encyclopedia*; and *Sentencing Practice.*

REFERENCE WORKS

Reference works can provide a useful starting point for any research project. As they tend to **8–18** cover a broad subject area and therefore will not contain too much detail on each individual topic, they are, however, ideal initial sources to provide background information and to place a research topic in context. Thus the text (and accompanying footnotes) should provide sufficient material to give any project a firm foundation and provide references to further sources which can then be consulted. As with text books, reference works are generally updated infrequently and tend to run to many editions, therefore it is important to make sure that the most up-to-date edition is consulted. Examples are Gloag and Henderson, *An Introduction to the Laws of Scotland,* 13th edn (Edinburgh: W. Green, 2012) and D.M. Walker, *Principles of Scottish*

Private Law, 4th edn (Oxford: Clarendon Press, 1988). D.M. Walker's *Legal History of Scotland*, published by W. Green, runs to seven volumes and is a detailed narrative account of the history of the Scottish legal system. Walker's earlier work, *The Oxford Companion to Law* (Oxford: Clarendon Press, 1980), is a single volume work which is becoming increasingly dated but is still useful, particularly as a starting point for a literature search.

CURRENT LAW DATA RETRIEVAL SYSTEM

8–19   Current Law has the most comprehensive range of information available in one paper data-retrieval system and is widely available throughout Scotland. It is an important and useful source of information. It covers legal developments since 1948 and is updated monthly. However, Current Law can be confusing to use initially due to its layout and component parts, but it is worth persevering and learning how the various parts are organised as it provides a very efficient way of locating and confirming certain types of legal information. For example Current Law uses a system of references to apply to its various constituent parts. The references appear in numerical form thus "82/4292". The numbers represent the year/paragraph number and not the page number.

8–20   Once a systematic approach to searching Current Law is adopted, information can be retrieved more quickly with this paper source than with many electronic databases and become a invaluable tool to the armoury of the legal researcher.

8–21   Prior to 1991, the Current Law service was provided in two formats: (i) Scottish Current Law and (ii) Current Law. The Scottish Current Law service included the English and Welsh service. The Current Law service excluded all purely Scottish material. From 1991 onwards the service has been called Current Law and now covers the law of England and Wales, Northern Ireland, Scotland and the EU. Matters applicable to the UK generally are included in the English section thus Scots lawyers and researchers must not overlook this section.

8–22   Current Law comprises separate yet linked and, in some cases, inter-dependent resources. These are listed below for convenience and discussed in turn at paras 8–23—8–34:

> ➢   Monthly Digests;
> ➢   Yearbooks;
> ➢   Case Citators;
> ➢   Legislation Citators;
> ➢   Current Law Statutes;
> ➢   Statutes Service Files.

> **NB** The European Current Law Monthly Digest and European Current Law Yearbook are discussed in para.10–48.

CURRENT LAW MONTHLY DIGESTS

8–23   These publications provide a monthly updating service. Each issue is divided into two parts, "Cases, Legislation, Books and Materials" and "Tables".

Cases, Legislation, Books and Materials

The subject headings covered in Current Law are listed at the beginning of each Monthly **8–24** Digest. Not every subject heading will appear in every issue. The subject areas covered in the issue are printed in bold type:

- ➤ Table of Abbreviations. This is a good place to look for new abbreviations. The Table lists abbreviations included in that issue of the Monthly Digest;
- ➤ Current Law Notes. These are brief notes arranged under subject headings. They are designed to provide an overview of recent developments in different fields of law. There is a separate section of Current Law Notes (Scotland);
- ➤ Digest. The material is arranged alphabetically by subject. The material consists of summaries of developments in the law such as cases, legislation, government department circulars, books and articles. The subject headings are divided into three sections: (i) UK, England and Wales and the EU; (ii) Northern Ireland; and (iii) Scotland.

Tables

A series of tables include the following: **8–25**

- ➤ Alphabetical table of SIs. This is a cumulative alphabetical list of SI digested in the current year;
- ➤ Alphabetical table of Scottish SIs. This is a cumulative alphabetical list of Scottish SIs digested in the current year;
- ➤ Cumulative index. This is arranged alphabetically within subject headings. Scottish entries are followed by an "S". The subject headings used here are greater in number and more specific than the broad subject headings in the Cases, Legislation, Books and Materials section;
- ➤ Dates of commencement. This gives dates of commencement and details of the instrument that brought the statute into force;
- ➤ EU legislation implemented by SIs. EU legislation implemented by SIs issued in the current year is listed in chronological order;
- ➤ EU legislation implemented by Scottish SIs. EU implemented by Scottish SIs issued in the current year is listed in chronological order;
- ➤ EU law. This details subject areas covering cases heard in the Court of Justice of the EU and the General Court and EU legislation which is digested in that month's digest;
- ➤ Legal publications. This includes books published that month which are arranged in alphabetical order of author. References to books can also be found under relevant subject headings;
- ➤ Progress of Bills covers Bills in the current parliamentary session at Westminster and is accurate on the date given at the top of the page. Government Bills are given in bold. The word "Commons" or "Lords" appears after the Bill's name to show where the Bill originated;
- ➤ Quantum of damages provides cumulative information on damages awarded in personal injuries cases reported in the current year. Information is given in tabular form under five headings: injury, age, case, award and reference. Scottish cases are in a separate Table, following the Table relating to English cases;
- ➤ Royal Assent. There are separate tables for England, Scotland, Wales and Northern Ireland;
- ➤ Progress of Scottish Bills. This covers Bills in the current Parliamentary session at Holyrood and is accurate on the date given at the top of the page. Government Bills are given in bold;

> ➤ Table of transcripts subsequently reported. This is a cumulative list of cases recently digested in Current Law as transcripts and subsequently reported elsewhere;
> ➤ Table of cases. This listing is cumulative and given in alphabetical order. It covers cases which have been digested or judicially considered in the current year. Cases which have been digested are in capital letters. Cases which have been judicially considered or commented on are in sentence case;
> ➤ Words and phrases judicially considered. This is a cumulative guide to words and phrases which have been judicially considered throughout the year.

8–26 Below is an extract (with annotations) from Monthly Digest Sept 1998 P. 198–199, Legal Aid:

---

[1]
LEGAL AID
693. Criminal legal aid—solicitors—employment [2]
SCOTTISH LEGAL AID BOARD (EMPLOYMENT OF SOLICITORS TO PROVIDE CRIMINAL LEGAL ASSISTANCE) REGULATIONS 1998, SI 1998 1938 (S.101); **[3]**
[4]   **[5]**
made under the Legal Aid (Scotland) Act 1986 s.28A, s.37. In force: October 1, 1998; £1.10. These Regulations provide for solicitors to be employed by the Scottish Legal Aid Board to give criminal legal assistance and to be used in the Sheriff Court district of Edinburgh. **[6]**

694. Expenses—modification—personal liability of legal aided person—competency of appeal [7]
[Legal Aid (Scotland) Act 1986 (c.47) s.18 (2).] **[8]**
In an action between two legally aided parties G was found liable in expenses.
The sheriff also refused G's motion under the Legal Aid (Scotland) Act 1986 s.18 (2) to modify his personal liability for expenses. G appealed seeking an order that the matter of modification be remitted to the sheriff for reconsideration. **[9]**
Held, refusing the appeal, that (1) where a sheriff might have erred in law it was incompetent for a sheriff principal to remit the case to the sheriff, and (2) it was not competent for an appellate court to review a decision on the modification of expenses, *Todd v. Todd* 1966 S.L.T. 50, [1966] C.L.Y. 13387 followed. **[10]**
Observed that *Todd v Todd* was not consistent with sound policy or the terms of the statute and ought to be reviewed by a larger court. ORTTEWELL v GILCHRIST 1998 S.C.L.R. 451, CGB Nicholson Q.C., Sheriff Principal, Shy Ct. **[11]**

695. Articles [12]
[13] No entry! No access! No justice!: J.L.S.S. 1998, 43(7) Supp, 2–3. (Proposed changes to civil legal aid scheme and implications of alternative means of funding litigation). **[14]**

Key:

[1]   Subject heading
[2]   Subject matter, catchphrases appear in bold
[3]   Title and citation of a SI
[4]   Enabling legislation
[5]   Date brought into force
[6]   Digest of contents
[7]   Subject matter, catchphrases appear in bold
[8]   Relevant legislation [in square brackets]
[9]   Facts

[10] Ratio decidendi
[11] Case name and citation
[12] Subject matter in bold
[13] Title of article and reference
[14] Summary of contents

Searching the Monthly Digest

The following ought to be borne in mind when searching the Monthly Digest: **8–27**

➢ All indexes are cumulative and they refer to the relevant paragraph in the Monthly Digest in which the item is mentioned. Always check the most recent issue of the Monthly Digest as it will contain information which will allow all the material for the current year to be accessed;
➢ Scottish items are identified by the letter "S" after the Current Law paragraph number;
➢ Matters applicable to the UK generally are included in the English section of Current Law;
➢ Not all digest headings are used in each Monthly Digest. They are not used if there is no current information;
➢ The Monthly Digests use two different referencing systems. This can result in the same reference being given in two different ways in the same volume. The Monthly Digest index refers to previous Monthly Digests as, e.g. Mar 442, the month and paragraph number, whereas other indexes in the Monthly Digest, e.g. alphabetical list of statutory instruments, refer to them as 373 3CL, i.e. paragraph and volume number for the Monthly Digest.

How to find out about recent developments on a particular subject

To find any developments over the last month check the relevant subject heading in the latest **8–28** Monthly Digest. If the subject heading is not listed it means that there have been no developments in the area for that month.

To find out about developments over the current year check the relevant subject heading in the **8–29** cumulative index at the back of the latest Monthly Digest. This will direct the researcher to the month and paragraph number, e.g. Mar 403. If the information there refers to Scotland the references will be followed by the letter "S". Then consult the March monthly Digest at para.403 to locate the information.

How to find a recent Scottish article on a subject

Locate the latest issue of the Monthly Digest. There, check the cumulative index under the **8–30** subject heading. Various sub-headings will exist and will be listed alphabetically. Check under "articles". If any of the references given are followed by an "S" the material concerns Scots law. Turn to the entry referred to locate the article.

CURRENT LAW YEARBOOKS

These are annual volumes which revise and consolidate the Monthly Digests. Items may be **8–31** regrouped and re-edited. They are not usually available until the middle of the following year. The Yearbooks are arranged by subject and contain summaries of all legal developments for that year. Over the years, the format of the Yearbooks has changed, the current format (published in two volumes since 1995) includes:

- ➤ Digest Headings in Use;
- ➤ Table of Cases;
- ➤ Table of Quantum of Damages Cases (with a separate table for Scottish cases);
- ➤ Alphabetical List of SIs for the Year;
- ➤ List of SI arranged alphabetically by subject headings;
- ➤ Numerical Table of SI for the Year;
- ➤ Alphabetical Table of Scottish SI;
- ➤ Numerical Table of Scottish SI;
- ➤ Table of Abbreviations;
- ➤ The Law summarised under Subject Headings, e.g. England, Scotland and the EU;
- ➤ Words and Phrases Table;
- ➤ Law Books published during the Year; and
- ➤ Index.

Searching the Yearbooks

8–32 If searching for information on a particular topic check under the appropriate subject heading. Under each subject heading there is a reference consisting of a year and a paragraph number, e.g. 96/6674S. These numerals refer to, (i) the 1996 Yearbook at, (ii) para.6674. The "S" denotes that it is Scottish material.

8–33 If the approximate date is known, check the appropriate Yearbook. If not, it is not necessary to check every Yearbook.

> **NB** In some earlier volumes the subject index has been consolidated at various times.

*1956 Scottish Current Law Yearbook Master Volume	contains entries for 1948–56
*1961 Scottish Current Law Yearbook Master Volume	contains entries for 1957–61
*1966 Scottish Current Law Yearbook Master Volume	contains entries for 1962–66
*1971 Scottish Current Law Yearbook Master Volume	contains entries for 1967–71
*1986 Scottish Current Law Yearbook	contains entries for 1972–86
*1990 Scottish Current Law Yearbook	contains entries for 1987–90
*From 1991 onwards each Yearbook should be checked	contains entries for each year
Check the latest Monthly Digest.	contains entries for current year

> **NB** The English version has been consolidated at different times.

If the researcher wished to discover if there have been any developments in the law of property in Scotland since 2009 the following steps should be undertaken:

- ➥ **Step 1**: Check the 2010, 2011, 2012 and 2013 Yearbooks in the Scottish section under "Property".
- ➥ **Step 2**: Check the most recent issue of the Monthly Digest, (at the time of writing this would be April 2014), in the index under the subject heading "Property" and look for

references followed by an "S". Once the 2014 Yearbook is issued this would be consulted instead of taking this step.

CURRENT LAW STATUTES SERVICE FILES

The Statutes Service Files allow access to a vast amount of information about recent legislative **8–34** developments. The contents section includes:

> ➢ A Chronological Table of Public General Acts which have received Royal Assent in the current year;
> ➢ A Chronological Table of Private Acts which have received Royal Assent in the current year;
> ➢ A list of recent White Papers and Green Papers;
> ➢ Separate cumulative Progress of Bills Tables for Public General Bills and Private Bills;
> ➢ A cumulative Table of Hansard references for Public Bills and Private Members' Bills currently before Westminster;
> ➢ Legislation not yet in force. This table lists alphabetically statutes which have been published in Current Law and remain on the statute book but which, in whole or in part, are not yet in force and for which no coming-into-force date has yet been fixed;
> ➢ Subject index. This lists all Acts in the current year;
> ➢ Statute citator cumulative monthly updates. Acts of the Scottish Parliament at Holyrood are followed by Acts of the Westminster Parliament. Use this part to update a search in the Statute Citator part of the Legislation Citator volumes;
> ➢ SI citator cumulative monthly updates. SI issued by Holyrood are followed by SI issued by Westminster. Use this part to update a search in the SI citator part of the legislation citator volumes;
> ➢ Alphabetical Table of Public General Acts 1700–present. This Table is cumulative and updated each year;
> ➢ Chronological Table of Statutes (1267–present);
> ➢ Table of Parliamentary Debates (1950–present). This lists Hansard references for substantive debates in both the House of Commons and the House of Lords for Public General Acts 1950–present;
> ➢ Commencement Orders. This section includes the Commencement Diary which notes, alphabetically by statute, the commencement of statutes from January of the current year as initiated by Orders and by statutory provisions. This section also includes a chronological Table of EU legislation implemented by SI. Commencement Orders issued appear in chronological order;
> ➢ Alphabetical Table of SI. This table lists all SI published in the current year;
> ➢ The full text of Public General Acts;
> ➢ The full text of Private Acts;
> ➢ The full text of Acts of the Scottish Parliament.

DICTIONARIES

Language is the everyday tool of the lawyer and the precise meaning of words is very important. **8–35** General English dictionaries are used but there are two types of dictionary which are more important for lawyers. Judicial dictionaries of words and phrases contain definitions given to words by the judiciary and legislation. Thus a judicial dictionary should be consulted in preference to mainstream publications to find out how a certain word has been legally defined. A legal dictionary (often referred to as a glossary) seeks to explain technical legal terms in a way that can be understood by a lay person. It is important to remember that while legal dictionaries provide guidance they are not authoritative.

Judicial dictionaries

Scottish

8–36 ➢ W.J. Stewart, *Scottish Contemporary Judicial Dictionary of Words and Phrases* (Edinburgh: W. Green, 1995). This is a dictionary of words and phrases interpreted by the Scottish courts. It claims to cover every case in which a word has been judicially considered between 1946 and 1993;

➢ A.W. Dalrymple and A.D. Gibb, *Scottish Judicial Dictionary: Dictionary of Words and Phrases* (Edinburgh: W. Green, 1946). This work is a dictionary of words and phrases interpreted by the higher Scottish courts between 1800–1944.

UK

8–37 ➢ D. Greenberg, *Stroud's Judicial Dictionary of Words and Phrases*, 8th edn (London: Sweet and Maxwell, 2013). This work consists of three volumes which are updated by annual cumulative supplements;

➢ *Words and Phrases Legally Defined*, 4th edn (London: Butterworths 2007).

Any search carried out using dictionaries can be updated by checking their date of publication and then consulting the Words and Phrases Tables in the Current Law Yearbooks, Monthly Digests, Halsbury's Laws or The Law Reports Index.

8–38 Westlaw and LexisNexis provide access to legal dictionaries and also enable searching for general words and phrases However, when searching a database results will be retrieved for every instance a word or phrase occurs in a case which will be considerably greater than the number of times when they are actually considered by the courts. Unless the word or phrase sought is specific rather than general such a search is best avoided.

Legal dictionaries and glossaries

Scottish

8–39 The classic dictionary of Scots law is Bell's *Dictionary and Digest of the Law of Scotland*, 7th edn (1890). More modern works include:

➢ S.R. O'Rourke, *Glossary of Legal Terms*, 5th edn (Edinburgh: W. Green, 2009);

➢ S. Styles (ed), *Glossary: Scottish and European Union Legal Terms and Latin Phrases*, 2nd edn (Edinburgh: Law Society of Scotland, LexisNexis UK, 2003);

➢ J. Trayner, *Latin Maxims and Phrases*, 4th edn (Edinburgh: W. Green, 1993);

➢ J. Trayner, *Latin Phrases and Maxims: Collected from the Institutional Writers On Scotch Law* (USA: Ulan Press, 2012).

NB The Judiciary of Scotland website—which can also be accessed from the Scottish Courts website (*http://www.scotcourts.gov.uk*)—contains a useful online glossary of more common Scottish legal terms which can be searched alphabetically, *http://scotland-judiciary.org.uk/29/0/Glossary* [accessed June 6, 2014].

English

Dictionaries of English Law are abundant. The majority provide holistic coverage, but certain **8–40** publications have a narrower focus and are tailored for the study of a specific area or aspect of law, e.g. B. Bix, *A Dictionary of Legal Theory* (Oxford: OUP, 2004). Mainstream works include:

> ➤ E.A. Martin and J. Law, *A Dictionary of Law*, 6th edn (Oxford: OUP, 2006);
> ➤ *Jowitt's Dictionary of English Law*, 3rd edn (London: Sweet & Maxwell 2010);
> ➤ M. Woodley, *Osborn's Concise Law Dictionary*, 11th edn (London: Sweet and Maxwell, 2009). An updated 2013 edition is as available as an app and ebook;
> ➤ L.B. Curzon, *The Longman Dictionary of Law*, 7th edn (Harlow: Longman, 2007).

NB Her Majesty's Court Service contains two glossaries. One contains common English legal terms *http://www.justice.gov.uk/courts/glossary-of-terms/glossary-of-terms-legal* [accessed June 6, 2014] and the other is an explanation of common Latin terms *http:// www.justice.gov.uk/courts/glossary-of-terms* [accessed June 6, 2014]. Both web pages can be searched alphabetically.

UK

W.J. Stewart and R. Burgess, *Collins Dictionary of Law*, 3rd edn (London: Harper Collins, **8–41** 2006) covers the law in England, Wales, Scotland and Ireland and is available in paper and as an ebook.

LEGAL TEXTS AND SEARCH STRATEGIES FOR THESE RESOURCES

Different types of legal texts

There are several different types of legal texts. The most important are discussed below. **8–42**

Textbooks

Textbooks aim to provide the student with an introduction to and explanation (and analysis) of **8–43** important facets of an area of law. Accordingly, textbooks are a prime resource. They explain key concepts without an understanding of which the student would struggle to put the law in context by forming a good understanding of the background to and the aims and objectives of the current law and possible future developments. To remain as up-to-date as possible textbooks will generally be produced in several editions in order to keep up with subsequent changes in the law. Hence the advice given throughout this book, to ensure that the most recent edition of a publication (if there is more than one) is consulted. Whilst it may prove tempting to purchase an older edition of a textbook this is not to be recommended given that the most recent edition has been authored with the purpose of providing a contemporary and comprehensive description and explanation of the relevant law. Students will be advised of the recommended text or texts for a specific subject of study by tutors who will provide a reading list based on a personal review of all recent publications in the field and an assessment of their relative strengths and weaknesses.

Casebooks

8–44 Casebooks (sometimes called cases and materials texts) are a type of textbook that contains excerpts from legal materials, such as cases, legislation, journal articles, books and official reports. Excerpts are accompanied by the author or authors' commentary which discusses the significance of the selected materials in the development of the law. They are, in essence, portable "mini libraries" about a specific subject and extremely useful. However, the primary materials referred to in casebooks should still be accessed and read to fully grasp the legal reasoning underpinning a court's judgment in cases considering a point of common law or rules of statutory interpretation.

Revision guides

8–45 Revision guides are designed to help students prepare for exams. There is currently one series dedicated to Scots law, the Law*Basics* series, published by W. Green. These publications are much shorter than recommended textbooks and, accordingly, will not contain sufficient depth to serve as a main textbook. However, a particular strength is the structured way in which information is presented to give a logical and clear framework within which the students can incorporate their own revision notes which will be based on the subject as taught by the tutor who will have placed emphasis on specific facets of the area of law under scrutiny.

Monographs

8–46 Monographs are formal works on a particular subject giving great detail and copious references to previous authoritative sources. Monographs are not the same as textbooks in that they assume that the reader already has a certain amount of subject knowledge and so discuss an area of law in greater depth. Whilst the content of monographs will vary, they will tend to digress from black letter law and consider policy issues or theoretical debates in the area concerned. Monographs are often cited in footnotes or references in textbooks or journal articles and can be located in order to obtain more detailed information after an initial literature search.

Practitioner texts

8–47 Practitioner texts are designed principally for use by the legal profession. However, they are also relevant to students studying for the Diploma in Legal Practice. They will therefore assume a great amount of prior knowledge. They contain detailed discussion of the particular area of law and tend to adopt a more practical, rather than theoretical, approach. A particular type of practitioner text is a "styles" book. These are works which contain templates for different types of legal documents commonly encountered by solicitors. One example is *Greens Practice Styles* which is published in four volumes and updated thrice yearly in loose-leaf and CD-ROM format.

Features of law textbooks

8–48 Law textbooks contain certain unique features which help the researcher locate valuable information in a self-contained, structured and coherent environment. These features include:

> ➢ The timescale of the publishing process means that most law books are at least six months out-of-date on the day they are published. However, a statement is usually given in the preface (as in *Legal Research Skills for Scots Lawyers*) of a date up to which the law can be taken as accurate. This alerts the reader of the date when research undertaken using the publication concerned must be brought up-to-date by consulting other resources, e.g. lecture materials provided by a tutor, the Scottish Courts website

or a subscription data base, such as Westlaw, to confirm that a recent case dealing with the relevant subject-matter has/has not occurred;

> A table of abbreviations. This provides the reader with (i) an understanding of commonly used legal abbreviations and (ii) those specific to a particular textbook;

> Table of cases. This lists, in alphabetical order of the first named party, all cases referred to in the publication and generally lists the relevant page number(s) in the text where the case is referred to. If consulting a textbook to locate information about a case or cases or for the purpose of checking a case citation or to find out if a case has an alternative citation, consult this table first;

> Tables of legislation. This is a chronological list of all Acts/SIs/Conventions, etc. referred to in the text. Page or paragraph number(s) in the text where the provisions are referred to may be given. It is also usual practice for the instruments to be listed separately.

Locating Textbooks

As stated in para.8–43, tutors, in the first instance, will identify relevant reading for a particular **8–49** subject of study and recommend a core textbook which ought to be purchased. In addition, a reading list detailing further reading will be provided. However, this is only the starting point. The legal researcher—no matter the stage of study—is required to use their growing research skills to locate further primary and secondary materials through personal endeavour and study. Textbooks, general reference works and encyclopaedias will provide references to further reading in footnotes, at the conclusion of a chapter and/or in bibliographies at the end of the book. These can initially be followed up by searching the researcher's institutional library collection via the library catalogue which will likely be available online. Some universities provide hyperlinks to other institutions' catalogues, enabling a search of the resources held there. Many universities also have a reciprocal arrangement whereby a matriculated student at one university can gain call and borrowing privileges at another by registering as a library member there also. Generally this will include access to databases subscribed to by the other university concerned.

Searching for textbooks within the UK and Ireland

It is a relatively straightforward process to search other UK and Irish university and specialist **8–50** libraries, including the British Library and the National Library of Scotland, online via COPAC. This resource provides free access to the merged online catalogues of over 70 library databases which can be searched by author(s) name) title or keyword.

COPAC is not a lending service thus it is best used to locate the whereabouts of a particular text. **8–51** The British Library and the National Library of Scotland are "libraries of deposit" (see the Legal Deposit Libraries Act 2003 ss.3and 4). The British Library must receive one copy of any work published in print in the UK within one month of its publication date. The National Library of Scotland is entitled to one copy of any work which it requests.

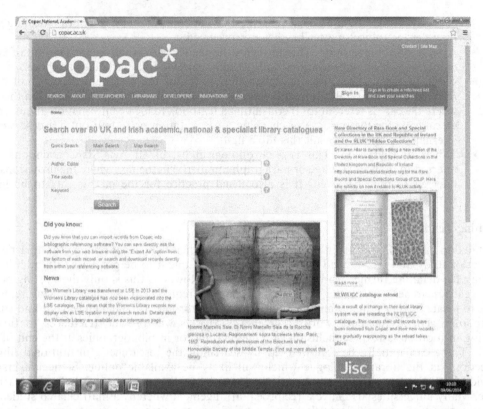

Inter-library loan

8–52 The inter-library loan system allows matriculated students at a UK institution (undergraduate and postgraduate) to request textbooks and other literature held by other institutions or the British Library Document Supply Centre. Policies on how this service operates will vary from institution to institution, but, generally, if an inter-library loan is requested with the support of a tutor the requesting institution rather than the student will cover the cost of delivery and then return of the materials, although the student will likely be required to pay a modest administration charge for using the service.

The Advocates Library

8–53 The Advocates Library was the precursor of the National Library of Scotland and has retained its copyright privileges for law publications when it gifted its non-law collections to the nation. The Advocates Library (which was inaugurated in 1689) therefore has a copy of every law book published in the United Kingdom. It is possible to search the catalogue of the Advocates Library online at *http://voyager.advocates.org.uk/* [accessed June 9, 2014]. It can be searched by title, author, subject and journal title.

The websites of legal booksellers can be consulted to locate forthcoming and recent publications **8–54** and also to view their back catalogue. Legal booksellers online catalogues include:

> ➢ Avizandum, *http://www.avizandum.co.uk/* [accessed June 9, 2014];
> ➢ Hammicks Legal Information Bookshop, *http://www.hammickslegal.com/live/* [accessed June 9, 2014];
> ➢ Wildy & Sons Ltd, *http://www.wildy.com* [accessed June 9, 2014].

Amazon, *http://www.amazon.co.uk/* [accessed June 9, 2014], whilst not a legal publisher or legal bookseller per se, is a further source which can be consulted to gather information about current and forthcoming legal publications. Avoid purchasing older editions of a work unless it is being sought for a specific purpose as it will not be up-to-date.

Legal publishers catalogues can also be found online. The publisher of *Legal Research Methods* **8–55** *for Scots Lawyers*, i.e. W. Green who, in common with the majority of publishers, lists forthcoming, recent and older publications still in print on their website *http://www.sweetandmaxwell.co.uk/wgreen/* [accessed June 9, 2014].

Legal bibliographies

Legal bibliographies contain lists of books grouped under subject headings. Examples of legal **8–56** bibliographies are:

> ➤ J. Winterton and E.M. Moys (eds.), *Information Sources in Law*, 2nd edn (Berlin: De Gruyter, 2012). This book is designed to provide a starting point for research in an unfamiliar area. It contains chapters written by information specialists in many different spheres including EU law;
> ➤ Scottish Current Law Yearbooks and Monthly Digests contain details of textbooks and articles. There is a list of law books published during the year at the end of the Yearbooks. The Monthly Digests are list recent publications;
> ➤ For information about older Scottish texts consult *An Introductory Survey of the Sources and Literature of Scots Law*, Publication of the Stair Society, No.1 (Stair Society, Edinburgh, 1936) (see below);
> ➤ For information on older UK texts consult *Legal Bibliography of the British Commonwealth of Nations*, 2nd edn (London: Sweet & Maxwell, 1955–8). Volume 5, published in 1957, covers Scots law up to 1956. D. Raistrick, *Lawyers' Law Books*, 3rd edn (London: Bowker Saur, 1997) contains bibliographical listings by subject. It also details encyclopaedias, periodicals and other texts. It concentrates on UK legal literature but does include material relating to other legal jurisdictions. There is a section on Scots law and various Scots terms appear, e.g. delict;
> ➤ *Law Books and Serials in Print*. The 2013 edition is published by Grey House Publishing with volume one detailing books published in English and currently in print.

The Stair Society

8–57 The Stair Society was instituted in 1934 to encourage the study and to advance the knowledge of the history of Scots law. The society publishes legal history materials which are listed on their website, *http://stairsociety.org/publications* [accessed June 24, 2014]. The website also contains a useful section of legal history links, *http://stairsociety.org/resources* [accessed June 24, 2014].

General bibliographic sources

The National Library of Scotland

8–58 The National Library of Scotland catalogues and databases can be searched online at, *http://www.nls.uk/catalogues/catalogues-plus-databases* [accessed June 9, 2014].

Resources include:

> ➢ Bibliography of Scotland. This is a database of material that has been written about Scotland and the Scottish people thus it excludes material published in Scotland if it has no Scottish content. It currently includes circa one hundred and forty thousand books, journal and periodical articles with approximately four hundred new books added on a monthly basis. Scottish Government and other official publications are also available. A search can be undertaken by selecting one of two options—the Bibliography of Scotland database, which contains materials published from 1987 onwards, or the Bibliography of the Scottish Book Trade database, which contains books and materials of all publication dates or both databases can be searched together. See *http:// www.nls.uk/catalogues/scottish-bibliographies-online/locations* [accessed June 9, 2014]. A search can be undertaken by author, title, subject, shelfmark, ISBN number and keyword;
> ➢ Main Catalogue. The main catalogue of printed books contains over three million records and covers printed material acquired by the library since 1801. A search can be undertaken as detailed above. See *http://main-cat.nls.uk/vwebv/searchBasic?sk = nls_en* [accessed June 9, 2014].

The British Library

The British Library's British National Bibliography is a complete listing of all books and journals titles published in the UK since 1950 which have been received and catalogued. It references all books regardless of whether or not the work is in print. A weekly list of new **8–59** additions to the bibliography can be accessed here, *http://www.bl.uk/bibliographic/natbibweekly.html* [accessed June 9, 2014].

THESES AND DISSERTATIONS

8–60 Theses and dissertations comprise student work submitted in part or full to gain an undergraduate or postgraduate degree at an academic institution. Many such works will be deposited in that institution's library in the reference section. Outwith a specific institution, postgraduate theses abstracts can be located by subscribing to Index to Theses at, *http://www.theses.com/* [accessed June 9, 2014], which holds approximately half a million UK and Irish theses from 1716 onwards. A copy of the full text thesis can be borrowed through the inter-library loan scheme. Alternatively, the relevant university can be contacted directly.

LEGAL JOURNALS

8–61 There are many different types of legal journals (sometimes called periodicals) and they are available in different formats and produced at different times and frequencies. Journals tend to be aimed at specific audiences (e.g. practitioner, academic and student) and tailored accordingly. The practitioner journals tend to be published frequently and aim to provide a current awareness service as well as practical information about developments in the law. Academic journals tend to be published less frequently and contain lengthy articles about more theoretical issues. Student journals generally contain short articles on recent legal developments.

8–62 Some journals are general in that they contain information on all areas of law. Others are restricted to one area. Journals also cater for different legal jurisdictions. There are Scottish legal journals, UK legal journals and journals which cover EU and international law.

8–63 There is no standard format for a legal journal. Some journals are produced as a collection of scholarly articles and are reasonably large publications, while others are slim pamphlets providing an updating service. Most journals are published in parts (called issues) which are subsequently consolidated into annual volumes. Some legal journals are only published electronically, but the majority are still paper-based although an increasing number are also available electronically. An example of an open source (free) electronic only journal is the European Journal of Law & Technology ("JILT") (1996–) which is available at, *http://www2.warwick.ac.uk/fac/soc/law/elj/jilt/* [accessed June 9, 2014].

8–64 In a law library, legal journals will be stored in alphabetical order. Usual practice is to separate the current edition from back issues of the journal. The latest editions will be placed where they are designed to be browsed. Older editions will be shelved elsewhere.

Scottish journals aimed at the profession

Journal of the Law Society of Scotland (J.L.S.S.) (1956–)	published monthly	*Contents*: professional information, articles, book reviews, news features, letters and interviews.
Scots Law Times (S.L.T.) (1893–)	published weekly	*Contents*: Articles, Acts of Adjournal/ Sederunt, appointments, book reviews, business changes, case commentaries, coming events, general information, law reports, letters, parliamentary news, and taxation.
Scottish Law Gazette (S.L.G.) (1933–)	published every second month by the Council of the Scottish Law Agents Society	*Contents*: articles, news, book reviews and book information.

English journals aimed at the profession

These include: *New Law Journal, Solicitors' Journal* and the *Law Society Gazette*. These are all **8–65** published weekly.

Scottish academic journals include:

Juridical Review (J.R.) (1889–)	published four times a year	*Contents:* articles, analysis of current legal developments and notes on cases. **8–66**
Edinburgh Law Review (EdinLR) (1996–)	published three times a year	*Contents:* articles, significant developments in the law and book reviews.

English academic journals include:

Law Quarterly Review (L.Q.R.) (1885–)	published six times a year	**8–67**
Modern Law Review (M.L.R.) (1937–)	published six times a year	
Cambridge Law Journal (C.L.J.) (1921–)	published every four months	
Oxford Journal of Legal Studies (O.J.L.S.)	published quarterly	

Specialist journals published in Scotland include:

SCOLAG (Scottish Legal Action Group) (1975–)	published monthly	This monthly journal contains articles, law updates and book reviews. **8–68**
Green's Business Law Bulletin Green's Civil Practice Bulletin, Green's Criminal Law Bulletin, Green's Employment Law Bulletin, Green's Family Law Bulletin, Green's Property Law Bulletin,	All published every two months	These are short updating bulletins which contain commentary about recent cases and legal developments.

UK-wide specialist journals include: *British Journal of Criminology, Journal of Law and Society,* and the *Criminal Law Review.*

Locating articles in legal journals

8–69 Locating legal journal articles can initially cause issues. Primarily, this is because university holdings of journals are, by necessity, selective and, secondly, there is no one electronic source holding all legal journal articles. Although searching has been made easier by linking many of the online subscription sources such as Westlaw or Heinonline directly to university library catalogues many online providers of full text journal articles only reference their own holdings. Westlaw's Legal Journal Index ("LJI") indexes circa 430 UK and EU related journals from 1986 onwards. However, this is not a full text service—only references to a journal article and/or an abstract are given unless the full-text of an article is held on Westlaw.

8–70 Westlaw and LexisNexis both have large collections of full text journals which do not overlap. The choice of database is therefore dependent on the subject matter of the journals which they contain. This is not a static list as both databases are constantly expanding their holdings so their holdings should be checked periodically to ensure familiarity with current content.

SEARCH STRATEGIES FOR FINDING ARTICLES IN JOURNALS

Locating journal articles in a law library with a full reference

8–71 If the researcher has been referred to an article by a tutor or found its details in a reference in a textbook this will comprise the full journal reference. A full reference for a journal article will include:

> ➢ Name of the author(s);
> ➢ Title of the articles;
> ➢ Reference with details of the date, volume number, title of the journal (usually in abbreviated form) and a page number.

If the full name of the journal is known check the library catalogue or proceed to the journals section to browse the shelves. Journals are generally shelved in alphabetical order with current issues normally stored in a different part of a library from older editions of journals.

8–72 If the reference to the journal title is in abbreviated from and the abbreviation is unfamiliar in the first instance consult:

> ➢ The list of abbreviations provided by the library;
> ➢ The Cardiff Index to Legal Abbreviations *http://www.legalabbrevs.cardiff.ac.uk* [accessed June 9, 2014].
> ➢ A general search engine, e.g. Google.

If looking for a journal of historic rather than current publication, D. Raistrick's *Index to Legal Citations and Abbreviations*, 2nd edn (London: Bowker-Saur, 1993) is a useful resource. Once armed with the name of the journal proceed as above.

8–73 If the library does not have the journal concerned enquire whether a copy can be accessed through the inter-library loan scheme.

8–74 Even without a full reference the desired article can still be located with a bit of perseverance. If the title of a publication is known, but the name of the author and/or the exact year of publication are unknown if the article has been published since 1986 Westlaw's Legal Journal Index ought to be consulted.

Locating journal articles online with a full reference

Check the library catalogue for the journal series. Many university libraries now link directly **8–75** from their catalogue to particular series of journals if they have the appropriate subscription. The password arrangements will depend on the particular institution's policies.

If a certain journal series does not appear in the catalogue of a particular institution, check the **8–76** journals section of Westlaw and other online sources to which access is given. If this is unsuccessful, enquire whether a copy of the article is available through the inter-library loan service.

Locating journal articles on a particular subject

Westlaw ⃠ subscription database
The best resource for tracing articles published in UK legal journals since 1986 is Westlaw's **8–77** LLJI. This is located on the "Journals" page where search options for the full-text articles held also appear. The LJI currently indexes over 1,000 legal journals from the UK and English language European journals. Westlaw also includes the Financial Journals Index (which ceased to be updated as of March 31, 2006) which indexes over 45 journals in areas, such as insurance, financial services, banking, construction, employment, property and health and safety and full text articles from journal titles published by Sweet and Maxwell and Tottel Publishing. This includes selected coverage of S.L.T. articles from 1997.

Articles can be searched for by using the basic search, advanced search or browsing options. **8–78**

Basic search

From the Welcome page, click the Journals link from the navigation bar at the top of the screen. **8–79** This will link to the Journals basic search page, where a search can be undertaken by entering the article title or author, or key subject terms into free text. Searching can be improved if the search techniques which Westlaw refer to as "Terms and Connectors" are used. See paras 2–58—2–59.

Advanced search

Select advanced search in the top right of the journals basic search page. In addition to the free **8–80** text, article title and author search fields a search can also be undertaken:

> ➢ For subject headings or keywords. However, note that this field only searches the article title and the abstract not the full text of the article;
> ➢ By journal title;
> ➢ By searching for articles discussing a particular case by entering the names of one or more parties in the cases cited field;
> ➢ By searching for articles referring to a particular Act or SI by entering its name in the legislation title field. A search can be restricted to individual sections of legislation (where abstracts or articles refer to a specific provision number) by entering the title, then additionally entering the section number in the legislation provision number field;
> ➢ By restricting a search by year of publication.

The results listed will show the article title, its citation and the subject and keywords applied to the abstract. There will also be a link to the LJI abstract and full text if available.

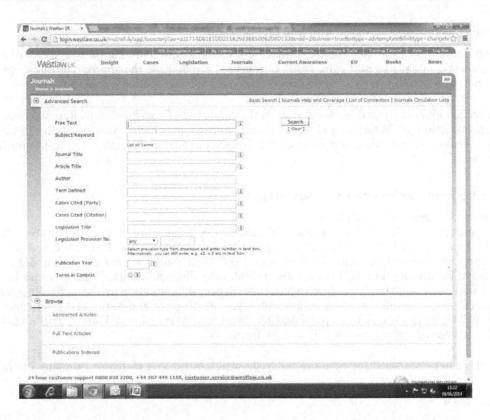

Browsing journal articles

8–81 Journals indexed in the LJI and those which appear in full text can be browsed from the basic search page alphabetically, by issue number or article title. This function can restrict a search to one series, e.g. if only S.L.T. articles are sought, select S.L.T. from the list of full text articles accessed by the link on the search page.

8–82 Once a choice has been made, a new search box appears and this enables a search within a single publication.

8–83 The LJI abstract contains:

> ➤ The title of the article;
> ➤ The author(s);
> ➤ A full reference to the article;
> ➤ The name of the journal. Clicking on it will display the publisher's details;
> ➤ The subject and keywords used to index articles;
> ➤ A brief abstract (this is very brief—usually only a few lines) about the subject of the article;
> ➤ If a case is referred to in the article and there is a case analysis available for that case, the name of the case and its citation will be hyperlinked;

> ➤ If a piece of legislation is cited, this will be hyperlinked unless it has been repealed.

If the full text is available in Westlaw this can be accessed by clicking on the citation immediately following the author's name.

LexisNexis ⁀ subscription database
Unlike Westlaw, LexisNexis only searches the journals it holds in full text. Select the journals **8–84** tab from the homepage. This opens up the journals search form. Enter the details of the publication sought in the enter search terms box.

Lawtel ⁀ subscription legal current awareness digest service
Lawtel indexes fewer journals than the Westlaw LJI and the majority of its coverage of journals **8–85** dates from 1998. Articles can be located by selecting the articles index on the home page.

Wiley Online Library ⁀ subscription
The Wiley Online Library is an online journal service from Wiley Publishing. It provides full- **8–86** text access to around twenty law journals. At the time of writing, a thirty day free trial giving access to certain legal publications is offered. See *http://onlinelibrary.wiley.com/subject/code/ 000076* [accessed June 9, 2014].

HeinOnline ⁀ subscription database of legal journals
This database holds a number of UK law journals in its Law Journal Library. However, its **8–87** Scots law holdings are currently limited. All journals held are full text and can be searched or browsed for. All holdings are image-based thus the original printed page is shown on the screen.

Index to Legal Periodicals and Books 📖 and ⁀ subscription indexing service
This index references legal periodicals and books which are published in Great Britain, Ireland, **8–88** US, Canada, Australia and New Zealand. However, the majority of material is American. The online version which is updated daily allows access to some journals in full text. Pre-1981 articles are referenced in the bound volumes. At the time of writing, a free trial giving access to certain legal publications is offered. See *http://www.ebscohost.com/academic/index-to-legal-periodicals-books* [accessed June 9, 2014].

Index to Foreign Legal Periodicals 📖 and ⁀ subscription indexing service
This is a US based index. It covers selected international and comparative law periodicals and **8–89** collections of essays. The paper volumes go back to 1960 and the online version contain material back to 1985.

Current Law Yearbooks

The Current Law Yearbooks and Monthly Digests contain details of journal articles under **8–90** subject headings.

Locating journal articles discussing a case

See paras 4–92—4–99. **8–91**

Locating journal articles discussing a piece of legislation

See paras 6–05—6–10. **8–92**

Locating non-law journal articles

Periodical Index Online ✇ subscription indexing service

8–93 This is an electronic index to millions of articles published in the arts, humanities and social sciences. It is a useful way of searching information contained in back issues of older journals, see *http://www.columbia.edu/cu/lweb/eresources/databases/2291867.html* [accessed June 9, 2014].

Zetoc ✇ indexing service which is free to some higher education institutions

8–94 *Zetoc* is a monitoring and search gateway that provides access to the British Library's Electronic Table of Contents database, containing details of approximately 20,000 current journals and 16,000 conference proceedings published per year. The database includes science, technology, medicine, engineering, business, law, finance and the humanities. The database covers the years from 1993 to date and is updated daily. The service which can be accessed here, *http://zetoc.-mimas.ac.uk/* [accessed June 9, 2014] is free for members of the Joint Information Systems Committee, a body sponsored by UK higher and further education institutions. See *http://www.jisc.ac.uk/* [accessed June 9, 2014].

British Humanities Index 📖 and ✇ subscription indexing service

8–95 The British Humanities Index provides abstracts from over 400 daily newspapers, weekly magazines and academic journals of international standing, with over half a million records dating back to 1962. It is updated monthly. See *http://www.csa.com/factsheets/bhi-set-c.php* [accessed June 9, 2014].

Social Sciences Citation Index and Arts & Humanities Citation Index ✇ subscription indexing services

8–96 Both of these indexes are available as part of the ISI Web of Knowledge platform. Both include not only the content of the articles, but also the reference lists and bibliographies included by the author. They also list how many times an article has been referenced or cited in another paper. A useful guide per documents held and how to search this database can be accessed here, *http://ip-science.thomsonreuters.com/m/pdfs/wos_workbook_en.pdf* [accessed June 9, 2014].

NEWSPAPER ARTICLES

8–97 All legal scholars, from the undergraduate student to the practitioner of many years standing, are required to keep abreast of current events. Primarily, reports and analysis of proposed changes in the law will be published in quality newspapers and reported in other media outlets. Of equal import, quality newspapers will highlight perceived issues concerning a current legal provision and report differing points of view on what alternative provisions, if any, should be enacted or whether a "bad" law ought to be repealed. Likewise, such publications will report on government policy and current proceedings in both domestic and EU courts.

8–98 Whilst newspaper articles in themselves are a weak secondary source, they may inter alia refer to policy documents, quote an authoritative legal source or direct the reader to further resources concerning the issue at hand. The majority of newspapers published in the UK offer a free website (the exception being *The Times* which is a subscription service if full text reports are sought) which, in addition to carrying that day's news, etc., may also provide search facilities to locate older reports and features.

Locating older newspaper articles

Older articles may also be available on the internet and dedicated websites that can be searched, **8–99**
e.g. if seeking a newspaper report on the background to and implications of the Defamation Act
2014 and the following is typed into a search engine—"Defamation Act 2013 The Times"—the
fourth hit yields an article dated January 16, 2014 entitled "What Does the Defamation Act
Mean for Academics?" which can be viewed here; *http://www.timeshighereducation.co.uk/
comment/opinion/defamation-act-2013-what-scientists-need-to-know/2010434.article* [accessed
June 9, 2014].

Amending the search terms to read, "Defamation Act 2014 The Guardian" the first hit dated **8–100**
December 31, 2013 is for an article entitled "Libel: New Defamation Act will Reverse 'Chilling
Effect' Ministers Claim" *http://www.theguardian.com/law/2013/dec/31/trivial-libel-claims-targeted-
new-law* [accessed June 10, 2014].

If specific information about the Act is sought the search terms used can be changed **8–101**
accordingly.

Both Westlaw and LexisNexis allow searching of selected quality newspapers. Westlaw includes **8–102**
the following Scottish newspapers: *Aberdeen Press and Journal* (from May 2004), *Dundee
Courier* (from July 2002), *Evening News* (October 1999), *Evening Times* (July 2002) *Herald* (from
January 2000) and *Scotsman* (from 1996). The British Humanities Index (see para.8–95) indexes
articles and features, but not news items and editorials. The papers it covers are the *Independen*t,
Guardian, *Financial Times*, *Observer*, *Times* (and any supplements) and *The Sunday Times.*

Locating current newspaper articles

In addition to consulting a specific publication's website to follow that day's news and current **8–103**
affairs the following are examples of free sites that provide access to the current issues of a
variety of domestic and foreign newspapers:

> ➢ Onlinenewspapers.com at *http://www.onlinenewspapers.com/* [accessed June 10, 2014]
> provides links to a large number of newspaper worldwide including a large number of
> Scottish newspapers;
> ➢ ABYZ News Links at *http://www.abyznewslinks.com/* [accessed June 10, 2014] is
> another site that links to a large number of newspapers in Scotland and from around
> the world.

News services

News services on the web in most jurisdictions are abundant. UK based services include: **8–104**

> ➢ BBC News—*http://www.bbc.co.uk/news/* [accessed June 10, 2014];
> ➢ The Huffington Post—*http://www.huffingtonpost.co.uk/* [accessed June 10, 2014];
> ➢ NewsNow—*http://www.newsnow.co.uk/h/* [accessed June 10, 2014];
> ➢ Reuters UK—*http://uk.reuters.com/* [accessed June 10, 2014]; and
> ➢ Sky News—*http://news.sky.com/uk* [accessed June 10, 2014].

Media outlets in every corner of the world will provide a news service which can be located
online. If a research project involves a comparative analysis of the law in another jurisdiction
with that of Scotland or the UK, a general internet search for national newspapers etc in a
specific country will likely yield a list of quality publications without difficulty.

CURRENT AWARENESS OF LEGAL DEVELOPMENTS IN SCOTLAND

Westlaw ⏺ subscription database

8–105 Westlaw provides a Current Awareness service which can be accessed by clicking the Current Awareness link at the top of the Welcome screen. It contains daily updates and notices of cases, legislation, and legal developments contained in or represented by official publications, press releases (including from the Scottish Government) and legal news (including from *The Scotsman* and *Herald*) relating to the UK. It is updated three times daily at 9am, 11am and 2pm. The information remains in Current Awareness for 90 days and can then be found by searching the Current Awareness Archive. This includes over 10 years of content.

8–106 To restrict a search to Scotland include the word "Scotland" in the subject/keyword box in the basic search function. Searching can be improved by using search techniques which Westlaw refer to as "Terms and Connectors". See paras 2–58—2–59. There is also a browse facility which allows a search within various date ranges, e.g. today or the last four days.

LexisNexis ⏺ subscription database

8–107 LexisNexis also offers a Current Awareness service which can be searched by clicking on the Current Awareness tab on the homepage.

Additional websites

8–108 The following websites contain regularly updated information about current legal developments in Scotland:

> The Firm—*http://www.firmmagazine.com/* [accessed June 10, 2014] provides news about legal developments within Scotland and the legal profession;

> Journalonline—*http://www.journalonline.co.uk/* [accessed June 10, 2014] is the online Journal of the Law Society of Scotland. It is updated daily and has an searchable archive back to August 2004;

> Scottish Legal News—*http://www.scottishlegal.com/* [accessed June 10, 2014] offers up-to-date news about legal developments and also practitioner orientated reports/information. A free daily email bulletin is provided upon registration. This site also has a searchable database.

> The Lawyer—*http://www.thelawyer.com/* [accessed June 10, 2014] is aimed at English practitioners. However it publishes news and articles of relevance to Scottish lawyers and researchers. This site also hosts articles from The Lawyer magazine. The service is free but registration is required.

> **NB** Scots Law News—*http://www.sln.law.ed.ac.uk/* [accessed June 10, 2014] provides short historical news items on many aspects of Scots law. It has a searchable archive beginning in January 1970 up until May 2013.

UK OFFICIAL PUBLICATIONS

8–109 UK official publications emanating from the UK Parliament at Westminster provide a vast amount of information and can be divided into two distinct categories: Parliamentary papers and non-Parliamentary publications.

Parliamentary papers at Westminster

The progress of Bills and Parliamentary debates as recorded in *Hansard* are classed as Parlia- **8–110** mentary papers and are discussed at various points in Ch.6. Other Parliamentary papers of interest to the researcher are Command papers, House of Commons papers and House of Lords papers.

Command papers

A Command paper is technically presented to Parliament "by the Command of Her Majesty", **8–111** but in practice they are usually presented by a Government Minister. They are documents which have been produced for Parliament to consider; they have not been produced by Parliament. There are many different types of Command Papers:

➢ White Papers (proposal for legislation put forward by the Government);
➢ Green Papers (consultation documents put forward by the Government);
➢ Reports of Royal Commissions;
➢ Reports of Committees of Inquiry;
➢ Annual reports and statistics produced by certain bodies;
➢ State Papers including Treaties; and
➢ Law Commission reports are (generally) published as Command papers.

There are six series of Command Papers. Each Command Paper is allocated a number; they are all numbered less than 10,000 and, apart from the first series, preceded with a different form of abbreviation for the word "Command":

*1833–1866	1–4222
*1870–1899	C.1 – C.9550
*1900–1918	Cd.1 – Cd.9239
*1919–1956	Cmd.1 – Cmd.9889
*1956–1986	Cmnd.1 – Cmnd.9927
*1986–	Cm.1 –

As the same numbers are used in the different series, it is important to note the precise abbreviation so as to locate the appropriate Command Paper.

All Command Papers from May 2005 onwards which originate in Government departments are **8–112** available at *https://www.gov.uk/government/publications?official_document_status = command_ and_act_papers* [accessed June 10, 2014]. The search facility enables a search by publication, topic, department, document status or by date.

The National Archives, at *http://tna.europarchive.org/20100402134329/http://www.opsi.gov.uk/* **8–113** *official-publications/command-papers/index.htm* [accessed June 10, 2014], provides a list of all command papers since 2001 with links to the Command Papers where known. The database can be searched alphabetically by department or by number if this is known.

House of Commons and House of Lords Papers

House of Commons and House of Lords Papers are documents that result from the work of **8–114** both Houses and that of their committees. They include:

> ➢ Votes and Proceedings (Commons) and the Minute (Lords) which are the formal, authoritative record of the decisions taken by each House;
> ➢ Select Committee reports and evidence;
> ➢ Register of Members' interests;
> ➢ Standing Orders (which are the rules for conducting business in both Houses); and
> ➢ Sessional Returns (which include statistics on the work of the Commons for each Parliamentary year).

House of Commons Papers are given a reference which consists of H.C., the relevant Parliamentary session (e.g. 2013/14) and the number of the paper. House of Lords Papers are numbered in a similar way, but with H.L. as the prefix.

8–115 House of Commons Papers are available on a dedicated Parliamentary website, see *http://www.parliament.uk/business/publications/commons/* [accessed June 10, 2014], and House of Commons Papers from the 2005–2006 Parliamentary session onwards, which originate in Government departments, are available at the TSO website

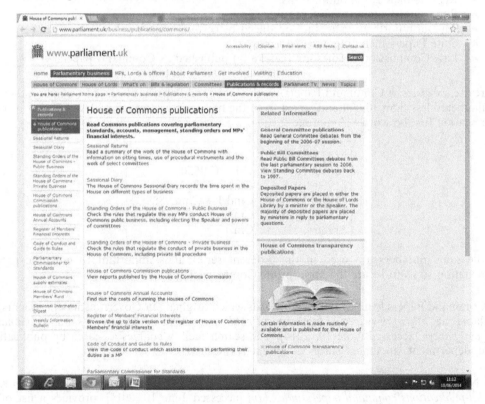

Aids to tracing official publications

8–116 Specific resources to locate the full text of the various Parliamentary papers have been detailed in previous chapters. For further information about Bills and *Hansard*, see Ch.6. For Command Papers and House of Commons and House of Lords Papers, see Ch.8.

Collections of Parliamentary publications 📖
The National Library of Scotland holds House of Commons Papers since 1715 and House of **8–117**
Lords papers since 1801.The British Library has received all TSO publications since 1962.

The United Kingdom Official Publications Database (UKOP) ⌁ subscription
UKOP, at *http://www.ukop.co.uk/* [accessed June 10, 2014], is the official catalogue of UK **8–118**
official publications. It combines the official catalogue of TSO with the Catalogue of Official
Publications Not Published by TSO, UKOP contains over 450,000 bibliographic records of
official publications from 1980 onwards and is updated daily. It catalogues all Parliamentary
and statutory publications (including Acts and SI), and the publications of over two thousand
public bodies. UKOP has the benefit of allowing users to trace Government publications
without having any knowledge of the departments that might have been involved in their
production.

Lawtel ⌁ subscription legal current awareness digest service
Lawtel offers a search facility for Command Papers, including White and Green Papers. Its **8–119**
holdings begin in 1984. It is updated daily and contains hypertext links to full text when this is
available from Government websites.

Justis Parliament ⌁ subscription service
This resource provides an index to the proceedings and publications of both Houses of Par- **8–120**
liament in Westminster from 1979 onwards.

British Official Publications Collaborative Reader Information Service (BOPRIS) ⌁
subscription
BOPCRIS is hosted by the University of Southampton and allows access to older official **8–121**
publications. It is a bibliographic database covering the period 1688–1995. It can search
approximately 39,000 selected British official publications within this period. It can be searched
by subject, but this is likely to retrieve a large number of results. The advanced search refines an
initial search by date, title or keywords. See *http://www.southampton.ac.uk/library/ldu/pro-
jects.html#18C* [accessed June 10, 2014].

Non-Parliamentary publications

Searching on the internet

These are official publications which are not presented to Parliament. This is not a particularly **8–122**
helpful definition, but this broad grouping of Government publications is vast and emerges from
a large number of public and official bodies. Problems of searching for this material can be
exacerbated by the fact that the bodies concerned change name from time to time during periods
of Government-inspired reorganisation of roles and/or responsibilities, e.g. until 1992, the
Nature Conservancy Council carried out broadly the same functions as those now undertaken
by its successor Scottish Natural Heritage, which has created under the auspices of The Natural
Heritage (Scotland) Act 1991. Likewise, The British Tourist Board, established by the Development of Tourism Act 1969, was renamed VisitBritain in 2003.

If the current name of the body is known an internet search will quickly locate its homepage **8–123**
where some such successor organisations may make reference to their previous incarnation and
name. If this is not the case, a further general search should be undertaken using the current
name of the body and the word "predecessor" after it.

Other sources of non-Parliamentary publications

8–124 Non-Parliamentary publications are included in TSO Daily List and shop, see *http://www.tsoshop.co.uk/* [accessed June 10, 2014], UKOP (para.8–118), and BOPCRIS (para.8–121).

8–125 The UK Government website *GOV.UK* enables a search for non-parliamentary publications here, *https://www.gov.uk/government/publications* [accessed June 24, 2014].

8–126 Certain libraries hold the Catalogue of British Official Publications Not Published by TSO which is issued bi-monthly and bound into annual volumes. This includes references to a large amount of material emerging from over 500 different organisations. UKOP (see para.8–118) includes this catalogue.

Sources of additional information about the workings of the UK Government

Westminster Parliament Publications and Records ⁀ free
8–127 The Westminster Parliament Publications and Records homepage, *http://www.parliament.uk/business/publications/*, contains a large amount of information including links to the House of Lords and House of Commons Hansard and their respective business papers and publications.

The Civil Service Yearbook 📖 and ⁀ subscription
8–128 This is published annually by TSO and is the official reference work for central Government in the UK providing the most authoritative source of up-to-date information on the Civil Service. See *http://www.tsoshop.co.uk/parliament/bookstore.asp?DI=328151* [accessed June 10, 2014].

The Directory of Westminster and Whitehall 📖
8–129 This directory describes itself as a consumers' guide to Parliament and the civil service. It contains information about inter alia MPs, their staff and constituencies, contact details for Government departments, listings of subject responsibility in Government departments and contact details for non-governmental organisations or agencies (quangos) to which Westminster has delegated certain powers. This directory can therefore be consulted to locate information about non-parliamentary publications from bodies such as VisitBritain, as detailed in paras 8–124—8–126.

Press releases from UK Government offices, ministerial departments and non-ministerial departments

8–130 Current and past press releases can be located on the dedicated websites for various UK Government Offices and Departments at Westminster. At the time of writing, the following Government Offices, Ministerial Departments and Non-Ministerial Departments operate. These can be accessed directly from the GOV.UK gateway at *https://www.gov.uk/government/organisations* [accessed June 10, 2014]. However, as with non-governmental bodies (see paras 8–124—8–126) periodic review and re-organisation of their functions and remits will likely lead to a name change at some point in the future.

8–131 Government offices:

➤ Prime Minister's Office, 10 Downing Street;
➤ Deputy Prime Minister's Office.

8–132 Ministerial departments:

➤ Attorney General's Office;

> Cabinet Office;
> Department for Business, Innovation and Skills;
> Department for Communities and Local Government;
> Department for Culture, Media & Sport;
> Department for Education;
> Department for Environment, Food & Rural Affairs;
> Department for International Development;
> Department for Transport;
> Department for Work and Pensions;
> Department of Health;
> Foreign and Commonwealth Office;
> HM Treasury;
> Home Office;
> Ministry of Defence;
> Ministry of Justice;
> Northern Ireland Office;
> Office of the Advocate General for Scotland;
> Office of the Leader of the House of Commons;
> Office of the Leader of the House of Lords;
> Scotland Office;
> UK Export Finance; and
> Wales Office.

Non-Ministerial Departments;   **8–133**

> The Charity Commission for England and Wales
> Competition and Markets Authority;
> Crown Prosecution Service;
> Food Standards Agency;
> Forestry Commission;
> Government Actuary's Department;
> HM Revenue and Customs;
> Land Registry;
> National Savings and Investments;
> The National Archives;
> National Crime Agency;
> Office of Fair Trading;
> Office of Rail Regulation;
> Office of Gas and Electricity Markets;
> Office of Qualifications and Examinations Regulation;
> Office of Qualifications and Examinations Regulation;
> Office for Standards in Education, Children's Services and Skills
> Ordnance Survey;
> Serious Fraud Office;
> Supreme Court of the United Kingdom;
> Treasury Solicitor's Department;
> UK Statistics Authority;
> UK Trade and Investment; and
> Water Services Regulation Authority.

Westlaw 🕭 subscription database

8–134 Westlaw also holds certain press releases with a legal connection from UK Government departments. To search this resource, select the current awareness tab from the homepage and click on document type and then enter the search terms and select press releases. This will retrieve press releases from the last 90 days.

HERMES 🕭 subscription database which is provided by Justis

8–135 This database contains selected press releases and other announcements from UK government departments since 2000.

SCOTTISH OFFICIAL PUBLICATIONS

8–136 Scottish official publications comprise Scottish Government and Scottish Parliament publications, most of which are issued in paper and electronic form.

NB The National Library of Scotland is a "library of deposit". This designation entitles this library to request a copy of all printed items published in the United Kingdom, and in the Republic of Ireland. See s.5 of the Legal Deposit Libraries Act 2003. As of April 6, 2013, s.3 inter alia of the Legal Deposit Libraries (Non-Print) Regulations 2013 extends the powers of the National Library of Scotland which can also request or "harvest" by downloading certain UK electronic publications. Visit the National Library of Scotland's homepage at *http://www.nls.uk/* [accessed June 9, 2014].

Scottish Parliament publications

8–137 Parliamentary publications as discussed throughout Ch.7 include: Bills, the Official Report, Minutes of proceedings (which formally record all items of business taken and the results of any decisions),the Business Bulletin and SPICe research publications.

8–138 The Parliament's business page at, *http://www.scottish.parliament.uk/ParliamentaryBusiness. aspx* [accessed June 9, 2014], and publications page at *http://www.scottish.parliament.uk/ abouttheparliament/15018.aspx* [accessed June 9, 2014], provide links to relevant documents grouped under specific headings.

NB A publication entitled "What's Happening in the Scottish Parliament?" was published between May 15, 1999 and July 3, 2004. This archive can be searched on the publications homepage.

8–139 Scottish Parliament publications are also listed in the Scottish Official Listings (see para.8–146), while TSO Daily List contains a more limited listing.

8–140 Most Parliamentary papers comprise reports of a Committee enquiry into a subject, e.g. subordinate legislation, or Bills before Holyrood.

Scottish Government publications

Scottish Government publications comprise a wide range of different types of documents, e.g. **8–141** policy documents, consultation papers, responses to consultation papers, annual reports of Executive Agencies and Scottish Law Commission documents all come within this rubric. Many Government publications are laid before the Holyrood parliament. The process for laying documents is set out in Ch.14 of the Parliament's Standing Orders. Documents may have to be laid before the Parliament because they require parliamentary scrutiny, such as Scottish SI. Alternatively, legislation may require that documents, such as the annual reports of certain public bodies be brought to the attention of Parliament

When a Scottish Government document is laid before the Holyrood Parliament it becomes part **8–142** of the "SG series" of papers (these are the equivalent of Command Papers at Westminster). These papers are numbered sequentially in a given year and are cited thus, Inspectorate of Prosecution in Scotland Annual Report 2011–12 SG/2012/168.

Confusingly, some Government documents, e.g. some Scottish Law Commission Reports which **8–143** are published jointly with the Law Commission, are laid before both Holyrood and Westminster and therefore have both a Command Paper number and an SG series number.

NB Prior to the Scotland Act 2012, the abbreviation SE was used to reflect the fact that the devolved administration was previously referred to as the Scottish Executive.

Full text Scottish Government directorate publications from 1999 onwards are generally **8–144** available online at, *http://www.scotland.gov.uk/Publications/Recent* [accessed June 9, 2014], and can be searched for by keyword, topic or year. Paper copies can be requested online from the Scottish Government Titles BookSource service. Postage and packing charges will apply. See *http://www.scotland.gov.uk/About/Information/PublicationCharges* [accessed June 9, 2014] for details.

Currently, the undernoted directorates work to the Scottish Cabinet which comprises the First **8–145** Minister, Cabinet Secretaries and Ministers:

- ➢ Learning and Justice;
- ➢ Finance;
- ➢ Enterprise, Environment and Digital;
- ➢ Health and Social Care;
- ➢ Governance and Communities;
- ➢ Strategy and External Affairs.

Listings of Scottish Official Publications

TSO Daily List contains details of some Scottish official publications. Details of Scottish official **8–146** publications are also available on UKOP.

Sources of additional information about the workings of the Scottish Parliament

Information about MSPs, their respective constituencies along with the details of the working of **8–147** the Parliament and the legislative process can be located on the Scottish Parliament homepage at, *http://www.scottish.parliament.uk/index.aspx* [accessed June 10, 2014].

Scottish Parliament Information Centre (SPICe) Research Briefings

8–148 SPICe research briefings and fact sheets can be accessed via the drop down menu on the homepage. These documents are objective re the issue(s) at hand and written by researchers in the SPICe. SPICe research briefings are primarily written for use by MSPs in support of Parliamentary business in Committees and in the Parliament Chamber. Research briefings from 1999 onwards can be browsed either by subject or by date of publication. Fact sheets contain information about various aspects of parliamentary business and about MSPs past and present.

Scottish Law Commission Papers

8–149 The Scottish Law Commission ("SLC") (and the Law Commission for England and Wales) were created by the Law Commissions Act 1965. The Chairman of the SLC is a Senator of the College of Justice and s/he is assisted by four Commissioners. The current Chairman is Lord Pentland. The primary purpose of the SLC is to recommend reforms to the law of Scotland. Since its inception the SLC has undertaken eight programmes of law reform. The current programme is due for completion at the end of 2014. The SLC also prepares Consolidation and Statute Law Repeals Bills for consideration by the Scottish Government/Parliament. To achieve these objectives, the SLC publishes consultation papers and then, post-consultation, prepares a report with recommendations for law reform. A draft Bill is usually appended to the report. The Scottish Government makes the final decision whether to adopt a report's proposals. A recent example of a SLC report being adopted by government is Report 209 (2007), *Rape and other Sexual Offences*, which was implemented in the Sexual Offences (Scotland) Act 2009.

8–150 The SLC website, at *http://www.scotlawcom.gov.uk/* [accessed June 10, 2014], contains details of current consultations, lists discussion papers issued since 1997 and all reports in full text reports issued since 1999. Some pre-1999 reports are also available. As all post 1999 SLC reports are laid before Holyrood, they are classified as Scottish Government publications.

> **NB** Joint SLC and Law Commission for England and Wales reports are published in a single document and are also classified as UK parliamentary papers.
>   See, e.g. Report 199 (2005) Unfair Terms in Contracts. The Law Commission for England and Wales website *http://www.lawcom.gov.uk/* provides a listing of consultation papers and reports and information about current consultations. Full text reports are available on the site from 1995 onwards.

Official statistical information about Scotland

8–151 The Scottish Government statistics homepage at *http://www.scotland.gov.uk/Topics/Statistics/* [accessed June 10, 2014], is a gateway to official statistical information about Scotland. Statistics can be sought under a variety of headings as shown below.

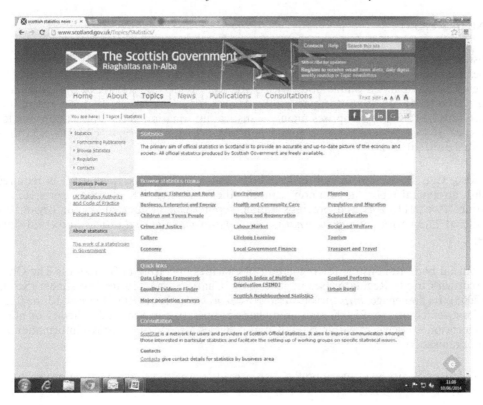

NB The "ScotStat" link aims to provide a network for and dialogue between users and providers of Scottish official statistics thus if statistical information is germane to the researcher's field of study it is also a useful resource for making contact with other like minded legal researchers.

Other statistical information about Scotland available online includes:

8–152

> ➢ National Records for Scotland (previously the General Register Office for Scotland) at *http://www.nrscotland.gov.uk/* [accessed June 24, 2014]. This site provides information about Scotland's population, including the 10 yearly census;
> ➢ The NHS Information Services Division provides access to archived and current information re health statistics for the Scottish population at *http://www.isdscotland.org* [accessed June 9, 2014];
> ➢ Scottish Neighbourhood Statistics, at *http://www.sns.gov.uk/* [accessed June 9, 2014], gives statistics on: health, education, unemployment, housing, crime and other social issues in Scotland. The quick search function provides a summary of statistics for any geographic area by entering the relevant postcode. More detailed information can be located using further search tools.

NB UK-wide statistical information is available from the UK National Statistics homepage *http://www.statistics.gov.uk/hub/index.html*.

ANNUAL REPORTS

8–153 Statistics concerning the work undertaken by both official and unofficial Scottish and UK bodies are often to be found in an organisation's annual report, e.g. the Scottish Criminal Cases Review Commission is a public body with a statutory remit (see s.194A of the Criminal Procedure (Scotland) Act 1995) to review alleged miscarriages of justice. Its most recent annual report, (2012/13), which comprises mainly statistical information about applications made and outcomes of case reviews, can be found here *http://www.sccrc.org.uk/ViewFile.aspx?id=585* [accessed June 10, 2014].

8–154 Likewise, Cats Protection (a non-official body but a registered UK charity) is required to publish an annual report in common with all other registered UK charities, per s.162 of the Charities Act 2011. This and previous annual reports can be located on the organisation's website at *http://www.cats.org.uk/what-we-do/about-us-index/annual-review/* [accessed June 9, 2014].

8–155 The official body responsible for regulation of charities operating in Scotland is The Office of the Scottish Charity Regulator (see in general the Charities and Trustee Investment (Scotland) Act 2005). Its homepage, *http://www.oscr.org.uk/search-charity-register/* [accessed June 9, 2014], enables a search of over 23,000 registered charities operating in Scotland, whether or not their main location is elsewhere within the UK and provides a range of statistical information about each organisation.

8–156 The following Scottish statutory bodies also provide a wealth of statistical information:

> ➤ The Scottish Legal Complaints Commission was created by the Legal Profession and Legal Aid (Scotland) Act 2007. Its remit is to:
>
> • "investigate complaints made by members of the public about services provided by legal practitioners in Scotland. It operates wholly independently of the legal profession, [and] provides a single gateway for taking a complaint forward and offers the services of trained mediators to aid resolution";
>
> ➤ Annual reports since its inception can be located at, *http://www.scottishlegal complaints.org.uk/resources/annual-report-accounts.aspx*, along with those of its predecessor the Scottish Legal Services Ombudsman whose reports are also available at *http://www.slso.org.uk* [accessed June 9, 2014];
> ➤ The Scottish Legal Aid Board. See *http://www.slab.org.uk/* [accessed June 9, 2014];
> ➤ The Scottish Committee Administrative Justice and Tribunals Council replaced the Scottish Committee Council on Tribunals in 2013. The annual reports of both bodies are available here at *http://ajtc.justice.gov.uk/scottish/publications-scottish.htm* [accessed June 9, 2014];
> ➤ The Crown Office and Procurator Fiscal Service, *http://www.copfs.gov.uk/* [accessed June 10, 2014] provides information about the operation of the criminal justice system in Scotland;
> ➤ Scottish Prison Service, see *http://www.sps.gov.uk/* [accessed June 9, 2014];
> ➤ Police Scotland, see *http://www.scotland.police.uk/* [accessed June 9, 2014], came into being on April 1, 2013, replacing previously autonomous regional police forces. It has yet to publish an annual report;
> ➤ Scottish Environment Protection Agency publishes its annual reports here, *http:// sepa.org.uk/about_us/publications/annual_reports.aspx* [accessed June 9, 2014].

LEGAL DIRECTORIES

The Scottish Law Directory: The White Book 2014 is an annual publication, published by **8–157** LexisNexis, which is currently in its 123rd edition. It contains an official list of certificated solicitors and is accompanied by a Fees Supplement which contains details of fee rates.

The Law Society of Scotland provides an online directory of Scottish solicitors at *http://* **8–158** *www.lawscot.org.uk/wcm/lssservices/find_a_solicitor/Core/directory.aspx* [accessed June 9, 2014]. It can be searched by name, location, postcode and category of legal practice work.

Scots Law Online, at *http://www.scottishlaw.org.uk/lawfirms/index.html* [accessed June 9, 2014], **8–159** provides a Scots law firm directory.

PROFESSIONAL SCOTTISH LEGAL BODIES AND ASSOCIATIONS

> Law Society of Scotland at *www.lawscot.org.uk/*, is the professional body for solicitors **8–160** and contains information about the profession and links to the daily updates of the Journal of the Law Society of Scotland at, *http://www.journalonline.co.uk* [accessed June 9, 2014];
> Scottish Young Lawyers' Association at *http://www.syla.co.uk/* [accessed June 9, 2014], is an association for lawyers up to 10 years post-qualification;
> Society of Writers to Her Majesty's Signet, at *http://www.thewss.co.uk/* [accessed June 9, 2014], is an independent association for lawyers;
> Scottish Law Agents Society, at *http://www.scottishlawagents.org/* [accessed June 9, 2014], is a society of solicitors who publish the *Memorandum Book* (a pocket size reference book which is updated and issued every year) and the *Scottish Law Gazette* (editor Kenneth Swinton) which is issued quarterly;
> Faculty of Advocates site at *http://www.advocates.org.uk* [accessed June 9, 2014], is the professional body for Scotland's advocates;
> The Society of Solicitor Advocates, at *http://www.solicitoradvocates.org/* [accessed June 9, 2014], was formed in 1990 and represents the interests of Scottish Solicitor Advocates;
> Scottish Paralegal Association, at *http://www.scottish-paralegal.org.uk/* [accessed June 9, 2014], represents the interests of Scottish paralegal practitioners;
> Society of Specialist Paralegals, at *http://www.specialistparalegals.co.uk/* [accessed June 9, 2014], is a UK wide organisation.

Information about Scottish Courts

The Scottish Courts website, at *http://www.scotcourts.gov.uk* [accessed June 9, 2014], provides **8–161** an abundance of useful information about the operation of the Scottish courts. As well as publishing opinions from the Court of Session, High Court of Justiciary and the Sheriff court, the site contains links to Rules of Court for the various courts and rules governing different types of legal actions. It also contains practice notes for the Court of Session, High Court of Justiciary and sheriff court.

Further, information for practitioners, such as the Rolls of Court (schedule of daily business) **8–162** for the Court of Session, High Court of Justiciary (both Trial and Appeal) and the sheriff courts, is also listed. The "Coming to Court" tab links to practical information for members of the public attending the courts (jurors, witnesses, victims of crime). Individual courts can then be located where the following information is available:

> ➤ Contact details—telephone numbers and addresses;
> ➤ How to get there—public transport and parking information;
> ➤ Customer information—what to do on arrival, who to report to, what to expect;
> ➤ Local facilities—e.g. disabled access to the court house, refreshments available on site or locally;
> ➤ Court opening times and local holidays;
> ➤ Local notices and public information;
> ➤ Searchable Daily Court Lists which are available online for 10 business days thereafter;
> ➤ Local street map; and
> ➤ Court photograph.

Styles books

8–163 There are many bespoke publications which provide styles for various documents commonly used by solicitors. These books are referred to as styles in Scotland and "precedents" in England. The initial styles book for general use, the *Scots Style Book*, was published between 1902–1905 and ran to seven volumes with an eighth volume of sheriff court styles appearing in 1911, largely compiled from earlier volumes. The styles were arranged in alphabetical order according to subject. In 1935, the 10 volume *Encyclopaedia of Legal Styles* was published. Again, the styles were arranged alphabetically according to subject. These works are now largely of historical interest. Examples of contemporary styles publications are:

> ➤ S.A. Bennett, *Style Writs for the Sheriff Court*, 4th edn (Edinburgh: Barnestoneworth, 2009);
> ➤ Green's *Litigation Styles* series published by Sweet and Maxwell (Edinburgh), which is a two volume loose-leaf compendium for use in the Court of Session and the sheriff court most recently published in June 2014. Green's *Styles* are regularly updated and includes a CD containing styles which can be downloaded. W. Green also publishes *Practice Styles*. This is also a two volume loose-leaf publication with a CD. It covers the following areas: agriculture and crafting; commerce, commercial conveyancing; domestic conveyancing; executry; family law; intellectual property; moveable property; trusts and wills.
> ➤ *Express Wills for Scotland* CD-ROM is also published by W. Green. This resource generates personalised wills automatically from a styles bank when instructions from an individual client are received and run through an interactive series of options. The ensuing will can then be edited and printed for final approval from the client.

Chapter 9

Selected UK Primary Sources of Law which Exclude Scots Law in Whole or Part

---

Significant abbreviations used in this chapter

- A.C.—Appeal Cases
- All ER—All England Law Reports
- Ch.—Chancery Division
- EU—European Union
- Fam.—Family Division
- Q.B.—Queen's Bench
- SI—Statutory Instrument
- W.L.R.—Weekly Law Reports

This chapter looks at selected UK primary sources of law which exclude Scots law, either wholly **9–01** or in part. The sources referred to have been selected as they are (i) generally accessible to the Scots-based researcher and (ii) good sources of persuasive authority. The principal series of English law reports are discussed as are further sources to locate recent English cases. The chapter also considers the merits of the major English legal encyclopaedia *Halsbury's Laws of England*.

LexisNexis ⏚ Subscription Database

The LexisNexis legal database excludes exclusively Scottish legislation from the Westminster **9–02** Parliament, although it does include a selection of Scottish law reports. Its "UK Parliament Acts" tab links to the revised form of all Acts of the Westminster Parliament relating to England and Wales from 1266 onwards that are currently in force. Public General Acts that are no longer in force do not appear in full text. However, if the Act ceased to have effect on or after January 1, 1999, a note explains why the enactment no longer applies. Acts that were made by the Westminster Parliament and apply to Scotland only are not included, although provisions of Scottish Acts that apply or are relevant to England and/or Wales are included. There is a separate tab which links to "Scottish Parliament Acts". This resource contains the revised form of Acts of the Scottish Parliament at Holyrood from 1999 to the present day. "UK (Westmister) Parliament Statutory Instruments" ("SI") contains the revised form of UK SIs, but does not include provisions that extend exclusively to Scotland. "Scottish Parliament SI" contains the revised form of Scottish SIs from 1999 onwards.

LexisNexis also offers access to Halsbury's Statute Citator which provides details of the current **9–03** status of statutes included in the Halsbury's Statutes series and Halsbury's SI Citator which does likewise for SI covered in the Halsbury's SI series.

Searching LexisNexis

Searching for an Act of Parliament

9–04   Choose the legislation tab from the homepage. This opens up the legislation search form. Select UK Parliament Acts from the Select Sources drop-down list. Go to the type field and select Statute from the drop-down list. If the name of the Act is unknown enter words or phrases in the enter search terms box. Boolean connectors to show the relationship of the terms (see paras 2–58—2–59) can also be used. If the title or part of the title is known, enter search terms in the legislation title field, giving the year if known. If only part of the title is entered, use Boolean connectors to link the search terms. If a particular section is sought, enter the number in the provision field prior to clicking on search.

Searching for a SI

9–05   Select the legislation tab from the homepage. This opens up the legislation search form. Then select UK Parliament SI from the Select Sources drop-down list. Go to the type field and select SI from the drop-down list. If the name of the SI is unknown, enter words or phrases in the enter search terms box. Use Boolean connectors to show the relation of the terms. If the SI number is known, enter the year in the legislation title field and the series number in the series number field. If the title or part of the title is known, enter search terms in the legislation title field, giving the year if known. If only part of the title is known, use Boolean connectors to link the search terms. Then click search.

LEGISLATION

Halsbury's Statutes of England and Wales 📖
9–06   This work is a collection of statutes which are arranged in broad subject headings. It consists of 50 volumes along with an updating service which has three parts: Cumulative Supplement, a Noter-up and Current Statutes Service. It contains statutes which relate to England and Wales or to the UK as a whole. Sections of UK statutes which relate to Scotland only are not included and statutes which relate only to Scotland are not included.

9–07   The full text of each statute is given along with annotations which clarify the legislation and refer to relevant case law. The text of the statute incorporates subsequent amendments (it is not, as in the Current Law Statutes, the original version). From 1993 onwards reference to West-minster Parliamentary debates is given. The volumes are arranged in alphabetical order, Vol.1 starts with Agriculture and Vol.59 ends with Wills. The volumes are re-issued periodically. At the start of each volume a statement is given that the publication represents the law up to a certain date. This statement must be viewed each time a volume is consulted with recourse then made to the updating service to check for any amendments made since the date given in the relevant volume. If other sources are available, e.g. Westlaw, these should also be consulted to ensure the search is as up to date as possible.

9–08   Each bound volume conforms to the following format:

> ➢   A list of headings in all the volumes;
> ➢   A table of contents for this volume;
> ➢   References and abbreviations;
> ➢   A table of statutes covering all the statutes printed in the volume in both alphabetical and chronological order;

> ➢ A table of SIs in alphabetical order; and
> ➢ A table of cases.

Within each subject heading there is:

> ➢ A table of contents;
> ➢ Cross references. These indicates where material has been categorised under a different heading and is therefore contained in a different volume;
> ➢ A preliminary note. This explains the legislative background to the subject area; and
> ➢ Annotated and amended versions of legislation.

At the end of each volume there is a subject index.

In addition to the volumes, there is the Current Statutes Service which is contained in loose-leaf **9–09** binders. The service includes the text of Acts passed since January 1, 1985, other than those included in the published volumes. It is arranged by volume number and subject.

The Current Statutes service consists of: **9–10**

> ➢ An Annual Cumulative Supplement. This publication records change which affect the published volumes. It is arranged by volume, subject and page order in the same way as the bound volumes. Updating material relating to Acts in the Current Statutes Service is given at the end of material for the corresponding volume title and is indicated thus, "S", following the volume number at the top of the page; and
> ➢ Noter-up. This records the effect of changes in the material in the volumes and Current Service Binders which have occurred since the publication of the last cumulative supplement. It is arranged by subject in the same way as the volumes and Cumulative Supplement. Again, the letter "S" indicates that the legislation is contained in one of the Current Service Binders. The Noter-up also contains an update for the publication *Is It in Force?* (see below). The Noter-up is updated four times a year.

Is It in Force? 📖
Halsbury's Statutes includes a bi-annual publication *Is it in Force?* This contains the com- **9–11** mencement dates of Acts of general application to England, Wales and Scotland passed since January 1 1980. Acts are listed in alphabetical order in the year in which they were passed. The publication also contains a Table of Statutes Not Yet in Force, which lists provisions of Acts passed prior to the three decades for which no commencement dates have yet been made.

Is it in Force? LexisNexis 🖱 subscription service
The online version of *Is It in Force?* is updated daily and contains links to the relevant com- **9–12** mencement orders.

Halsbury's Statutes also includes the following paperback volumes: **9–13**

> ➢ *Statutes Citator.* Part 1 contains an alphabetical list of statutes published in Halsbury's Statutes. It does not include statutes repealed before 1929. Part 2 shows the current status of these statutes and is arranged chronologically and then alphabetically within each year;
> ➢ *Consolidated Index.* This annual publication contains alphabetical and chronological lists of all statutes contained in Halsbury's Statutes and guides the researcher to specific statutes in the main volumes. It also contains a consolidated index to the current

volumes and Current Statutes Service up to 2006. Volumes published subsequently are covered by their own indexes;

➢ *Consolidated Table of SIs*. This is a guide to secondary legislation which has been made or has effect under any Act in Halsbury's Statutes;

➢ *Consolidated Table of Cases*. This contains both an alphabetical list of cases that appear in Halsbury's Statutes and a listing of the cases under the statutes to which they relate. Volumes reissued after June 1, 2006 are covered by their own Tables of Cases; and

➢ *Destination Tables*. These cover all Consolidation Acts passed between 1957 to the present date and are published periodically.

9–14 *How to Use Halsbury's Statutes*

Consolidated Index
↓
Relevant volume (begin here if the subject area is known)
↓
Update by checking the Cumulative Supplement
↓
Update by checking the Noter-up

9–15 The search is being undertaken to yield information on offences/cruelty to badgers.

↳ Browse either the spines of the hardback volumes which list the subject headings contained in each volume or look in the Consolidated Index. This will allow access under several different routes. In the above example the following information was gleaned under the Index heading "badgers";

↳ Entry: cruelty to, offences of, 2 590

• Use the numerical reference to locate the information. 2 590 means Vol.2 p.590;

↳ This leads to the text of the Protection of Badgers Act 1992 (c.51), s.2 is headed "Cruelty";

↳ Check whether this information is still current. To do so check the beginning of the volume for a reference to a date. On one of the first pages will be a statement: "This volume states the law as at ...". To update the information given in the volume go to the Cumulative Supplement. This provides updated information from the date of the bound volume to the date of the Cumulative Supplement, e.g. turn to the entry for Vol.2, Animals. In this section any changes appear in the page order of Vol.2. The original reference was to p.590. If the entry in the Cumulative Supplement does not refer to this page number then no amendments have been made to s.2 at the time of publication.

↳ In order to check for any subsequent developments consult the Noter-up. Turn to the entry for Vol.2, Animals. Check at the end of the section for Vol.2. If there is no mention of s.2 it can be presumed no amendments have been made unless any change is very recent. For the sake of completeness and accuracy consult a legal database, e.g. LexisNexis, that is updated on a daily basis.

Halsbury's SI 📖

9–16 This service provides information about every SI of general application in England and Wales. It does not include provisions that extend exclusively to Scotland. It does not reproduce every SI in full text. Those which are regarded as of little general importance are summarised.

Halsbury's SI consists of several volumes (28 at the time of writing) which are arranged by **9–17** subject in a similar format to Halsbury's Statutes and Halsbury's Laws. Volume 1 commences with a section about SIs. The rest of the work is alphabetical by subject, from agriculture to wills. At the beginning of each volume is the date at which the law is stated in that volume. If seeking an SI on a specific subject go to the relevant volume, e.g. Vol.9 for health and safety. Alternatively, if unsure of the relevant subject heading, check the detailed subject index in the separate paperback Consolidated Index. This will direct the reader to the relevant volume. Turn to the health and safety section. It has a table, referred to as an "arrangement" showing contents of the section. If the section concerned is large it is split into parts. A list of cross-references is provided to enable the reader to see where material has been categorised under a different subject heading, e.g. slaughterhouses are dealt with under the separate headings "animals" and "food".

A preliminary note explains the legislative background to the subject area. This is followed by **9–18** cross-references to Halsbury's Statutes. The next part of the volume contains a chronological list of SIs. This shows instruments in the subject area. It lists: year and number of the instrument; full title; remarks indicating if it is an amending instrument; and a reference to a page number where the instrument is either printed in full or summarised.

There is also a Table of Instruments No Longer in Operation. This lists instruments which have **9–19** ceased to have effect since the last re-issue of the volume.

The texts of the SI are printed in amended form. Where amendments have been printed the **9–20** added or substituted words appear in square brackets. Omissions are indicated by three dots. Each volume has a subject index at the end.

The service is kept up-to-date by re-issuing the volumes periodically. Between re-issues it is **9–21** updated on a monthly basis through the Service. This is a loose-leaf work that consists of two binders. Binder 1 contains the following information:

- ➤ A chronological list of all SIs in the main volumes and in the Service and the subject heading under which they can be found;
- ➤ A Table of Statutes which lists all the enabling legislation under which SIs in Halsbury's SI;
- ➤ An Annual Cumulative Supplement. This updates the bound volumes and contains changes made since they were published. It contains a chronological list of new instruments, table of instruments no longer in operation, a noter-up to pages of the main volumes and summaries of new instruments;
- ➤ Monthly Survey. This contains updates subsequent to the last Annual Cumulative Supplement. It is divided into two sections: summaries of SIs which are arranged numerically and a key which relates the numbers to subject headings.

There is a separate paperback Annual Consolidated Index and Alphabetical List of SIs which is published on an annual basis. This contains a consolidated version of all the subject indexes to the current volumes. It also covers information in the current Annual Supplement. This means that the Consolidated Index is never more than a year out of date. The Alphabetical List contains references to all SI which are included in the Service in alphabetical order. This is very useful if seeking the number for a SI when only the title is known.

The ways in which SI can be located are as follows: **9–22**

➢ Subject matter:

- Start at either the Annual Consolidated Index or the volume subject index
  ↓
  relevant volume and page reference
  ↓
  update by using Annual Cumulative Supplement and the Monthly Survey.

➢ Number:

- Start by looking at the chronological list in Binder 1 of the Service. This lists all SIs in Halsbury's SI. This will provide the relevant heading;
- Turn to the relevant volume. Check the chronological list in this volume. This will lead to the SI. If the instrument is very recent, check the Monthly Survey and the additional texts in Binder 2.

➢ Title:

- Consult the Alphabetical List of SIs. This will indicate the number of the instrument and the relevant subject heading. The bound volume can then be consulted and the SI located by checking the chronological list at the beginning of the subject area.

➢ Enabling power:

- To find out if any SIs have been made under an Act, check the Table of Statutes in Binder 1. This lists all the enabling powers under which the instruments included in Halsbury's SI have been made. It also references the appropriate subject heading. This allows the reader to access the SIs (if any) in the bound volumes.

LAW REPORTS

9–23 In England and Wales, the law reports are the most authoritative series of law reports. Publication has traditionally tended to be slow and weekly law reports appeared to fill in the gap. The two most widely used weekly series are the Weekly Law Reports (W.L.R.) and the All England Law Reports (All E.R.).

9–24 A system of media neutral citation was introduced from January 11, 2001. This means that judgments deriving from the High Court (all divisions), the Court of Appeal (civil and criminal divisions), the Supreme Court, (previously the House of Lords) and the Privy Council have been issued with unique judgment numbers. Cases are referenced to case number and paragraph number (instead of page number). This system means that case references are completely independent of published reports. The reason it has been adopted is to make it easier to cite and trace unreported judgments.

9–25 Examples of numbering of post-January 11, 2001 judgments:

➢ Court of Appeal (Civil Division) [2012] EWCA Civ 185;
➢ Court of Appeal (Criminal Division) [2014] EWCA Crim 53;
➢ High Court (Administrative Court) [2013] EWHC 249 (Admin) (pre-January 12, 2002) (From January 12, 2002, all High Court judgments were provided with a media neutral citation by virtue of the allocation of a unique number from a central register. This applies to: Administrative Court, Admiralty Chancery Division, Commercial Court,

Family Division, Patents Court, Queen's Bench Division, Technology and Construction Court. After this date, no suffix was added after the EWHC abbreviation as the numbering is sequential. However, the Admin suffix was retained for legacy material, i.e. judgments delivered between January 11, 2001 and January 12, 2002);

➢ House of Lords [2001] UKHL 6;
➢ Supreme Court [2014] UKSC 9;
➢ Privy Council [2014] UKPC 1.

Each of these unique judgment numbers represents a case number allocated by the court, and must appear as the first in any string of citations, e.g. para.15 in *Charnock & Ors v Rowan & Ors*, the second numbered judgment of the year in the Civil Division of the England and Wales Court of Appeal and the second reported case in Civ. in 2012, would be cited: *Charnock & Ors v Rowan & Ors* [2012] EWCA Civ 2 at [15].

The Law Reports 📖
This series started in 1865 and is published by the ICLR. It is the most authoritative series of **9–26** English law reports and should be cited in preference to other reports where there is a choice. The judge is given the opportunity to check the text before publication. They are also the only reports to include a summary of the argument of counsel. It was originally published in several different series but is now published in four series:

➢ Appeal Cases (A.C.);
➢ Queen's Bench (Q.B.) (this becomes King's Bench if a king is on the throne);
➢ Chancery Division (Ch.);
➢ Family Division (Fam.)

All these different parts usually appear together under "L" for Law Reports in a law library.

The Law Reports cover cases heard in: **9–27**

➢ Supreme Court (previously the House of Lords);
➢ Privy Council;
➢ The Court of Appeal (Criminal and Civil Divisions);
➢ Chancery Division;
➢ Family Division;
➢ Employment Appeal Tribunal; and
➢ Court of Justice of the EU.

The Law Reports 🖱 subscription
Electronic versions of the Law Reports are available on three subscription online databases: **9–28** LexisNexis, Justis and Westlaw.

The Law Reports Index 📖
The Law Reports Index provides a continuous indexing system from 1951 to date. This includes **9–29** all significant cases reported in: Law Reports; Weekly Law Reports; and Industrial Case Reports. It also includes references to cases reported in: All England Commercial Cases; All England European Cases; All England Law Reports; Criminal Appeal Reports; Lloyd's Law Reports; Local Government Reports; Road Traffic Reports; Tax Cases; and Simon's Tax Cases.

There are currently seven volumes. They are referred to as the "Red Indexes". The six volumes **9–30** are: 1951–60, 1961–70, 1971–80, 1981–90, 1991–00, 2001–05, 2006–10. Subsequent decisions are listed in supplements known as the "Pink Book". Supplements are published three times a year and are free if a subscription to the Weekly Law Reports is held.

Red Index
↓
Pink Index
↓
Weekly Law Reports

9–31 The Red Index consists of the following tables of information:

➢ Cases reported;
➢ Subject matter—includes 'Words and Phrases' as a heading;
➢ Cases judicially considered;
➢ Statutes judicially considered;
➢ SIs judicially considered;
➢ Standard forms of Contract judicially considered;
➢ EU enactments judicially considered;
➢ Overseas enactments judicially considered; and
➢ International Conventions judicially considered.

The Weekly Law Reports (W.L.R.) 📖
9–32 This series was first published in 1953. It is published 45 times a year. The law reports for each year are published in four volumes. Volumes 1a and 1b contain cases which do not merit inclusion in the Law Reports. Volume 2 (January–June) and Vol.3 (July–December) cover cases which will be subsequently published in the law reports.

9–33 The annual volumes contain the following information:

➢ List of judges;
➢ Cases—accessible by either party's name;
➢ Subject Matter Index which includes a 'Words and phrases' heading; and
➢ Case reports.

The Weekly parts contain the update of The Law Reports Index, namely:

➢ Cases judicially considered;
➢ Statutes judicially considered;
➢ SIs judicially considered;
➢ EU enactments judicially considered; and
➢ Overseas enactments judicially considered.

The Weekly Law Reports (W.L.R.) 💾 subscription
9–34 Electronic versions of the W.L.R. are available in Justis UK and Westlaw. Also see the W.L.R. Daily as detailed in para.9–32.

All England Law Reports (All ER) 📖
9–35 This series began in 1936. It is published 48 times a year in weekly parts. The annual volumes contain the following information:

➢ List of judges;

> ➤ Table of cases—accessible by either party's name;
> ➤ Digest of cases accessible via subject matter; and
> ➤ Supreme Court Petitions—details of the results of any petitions for leave to appeal.

The case reports contain references to *Halsbury's Laws of England*, Halsbury's Statutes of England and Wales and Halsbury's SI.

There are two sub-series: **9–36**

> ➤ All England Commercial Cases 1999–present. This series is published in the same format as the general series, but contains cases of interest to lawyers who specialise in commercial law; and
> ➤ All England European Cases 1995–present. This series contains judgments with headnotes and words of reference from the Court of Justice of the EU and the General Court.

There are three volumes of Consolidated Tables and Index covering the period 1936–2013. These include Commercial Cases and European Cases. Volume 1 contains:

> ➤ A table of cases reported and judicially considered;
> ➤ A table of practice directions and notes;
> ➤ A table of statutes judicially considered; and
> ➤ A table of words and phrases judicially considered.

Volumes 2 and 3 contain a subject index which provides the names and references of a case pertaining to a specific topic.

All England Law Reports (All ER) ⌁ subscription
The electronic version of the All ER, All England Commercial Cases and All England EU Cases   **9–37**
is available in LexisNexis.

The Times Law Reports 📖
The Times Law Reports were published from 1884 until 1952, when the W. L.R. started   **9–38**
publication. The early reports were based on those published in *The Times* newspaper, while later reports provided transcripts of the judgments. These were published in annual volumes.

The Times newspaper still publishes law reports. However, these only comprise summaries of   **9–39**
cases. To access *The Times* online a subscription is required.

Since 1990, The Times Law Reports in their current format have also been published in annual   **9–40**
volumes. In addition to the reports, the volumes contain:

> ➤ A cumulative table of cases reported;
> ➤ A cumulative table of cases referred to;
> ➤ A cumulative table of legislation; and
> ➤ A cumulative subject index.

The Times Law Reports ⌁ subscription
Online versions of the Times Law Reports are available from Justis (1990 onwards) and Lex-   **9–41**
isNexis (1988 onwards).

The Digest (formerly The English & Empire Digest) 📖

9–42 *The Digest* provides access to case law from multi jurisdictions from the 16th century to the present day. Jurisdictions include: England and Wales; Scotland (selected cases); Ireland; Canada; Australia; New Zealand; and other Commonwealth countries. The current edition consists of 52 main volumes organised by subject. The volumes contain annotated summaries of over half a million cases. *The Digest* is generally considered to be the most widely available source of information about Scottish cases digested in England.

9–43 *The Digest* is a sister publication to *Halsbury's Laws* and enjoys a similar format. Cross-references are given to Halsbury's Statutes and Halsbury's Laws. It is updated by re-issued volumes, an Annual Cumulative Supplement and a Quarterly Survey of recent developments. In order to facilitate searching there are Consolidated Tables of Cases and a two volume Consolidated (Subject) Index.

SOURCES OF RECENT ENGLISH CASES

BAILII ⌐ free
9–44 The BAILII site, as detailed in previous chapters, is a free and full text searchable database. It is updated on a daily basis.

UK Supreme Court website ⌐ free
9–45 This website is updated on a daily basis. Judgments are also available on BAILLI.

Judgments of the Privy Council ⌐ free
9–46 All judgments of the Privy Council from 1996 onwards along with some selected earlier judgments are available, at *http://jcpc.uk/decided-cases/index.html* [accessed June 10, 2014]. Judgments are also available on BAILLI.

The Register of Judgments, Orders and Fines ⌐ search fee payable
9–47 The Register of Judgments, Orders and Fines is a statutory public register operated by a not-for-profit company on behalf of the UK Parliament Ministry for Justice per England and Wales. Registers for Scotland, Northern Ireland, Ireland, Jersey and the Isle of Man are also held at *http://www.trustonline.org.uk/* [accessed June 24, 2014]

9–48 The Register for England and Wales can be searched under the following headings:

> ➢ County Court Judgments, Administration Orders and Child Support Agency Orders;
> ➢ High Court Judgments;
> ➢ Magistrates Courts Fines Defaults; and
> ➢ Tribunal Awards.

For the other jurisdictions, the undernoted judgments are recorded:

> ➢ Scotland—Small claims and summary cause decrees;
> ➢ Northern Ireland—Small claims judgments and undefended actions;
> ➢ Ireland—Money judgments from circuit and district courts;
> ➢ Isle of Man—Default money judgments;
> ➢ Jersey—Money judgments from the Petty Debts and Royal Court.

The Weekly Law Reports (W.L.R.) Daily ⌐₰ free

This resource provides a free case summary service from the ICLR. The cases reported are cases **9–49** deemed to be worthy of inclusion in the W.L.R., the Law Reports or the Industrial Cases Reports. Summaries of recently decided cases, which appear within 24 hours of the judgment being handed down, can be searched via the homepage.

Daily Cases ⌐₰ subscription

Daily Cases is provided by Justis. It is a fully searchable database incorporating the W.L.R. (see **9–50** above). It includes judgments, since 1999 of the Supreme Court (House of Lords), the Privy Council, the Court of Appeal, all Divisions of the High Court, the Courts-Martial Appeal Court, the Restrictive Practices Court, the Employment Appeal Tribunal and the Court of Justice of the EU. Only cases that develop or clarify a point of law or that set legal precedent are included. Practice Directions, Practice Notes and Practice Statements are also covered. The database is updated most working days.

HALSBURY'S LAWS OF ENGLAND 📖

As detailed in various chapters, this encyclopaedia is the foremost compendium of English law **9–51** and is the English equivalent of *The Laws of Scotland: Stair Memorial Encyclopaedia*. However, *Halsbury's Laws* has been in existence for far longer than its Scottish counterpart and is widely regarded as the best starting point when undertaking research on a UK-wide or English legal problem. This publication does not contain primary material; rather it provides a commentary on the law of England from the scholarly viewpoint of experts, ranging from the academic to the practitioner. The current edition (5th edn) consists of over 80 main volumes which are kept up-to-date by the re-issue of individual volumes, as and when required. In addition, there is an annual Cumulative Supplement (two volumes) and monthly Current Service binders. A volume summarising legal developments in the previous 12 months is also published each May.

> **NB** This work is to be distinguished from Halsbury's Statutes which contains annotated versions of the text of Acts of Parliament only.
> *Halsbury's Laws* does not include exclusively Scottish material.

Component parts of Halsbury's Laws

Individual volumes

References used to locate materials throughout are to volume and paragraph number.   **9–52**

The following information is given at the beginning of each volume: **9–53**

- ➢ The date at which the law is stated;
- ➢ Table of contents;
- ➢ Table of references and abbreviations;
- ➢ Table of statutes;
- ➢ Table of SIs; and
- ➢ Table of cases.

At the end of each volume there is a detailed index for each subject covered by that volume and a words and phrases index. This lists words and phrases which have been explained or defined in the volume.

Annual Cumulative Supplement

9–54 The two-volume Annual Cumulative Supplement brings the work up-to-date to within a year. It provides an account of the changes which have taken place since publication of the bound volumes. Each annual Cumulative Supplement supersedes the previous supplement thus the researcher must ensure that they are consulting the most recent edition. The Cumulative Supplement is arranged in the same way as the volumes.

The Current Service

9–55 This resource is contained in two loose-leaf binders and updated monthly to give details of developments in the law which have taken place since the date of the last Cumulative Supplement. Binder 1 contains the following information:

> ➤ The Monthly Review. This is published in a journal format. Its prime function is to update *Halsbury's Laws*. However, it can also be consulted if information on a specific and known recent developments is sought;
> ➤ Tables of cases (includes a quantum of damages table), statutes and SIs; and
> ➤ A cumulative index to the Monthly Reviews. This cross-references the Reviews to the bound volumes and the Cumulative Supplement.

Binder 2 contains the following information:

> ➤ Commencement of Statutes Table. This lists statutes which were not in force (wholly or partially) when the latest Cumulative Supplement was published. It specifies commencement dates for statutes or states "no date" as appropriate;
> ➤ Destination Tables for Consolidation Acts;
> ➤ Personal Injury Section which includes various model letters;
> ➤ Practice Directions relating to the English courts;
> ➤ Table of Articles which relates recent articles to the Halsbury subject headings;
> ➤ Words and Phrases Judicially Interpreted;
> ➤ EU materials; and
> ➤ Noter-up. This sets out the latest developments in the same format as the Cumulative Supplement.

The Annual Abridgement

9–56 The Annual Abridgement has been published annually since 1974. The Monthly Review contains summaries of cases and legislation which, for reasons of space, are not included in the Cumulative Supplement which only contains details of the effects of these developments on the previous law. The summaries of the cases and legislation are consolidated from the Monthly Reviews into an Abridgement volume.

Consolidated Tables of Statutes, etc.

9–57 These volumes contain:

> ➤ Consolidated Tables of statutes;
> ➤ SIs;
> ➤ Procedural materials;
> ➤ EU materials;
> ➤ Treaties and Conventions;
> ➤ Non-statutory rules and regulations; and

> ➢ Codes of Practice and reports. These list the piece of legislation and the relevant reference for it in *Halsbury's Laws*. This enables the researcher to access same if the title of a piece of legislation is known but the correct subject area is not.

Consolidated Table of Cases

These volumes lists all the cases (including cases from the Court of Justice of the EU) referred to in *Halsbury's Laws* in alphabetical order of claimant (previously referred to as plaintiff). This allows *Halsbury's Laws* to be searched swiftly if only the name of a case is known. There is also a chronological table of EU cases.   **9–58**

Consolidated Index Volume

This resource provides a detailed subject index and a Table of Words and Phrases which includes words which are defined or explained in *Halsbury's Laws,* e.g. if the purpose of the search is to extract information as to whether "marine pollution" has been judicially defined, consult the Table of Words and Phrases under "M". There the following entry is given: "marine" (pollution) 43(1), 39n1.   **9–59**

Turn to Vol.43(1), para.39 and note 1 to locate information about discussion of the definition of "marine pollution".   **9–60**

NB Information in the volumes may quickly become out-of-date so the date of publication of a volume must always be confirmed. Binder 1 of the Current Service will provide contemporary information with regard to any changes.

Using Halsbury's Laws   **9–61**

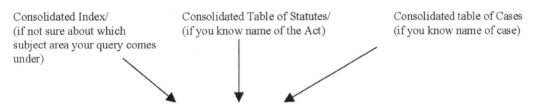

Consolidated Index/ (if not sure about which subject area your query comes under)

Consolidated Table of Statutes/ (if you know name of the Act)

Consolidated table of Cases (if you know name of case)

Relevant volume (you could start here if you know the subject area)

Cumulative Supplement ⟶ Annual Abridgment for more detail of developments in Cumulative Supplement

Noter-Up ⟶ Index to Monthly Review

Monthly Reviews for more detail of developments in the Noter-Up

Halsbury's Laws of England ◷ subscription

9–62 *Halsbury's Laws of England* are also available online as part of the LexisNexis legal database. From the home page select Commentary from the tab along the top of the homepage. This opens up the Commentary search page. Click on the downward arrow beside the Select Source box and click on *Halsbury's Laws*. Then use the enter search terms box to carry out a free text search. This will search the whole encyclopaedia. Alternatively, select browse on the Commentary search page where *Halsbury's Laws* is listed. Click on *Halsbury's Laws* then browse an alphabetical list of the subject headings used in the paper version. There, either go straight to a subject or tick one or more subjects and then enter the search terms in to the quick search box or return to the commentary search box where the search will be restricted to the chosen subject areas. The text from the original paper volume will appear on the screen with any monthly updates appearing at the end of the main text.

Chapter 10
European Union Law

Significant abbreviations used in this chapter

- COM-Official publication of the European Commission
- CMLR-Common Market Law Reports
- ECLAS-European Commission Library Catalogue
- E.C.R.-European Court Reports
- EDC-European Documentation Centres
- EU-European Union
- EC-European Community
- EEC-European Economic Community
- LJI-Legal Journals Index (Westlaw)
- MEP-Member of the European Parliament
- O.J.-Official Journal of the European Union
- SI-Statutory Instrument

INTRODUCTION

EU law is an integral and major source of Scots and UK law. Whilst figures vary, commentators **10–01** agree that the majority of Acts and SIs passed by both the Westminster and Holyrood Parliaments only require to be legislated for to enact the United Kingdom's obligations as a member state of the EU. (Daniel Hannen, a UK member of the European Parliament speaking on the BBC current affairs programme "Question Time" in May 2009, suggested that the figure is 84 percent, whereas the EU Commission Vice-President Viviane Reding, when delivering the Mackenzie-Stewart annual lecture at the University of Cambridge's Faculty of Law on February 17, 2014, suggests the figure is 70 percent, see *http://www.theguardian.com/world/2014/feb/17/eurozone-countries-united-states-europe-viviane-reding* [accessed June 10, 2014]). Whatever the actual percentage, it is a significant one, therefore it is essential that the Scots legal researcher cultivates a sound and rounded understanding of the primary and secondary sources of EU law, where to locate them and how these instruments impact on domestic law making.

Whilst this chapter does not provide an exhaustive overview of the EU institutions involved in **10–02** the EU law-making process (many dedicated EU texts do this admirably), it does discuss key features of the EU institutions, the EU legal system and legislative provisions, texts and other documents of relevance to undergraduate and post-graduate students and practitioners who wish to update their knowledge of this dynamic area of law. Alternative search strategies, which can be employed to locate both official and unofficial materials, are also the subject of scrutiny.

The researcher new to EU law will initially likely be impressed by the breadth and volume of **10–03** official publications freely available online from databases hosted by EU institutions and the

241

ease with which they can be searched when compared with official electronic sources in the UK which tend to require a more precise search strategy at the outset. However, as ever, an abundance of anything may, in turn, begat problems. In particular the following factors can be the cause of frustration:

> The sheer volume of material emerging from EU institutions may hamper a search if details of a specific document or documents are incomplete;
> The time delay in publication of some key sources; and
> The bespoke terminology used for indexing systems of primary and secondary sources of law.

Terminology

10–04 One further cause of (initial) confusion may be the legal significance between and the meaning of the acronyms EEC, EC, EU and the terms "Community law" and "Union law", all of which have to be briefly considered in their historical context as they refer to different and progressive periods of development of the "European Project".

10–05 "EEC" is the abbreviated form for the "European Economic Community", which refers to the agreement reached by the six founding member states to create, inter alia, a common trading market through economic integration. This agreement culminated in the founding Treaty, the Treaty of Rome 1957. This document has been amended many times in the intervening years and the number of member states has increased incrementally from the original six to 28, with Croatia becoming the most recent member on July 1, 2013.

10–06 The Treaty on European Union (the Maastricht Treaty) which came into force in November 1993 renamed the EEC the European Community ("EC") and established the European Union ("EU").

10–07 The EU originally consisted of three distinct "pillars". The first pillar was the "EC" pillar which was governed by EC institutions and community law. The other pillars, Common Foreign and Security Policy and Co-operation in Justice and Home Affairs were not subject to the jurisdiction of the institutions and functioned by way of voluntary intergovernmental co-operation between some member states. On December 1, 2009 the Treaty of Lisbon entered into force at which point the pillar structured was dismantled, with the powers and remit of all three, in most instances, consolidated in a single EU entity subject to the jurisdiction of the institutions and the Court of Justice of the EU (previously called the European Court of Justice). The EU is based on the rule of law (see *http://europa.eu/about-eu/basic-information/decision-making/treaties/index_en.htm* [accessed June 12, 2014]).

Executive and legislative EU institutions

10–08 Since the inception of the EEC in 1957, three principal institutions have held executive and legislative powers and their remit and functions are detailed below:

> *The Council of the EU* comprises elected representatives of the domestic governments of all member states and is the body, in common with the European Parliament, involved in enacting the vast majority of EU legislation. It meets on a regular, ad-hoc basis with the relevant domestic government minister from each member state in attendance, depending on the subject matter under discussion, e.g. if the common fisheries policy is under scrutiny, the minister within whose remit fishing and fish stock conservation falls or his/her representative will attend, curiously even if a member state is land-locked

with no fishing fleet. For further information on the work undertaken by the Council of the EU see, *http://europa.eu/about-eu/institutions-bodies/european-council/index_en.htm* [accessed June 11, 2014];

➢ *The European Parliament* is elected every five years by voters in all member states who vote for a political party or individual of choice on a regional basis. Currently, Scotland is designated a region and returns six Members of the European Parliament ("MEPs"). The European Parliament shares certain legislative powers with the Council. For further information see, *http://europa.eu/about-eu/institutions-bodies/european-parliament/index_en.htm* [accessed June 11, 2014];

➢ *The European Commission* is the executive branch of the EU and comprises 28 Commissioners, one from each Member State, with a term of office lasting five years. Individual Commissioners can be re-appointed at the expiry of their term of office. This body's primary function is to ensure the terms of the current EU Treaty is observed and initiate legal proceedings against any Member State in breach of any EU obligation. It also drafts legislative proposals which are subsequently approved or vetoed by the Council of the EU (and the European Parliament if it has legislative powers in the area concerned). In certain circumstances it can enact legislation (see para.10–11 below). For further information see, *http://europa.eu/about-eu/institutions-bodies/european-commission/index_en.htm*.

NB The fourth institution of relevance, the Court of Justice of the EU and its subordinate court, the General Court, are discussed at various points throughout this chapter.

EU LEGISLATION

As detailed in para.10–08 above, the "actors" involved in the EU legislative process are com- **10–09** pletely different from those of either the UK Parliament at Westminster or the Scottish Parliament at Holyrood. The types and format of EU legislation are also different (see paras 10–11 and 10–16 below).

The Treaty in force at any point in time is considered to be primary legislation. As it has been **10–10** agreed by all current member states, it provides the legislative base for any action taken on an EU basis. In essence, if the Treaty does not confer power on the EU to act and it did so, any provision made would be considered ultra vires, that is, beyond the powers of the Treaty. Accordingly, any such provision would be null and void and have no legal effect whatsoever. The Treaty comprises "Articles" rather than sections, e.g. art.16 of the part of the Treaty concerned with the functioning of the EU states the following:

1. Everyone has the right to the protection of personal data concerning them;
2. The European Parliament and the Council, acting in accordance with the ordinary legislative procedure, shall lay down the rules relating to the protection of individuals with regard to the processing of personal data by Union institutions, bodies, offices and agencies, and by the Member States when carrying out activities which fall within the scope of Union law, and the rules relating to the free movement of such data. Compliance with these rules shall be subject to the control of independent authorities.

Article 16 will provide the legal basis for any action taken in the sphere of the protection of personal data within the EU. To do this, the EU must enact a piece of secondary or delegated legislation.

10–11 There are three types of EU secondary legislation:

➤ **Regulations** are "directly applicable" EU instruments. This means that as soon as they have been enacted by the relevant institution(s) they become effective immediately in all Member States, i.e. the respective Member State Parliaments do not have to pass domestic legislation to bring them into effect within their legal system. Accordingly, they have instant binding legal effect in every Member State. Regulations can be enacted either jointly by the Council of the EU and European Parliament, or by the Commission to whom the Council has delegated legislative authority in specific circumstance.

An example of the latter is Commission Regulation (EU) No.1210/2011 of November 23 2011... to determine the volume of greenhouse gas emission allowances to be auctioned prior to 2013. The full text of this Regulation can be accessed here, *http://eur-lex.europa.eu/LexUriServ/LexUriServ.do?uri=OJ:L:2011:308:0002:0014:EN: PDF* [accessed June 11, 2014].

At the time of writing, there is a proposal for a Regulation of the European Parliament and Council on the protection of personal data (COM 2012 11). If it is duly passed by both of these bodies it will become the law in a member states on the day stipulated for it to come into force.

➤ **Directives**, unlike Regulations, only become effective in each member state after their respective Parliaments have passed some form of domestic legislation to bring them into force within their jurisdictions. Directives generally stipulate that each member state has up to two years to do so. Once this has been achieved, the Directive, via the domestic legislation concerned, is "transposed" and has binding legal effect in that jurisdiction.

An example of a recent Directive is Directive 2012/12/EU of the European Parliament and of the Council of April 19 2012 relating to fruit juices and certain similar products intended for human consumption. The full text of this Directive can be accessed here, *http://eur-lex.europa.eu/LexUriServ/LexUriServ.do?uri=OJ:L:2012: 115:0001:0011:EN:PDF* [accessed June 11, 2014].

Article 2 of this Directive requires member states to "adopt the laws, regulations and administrative provisions necessary to comply with this Directive before 28 October 2013."

The Westminster Parliament met the deadline for transposition by passing the Fruit Juices and Fruit Nectars (England) Regulations 2013 No.2775 on October 28, 2013, although they did not came into force until November 20, 2013. They Holyrood Parliament separately enacted the Fruit Juices and Fruit Nectars (Scotland) Regulations 2013 No.305 which also came into force on November 20, 2013.

➤ **Decisions** are neither directly applicable nor of binding legal effect on each member state. Rather, they apply (thus are fully binding) upon specific individuals or bodies within the EU when delivered. These instruments can be enacted by the EU Council/ Parliament or the Commission.

For an example of a recent decision, see the Commission Implementing Decision 2013/470/EU of September 20, 2013 as regards the animal health requirements relating to scrapie for trade in and imports into the Union of semen, ova and embryos of animals of the ovine and caprine species. The full text of this decision can be accessed here, *http://eur-lex.europa.eu/LexUriServ/LexUriServ.do?uri=OJ:L:2013:252:0032: 0050: EN:PDF* [accessed June 12, 2014].

Citation of EU legislation

Primary legislation

As detailed above, the EU Treaty in force at any point in time is the primary source of EU law. **10–12** The citation convention for Treaties is as published in the Official Journal of the European Union ("O.J."). The citation for the most recent consolidated version of the Treaty of Lisbon is O.J. C 83 of March 30, 2010. This can also be expressed thus, 2010/C 83/01 O.J.

The O.J. can be accessed here; http://eur-lex.europa.eu/oj/direct-access.html?locale = en **10–13** [accessed June 11, 2014].

The O.J. is, as its name suggests, the official publication of EU provisions. It is published daily **10–14** and comprises two related series, one for secondary legislative provisions, "L", the other for information and notices, "C", which includes Treaties and summaries of judgments of the Court of Justice. A supplement for public procurement "S" is published separately. See *http://publications.europa.eu/official/index_en.htm* [accessed June 11, 2014]. When citing EU provisions, individual institutional referencing conventions will most likely stipulate that the O.J. reference ought to be used in preference to any other form of citation.

Secondary legislation

The citation convention for secondary legislation comprises: **10–15**

> ➤ The institutional origin (Commission or Council or European Parliament and Council);
> ➤ The form (Regulation or Directive etc.);
> ➤ The number;
> ➤ The year of enactment; and
> ➤ Date passed.

NB Regulations are cited by their number first followed by the year whereas Directives and Decisions cite the year followed by the number. Hence—

> ➤ Commission Regulation (EU) No 1210/2011 of November 23 2011, to determine the volume of greenhouse gas emission allowances to be auctioned prior to 2013;
> ➤ Directive 2012/12/EU of the European Parliament and of the Council of April 19 2012, relating to fruit juices and certain similar products intended for human consumption; and
> ➤ Commission Implementing Decision 2013/470/EU of September 20, 2013, as regards the animal health requirements relating to scrapie for trade in and imports into the Union of semen, ova and embryos of animals of the ovine and caprine species.

ANATOMY OF A DIRECTIVE WITH ANNOTATIONS

The excerpt from this Directive "Council Directive 91/676/EEC of 12 December 1991 con- **10–16** cerning the protection of waters against pollution caused by nitrates from agricultural sources" which is still in force was enacted prior to the Treaty of Lisbon 2009 when the designation "EU" replaced "EEC" or "EC" in the citation (see para.10–04). It gives a comprehensive overview of the component parts of such instruments and, further, illustrates the longevity of some (now) EU instruments. It was transposed in the UK by the Protection of Water Against Agricultural

Nitrate Pollution (England and Wales) Regulations 1996 No.888 and the Protection of Water Against Nitrate Pollution (Scotland) Regulations 1996 No.1564, both of which are also still in force.

NB Regulations are produced in a similar format.

---

31. 12 91 [2] Official Journal of the European Communities [1] No L375/1

II

(Acts whose publication is not obligatory)

COUNCIL

COUNCIL DIRECTIVE

of 12 December 1991 [3]

concerning the protection of waters against pollution caused by nitrates from agricultural sources

(91/676/EEC) [4]

COUNCIL OF THE EUROPEAN COMMUNITIES
[5]

Having regard to the Treaty establishing the European Economic Community, and in particular Article 130s thereof, [6]

Having regard to the proposal from the Commission (¹)

Having regard to the opinion of the European Parliament (²)

Having regard to the opinion of the Economic and Social Committee (³), [7]

Whereas the nitrate content of water in some areas of Member States is increasing and is already high as compared with standards laid down in Council Directive 75/440/EEC of 16 June 1975 concerning, the quality required of surface water intended for the abstraction of drinking water in the Member States (⁴), as amended by Directive 79/869/EEC (⁵), and Council Directive 80/778/EEC of 15 July 1980 relating to the quality of Crater intended for human consumption (⁶), as amended by 1985 Act of Accession;

Whereas the fourth programme of action of the European Economic Communities on the environment (⁷) indicated that the Commission intended to make a proposal for a

Directive on the control and reduction of water pollution resulting from the spreading or discharge of livestock effluents and the excessive use of fertilizers; [8]

Whereas the reform of the common agricultural policy set out in the Commission's green paper 'Perspectives for the common agricultural policy' indicated that, while the use of nitrogen-containing fertilizers and manures is necessary for Community agriculture, excessive use of fertilizers constitutes an environmental risk, that common action is needed to control the problem arising from intensive livestock production and that agricultural policy must take greater account of environmental policy;

Whereas the Council resolution of 28 June 1988 of the protection of the North Sea and of other waters in the Community (⁸) invites the Commission to submit proposals for measures at Community level;

Whereas the main cause of pollution from diffuse sources affecting the Community's waters in nitrates from agricultural sources;

Whereas it is therefore necessary, in order to protect human health and living resources and aquatic ecosystems and to safeguard other legitimate uses of water, to reduce water pollution caused or induced by nitrates from agricultural sources and to prevent further such pollution; whereas for this purpose it is important to take measures

---

(¹) OJ No C 54, 3. 3. 1989, p. 4 and OJ No C 51, 2. 3. 1990, p. 12.
(²) OJ No C 158, 26. 6. 1989, p. 487.
(³) OJ No C 159, 26. 6. 1989, p. 1.
(⁴) OJ No L 194, 25. 7. 1975, p. 26.

(⁵) OJ No L 271, 29. 10. 1979, p. 44.
(⁶) No L 229, 30. 8. 1980, p. 11.
(⁷) OJ No C 328, 7. 12. 1987, p. 1.
(⁸) OJ No C 209, 9. 8. 1988, p. 3.

concerning the storage and the application on land of all nitrogen compounds and concerning certain land management practices;

Whereas since pollution of water due to nitrates on one Member State can influence waters in other Member States, action at Community level in accordance with Article 130r is therefore necessary;

Whereas, by encouraging good agricultural practices, Member States can provide all waters with a general level of protection against pollution in the future;

Whereas certain zones, draining into waters vulnerable to pollution from nitrogen compounds, require special protection;

Whereas it is necessary for Member States to identify vulnerable zones and to establish and implement action programmes in order to reduce water pollution from nitrogen compounds in vulnerable zones;

Whereas such action programmes should include measures to limit the land-application of all nitrogen-containing fertilizers and in particular to set specific limits for the application of livestock manure;

Whereas it is necessary to monitor waters and to apply reference methods of measurement for nitrogen compounds to ensure that measures are effective;

Whereas it is recognized that the hydrogeology in certain Member States is such that it may he many years before protection measures lead to improvements in water quality;

Whereas a Committee should be established to assist the Commission on matters relating to the implementation of this Directive and to its adaptation to scientific and technical progress;

Whereas Member States should establish and present to the Commission reports on the implementation of this Directive;

Whereas the Commission should report regularly on the implementation of this Directive by the Member States, HAS ADOPTED THIS DIRECTIVE: [9]

Article 1 [10]

This Directive has the objective of:

— reducing water pollution caused or induced by nitrates from agricultural sources; and
— preventing further such pollution.

Article 2

For the purpose of this Directive:

(a) 'groundwater': means all water which is below the surface of the ground in the saturation zone an direct contact with the ground or subsoil;

(b) 'freshwater': means naturally occurring water having a low concentration of salts, which is often acceptable as suitable for abstraction and treatment to produce drinking water;

(c) 'nitrogen compound': means any nitrogen-containing substance except for gaseous molecular nitrogen;

(d) 'livestock': means all animals kept for use or profit;

(e) 'fertilizer': means any substance containing a nitrogen compound or nitrogen compounds utilized on land to enhance growth of vegetation; it may include livestock manure, the residues from fish farms and sewage sludge;

(f) 'chemical fertilizer: means any fertilizer which is manufactured by an industrial process;

(g) 'livestock manure': means waste products excreted by livestock or a mixture of litter and waste products excreted by livestock, even in processed form;

(h) 'land application': means the addition of materials to land whether by spreading on the surface of the land, injection into the land, placing below the surface of the land or mixing with the surface layers of the land;

(i) 'eutrophication': means the enrichment of water by nitrogen compounds, causing an accelerated growth of algae and higher forms of plant life to produce an undesirable disturbance to the balance of organisms present in the water and to the quality of the water concerned;

(j) 'pollution': means the discharge, directly or indirectly, or nitrogen compounds from agricultural sources into the aquatic environment, the results of which are such as to cause hazards to human health, harm to living resources and to aquatic ecosystems, damage to amenities or interference with other legitimate uses of water;

(k) 'vulnerable zone': means an area of land designated according to Article 3(2).

Article 3

1. Waters affected by pollution and waters which could be affected by pollution if action pursuant Article 5 is not taken shall be identified by the Member States in accordance with the criteria set out in Annex I.

2. Member States shall, within a two-year period, following the notification of this Directive, designate as vulnerable zones all known areas of land in their territories which drain into the waters identified according to paragraph 1 and which contribute to pollution. They shall notify the Commission of this initial designation within six months.

3. When any waters identified by a Member State in accordance with paragraph 1 are affected by pollution

from waters from another Member State draining directly or indirectly in to them, the Member States whose waters affected may notify the other Member States and the Commission of the relevant facts.

The Member States concerned shall organise, where appropriate with the Commission, the concentration necessary to identify the sources in question and the measures to be taken to protect the waters that are affected in order to ensure conformity with this Directive.

4. Member States shall review if necessary revise or add to the designation of vulnerable zones as appropriate, and at least every four years, to take into account changes and factors unforeseen at the time of the previous designation. They shall notify the Commission of any revision or addition to the designations within six months.

5. Member States shall be exempt from the obligation to identify specific vulnerable zones, if they establish and apply action programmes referred to in Article 5 in accordance with this Directive throughout their national territory.

Article 12 **[11]**

1. The Member States shall bring into force the laws, regulations and administrative provisions necessary to

---

(¹) This Directive was notified to the Member States on 19 December 1991.

comply with this Directive within two years of its notification (¹). They shall forthwith inform the Commission thereof.

2. When Member States adopt these measures, they shall contain a reference to this Directive or shall be accompanied by such reference on the occasion of their official publication. The methods of making such a reference shall be laid down by the Member States.

3. Member States shall communicate to the Commission the texts of the provisions of national law which they adopt in the field governed by this Directive.

Article 13

This Directive is addressed to the Member States.

Done at Brussels, 12 December 1991.

For the Council

The President

J.G.M. ALDERS

ANNEX 1 **[12]**

CRITERIA FOR IDENTIFYING WATERS REFERRED TO IN ARTICLE 3(1)

A. Waters referred to in Article 3 (1) shall be identified making use, inter alia, of the following criteria:

1. whether surface freshwaters, in particular those used or intended for the abstraction of drinking water, contain or could contain, if action pursuant to Article 5 is not taken, more than the concentration of nitrates laid down in accordance with Directive 75/440/EEC;

2. whether groundwaters contain more than 50 mg/1 nitrates or could contain more than 50 mg/1 nitrates if action pursuant to Article 5 is not taken;

3. whether natural freshwater lakes, other freshwater bodies, estuaries, coastal waters and marine waters are found to be eutrophic or in the near future may become euthropic if action pursuant to Article 5 is not taken.

B. In applying these criteria, Member States shall also take account of:

1. the physical and environmental characteristics of the waters and land;

2. the current understanding of the behaviour of nitrogen compounds in the environment (water and soil);

3. the current understanding of the impact of the action taken pursuant to Article 5.

10–17 *Key:*

[1]   Official Journal series, issue and page—note the title has now changed to the *Official Journal of the European Union*.

[2]   Date of publication.

[3]   Date of adoption.

[4] Number of the Directive which comprises the year of enactment, running number and the institutional treaty basis of the Directive.

[5] The enacting authority.

[6] The legal basis (treaty) for the Directive.

[7] The legislative procedure.

[8] The series of paragraphs beginning with the word "whereas" are referred to as recitals. They state the main policy considerations that lie behind the Directive.

[9] This is usually printed in capital letters and represents the end of the first part of the Directive.

[10] The substantive part of the Directive. The parts of European legislation are referred to as articles and not as sections.

[11] Provision concerning when the Directive is to be brought into force.

[12] Additional information at the end of a Directive will be contained in annexes (the equivalent of schedules in UK legislation).

EU COURT STRUCTURE

There are two Courts which interpret and enforce EU law—the previously mentioned Court of **10–18** Justice of the EU and the General Court. Both are situated in Luxembourg. The Courts' homepage, CURIA, provides a gateway to specific information about each Court and other resources, including case law. See *http://curia.europa.eu/jcms/jcms/Jo2_6999/* [accessed June 11, 2014].

A précis of the operation of each Court is detailed below. **10–19**

Court of Justice of the EU

> ➢ One judge from each member state is appointment to the Court for a six year term of **10–20** office. The tenure of each judge can be renewed at the end of a six year period;

> ➢ The Court is assisted by nine "Advocates-General" who give an "Opinion" on cases yet to come before the Court. These Opinions are not binding on the Court, but are generally followed. Advocates-General are also appointed for a (renewable) period of six years;

> ➢ The most common types of cases pled before the Court of Justice are as follows:

  • Requests for a preliminary ruling—when member state national courts ask the Court of Justice to interpret a point of EU law;

  • Actions for failure to fulfil an obligation—brought against EU governments for not transposing/applying EU law;

  • Actions for annulment—against EU laws thought to violate the EU treaties or fundamental rights;

  • Actions for failure to act—against EU institutions for failing to make decisions required of them;

  • Direct actions—brought by individuals, companies or organisations against EU decisions or actions.

*The Court of Justice will also hear appeals from the General Court on a point of law only.

For further information, see *http://europa.eu/about-eu/institutions-bodies/court-justice/index_* **10–21** *en.htm* [accessed June 11, 2014].

The General Court

10–22
> Currently comprises 28 judges, (one from each member state), who are appointed for a six year (renewable) term;
> Advocates-General are not appointed;
> The General Court hears, inter alia, actions brought by: private citizens or companies (natural or legal persons) against the EU including cases concerning EU competition law; Member States against the Commission; and Member States against the Council.

NB When referring to either Court, avoid using the term "European Court" in any context as this appellation could refer to other judicial bodies outwith the EU, e.g. the European Free Trade Association Court or the European Court of Human Rights.

EU CASE LAW

10–23 There are four fundamental initial distinctions to be drawn between EU case law and reported cases in Scotland and England:

> EU cases are reported in a different format. Compare and contrast the anatomy of the Scottish case detailed in para.3–46 and the EU cases in para.10–25.
> There is no strict doctrine of stare decisis (see para.3–02) in either the Court of Justice or the General Court;
> The Court of Justice and the General Court adopt a "purposive" approach to statutory interpretation, i.e. the prime and guiding principle is to consider, in light of any ambiguity in the text, the purpose for which each provision was enacted. Thus, the permissive and variable domestic UK-wide approaches to statutory interpretation (see para.5–53), are generally alien concepts, although the domestic "mischief rule"* adopts a (broadly) purposive approach. This disparity may give rise to differing interpretations of the same piece of EU secondary legislation depending upon whether a domestic or EU court is called to interpret it. However, all UK courts are bound to follow judgments of the Court of Justice and are therefore required to interpret domestic legislation enacted to transpose an EU Directive or Decision in a purposive way;
> It is common for EU case law to be referred to by a nickname (also known as a soubriquet). This has arisen because the names of parties often tend to be long and difficult to remember, e.g. the German phrase for a limited liability company is "gesellschaft mit beschränkter hafting" which may or may not be abbreviated to "Gmbh".
>   The use of nicknames, however, is not without issue as they are seldom referred to in indexes of cases and problems can also arise if the same nickname has been given to more than one case emanating from the same parties. An example of a nickname being used to describe a case is Case C-415/93 *Union Royale Belge de Societes de Football Association ASBL v Jean-Marc Bosman* [1995] E.C.R. I-4921 which is commonly referred to as "The Bosman ruling".

*The "mischief rule" can be applied by a UK court if a domestic legislative provision is ambiguous as to its meaning, i.e. the intention of Parliament is unclear. In doing so, a court is said to "advance the remedy to suppress the mischief" concerned. This means that the court considers why the provision was enacted, i.e. considers the deficiency, if any, in the previous law which moved Parliament to legislate to remedy same. This "rule" of statutory interpretation was established in *Heydon's Case* (1584) 76 ER 637.

Citing an EU case

EU case citations comprise the following:

10–24

> ➢ A case number/year*;
> ➢ The names of the parties;
> ➢ The year of the judgment;
> ➢ A citation of the case report series and a page number.

Case 6/64 *Costa v ENEL* [1964] E.C.R. 585. E.C.R. is the abbreviation for the European Court Reports series.
*The year referred to is the year that application was made to the court. It does not necessarily mean that the case will appear (be reported) in the case report series published for that year.

NB Prior to 2009 when the Lisbon Treaty came into force and the EU courts were renamed, the predecessor to the General Court was the Court of First Instance which started to issue judgments in 1990. Thereafter, in order to distinguish cases heard by the Court of First Instance and the then European Court of Justice, the prefix "C" was added to cases from the European Court of Justice and the prefix "T" was added to cases from the Court of First Instance.

If the letter "P" appeared after the year it denotes that the case was appealed from the Court of First Instance to the European Court of Justice. For example see Case C-113/04 P *Technische Unie BV v Commission of the European Communities* [2006] E.C.R. I-08831.

Unhelpfully, while the above is the usual style of citation it is common to see citations of EU cases omitting the case number altogether or placing it after the names of the parties.

Post-Lisbon, cases heard by the Court of Justice and the General Court continue to use the same prefixes.

ANATOMY OF A PRE-LISBON CASE REPORTED IN THE E.C.R. WITH ANNOTATIONS

Case C-83/97 [1]

10–25

Commission of the European Communities [2]

v

Federal Republic of Germany

(Failure to fulfil obligations—Failure to transpose Directive 92/43/EEC)

Opinion of Advocate General Fennelly delivered on 23 October 1997....................................I—7192
Judgment of the Court (Fifth Chamber) 11 December 1997...I—7195

Summary of the Judgment [3]

Acts of the institutions — Directives — Implementation by the Member States — Mere administrative practices not sufficient
(EC Treaty, Art. 189, third para.)

Mere administrative practices, which by their nature are alterable at will by the administration and are not given the appropriate publicity, cannot be regarded as constituting the proper fulfilment of a Member State's obligations under Article 189 of the Treaty.

I—7191 [4]

OPINION OF ADVOCATE GENERAL [5]
FENNELLY

delivered on 23 October 1997*

1. Council Directive 92/43/EEC of 21 May 1992 on the conservation of natural habitats and of wild fauna and flora[1] (hereinafter 'the Directive') was notified to the Federal Republic of Germany on 5 June 1992. Article 23(1) required Member States to 'bring into force the laws, regulations and administrative provisions necessary to comply with this Directive within two years of its notification [and] forthwith [to] inform the Commission thereof'. For Germany, this deadline therefore expired on 5 June 1994.

2. In the absence of any indication that the Directive had been transposed into German law, the Commission opened the pre-litigation stage of the procedure provided by Article 169 of the Treaty establishing the European Community ('the Treaty') by sending a letter of formal notice on 9 August 1994. Germany did not contest the complaint in its reply of 6 October 1994. The Commission issued a reasoned opinion on 28 November 1995, to the effect that in failing to adopt the necessary provisions, Germany was in breach of its obligations under the Directive, and setting a two-month deadline for compliance. The present proceedings were initiated pursuant to Article 169 of the Treaty by an application registered at the Court on 24 February 1997.

3. In its application, the Commission observes that, as far as it is aware, not all the provisions necessary to comply with the Directive have been adopted or notified, and that the defendant neither answered nor complied with the reasoned opinion. On this ground, it requests the Court to hold that Germany is in breach of its obligations under the Treaty, and in particular the third paragraph of Article 189 and the first paragraph of Article 5 thereof.

4. In its defence, Germany admits that it has not adopted all the necessary measures to comply with its obligations under the Directive. It adds by way of complementary information that the Directive is directly applied by the competent public authorities, and that the existing national provisions are interpreted in conformity therewith. Furthermore, a bill to amend the Bundesnaturschutzgesetz (Federal law on nature protection) has been submitted to the Bundestag (Federal Assembly, lower house of parliament); the legislative procedure was scheduled to be completed by Autumn 1997.

5. The Directive is predicated on the statement in the first recital in the preamble that, 'the preservation, protection and improvement of the quality of the environment, including the conservation of natural habitats and of wild fauna and flora, are an essential objective of general interest pursued by the Community'. The fourth recital notes that, as 'the threatened habitats and species form part of the Community's natural heritage and the threats to them are often of a transboundary nature, it is necessary to take measures at Community level in order to conserve them'. This Directive is closely linked to Council Directive 79/409/EEC of 2 April on the conservation of wild birds[2] (hereinafter 'the Birds Directive').[3] The definition of the obligation to transpose the Birds Directive laid down by the Court from its earliest judgments in this area seems to me to be applicable, *mutatis mutandis*, to the obligation to transpose the present Directive. In *Commission v Belgium*, for example, the Court held that transposition 'does not necessarily require the provisions of the directive to he enacted in precisely the same words in a specific express legal provision national law; a general legal context may be sufficient if it actually ensures the full application of the directive in a sufficiently clear and precise manners'.[4] It added a proviso to this general statement which is especially relevant in the present proceedings, to the effect that 'a faithful transposition becomes particularly important in a case such as this in which the management of the common heritage is entrusted to the Member States in their respective territories'.[5]

6. Germany has expressly admitted its failure to adopt all of the necessary provisions to comply with the Directive; it has not contended that the action of the public authorities, or the interpretation of the relevant national provisions, ensures such compliance, and, indeed, the Court has consistently held that '[mere] administrative practices, which by their nature are alterable at will by the authorities and are not given the appropriate publicity, cannot he regarded as constituting the proper fulfilment of obligations under the Treaty'.[6] In these circumstances, I am of the opinion that the Commission should be granted the declarations which it has requested both on the merits and as regards costs.

---

* Original language: English

[1] — OJ 1992 L 206, p. 7.

[2] — OJ 1979 L 103, p. 1.

[3] — See paragraph 70 of my Opinion in Case C-44/95 *Royal Society for the Protection of Birds* [1996] ECR I-3802, at pp. I-3832 and I-3833.

[4] — Case 247/85 [1987] ECR 3029, paragraph 9 of the judgment.

[5] — Loc. Cit.

[6] — Case C-334/94 *Commission v France* [1996] ECR I-1307, paragraph 30 of the judgment.

Conclusion

7. In the light of the foregoing, I recommend to the Court that it:

(1)   Declare that, by failing to adopt the laws, regulations and administrative provisions necessary to comply with Council Directive 92/43/EEC of 21 May 1992 on the conservation of natural habitats and of wild fauna and flora within the deadline set, the Federal Republic of Germany has failed to comply with its obligations under the EC Treaty;

(2)   Order the Federal Republic of Germany to pay the costs.

COMMISSION v GERMANY

JUDGMENT OF THE COURT (Fifth Chamber) [6]

11 December 1997*

In Case C-83/97,

Commission of the European Communities, represented by Götz zur Hausen, Legal Adviser, acting as Agent, with an address for service in Luxembourg at the office of Carlos Gómez de la Cruz, of its Legal Service, Wagner Centre, Kirchberg, [7]

applicant,

v

Federal Republic of Germany, represented by Ernst Rösder, Ministerialrat in the Federal Ministry of Economic Affairs, and Bernd Kloke, Oberregierungsrat in the same ministry, acting as Agents, D-53107 Bonn,

defendant,

APPLICATION for a declaration that, by failing to adopt within the prescribed period the laws, regulations and administrative provisions necessary to comply with Council Directive 92/43/EEC of 21 May 1992 on the conservation of natural habitats and of wild fauna and flora (OJ 1992 L 206, p. 7), the Federal Republic of Germany has failed to fulfil its obligations under the EC Treaty, [8]

* Language of the case: German. [9]

COMMISSION v GERMANY

THE COURT (Fifth Chamber),

composed of. C. Gulmann (Rapporteur), President of the Chamber, M. Wathelet, J. C. Moitinho de Almeida, J.-P. Puissochet and L. Sevón, Judges, [10]

Advocate General: N. Fennelly,
Registrar. R. Grass, [11]

having regard to the report of the Judge-Rapporteur, [12]

after hearing the Opinion of the Advocate General at the sitting on 23 October 1997, gives the following

Judgment [13]

1. By application lodged at the Registry of the Court of justice on 24 February 1997, the Commission of the European Communities brought an action under Article 169 of the EC Treaty for a declaration that, by failing to adopt within the prescribed period the laws, regulations and administrative provisions necessary to comply with Council Directive 92/43/EEC of 21 May 1992 on the conservation of natural habitats and of wild fauna and flora (OJ 1992 L 206, p. 7, 'the directive'), the Federal Republic of Germany has failed to fulfil its obligations under the EC Treaty.

2. In accordance with Article 23 of the directive, the Member States were to bring into force the laws, regulations and administrative provisions necessary to comply with it within two years of its notification, and forthwith to inform the Commission thereof. Since the directive was notified to the Federal Republic of Germany on 5 June 1992, the period allowed for its implementation expired on 5 June 1994.

3. On 9 August 1994, not having been notified or otherwise informed of any measures to transpose the directive into German law, the Commission give the Federal Government formal notice under Article 169 of the Treaty to submit its observations in that regard within two months.

4. By letter of 25 October 1994 the Federal Government replied that the German authorities were drafting the provisions necessary to comply with the directive and that, pending their adoption, the directive was to be applied under the legal rules in force. However, the Federal Government asserted that the provisions of the directive concerning the conservation of natural habitats were not yet relevant for areas of Community interest, that the provisions relating to protection of species had already been to a large extent transposed by the federal law on the protection of nature then in force and, generally, that in certain places the directive was unclear, which complicated its transposition.

5. On 28 November 1995, not having received any communication of the promised transposition measures, the Commission sent the Federal Government a reasoned opinion requesting it to take the necessary measures to comply therewith within two months from its notification. That reasoned opinion went unanswered.

6. Accordingly, the Commission decided to bring the present action.

7. The Federal Government does not deny that it has not adopted all the measures necessary for implementation of the directive. It states, however, that since the passing of the deadline for transposition, the directive has been directly applied by the competent authorities and existing national provisions have been interpreted in accordance with Community law. It goes on to say that a law designed *inter alia* to implement the directive is in the process of being adopted.

8. Since the directive has not been transposed into national law by the Federal Republic of Germany within the prescribed period, the action brought by the Commission must be held to be well founded.

9. It has consistently been held that mere administrative practices, which by their nature are alterable at will by the administration and are not given the appropriate publicity, cannot be regarded as constituting the proper fulfilment of a Member State's obligations under Article 189 of the EC Treaty (see, *inter alia*, Case C-242/94 *Commission* v *Spain* [1995] ECR I-3031, paragraph 6).

10. It must therefore he held that, by failing to adopt within the prescribed period the laws, regulations and administrative provisions necessary to comply with the directive, the Federal Republic of Germany has failed to fulfil its obligations under Article 23 of the directive.

Costs

11. Under Article 69(2) of the Rules of Procedure, the unsuccessful party is to be ordered to pay the costs if they have been applied for in the successful party's pleadings. Since the Commission has applied for costs and the defendant has been unsuccessful, the Federal Republic of Germany must be ordered to pay the costs.

COMMISSION v GERMANY

On those grounds, **[14]**

THE COURT (Fifth Chamber)

hereby:

1.   Declares that, by failing to adopt within the prescribed period the laws, regulations and administrative provisions necessary to comply with Council Directive 92/43/EEC of 21 May 1992 on the conservation of natural habitats and of wild fauna and flora, the Federal Republic of Germany has failed to fulfil its obligations under Article 23 of that directive;

2.   Orders the Federal Republic of Germany to pay the costs.

| Gulmann | Wathelet | Moitinho de Almeida |
| Puissochet | Sevón |

Delivered in open court in Luxembourg on 11 December 1997.

R. Grass · C. Gulmann

Registrar · President of the Fifth Chamber

Key: **10–26**

[1] Case number.

[2] Names of the parties.

[3] Summary of Judgment. This is similar to the headnote in UK cases. It can be a useful guide to the subject matter of the case but it has no binding force of law.

[4] The page number in the E.C.R. The full citation for this case in Case C-83/97: *Commission of the European Communities v Federal Republic of Germany* [1997] E.C.R. I-7191.

[5] Opinion of the Advocate General, see para.10–20.

[6] The current composition of the E.C.J. is 27 judges. The court can sit as a full court, in plenary session with 13 judges or it can also sit with smaller numbers of judges in groups which are referred to as "Chambers".

[7] The parties and their legal advisers.

[8] The section beginning with "APPLICATION" outlines the legal issue(s). The wording would depend on the type of case e.g. a reference or an action.

[9] The authentic version of the case is in the language used in the case itself. The E.C.J. identifies the original language in a footnote.

[10] Details of the composition of the court in this case.

[11] The Registrar is a close equivalent to the clerk of court in the UK system except that he is considered as more important. He deals with the procedure and administration of the court.

[12] Until 1994, the Report of the Judge-Rapporteur was published with the rest of the case in the E.C.R. It is a report for the hearing which gives the background to the dispute, the legislative framework, details of the procedure adopted and a summary of the written observations submitted to the court.

[13] Judgment. Single judgments are given in all decisions. There is no publication of dissenting judgments. Judgments are brief (by UK standards) consisting of a series of short paragraphs.

[14] The actual ruling of the court is always at the end of the judgment and usually starts with the words "On those grounds". As in this case, the rulings tend to be short.

ANATOMY OF A POST-LISBON CASE REPORTED IN THE E.C.R. WITHOUT ANNOTATIONS

The case report below can also be viewed online at EUR-LEX homepage *http://eur-lex.europa.* **10–27**
eu/homepage.html [accessed June 24, 2014] where recent cases appear thus:

Date	Case	Parties	Type of document	Text	
2014/02/13	C-18/13	MAKS PEN	Judgment of the Court	html	Bibliographic notice

Older case law can be located in the EUR-LEX database by using the search function at the foot of the homepage.

10–28 Cases can be searched for by; year, case number, Advocate-General's Opinion and court.

JUDGMENT OF THE COURT (Seventh Chamber)

13 February 2014*

*Language of the case: Bulgarian.

(Taxation—Common system of value added tax—Directive 2006/112/EC—Deduction of input tax—Supplies made—Tax inspection—Supplier not having the necessary resources—Concept of tax evasion—Obligation to make a finding of tax evasion of the court's own motion—Requirement that the service actually be supplied—Requirement to keep accounts in sufficient detail—Legal proceedings—National court prohibited from classifying the tax evasion as a criminal offence and adversely affecting the applicant's situation)

In Case C-18/13,

REQUEST for a preliminary ruling under Article 267 TFEU from the Administrativen sad Sofia-grad (Bulgaria), made by decision of 11 December 2012, received at the Court on 14 January 2013, in the proceedings

Maks Pen EOOD

v

Direktor na Direktsia 'Obzhalvane i danachno-osiguritelna praktika' Sofia, formerly Direktor na Direktsia 'Obzhalvane i upravlenie na izpalnenieto' Sofia,

THE COURT (Seventh Chamber),

composed of J.L. da Cruz Vilaça, President of the Chamber, G. Arestis and J.-C. Bonichot (Rapporteur), Judges,
Advocate General: J. Kokott,
Registrar: A. Calot Escobar,

having regard to the written procedure,

after considering the observations submitted on behalf of:
— the Direktor na Direktsia 'Obzhalvane i danachno-osiguritelna praktika' Sofia, formerly Direktor na Direktsia 'Obzhalvane i upravlenie na izpalnenieto' Sofia, by A. Georgiev, acting as Agent,
— the Bulgarian Government, by E. Petranova and D. Drambozova, acting as Agents,
— the Greek Government, by K. Paraskevopoulou and M. Vergou, acting as Agents,
— the European Commission, by C. Soulay and D. Roussanov, acting as Agents,

having decided, after hearing the Advocate General, to proceed to judgment without an Opinion, gives the following

Judgment

1 This request for a preliminary ruling concerns the interpretation of Article 63, Article 178(a), subparagraph (6) of Article 226, and Articles 242 and 273 of Council Directive 2006/112/EC of 28 November 2006 on the common system of value added tax (OJ 2006 L 347, p. 1).

2 The request has been made in proceedings between Maks Pen EOOD ('Maks Pen') and the Direktor na Direktsia 'Obzhalvane i danachno-osiguritelna praktika' Sofia, formerly Direktor na Direktsia 'Obzhalvane i upravlenie na izpalnenieto' Sofia (Director of the 'Appeals and Enforcement' Directorate, for Sofia, of the central office of the National Public Revenue Agency), regarding the refusal of the right to deduct value added tax ('VAT'), in the form of a tax credit, on invoices drawn up by some suppliers to Maks Pen.

Legal context

European Union law

3 Under Article 62 of Directive 2006/112:
'For the purposes of this Directive:
(1) "chargeable event" shall mean the occurrence by virtue of which the legal conditions necessary for VAT to become chargeable are fulfilled;
(2) VAT shall become "chargeable" when the tax authority becomes entitled under the law, at a given moment, to claim the tax from the person liable to pay, even though the time of payment may be deferred.'

4 Article 63 of that directive provides:
'The chargeable event shall occur and VAT shall become chargeable when the goods or the services are supplied.'

5 Article 167 of that directive provides:
'A right of deduction shall arise at the time the deductible tax becomes chargeable.'

6 Article 168 of that directive provides:
'In so far as the goods and services are used for the purposes of the taxed transactions of a taxable person, the taxable person shall be entitled, in the Member State in which he carries out these transactions, to deduct the following from the VAT which he is liable to pay:
(a) the VAT due or paid in that Member State in respect of supplies to him of goods or services, carried out or to be carried out by another taxable person;
...'

7 Under Article 178 of Directive 2006/112:
'In order to exercise the right of deduction, a taxable person must meet the following conditions:
(a) for the purposes of deductions pursuant to Article 168(a), in respect of the supply of goods or services, he must hold an invoice drawn up in accordance with Articles 220 to 236 and Articles 238, 239 and 240;
...'

8 Article 220(1) of Directive 2006/112, which is in Chapter 3, headed 'Invoicing', of Title XI thereof, provides that every taxable person is to ensure that an invoice is issued, either by himself or by his customer or, in his name and on his behalf, by a third party, in respect of supplies of goods or services which he has made to another taxable person or to a non-taxable legal person.

9 Article 226 of Directive 2006/112 lists the only details which, without prejudice to the particular provisions laid down in that directive, are required for VAT purposes on invoices issued pursuant to Articles 220 and 221 of that directive.

10 Article 242 of that directive is worded as follows:
'Every taxable person shall keep accounts in sufficient detail for VAT to be applied and its application checked by the tax authorities.'

11 Article 273 of the same directive provides:
'Member States may impose other obligations which they deem necessary to ensure the correct collection of VAT and to prevent evasion, subject to the requirement of equal treatment as between domestic transactions and transactions carried out between Member States by taxable persons and provided that such obligations do not, in trade between Member States, give rise to formalities connected with the crossing of frontiers.
The option under the first paragraph may not be relied upon in order to impose additional invoicing obligations over and above those laid down in Chapter 3.'

Bulgarian law

12 In accordance with Article 70(5) of the Law on value added tax (Zakon za danak varhu dobavenata stoynost, 'Law on VAT'), unlawfully invoiced VAT cannot be deducted.

13 Article 12 of the regulation implementing the Law on VAT is headed 'Date on which the chargeable event takes place where there is a supply of goods or services'. Paragraph 1 of that article, in the version applicable to the dispute in the main proceedings, provides as follows:
'... the service is considered to be supplied, within the meaning of the law, at the date on which the conditions for recognition of the revenue arising from that supply are satisfied in accordance with the Law on Accounting and the applicable accounting standards.'

14 Pursuant to Article 160(1), (2) and (5) of the Tax and Social Security Procedure Code (Danachno-osiguritelen protsesualen kodeks):

'1. The court shall rule on the substance of the case and it may annul the amended notice in its entirety or in part, alter that notice or even dismiss the action.

2. The court shall assess whether the amended notice complies with the law and its validity by checking whether that notice was issued by a competent department, in the required form, and whether it complies with the substantive and procedural provisions.

...

5. A judicial decision cannot provide that an amended notice is to be altered to the detriment of the applicant.'

15 Article 17(1) of the Code of Civil Procedure (Grazhdanskiya protsesualen kodeks) provides as follows:

'The court shall rule on all the issues relevant to the outcome of the proceedings, apart from the issue of whether an offence has been committed.'

The dispute in the main proceedings and the questions referred for a preliminary ruling

16 Maks Pen is a company registered under Bulgarian law which operates as a wholesaler of office supplies and advertising material.

17 The tax inspection to which it was subject in respect of the tax period from 1 January 2007 to 30 April 2009 inclusive led the tax authorities to contest the validity of the VAT deduction made on the basis of the tax included in the invoices of seven of its suppliers.

18 In respect of some of the suppliers themselves, or their sub-contractors, it was not possible to establish from the information requested of them during that inspection that they had the necessary resources to have made the supplies invoiced. Taking the view that either it was not proven, in respect of some of the sub-contractors, that the transactions in question had actually been carried out, or that those transactions were not carried out by the service providers referred to on the invoices, the tax authorities drew up an amended tax assessment notice contesting the deductibility of the VAT included in the invoices of those seven undertakings.

19 Maks Pen challenged that amended notice before the Direktor na Direktsia 'Obzhalvane i upravlenie na izpalnenieto' Sofia, then before the referring court, submitting that it possessed invoices and contractual documents in due form, that those invoices had been paid by bank transfer, that they were registered in the accounting records of the suppliers, that those suppliers had declared the VAT relating to those invoices, that there was therefore evidence that the supplies at issue had actually taken place and that, further, it was not disputed that Maks Pen itself had made supplies subsequent to the provision of those services.

20 The tax authorities submitted that it was not sufficient to hold invoices in due form to qualify for a right to deduct, where, in particular, the private documents presented in support of the invoices by the suppliers concerned were not reliably dated and had no probative value, and the sub-contractors had not declared the workers whose services they had used or the services supplied. Before the referring court, the tax authorities relied on new evidence, first, by challenging the validity of the signature of representatives of two of the suppliers and, secondly, by pointing out that one of them had not included in its accounting records or in its tax returns the invoices of one of the sub-contractors whose services it had used. While the tax authorities conceded that the services invoiced had been supplied to Maks Pen, they submitted that those services were not however provided by the suppliers mentioned in those invoices.

21 In those circumstances the Administrativen sad Sofia-grad decided to stay the proceedings and to refer to the Court the following questions for a preliminary ruling:

'(1) Are circumstances of fact in which the service provider named on the invoice or its subcontractor do not have the personnel, equipment or assets that would be required to provide the service, the costs of actually providing the service are not documented and no such costs are entered in its accounts, and documents submitted as evidence of the consideration due and of provision of the service in respect of which a VAT invoice was issued and the right to deduct input tax was exercised, in the form of a contract and a record of acceptance and delivery, were false in so far as concerns the identification of the persons who signed them as the suppliers, to be treated as relating to 'tax evasion' for the purposes of the right of deduction under European Union law?

(2) Does it follow from the obligation incumbent on a court under European Union law and the case-law of the Court of Justice ... to refuse the right to deduct input tax in the case of tax evasion that a national court also has a duty to establish the existence of tax evasion of its own motion, in circumstances such as those at issue in the main proceedings, to the extent that—taking into account its obligations under national law to give a ruling on the substance of the dispute, to comply with the prohibition on altering the position of the claimant, to observe the principles of the rights of the defence and legal certainty and to apply the relevant legal provisions of its own motion—it must assess new facts put before it for the first time, as well as all evidence, including that relating to fictitious transactions, false documents and documents the contents of which are inaccurate?

(3) In the context of the obligation of the court to refuse the right to deduct input tax in the event of tax evasion, does it follow from Article 178(a) of ... Directive 2006/112 ... that the service must actually have been provided by the service provider named on the invoice or its subcontractor in order for the right of deduction to be exercised?

(4) Does the requirement under Article 242 of Directive 2006/112 to keep detailed accounts for the purposes of verification of the right to deduct input tax mean that the corresponding accounting legislation of the Member State in question, which provides for consistency with the international accounting standards applicable under European Union law, must also be observed, or does it refer only to the requirement to keep the VAT accounting documents prescribed in that directive: invoices, VAT returns and recapitulative statements?
In the event that the second alternative is correct:

Does it follow, from the requirement in subparagraph (6) of Article 226 of Directive 2006/112 that invoices must state the 'extent and nature of the services rendered', that, when services are provided, invoices or a document issued in connection with them must contain details of the actual provision of the service, i.e. objective, verifiable facts that serve as proof both that the service was in fact provided and that it was rendered by the service provider named on the invoice?

(5) Is Article 242 of Directive 2006/112, which lays down the requirement to keep detailed accounts for the purposes of checking the right to deduct input tax, in conjunction with Article 63 and Article 273 of that directive, to be interpreted as precluding a national provision under which a service is deemed to have been provided at the time when the conditions governing recognition of revenue arising from that service are satisfied in accordance with the relevant accounting legislation, which provides for consistency with the international accounting standards applicable under European Union law and the principles of documented evidence for business transactions, the precedence of substance over form and the comparability of revenue and costs?'

Consideration of the questions referred

The first and third questions

22 By its first and third questions, which can be examined together, the referring court asks, in essence, whether Directive 2006/112 must be interpreted as precluding a taxable person from deducting VAT on the invoices issued by a supplier where, although the supply was made, it is apparent that it was not actually made by that supplier or by its subcontractor, inter alia because they did not have the personnel, equipment or assets required, there was no record of the costs of supplying the service in their accounts and the identification of persons signing certain documents as suppliers was shown to be inaccurate.

23 It should be borne in mind that, according to settled case-law, the right of taxable persons to deduct VAT due or already paid on goods purchased and services received as inputs from the VAT which they are liable to pay is a fundamental principle of the common system of VAT established by the relevant European Union legislation (see Case C-285/11 *Bonik* [2012] ECR, paragraph 25 and the case-law cited).

24 In that regard, the Court has consistently held that the right of deduction provided for in Article 167 et seq. of Directive 2006/112 is an integral part of the VAT scheme and in principle may not be limited. In particular, the right of deduction is exercisable immediately in respect of all the taxes charged on transactions relating to inputs (see *Bonik*, paragraph 26 and the case-law cited).

25 In addition, it is apparent from the wording of Article 168(a) of Directive 2006/112 that, in order to have a right of deduction, it is necessary, first, that the interested party be a taxable person within the meaning of that directive and, second, that the goods or services relied on to give entitlement to that right be used by the taxable person for the purposes of his own taxed output transactions, and that, as inputs, those goods or services must be supplied by another taxable person (see *Bonik*, paragraph 29 and the case-law cited). Where those conditions are fulfilled, entitlement to deduction cannot in principle be refused.

26 That said, it must be borne in mind that the prevention of tax evasion, tax avoidance and abuse is an objective recognised and encouraged by Directive 2006/112. In that connection, the Court has held that European Union law cannot be relied on for abusive or fraudulent ends. It is therefore for the national courts and authorities to refuse the right of deduction, if it is shown, in the light of objective evidence, that that right is being relied on for fraudulent or abusive ends (see *Bonik*, paragraphs 35 to 37 and the case-law cited).

27 While that is the position where tax evasion is committed by the taxable person himself, the same is also true where a taxable person knew, or should have known, that, by his acquisition, he was taking part in a transaction connected with the evasion of VAT. He must therefore, for the purposes of Directive 2006/112, be regarded as a participant in that evasion, whether or not he profits from the resale of the goods or the use of the services in the context of the taxable transactions subsequently carried out by him (see *Bonik*, paragraphs 38 to 39 and the case-law cited).

28 Accordingly, a taxable person cannot be refused the right of deduction unless it is established on the basis of objective evidence that that taxable person—to whom the supply of goods or services, on the basis of which the right of deduction is claimed, was made—knew or should have known that, through the acquisition of those goods or services, he was participating in a transaction connected with the evasion of VAT committed by the supplier or by another trader acting upstream or downstream in the chain of supply of those goods or services (see *Bonik*, paragraph 40 and the case-law cited).

29 Since the refusal of the right of deduction is an exception to the application of the fundamental principle constituted by that right, it is incumbent upon the competent tax authorities to establish, to the requisite legal standard, that the objective evidence to which the preceding paragraph of this judgment refers is present. It is for the national courts subsequently to determine whether the tax authorities concerned have established the existence of such objective evidence (see, to that effect, *Bonik*, paragraphs 43 and 44).

30 It should be borne in mind in that regard that, in proceedings brought under Article 267 TFEU, the Court has no jurisdiction to check or to assess the factual circumstances of the case in the main proceedings. In the main proceedings, it is therefore for the referring court to carry out, in accordance with the rules of evidence under national law, an overall assessment of all the evidence and factual circumstances of those proceedings in order to determine, in the light of the objective evidence provided by the tax authorities, whether Maks Pen knew or should have known that a transaction relied on to give entitlement to the right to deduct was connected with tax evasion committed by its suppliers.

31 In that regard, if it were simply to be the case that, in the main proceedings, a supply made to Maks Pen was not actually made by the supplier mentioned on the invoices or by its sub-contractor, inter alia because they did not have the personnel, equipment or assets required, there was no record of the costs of making the supply in their accounts and the identification of persons signing certain documents as suppliers was shown to be inaccurate, that would not, in itself, be sufficient ground to exclude the right to deduct relied on by Maks Pen.

32 In those circumstances, the answer to the first and third questions is that Directive 2006/112 must be interpreted as precluding a taxable person from deducting the VAT included in the invoices issued by a supplier where, although the supply was made, it is apparent that the supply was not actually made by that supplier or by its sub-contractor, inter alia because they did not have the personnel, equipment or assets required, there was no record of the costs of making the supply in their accounts and the identification of persons signing certain documents as the suppliers was shown to be inaccurate, subject to the twofold condition that such facts constitute fraudulent conduct and that it is established, in the light of objective evidence provided by the tax authorities, that the taxable person knew or should have known that the transaction relied on to give entitlement to the right to deduct was connected with that fraud, which it is for the referring court to determine.

The second question

33 By its second question, the referring court asks, in essence, whether European Union law requires that that court establish the existence of tax evasion of its own motion in circumstances such as those of the case in the main proceedings, on the basis of new facts relied on for the first time before it by the tax authorities and on all the evidence, even though, by carrying out such an examination, it would fail to comply with obligations imposed on it by the applicable national law.

34 As observed in paragraph 26 above, European Union law requires of the national courts and authorities that they refuse entitlement to the right to deduct where it is established, in the light of objective evidence, that that right is being relied on for fraudulent or abusive ends. Moreover, even though European Union law is not relied upon by the parties, the national court must raise of its own motion points of law based on binding European Union law rules where, under national law, the national courts must or may do so in relation to a binding rule of national law (see, to that effect, Case C-2/06 *Kempter* [2008] ECR I-411, paragraph 45 and the case-law cited).

35 Therefore, although, as the referring court itself states at paragraph 72 of its request for a preliminary ruling, it is apparent from Article 160(2) of the Tax and Social Security Procedure Code that that court is required to determine whether there is tax evasion when it examines of its own motion whether the amended tax notice contesting the VAT deduction made by the taxable person is in conformity with national law, it must also raise of its own motion the requirement of European Union law referred to in the preceding paragraph of this judgment, in accordance with the objective of Directive 2006/112 of preventing any tax evasion, tax avoidance and abuse.

36 It must be recalled, in this connection, that it is for the national court to interpret the national law, so far as possible, in the light of the wording and the purpose of the directive concerned in order to achieve the result sought by the directive, which requires that it does whatever lies within its jurisdiction, taking the whole body of domestic law into consideration and applying the interpretative methods recognised by that law (see, to that effect, Case C-212/04 *Adeneler and Others* [2006] ECR I-6057, paragraph 111). It is therefore for the national court to ascertain whether the rules of

national law on which it is relying and which, in its view, might be contrary to the requirements of European Union law, can be interpreted in accordance with the objective of preventing tax evasion on which those requirements are based.

37 In this respect, admittedly, European Union law cannot oblige a national court to apply European Union legislation of its own motion where this would have the effect of disregarding the principle, enshrined in its national procedural law, of the prohibition of *reformatio in peius* (Case C-455/06 *Heemskerk and Schaap* [2008] ECR I-8763, paragraph 46). However, it is not obvious, in any event, that, in a dispute such as that in the main proceedings which, from its origin, concerns the right to deduct the VAT included in a number of specific invoices, such a prohibition can apply to the submission by the tax authorities during court proceedings of new evidence which, concerning those same invoices, cannot be regarded as adversely affecting the situation of the taxable person who is relying on that right to deduct.

38 Moreover, even if a rule of national law were to classify the tax evasion as a criminal offence, where only a criminal court could make that classification, it is not obvious that such a rule would preclude the court responsible for assessing the legality of an amended tax notice which contests the VAT deduction made by a taxable person from being able to rely on objective evidence submitted by the tax authorities to establish the existence, in the particular case, of tax evasion, where, pursuant to another provision of national law, such as Article 70(5) of the Law on VAT, VAT which is 'unlawfully invoiced' cannot be deducted.

39 Accordingly, the answer to the second question is that, where the national courts must or may raise of their own motion points of law based on binding rules of national law, they must do so in relation to a binding rule of European Union law such as that which requires that national courts and authorities refuse entitlement to the right to deduct VAT where it is established, in the light of objective evidence, that that right is being relied on for fraudulent or abusive ends. It is incumbent on those courts, in the assessment of whether that right to deduct was relied on for fraudulent or abusive ends, to interpret the national law, so far as possible, in the light of the wording and the purpose of Directive 2006/112, in order to achieve the result sought by that directive, which requires that they do whatever lies within their jurisdiction, taking the whole body of domestic law into consideration and applying the interpretative methods recognised by that law.

The fourth and fifth questions

40 By its fourth and fifth questions, which can be examined together, the referring court asks, in essence, whether Directive 2006/112, by requiring in particular, pursuant to Article 242 thereof, that any taxable person keep accounts in sufficient detail to allow VAT to be applied and its application checked by the tax authorities, must be interpreted as not precluding the Member State concerned from requiring that any taxable person observe in that regard all the national accounting rules consistent with international accounting standards, including a provision of national law according to which a service is deemed to have been supplied at the time when the conditions governing recognition of the revenue arising from that service are satisfied.

41 Under the common system of VAT, Member States are required to ensure compliance with the obligations to which taxable persons are subject and they enjoy in that respect a certain measure of latitude, inter alia, as to how they use the means at their disposal. Among those obligations, Article 242 of Directive 2006/112 provides, inter alia, that every taxable person is to keep accounts in sufficient detail to permit VAT to be applied and its application checked by the tax authority (see, to that effect, Case C-188/09 *Profaktor Kulesza Frankowski, Józwiak, Orlowski* [2010] ECR I-7639, paragraphs 22 and 23).

42 In addition, pursuant to the first paragraph of Article 273 of Directive 2006/112, Member States may impose other obligations which they deem necessary to ensure the correct collection of VAT and to prevent evasion. That option, which can only be made use of provided it does not affect trade between Member States, may not, furthermore, as stated in the second paragraph of that article, be relied upon in order to impose additional obligations over and above those laid down in that directive.

43 Moreover, that option cannot authorise the Member States to adopt measures which go further than is necessary to attain the objectives of ensuring the correct levying and collection of the tax and the prevention of tax evasion (*Profaktor Kulesza, Frankowski, Józwiak, Orlowski*, paragraph 26).

44 Provided that they comply with those limits, European Union law does not preclude additional national accounting rules which are established by reference to international accounting standards applicable within the European Union under the conditions provided for by Regulation (EC) No 1606/2002 of the European Parliament and of the Council of 19 July 2002 on the application of international accounting standards (OJ 2002 L 243, p. 1).

45 As regards the issue of whether those national accounting rules may provide that a service is deemed to have been supplied at the time when the conditions governing recognition of the revenue arising from that service are satisfied, it

must be held that the effect of that rule would be to render VAT chargeable in respect of such a supply only once the costs incurred by the supplier or its sub-contractor have been entered in the accounts of those traders.

46 It must be recalled that, under Article 167 of Directive 2006/112, a right of deduction arises at the time the tax becomes chargeable and that, under Article 63 of that directive, VAT becomes chargeable when the services are supplied. Therefore, subject to the specific situations referred to in Articles 64 and 65 of that directive, which are not at issue in the main proceedings, the time when the tax becomes chargeable, and thus deductible for the taxable person, cannot be determined, generally, by the completion of formalities such as the entering, in the supplier's accounts, of the costs borne by them in respect of the supply of their services.

47 Further, any failure by the service provider to complete certain accounting requirements cannot call in question the right of deduction to which the recipient of services supplied is entitled in respect of the VAT paid for those services, where the invoices relating to the services supplied contain all the information required by Article 226 of Directive 2006/112 (see, to that effect, Case C-324/11 *Tóth* [2012] ECR, paragraph 32).

48 Having regard to the foregoing, the answer to the fourth and fifth questions is that Directive 2006/112, by requiring in particular, pursuant to Article 242 thereof, that any taxable person keep accounts in sufficient detail to allow the VAT to be applied and its application checked by the tax authorities, must be interpreted as not precluding the Member State concerned, within the limits provided for in Article 273 of that directive, from requiring that any taxable person observe in that regard all the national accounting rules consistent with international accounting standards, provided that the measures adopted to that effect do not go beyond what is necessary to attain the objectives of ensuring correct levying and collection of the tax and preventing tax evasion. In that regard, Directive 2006/112 precludes a national provision according to which a service is deemed to have been supplied at the time when the conditions governing recognition of the revenue arising from that service are satisfied.

Costs

49 Since these proceedings are, for the parties to the main proceedings, a step in the action pending before the national court, the decision on costs is a matter for that court. Costs incurred in submitting observations to the Court, other than the costs of those parties, are not recoverable.

On those grounds, the Court (Seventh Chamber) hereby rules:
1. Council Directive 2006/112/EC of 28 November 2006 on the common system of value added tax must be interpreted as precluding a taxable person from deducting the value added tax included in the invoices issued by a supplier where, although the supply was made, it is apparent that it was not actually made by that supplier or by its sub-contractor, inter alia because they did not have the personnel, equipment or assets required, there was no record of the costs of making the supply in their accounts and the identification of persons signing certain documents as the suppliers was shown to be inaccurate, subject to the twofold condition that such facts constitute fraudulent conduct and that it is established, in the light of the objective evidence provided by the tax authorities, that the taxable person knew or should have known that the transaction relied on to give entitlement to the right to deduct was connected with that fraud, which it is for the referring court to determine.
2. Where the national courts must or may raise of their own motion points of law based on binding rules of national law, they must do so in relation to a binding rule of European Union law such as that which requires that the national courts and authorities refuse entitlement to the right to deduct value added tax where it is established, in the light of objective evidence, that that right is being relied on for fraudulent or abusive ends. It is incumbent on those courts, in the assessment of whether that right to deduct was relied on for fraudulent or abusive ends, to interpret the national law, so far as possible, in the light of the wording and the purpose of Directive 2006/112, in order to achieve the result sought by that directive, which requires that they do whatever lies within their jurisdiction, taking the whole body of domestic law into consideration and applying the interpretative methods recognised by that law.
3. Directive 2006/112, by requiring in particular, pursuant to Article 242 thereof, that any taxable person keep accounts in sufficient detail to allow the value added tax to be applied and its application checked by the tax authorities, must be interpreted as not precluding the Member State concerned, within the limits provided for in Article 273 of that directive, from requiring that any taxable person observe in that regard all the national accounting rules consistent with international accounting standards, provided that the measures adopted to that effect do not go beyond what is necessary to attain the objectives of ensuring the correct levying and collection of the tax and preventing tax evasion. In that regard, Directive 2006/112 precludes a national provision according to which a service is deemed to have been supplied at the time when the conditions governing recognition of the revenue arising from that service are satisfied.

[Signatures]

Official Sources of EU Legislation

The Official Journal of the European Union (previously Communities) ("O.J.")

The O.J. is the official gazette of the EU. It is published every working day and contains a vast **10–29** amount of material. It is published in all EU official languages. At the time of writing, the EU recognises 24 official languages. The O.J. contains all secondary legislation (regulations, directions, decisions) in full text along with proposed legislation, official announcements and information about the activities of the EU institutions. The O.J. is available in paper form, CD ROM and online. See *http://publications.europa.eu/official/index_en.htm* [accessed June 11, 2014] for the online version.

Anatomy of the O.J.

The O.J. comprises three separate series: **10–30**

> ➢ The "L" series contains the full authoritative text of legislation whose publication is obligatory and virtually all other legislation adopted. In addition, the Directory of EU Legislation in Force is published as part of the O.J. "L" series. This Directory lists references to the initial texts and to any subsequent amendments and can be accessed here *http://eur-lex.europa.eu/oj/direct-access.html* [accessed June 24, 2014];
> ➢ The "C" series, "Information and Notices", covers a wide range of information including; summaries of judgments of the Court of Justice and the General Court (and its predecessors) minutes of Parliamentary meetings, reports of other EU institutions, e.g. the Court of Auditors, Parliamentary written questions and answers from the Council or Commission and statements from EU bodies, such as the Economic and Social Committee and the Committee of the Regions. The debates of the plenary sessions and oral questions from the European Parliament are also published in the O.J;
> ➢ Monthly indexes to the "L" and "C" series are subsequently collated in an annual index. The alphabetical index is organised by subject and the methodological index is listed by number;
> ➢ The "CE" series, is an electronic sub-series of the "C" series and publishes the pre-paratory materials in the legislative process;
> ➢ The "S" series is a supplement to the O.J. and contains invitations to tender for public works, services and supply contracts. This series is only available online via the Tenders Electronic Daily database, (see *http://ted.europa.eu/TED/main/HomePage.do* [accessed June 11, 2014]) or on CD Rom.

NB Full text authoritative case reports from the Court of Justice and the General Court are not published in the O.J. Judgments and Opinions are published on the CURIA website with the majority subsequently appearing in the European Case Reports ("E.C.R."). See *http://curia.europa.eu/* [accessed June 12, 2014].

O.J. citation

Each issue of the "L", "C" and "S" series is numbered sequentially beginning with "1" at the **10–31** start of every calendar year. There is no standard citation convention for references in the O.J. A commonly used format is:

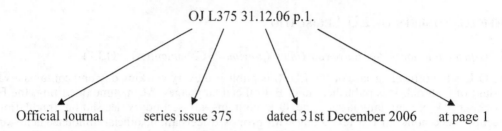

OJ L375 31.12.06 p.1.

Official Journal   series issue 375   dated 31st December 2006   at page 1

However, the fourth edition of the *Oxford Standard for the Citation of Legal Authorities* ("OSCOLA") recommends—[year] O.J. series number/page, e.g. [2006] OJ L375/1. See *http:// www.law.ox.ac.uk/published/OSCOLA_4th_edn.pdf* [accessed June 11, 2014].

Eur-lex free

10–32 The EUR-Lex website offers structured access to a vast amount of EU legal resources and is arranged by collections. At the time of writing, the website is being re-designed. Thus the details given below may or may not be accurate at the time of publication. In any event, it would seem logical to presume that additional materials rather than fewer may appear in due course. See *http://eur-lex.europa.eu/en/index.htm* [accessed June 11, 2014].

> O.J. "L" and "C" series since 1998 in full text. As of July 1, 2013, the electronic version of the O.J. is regarded as "authentic", i.e. it produces legal effects. See Regulation (EU) No.216/2013;
> EU primary legislation—the Treaties (including consolidated versions) in full text;
> International agreements. All the instruments generated by the EU in the exercise of their international responsibilities in full text;
> Legislation in force. The full consolidated version of secondary legislation is contained in the Directory of EU Legislation in Force. It is grouped into twenty categories which are further divided into sub-categories;
> Preparatory acts. Legislative proposals and other Commission communications to the Council and other institutions;
> Case law from 1954 onwards;
> Parliamentary questions. There is a link to the European Parliament website where the texts of the questions and answers of the three most recent legislative terms are available.

Searching EUR-Lex

10–33 The site has a "simple" search function which offers the following options:

> A general search with options to search by free text, date/time, author, classification heading or keywords;
> Search by document number using natural numbers or CELEX number. CELEX is the database holding the resources available on EUR-Lex. All documents held have a unique number, e.g. 32007R0967 refers to Regulation (EC) No.967/2007 of August 17, 2007 on the issue of system B export licences in the fruit and vegetables sector (table grapes) O.J. L 215, 18.8.2007.
> Search by file category with options to search by Treaty, legislation, preparatory acts, cases or parliamentary questions;
> Search by publication reference from the O.J. or the E.C.R.

NB EUR-Lex states that the advanced search function, which operates using Boolean connectors (see paras 2–58—2–59), was "developed for the needs of professional user". In most circumstance, the "simple" search function will locate the required documents.

Commercial sources of EU legislation

Commercial databases
There are several commercial databases which contain EU legislation. Most undergraduate and **10–34** post-graduate law students will have access to one or more of the following:

> ➤ Justis ⚲ subscription database;
> ➤ LexisNexis ⚲ subscription database; and
> ➤ Westlaw ⚲ subscription database.

The Encyclopaedia of European Union Law

This service published by Sweet and Maxwell comprises eight loose-leaf volumes which inter alia **10–35** contain:

> ➤ The Treaties/secondary legislation;
> ➤ All EU association agreements; and
> ➤ Rules of procedure for the Court of Justice/General Court and Institutions.

Each distinct part is contained in a colour-coded section. A contents listing is provided for each section. This service is updated four times a year.

Collections of EU legislation

10–36 Commercial publications include *Blackstone's EU Treaties & Legislation 2013–2014*, 24th edn (Oxford: OUP, 2013). This is an annual publication without annotations.

10–37 The EU Commission also provides a dedicated website EUdralex where EU pharmaceutical legislation currently in force for human and animal use is freely available. A CD containing the same information can also be obtained free of charge. See *http://ec.europa.eu/health/documents/ eudralex/index_en.htm* [accessed June 22, 2014].

Aids to finding EU legislation

EUR-Lex ✤ free
10–38 As detailed above in para.10–32, the EUR-Lex "simple" search facility provides a comprehensive set of search tools.

Searching by document number

10–39 If the reference details are known, go to natural number (located under the heading Search by document number) and then enter the year and number in to the search field.

10–40 If the reference details are not known, select legislation listed under Search by file category. This page opens up various options depending on the amount of information known. A search can be undertaken by free text, date or time span, author, classification headings or keywords. If the keyword option is selected a list of possible keywords are offered which, in turn, reveal further options to select from. This is achieved by linking through to a multilingual thesaurus EUROVOC which contains terms and phrases in 23 of the 24 official EU languages, including English.

10–41 The search results achieved will provide further options: Bibliographic notice, bibliographic notice + text, .html or .pdf. The last two options will provide a full text version of the legislation. However, the option containing the most information is the bibliographic notice + text listing. This retrieves additional information such as amending or amended legislation which can be accessed via hyperlink. If the piece of legislation has been amended and a consolidated version has been created an initial search will retrieve the original version. The bibliographic notice will alert the researcher to the fact that there is a consolidated version and there will be a link to it.

Legislation in force

10–42 This feature of EUR-Lex provides a gateway to the Directory of EU legislation and agreements, *http://eur-lex.europa.eu/browse/directories/legislation.html* [accessed June 24, 2014]. Twenty bespoke chapters which are divided into sections and, where applicable, sub-sections can be searched. Once a section has been selected, a list of all titles of acts in force as classified in that section becomes visible. Where consolidated texts are provided these list subsequent amendments.

Finding EU Legislation on a specific subject online

EUR-Lex ✤ free
10–43 See para.10–33 above.

Legislation in force: legislation under preparation

This web address *http://europa.eu/eu-law/legislation/index_en.htm* [accessed June 11, 2014] links **10–44**
directly to EUR-Lex per legislation in force and to PreLex for legislation under preparation.
PreLex holds documentation on the significant stages of the EU decision making process
between the relevant institutions and includes:

> ➢ The stage the procedure has reached;
> ➢ The decisions taken by the institutions involved;
> ➢ Names of the relevant persons; and
> ➢ Name of the Directorate(s) responsible for the proposed legislation.

General Report—activities of the EU 📖 and ᷠ free
This is an annual publication arranged by subject matter. It is available on the EUROPA **10–45**
website at *http://europa.eu/publications/reports-booklets/general-report/index_en.htm* [accessed
June 11, 2014].

NB The Bulletin of the EU which detailed the major activities of EU institutions was
published monthly until August 31, 2009. These publications have been archived and can
be accessed here *http://ec.europa.eu/archives/bulletin/en/welcome.htm* [accessed June 24,
2014].

Commercial databases

> ➢ Justis ᷠ subscription database;   **10–46**
> ➢ LexisNexis ᷠ subscription database;
> ➢ Westlaw ᷠ subscription database.

Loose-leaf encyclopaedias and texts 📖

> ➢ D. Vaughan, A. Robertson, *Law of the European Union* is published in loose-leaf **10–47**
> format by Oxford University Press. The most recent update was published in August
> 2013.
> ➢ *The Laws of Scotland: Stair Memorial Encyclopaedia* (see para.8–04).

European Current Law Issues and Yearbook 📖
This resource is published by Sweet and Maxwell and provides information about recent legal **10–48**
developments throughout Europe. It consists of monthly digests which are subsequently consolidated into Yearbooks. The information contained in European Current Law is divided into
four sections which can be searched by subject or by country.

> ➢ *Focus.* This contains short articles about developments in a specific subject area or
> jurisdiction;
> ➢ *The EU.* This section contains details of legislation, cases (from the Court of Justice
> and the General Court), books and articles arranged under subject headings;
> ➢ *National Jurisdictions.* Digests of legislation and cases and lists of legislation recently
> passed are arranged under subject headings and referenced to particular Member
> States;
> ➢ *Reference Section.* This includes a glossary of courts in all Member States, a list of
> abbreviations, Treaty provisions referred to in cases and legislation digested in the

volume, cumulative lists of legislation digested and cases reported and a cumulative subject index.

Current status of EU legislation

EUR-Lex ⌐ free

10–49 See para.10–33.

Commercial Databases

10–50
> ➢ Justis ⌐ and CD Rom subscription database;
> ➢ LexisNexis ⌐ subscription database; and
> ➢ Westlaw ⌐ subscription database.

Tracing if a Directive has been implemented in national law by Member States

N-Lex ⌐ free

10–51 N-Lex provides a gateway to the national law of member states. It allows users to search national databases where details of the implementation or otherwise of directives can be located. See *http://eur-lex.europa.eu/n-lex/index_en.htm* [accessed June 11, 2014].

European Commission Website ⌐ free

10–52 The EU Commission monitors the implementation of directives by each member state. Every two months the measures taken to date by each Member State to transpose a specific directive are scrutinised. If a member state has implement a measure but failed to inform the Commission it will likely find itself on the receiving end of a notice for "infringement by non-communication". The number of notices sent by the Commission to each member state from 2005 to the present day can be located, by year, here *http://ec.europa.eu/eu_law/directives/directives_communication_en.htm* [accessed June 11, 2014].

10–53 If the Member State concerned does not respond or its observations are deemed inadequate by the Commission the matter will be referred to the Court of Justice.

10–54 This resource thus provides statistical information only. To track implementing measures notified by member states for specific directives a search is undertaken by CELEX number. To do this access CELEX here *http://eur-lex.europa.eu/RECH_celex.do?ihmlang = en* [accessed June 11, 2014], e.g. Directive 2012/3/EU of February 9, 2012 amending Directive 98/8/EC of the European Parliament and of the Council to include bendiocarb as an active substance in Annex I thereto.

10–55 In the search field enter:

> ➢ The "sector" code this is "7";
> ➢ The year in "yyyy" format (four digits);
> ➢ The type of document: "L";
> ➢ The Directive number (four digits).

To find out which Member States have/have not transposed Directive 2012/3/EU enter "72012L0003" then click search.

10–56 In the results page (see below), click "Bibliographic Notice + MNE" where the individual member states national "execution measures" can be accessed.

Results page

72012L0003

The fact that there is a reference to national execution measures does not necessarily mean that these measures are either comprehensive or in conformity.
NATIONAL PROVISIONS COMMUNICATED BY THE MEMBER STATES CONCERNING:
Commission Directive 2012/3/EU of 9 February 2012 amending Directive 98/8/EC of the European Parliament and of the Council to include bendiocarb as an active substance in Annex I thereto Text with EEA relevance

Bibliographic notice + NEM

Westlaw ⚘ subscription database
When a Directive is located in the EU law section of Westlaw and the link to the Directive **10–57** accessed, a link on the left of the screen headed "Document outline" will be visible. Click on the option below this heading for national measures. A list of Member States will appear. These can then be accessed individually, if necessary, to obtain details of the implementing legislation in each member state.

EU Legislation Implementator 📖
This feature is part of Halsbury's SI (available on LexisNexis) and provides information on **10–58** Westminster legislation implementing EU directives. It is divided into two parts. The first part provides a chronological list of EU Directives (or Decisions) and an indication of if, when and how they have been implemented. The second part is a chronological list of UK legislation, indicating the EU Directives (or decisions) that each provision implemented.

Current Law Monthly Digest 📖
The Current Law Monthly Digests contain tables of EU legislation implemented by SIs and **10–59** Scottish SIs.

Official EU Documents

European Union working documents are published as "COM" documents. Legislative pro- **10–60** posals will first be published as COM documents and will later appear in the C series of the O.J.

COM documents can be located in the EUR-Lex database in the preparatory acts page. Other **10–61** documents published by EU institutions detailing or discussing the early stages of legislative proposals and Opinions of official EU advisory bodies, e.g. the European Economic and Social Committee, see *http://europa.eu/about-eu/institutions-bodies/ecosoc/index_en.htm* [accessed June 12, 2014], and the Committee of the Regions, see *http://cor.europa.eu/en/about/Pages/index.aspx* [accessed June 12, 2014], can also be accessed from this page.

Information about EU legislative proposals and their progress through the law-making pro- **10–62** cedure can also be located on the European Parliament's Legislative Observatory website at *http://www.europarl.europa.eu/oeil/home/home.do* [accessed June 11, 2014]. This resource is updated daily and can be searched under, inter alia, the following headings:

> ➤ EU Parliamentary term;
> ➤ Year;
> ➤ Procedure type;
> ➤ Procedure status;
> ➤ Rapporteur;
> ➤ Parliamentary committee;
> ➤ Legal basis; and
> ➤ Type of legislative act.

10–63 COM documents can also be located by consulting:

> ➤ LexisNexis ⌁ subscription database;
> ➤ Justis ⌁ subscription database; and
> ➤ Westlaw 8 subscription database.

NB Pre-lex at *http://ec.europa.eu/prelex/apcnet.cfm?CL=en* [accessed June 11, 2014] is a site that monitors the decision-making process between institutions which allows the researcher to track a proposal through all required legislative stages. This website also provides links to relevant background documents and other papers.

10–64 Further online resources detailing consideration of EU legislative proposals are; the Westminster Parliament's House of Lords EU Select Committee and House of Commons European Scrutiny Committee and the Holyrood Parliament European and External Relations Committee. For example:

> ➤ The House of Lords Committee has considered such proposals and formally reported on them since 1974. Its debates and reports, current and historic are available at *http://www.parliament.uk/business/committees/committees-a-z/lords-select/eu-select-committee-/* [accessed June 11, 2014].
> ➤ The House of Commons Committee considers all draft EU legislative proposals. This committee has the power to question the government on specific proposals and/or to recommend that certain proposals are debated in the House of Commons.
> The committee's homepage, at *http://www.parliament.uk/business/committees/committees-a-z/commons-select/european-scrutiny-committee/role/* [accessed June 11, 2014], provides links to committee publications and government responses to questions and any debates held.
> ➤ The Scottish Parliament European and External Relations Committee first sat on June 1, 2011. Its homepage, at *http://www.scottish.parliament.uk/parliamentarybusiness/CurrentCommittees/29814.aspx* [accessed June 11, 2014], states that its remit is to "consider and report on issues relating to the EU". Legislative proposals may be considered, however the main business of the committee is to consider EU policy objectives.
> Scrutiny of EU-related legislative provisions are more fully discussed at the Subordinate Legislation Committee *http://www.scottish.parliament.uk/parliamentarybusiness/PreviousCommittees/64264.aspx* [accessed June 11, 2014].
> This committee issues reports four times a year detailing the Scottish SIs it has considered in the reporting period and the recommendations, if any, made for each. A recent example of a Scottish SI considered in light of an EU obligation where concern was expressed by the committee is The Energy Performance of Building (Scotland) Amendment (No.2) Regulations 2012 No.208. An amended Scottish SI was duly

enacted to address the concerns expressed by the committee. This amended instrument came fully into force as of January 9, 2013.

SOURCES OF EU CASE LAW

There are three bespoke series of EU law reports: **10–65**

Title	**European Court Reports**
Abbreviation	E.C.R.
Citation	Case C-41/93 *French Republic v Commission of the European Communities* [1994] E.C.R. I-1829.
Period covered	1954 to present.
Publisher	Publications Office of the European Union.
Comments	This is the official series of European law reports.
	The reports are generally published in all the official languages of the EU.
	The production of multiple translations of cases can mean that the English version may appear some time after the date of the judgment.
	The reports include the Advocate General's Opinion alongside the decision. This is particularly useful as it is the Advocate General's Opinion which tends to contain the reasoned legal argument in EU cases.
Available in	Paper.
Coverage	All cases heard by the former European Court of Justice (ECJ) and the Court of First Instance were reported until 1988. As of 1989, certain cases have been published in summary form only. From 1/05/2004 onwards the following have not been published in the E.C.R.: judgments delivered, other than in preliminary ruling proceedings, by Chambers of three Judges, judgments delivered, other than in preliminary ruling proceedings, by Chambers of five Judges ruling without an Advocate General's Opinion and orders.
Format	Indexed by subject matter and in the final volume of the year there is a chronological table of cases.
	Since 1990 the reports have been divided into two sections: section I for the Court of Justice (formerly the ECJ) and section II for the General Court (formerly the Court of First Instance).

Title	**Common Market Law Reports**
Abbreviation	C.M.L.R.
Citation	Original: T-194/94 *Carvel & Guardian Newspaper Ltd v Council* [1995] 3 C.M.L.R. 359.
	Since 2001 a case number as opposed to a page number has featured in the citation e.g. C-321/03 *Dyson Ltd v Registrar of Trade Marks* [2007] 2 C.M.L.R. 14
	Thus "14" refers to case number 14 of the second volume of the 2007 Common Market Law Reports.
Period covered	1962 to present.
Publisher	Sweet and Maxwell.
Comments	Although they are not official reports, this series enjoys the advantage of appearing more speedily than the E.C.R. It is published weekly.
Available in	Paper and online via Westlaw.
Coverage	Decisions from the Court of Justice and the General Court, Commission decisions and decisions of national courts concerning EU law. All cases of significance are reported.
Format	Indexed alphabetically by case name, subject and legislative provision(s). It also contains tables of Treaties and Regulations judicially considered, cases judicially considered, secondary legislation cited and abbreviations.
Title	**All England Law Reports European Cases**
Abbreviation	All ER (EU)—previously (EC)
Citation	C-280/00 *Altmark Trans GmbH v Nahverkehrsgesellschaft Altmark GmbH* [2005] All ER (EC) 610.
Period covered	1995 to present.
Publisher	LexisNexis.
Available in	Paper, and online via LexisNexis.
Coverage	Decisions from the Court of Justice and the General Court.

Court of Justice Website (CURIA)

The CURIA homepage at *http://curia.europa.eu/jcms/jcms/j_6/* [accessed June 11, 2014] pro- **10–66** vides a gateway to the official electronic version of opinions and judgments of the Court of Justice. However, the definitive version of EU case law is the report of a specific case as published in the E.C.R. or the O.J. If there is any difference in the text as published in the CURIA version and these sources, the latter are to be considered authoritative.

The CURIA website also offers inter alia the following features: **10–67**

> ➤ The Institution tab provides a wealth of background information about the operation of the Court of Justice, including annual reports and statistical information;
> ➤ The Civil Service Tribunal tab links to first instance decisions concerning disputes between the EU and its employees (previously referred to as "staff cases"), appeals from which are heard by the General Court;
> ➤ The Library and Documentation tab is a gateway in itself as it provides direct access to the Court's library collection which includes documents pertaining to national, EU and international law; and
> ➤ The Press Releases tab links to media releases outlining the salient points of recent judgment of the Court of Justice or the General Court.

EUR-Lex ⌁ free

10–68 This website contains nearly three million documents which can be searched for by category. Court Opinions and judgments since 1954 can be accessed here *http://eur-lex.europa.eu/browse/ institutions/justice.html* [accessed June 24, 2014]:

> ➢ Recently decided cases from all EU courts are listed first by date of judgment; and
> ➢ The search boxes at the bottom of the screen allow a search for earlier cases to be undertaken by case number and year.

Westlaw ⌁ subscription database

10–69 Westlaw offers access to EU case law and also to the C.M.L.R.

LexisNexis ⌁ subscription database

10–70 LexisNexis offers access to EU case law and also to the All England Law Reports European Cases.

SECONDARY SOURCES OF INFORMATION ABOUT RECENT EU LEGISLATIVE AND POLICY DEVELOPMENTS

EUROPA Newsroom ⌁ free

10–71 This website, available at *http://europa.eu/newsroom/index_en.htm* [accessed June 11, 2014], has incrementally replaced prior and incorporated current stand alone webpages for the EU institutions and bodies listed below. The EUROPA Newsroom homepage, which is updated on a daily basis, provides direct access to information concerning current legal developments within the EU, including recent press releases and statements from these EU entities. To locate older press releases access the EUROPA Newsroom archive database here *http://europa.eu/newsroom/ press-releases/databases/index_en.htm* [accessed June 11, 2014].

10–72 The current generic address for each homepage is listed for convenience:

> ➢ Committee of the Regions—*http://cor.europa.eu/en/Pages/home.aspx* [accessed June 11, 2014];
> ➢ Council of the EU and European Council—*http://www.consilium.europa.eu/home page?lang=en* [accessed June 11, 2014];
> ➢ Court of Justice of the European Union—*http://europa.eu/about-eu/institutions-bodies/ court-justice/index_en.htm* [accessed June 11, 2014];
> ➢ European Central Bank—*http://www.ecb.europa.eu/home/html/index.en.html* [accessed June 11, 2014];
> ➢ European Commission (Rapid database)—*http://europa.eu/rapid/search.htm* [accessed June 11, 2014];
> ➢ European Court of Auditors—*http://www.eca.europa.eu/en/Pages/ecadefault.aspx* [accessed June 11, 2014];
> ➢ European Data Protection Supervisor—*https://secure.edps.europa.eu/EDPSWEB/edps/ EDPS?lang=en* [accessed June 11, 2014];
> ➢ European Economic and Social Committee—*http://www.eesc.europa.eu/?i=portal. en.home* [accessed June 11, 2014];
> ➢ European Ombudsman—*http://www.ombudsman.europa.eu/start.faces* [accessed June 11, 2014];

> European Parliament—*http://europa.eu/about-eu/institutions-bodies/european-parliament/ index_en.htm* [accessed June 11, 2014];
> Eurostat Statistical Office—*http://epp.eurostat.ec.europa.eu/portal/page/portal/eurostat/ home/* [accessed June 11, 2014].

EU Observer ⌐ free

This unofficial website provides a free online news service concerning EU related issues. The **10–73** homepage provides up-to-date commentary on current EU affairs and the site is easily navigated by topic by selecting from the various tabs at the top of the homepage. A free newsletter can be subscribed to which offers, daily, twice daily or weekly delivery. See *http://euobserver.-com/* [accessed June 11, 2014].

Other online unofficial sources

EU activity and legal developments are reported in many national, European-based and **10–74** international online publications. In-depth and critical coverage is to be found in the following:

> The European Voice website. Free to access and, in addition, a paid subscription service is available for a print copy delivered 45 times a year. *http://www.european voice.com/* [accessed June 11, 2014];
> EuroNews ⌐ free *http://www.euronews.com* [accessed June 11, 2014];
> BBC World Service Europe Today ⌐ free *http://www.bbc.co.uk/worldservice/ programmes/europetoday/index.shtml* [accessed June 11, 2014].

A selection of journals containing legal information about the EU

> Common Market Law Review (C.M.L.Rev.) Published bi-monthly;   **10–75**
> European Law Review (E.L.Rev.) Published bi-monthly;
> Journal of Common Market Studies (J.C.M.S.) Published four times a year;
> The International and Comparative Law Quarterly (I.C.L.Q.) Published four times a year;
> European Law Journal (E.L.J.) Published four times a year; and
> The Yearbook of European Law (Y.E.L.) This is an annual publication which contains tables of abbreviations, articles, annual surveys, book reviews, tables of cases, decisions and communications, legislation, treaties and rules of procedure, international conventions and agreements, national legislation and an index.

Journals concentrating on specific aspects of EU law include:

> European Business Law Review (E.B.L.R.) Published 11 times a year;
> European Competition Law Review (E.C.L.R.) Published eight times a year;
> European Environmental Law Review (E.E.L.R.) Published 11 times a year;
> European Intellectual Property Review (E.I.P.R.) Published monthly; and
> European Public Law (E.P.L.) Published four times a year.

Finding sources of articles concerning EU law

Westlaw ⌐ subscription database

The Westlaw UK Journals database contains the Legal Journals Index (LJI) and a significant **10–76** number of full-text articles. The LJI currently indexes hundreds of legal journals from the UK and English language European journals (see para.8–69).

European Commission Library Catalogue (ECLAS) ⌐ free

10–77 The ECLAS database, at *http://ec.europa.eu/eclas/F* [accessed June 11, 2014], can be searched to locate articles on European law and policy available in both electronic and paper form.

European Integration Current Contents ⌐ free

10–78 This online service, which began in 1999, provides access to the tables of contents of over 100 journals of relevance to European Integration. Its database holds information about approximately 45,000 articles pertaining to law, human rights, economics, history and political sciences in this sphere. See *http://archive.is/wanbo* [accessed June 11, 2014].

10–79 Check the subject index at the end of the Yearbooks. There is also an alphabetical list by title (see para.8–31 and para.10–48).

General sources of EU legal information

General Report on the Activities of the European Union 📖 and ⌐

10–80 This is an annual publication produced by the Secretariat-General of the EU Commission. It reviews the previous year's legal and policy developments. It is available in paper format (for a fee), but is free as a .pdf file or ebook (see *http://europa.eu/publications/reports-booklets/general-report/index_en.htm* [accessed June 11, 2014]). Reports from 1997 onwards are available in full text.

SCADPLUS ⌐ free

10–81 This easily searched website, see *http://europa.eu/legislation_summaries/index_en.htm* [accessed June 11, 2014], provides fact sheets which summarise EU legislation. The fact sheets are divided into 32 subject areas. There are summaries of existing measures and also follow-up information about new legislative proposals. The dates that appear at the bottom of each summary correspond to the date of the last substantial modification, e.g. the introduction of an amending or a related act. The SCADPLUS database holds over 3,000 fact sheets and the site is updated daily.

10–82 A search for a specific fact sheet can be undertaken here *http://europa.eu/scadplus/query_en.html* [accessed June 11, 2014].

European Parliament Fact Sheets ⌐

10–83 This official website holds fact sheets from 1979 onwards which have been, where necessary, revised. See *http://www.europarl.europa.eu/aboutparliament/en/displayFtu.html* [accessed June 11, 2014]. These documents are generally brief and to the point. Thus if an in-depth explanation of a specific policy or legislative measure is sought another source, e.g. the European Parliament homepage, at *http://www.europarl.europa.eu/portal/en* [accessed June 11, 2014], ought to be consulted.

10–84 A search can be undertaken on the fact sheet homepage under the following headings:

> ➢ How the European Union works;
> ➢ Citizens' Europe;
> ➢ The internal market;
> ➢ Economic and Monetary Union;
> ➢ Sectoral policies; and
> ➢ The EU's external relations.

European Union External Action ⌁ free

This website at *http://eeas.europa.eu/index_en.htm* [accessed June 11, 2014] provides information **10–85** on the EU's external relations, foreign policy, humanitarian aid and other areas of the EU's global role.

Europe in the UK ⌁ free

This website is, strictly speaking, a non-legal resource given that its prime function is to act as a **10–86** gateway for general resources of interest to teachers, researchers, students and the business community. That said, its "News and Events" tab, which can be accessed from the homepage, does contain information about selected current or pending legal issues (see *http://www.europe.org.uk/*).

EU local offices and information points

"Local" offices and information points are located in all Member States. Their purpose is to **10–87** disseminate information to the general public about the work undertaken by the Commission and take soundings in each Member State per current developments regarding EU law and policy. The generic website at *http://ec.europa.eu/contact/local_offices_en.htm* [accessed June 11, 2014] provides a search function which provides a direct link to each Member State's own website. The UK homepage, *http://ec.europa.eu/unitedkingdom/about_us/index_en.htm* [accessed June 11, 2014], provides a further link to information about the Representative Office based in Edinburgh (9 Alva Street, Edinburgh EH2 4PH).

Europe Direct

The Europe Direct homepage offers access to a "central" information service and "local" **10–88** information services (see *http://europa.eu/europedirect/introducing/index_en.htm* [accessed June 11, 2014]).

The central information service offers, by telephone or email: **10–89**

- ➤ Contact details for EU bodies at EU/national level;
- ➤ Information about EU citizens' legal rights;
- ➤ A response to general questions about the EU; and
- ➤ Information about how to access certain EU publications in paper format by post free of charge.

The local information services option provides a link to an interactive geographic map detailing the location of European Documentation Centres ("EDC") in each Member State. EDCs are authorised by the Commission to receive copies of official EU documents and publications, including EU legal provisions which can be accessed free of charge by members of the public.

The following UK institutions are designated EDCs: **10–90**

Scotland:

- ➤ University of Aberdeen, Taylor Library & EDC, Dunbar Street, AB24 3UB;
- ➤ University of Edinburgh, Old College, South Bridge, EH3 9YL;
- ➤ University of Glasgow, Hillhead Street, Glasgow, G12 8QB;

England and Wales:

- ➢ Aberystwyth University, Law Library Hugh Owen Library Aberystwyth Penglais Campus Aberystwyth, Ceredigion, SY23 3DZ;
- ➢ Cardiff University, Guest Building, Colum Drive, Cardiff, CF24 ODE;
- ➢ Leeds Metropolitan University, Leslie Silver Building, Calverley Street, Leeds, LS1 3ES;
- ➢ London School of Economics and Political Science, 10 Portugal Street, London, WC2A 2HD;
- ➢ Loughborough University, University Library, Loughborough, Leicestershire, LE11 3TU;
- ➢ Queen Mary & Westfield College London, Mile End Road, London, E1 4NS;
- ➢ Sheffield Hallam University, Howard Street, Sheffield, S1 1WB;
- ➢ The British Library, St. Pancras, 96 Euston Road, London, NW1 2DB;
- ➢ University of Bath Library & Learning Centre, Claverton Down, Bath, BA2 7AY;
- ➢ University of Birmingham, Edgbaston, Birmingham, B15 2TT;
- ➢ University of Bradford, Richmond Road, Bradford, BD7 1DP;
- ➢ University of Cambridge, West Road, Cambridge, CB3 9DR;
- ➢ University of Coventry, Gosford Street, Coventry, CV1 5PN;
- ➢ University of Durham, Stockton Road, Durham, DH1 3LY;
- ➢ University of Essex, Wivenhoe Park, Colchester, C04 3UA;
- ➢ University of Exeter, Stocker Road, Exeter, EX4 4PT;
- ➢ University of Hull, Cottingham Road, Hull, HU6 7RX;
- ➢ University of Keele, Staffordshire, ST5 5BG;
- ➢ University of Kent, Templeman Library, Canterbury, Kent, CT2 7NU;
- ➢ University of Lancaster, Bailrigg, Lancaster, LA1 4YH;
- ➢ University of Leeds, Brotherton Library, Leeds, LS2 9JT;
- ➢ University of Leicester, University Road, Leicester, LE1 7RH;
- ➢ University of Northumbria, Ellison Place, Newcastle upon Tyne, NE1 8ST;
- ➢ University of Nottingham, Nottingham, NG7 2RD;
- ➢ University of Oxford Bodleian Law Library, St Cross Building, Manor Road, Oxford, OX1 3UR;
- ➢ University of Portsmouth, Cambridge Road, Portsmouth, PO1 2ST;
- ➢ University of Reading, Whiteknights, Reading, RG6 6AE;
- ➢ University of Southampton, Highfield, Southampton, SO17 1BJ;
- ➢ University of Surrey, Guildford, GU2 5XN;
- ➢ University of Sussex, The Library, Brighton, BN1 9QL;
- ➢ University of Warwick, Gibbet Hill Road, Coventry, CV4 7AL;
- ➢ University of Wolverhampton, St Peter Square, Wolverhampton, WV1 1RH.

Northern Ireland:

- ➢ Queen's University of Belfast, University Road, Belfast, BT7 1LS.

NB The email address for each institution can be accessed via a general internet search or by visiting the homepage of the institution concerned.

Further Reading

10–91   ➢ R. Schutze, *An Introduction to EU Law* (Cambridge: Cambridge University Press, 2012)

Chapter 11
International Law

Significant abbreviations used in this chapter

- Cmnd, Cm.—Government publications presented to Parliament (UK)
- ECHR—European Convention on Human Rights
- ECtHR—European Court of Human Rights
- EU—European Union
- FLAG—Foreign Law Guide
- ICC—International Criminal Court
- ICJ—International Court of Justice
- LJI—Legal Journals Index (Westlaw)
- OSCOLA—Oxford Standards for Citation of legal Authorities
- SI—Statutory Instrument

The phrase "international law" can be used to identify a series of non-domestic, rule-based legal **11–01** regimes that sovereign states become part of via treaties or conventions which, once ratified, are considered binding in legal relations between the signatory states concerned.

There is a distinction to be drawn between "public" international law and "private" interna- **11–02** tional law. Public international law concerns specific relationships between sovereign states and international organisations, e.g. the Council of Europe (see below) and is the focus of this chapter. Private international law, on the other hand, is concerned with legal relations where there exists what is colloquially referred to as, a "conflict of laws". This means that issues of jurisdiction require to be determined as to which sovereign state may hear a dispute between private parties where more than one jurisdiction is involved and which sovereign state's law is to be applied to the dispute. The "rules" of private international law are not discussed in this chapter.

> **NB** EU law (see Ch.10) involves issues of "supranational" law, a species of international law, where sovereign states cede some of that sovereignty by ratifying a treaty (currently the Treaty of Lisbon) that details the legal powers enjoyed by the EU to make law for application in all states party to the treaty.

Public international law has a significant impact upon (the study of) Scots law given that it **11–03** involves examining the relationship between two or more legal systems. The research skills required to investigate public (and private) international law are principally the same as other areas of Scots law, with the addition of the ability to locate and interpret the international conventions or other legal instruments detailing the rules governing the relationship concerned. How to search for conventions is discussed below.

11–04 The purpose of this chapter is to introduce the reader to this increasingly important area of law and to highlight the differences between domestic legal sources and sources of international law. Accordingly, it begins by discussing some of the main sources and suggests ways of locating the materials referred to efficiently. The chapter concludes by discussing a particular aspect of public international law, human rights law, and explains the significance of the European Convention on Human Rights ("ECHR") and case law emanating from the European Court of Human Rights ("ECtHR") which gives judgments on the extent of these rights.

11–05 It is vital at the outset to be aware that the ECHR is NOT a piece of EU legislation and that human rights cases under the ECHR are NOT heard by the Court of Justice of the EU. Rather, the ECHR is an international (NOT supranational) convention created under the auspices of the Council of Europe. This point is emphasised to stop the reader falling into error, as many students have done in the past, by confusing the EU with this international organisation. The Council of Europe website even has a dedicated page *http://www.coe.int/aboutCoe/index.-asp?page=nepasconfondre&l=en* [accessed June 11, 2014] entitled "Do not get confused" which succinctly explains the differing role and remit of these two bodies.

SOURCES OF INTERNATIONAL LAW

International law concerns relationships between states, but the legal rules determining specific **11–06** rights and obligations are not made by a parliamentary body. Rather, international law is based on the goodwill of signatory states who agree to abide by a specific convention or treaty's provisions. However, if a state chooses not to ratify a legal instrument it has signed in accordance with its own domestic procedures for doing so, it is not bound by that instrument.

The Council of Europe Convention on Cybercrime illustrates that although a sovereign state **11–07** signs up to an instrument there may be a delay before it ratifies it, or in some cases, ratification is still awaited, over a decade after signature.

Convention on Cybercrime

http://conventions.coe.int/Treaty/Commun/print/ChercheSig.asp?NT = 185&CL = ENG [accessed June 12, 2014].

CETS No.185

Treaty open for signature by the member States and the non-member States which have participated in its elaboration and for accession by other non-member States

Opening for signature	Entry into force
Place: Budapest Date : 23/11/2001	Conditions: 5 Ratifications including at least 3 member States of the Council of Europe Date : 1/7/2004

Members of the Council of Europe

	Signature	Ratification	Entry into force	Notes	R.	D.	A.	T.	C.	O.
Argentina										
Australia		30/11/2012 a	1/3/2013		X		X			
Canada	23/11/2001									
Chile										
Colombia										
Costa Rica										
Dominican Republic		7/2/2013 a	1/6/2013			X	X			
Israel										
Japan	23/11/2001	3/7/2012	1/11/2012		X	X	X			
Mauritius		15/11/2013 a	1/3/2014				X			
Mexico										
Morocco										
Panama		5/3/2014 a	1/7/2014				X			
Philippines										
Senegal										

| South Africa | 23/11/2001 | | | | | | | | | |
| United States of America | 23/11/2001 | 29/9/2006 | 1/1/2007 | | X | X | X | | | |

Total number of signatures not followed by ratifications:	11
Total number of ratifications/accessions:	42

Status as of: 18/3/2014										
States of the Council of Europe										
	Signature	Ratification	Entry into force	Notes	R.	D.	A.	T.	C.	O.
Albania	23/11/2001	20/6/2002	1/7/2004				X			
Andorra	23/4/2013									
Armenia	23/11/2001	12/10/2006	1/2/2007				X			
Austria	23/11/2001	13/6/2012	1/10/2012		X	X	X			
Azerbaijan	30/6/2008	15/3/2010	1/7/2010		X	X	X	X		
Belgium	23/11/2001	20/8/2012	1/12/2012		X	X	X			
Bosnia and Herzegovina	9/2/2005	19/5/2006	1/9/2006				X			
Bulgaria	23/11/2001	7/4/2005	1/8/2005		X	X	X			
Croatia	23/11/2001	17/10/2002	1/7/2004				X			
Cyprus	23/11/2001	19/1/2005	1/5/2005				X			
Czech Republic	9/2/2005	22/8/2013	1/12/2013		X	X	X			
Denmark	22/4/2003	21/6/2005	1/10/2005		X		X	X		
Estonia	23/11/2001	12/5/2003	1/7/2004				X			
Finland	23/11/2001	24/5/2007	1/9/2007		X	X	X			
France	23/11/2001	10/1/2006	1/5/2006		X	X	X			
Georgia	1/4/2008	6/6/2012	1/10/2012				X			
Germany	23/11/2001	9/3/2009	1/7/2009		X	X	X			
Greece	23/11/2001									
Hungary	23/11/2001	4/12/2003	1/7/2004		X	X	X			
Iceland	30/11/2001	29/1/2007	1/5/2007		X		X			
Ireland	28/2/2002									
Italy	23/11/2001	5/6/2008	1/10/2008				X			
Latvia	5/5/2004	14/2/2007	1/6/2007		X		X			
Liechtenstein	17/11/2008									
Lithuania	23/6/2003	18/3/2004	1/7/2004		X	X	X			
Luxembourg	28/1/2003									
Malta	17/1/2002	12/4/2012	1/8/2012			X				
Moldova	23/11/2001	12/5/2009	1/9/2009			X	X	X		
Monaco	2/5/2013									
Montenegro	7/4/2005	3/3/2010	1/7/2010	55	X		X			

Netherlands	23/11/2001	16/11/2006	1/3/2007				X	X		
Norway	23/11/2001	30/6/2006	1/10/2006		X	X	X			
Poland	23/11/2001									
Portugal	23/11/2001	24/3/2010	1/7/2010			X	X			
Romania	23/11/2001	12/5/2004	1/9/2004				X			
Russia										
San Marino										
Serbia	7/4/2005	14/4/2009	1/8/2009	55			X			
Slovakia	4/2/2005	8/1/2008	1/5/2008		X	X	X			
Slovenia	24/7/2002	8/9/2004	1/1/2005				X			
Spain	23/11/2001	3/6/2010	1/10/2010			X	X			
Sweden	23/11/2001									
Switzerland	23/11/2001	21/9/2011	1/1/2012		X	X	X			
The former Yugoslav Republic of Macedonia	23/11/2001	15/9/2004	1/1/2005				X			
Turkey	10/11/2010									
Ukraine	23/11/2001	10/3/2006	1/7/2006		X		X			
United Kingdom	23/11/2001	25/5/2011	1/9/2011		X		X			

(55) Date of signature by the state union of Serbia and Montenegro.
    a: Accession – s: Signature without reservation as to ratification – su: Succession – r: Signature "ad referendum".
    R.: Reservations – D.: Declarations – A.: Authorities – T.: Territorial Application – C.: Communication – O.: Objection.
Source : Treaty Office on http://conventions.coe.int [accessed June 12, 2014].

Where the rules of public international law come from

The obvious question to pose is if there is no legislature, where do the rules of public inter- **11–08** national law come from? Article 38(1) of the Statute of the International Court of Justice, which is part of the Charter of the United Nations, has come to be regarded as a statement of the sources of international law. It states that the court shall apply: international conventions; international custom; general principles of law recognised by civilised nations; judicial decisions and the teaching of respected jurists.

For a detailed discussion of the sources of international law consult I. Brownlie, *Brownlie's* **11–09** *Principles of Public International Law*, 8th edn (Oxford: Clarendon Press, 2012.

There are two international courts of significance. The longer established of the two, the pre- **11–10** viously mentioned International Court of Justice, deals with civil matters: principally disputes between States. Unlike UK courts, it does not adopt a system of binding precedent and it does not enjoy jurisdiction over States in the same way as national courts have jurisdiction over individuals within a State (see *http://www.icj-cij.org/homepage/index.php* [accessed June 12, 2014]).

11–11 The International Criminal Court commenced work in 2002 under the authority of the Rome Statute of the International Criminal Court and hears cases concerning genocide, crimes against humanity, war crimes and crimes of aggression, but only those committed on the territory of, or by one of the nationals of, one of the States who agreed to the setting up of the court or under the authority of the United Nation's Security Council. The International Criminal Court's homepage can be consulted here, *http://www.icc-cpi.int/en_menus/icc/Pages/default.aspx* [accessed June 12, 2014].

11–12 At the time of writing, 122 sovereign states are party to this statute.

11–13 One difference in researching international law, as opposed to domestic or EU law, is the pre-eminence of electronic material. It is an increasingly important medium in all areas of law, but none more so than international law. A list of online gateways to international law materials is included at para.11–45.

Primary sources of international law

Treaties

11–14 The Vienna Convention on the Law of Treaties 1969, art.2(1)(a) defines a treaty as "an international agreement concluded between States in written form and governed by international law, whether embodied in a single instrument or in two or more related instruments and whatever its particular designation". Treaties are thus different from domestic legislation as they do not have a defined territorial jurisdiction. They only apply to States which agree to accede to them. A treaty can be between two states (bilateral) or several states (multilateral). Some international organisations are able to make treaties with States, but individuals do not have the capacity to make treaties. Treaties can also be referred to as Conventions, Covenants, Pacts, Agreements or Charters. A Protocol tends to refer to an agreement reached subsequent to a treaty which has amended the original treaty.

11–15 Treaties are divided into articles and paragraphs, as opposed to sections as used in domestic Acts of Parliament. As detailed in para.11–06, treaties do not automatically come into force at the moment the parties reach agreement. Thus the mere act of signing a treaty does not bind a state to ratify it at a later date. Signature only indicates an intention to ratify. There can also be a considerable period of time between the signature of a treaty and its coming into force. Individual treaties will specify different periods. It is normal for a treaty to come into force after it has been ratified by a certain number of signatories. The Convention on Cybercrime shown in para.11–07 illustrates this norm.

Citation of treaties

11–16 The usual way of referring to treaties is by their title and the year of signature/adoption, e.g. the Vienna Convention on the Law of Treaties 1969. A full citation will include a reference to the relevant treaty series where the treaty appears. The possible citations for this treaty include:

> ➤ 1155 U.N.T.S. 331 refers to the United Nations Treaty Series, Vol.1155 and p.331;
> ➤ U.K.T.S. 58 (1980), Cmnd. 7964 relates to the entry in the United Kingdom Treaty Series. This series forms a sub-series to the Command Papers. Treaties are referred to by the treaty series number, a Command Paper number and the date of issue (treaties are only published in this series after ratification);
> ➤ (1969) 8 I.L.M. 679 refers to *International Legal Materials*, 1969, Vol.8 and p.679.

Information about the citation of international legal materials is provided by the Oxford Standard for Citation of Legal Authorities ("OSCOLA").

Selected collections of treaties and dedicated websites

United Nations Treaty Collection

The Consolidated Treaty Series covers the period 1628–1920 and the League of Nations Treaty **11–17** Series covers 1920–1946. The major series of modern treaties is the United Nations Treaty Series which includes material from 1946 onwards and comprises the treaties and international agreements which have been published by the Secretariat of the United Nations. The collection currently has over 200,000 treaties and related material which have been published in over 2,660 volumes. The United Nations Treaty Series can be searched online at *https://treaties.un.org/ Pages/UNTSOnline.aspx?id=1* [accessed June 11, 2014]. A search can be undertaken by: date, party, title, subject terms, registration number or a combination of these features.

The collection also allows full access to Multilateral Treaties deposited with the Secretary- **11–18** General of the United Nations and provides current information on the status of major multilateral instruments. It is updated on a weekly basis allowing the researcher to confirm the status of instruments as the process of signature and ratification by individual States takes place.

The United Kingdom Treaty Series *FREE*

This series comprises the UK's national collection of treaties as published by the Foreign and **11–19** Commonwealth Office at *https://www.gov.uk/uk-treaties* [accessed June 11, 2014]. The series begins in 1892 and forms a sub-series to the Command Papers. Treaties are published in this series only after ratification by the United Kingdom.

International Legal Materials *SUBSCRIPTION*

This is an excellent source of information about Treaties and international law in general. See **11–20** *http://www.asil.org/resources/international-legal-materials* [accessed June 11, 2014].

The Council of Europe Treaty Office *FREE*

The Council of Europe Treaty Office website allows access to treaties and agreements of the **11–21** Council of Europe. See *http://conventions.coe.int/* [accessed June 11, 2014]. The official versions of the treaties are contained in the European Treaty Series ("ETS") 1949–2003 and the Council of Europe Treaty Series ("CETS") 2004 onwards. The Council of Europe was established by the Statute of the Council of Europe in 1949. Its aim, as stated in art.1(b), is to encourage progressive European agreement on economic, social, cultural, scientific, legal and administrative matters and to maintain and work towards the further realisation of human rights and fundamental freedoms. Its principal and most widely known achievement is the European Convention on Human Rights. See paras 11–47 and 11–49.

NB When a treaty is incorporated into UK law it is common practice to include the text of the original treaty in a Schedule to the Act of the Westminster or Statutory Instrument concerned. However, the ease with which these can be located when only the name of the treaty is known depends on how closely the short title of the UK legislation matches the treaty title.

There are compendiums of important treaties aimed at the student market available for pur- **11–22** chase, such as *Blackstone's International Law Documents*, 11th edn (Oxford: OUP, 2013). This text does not contain any annotations thus is suitable for use in examinations if this is permitted.

Another widely-used text which includes both primary materials and useful commentary is D.J. Harris, *Cases and Materials on International Law*, 7th edn (London: Sweet & Maxwell, 2010).

Custom

11–23 Custom has traditionally been regarded as one of the most important sources of public international law. However, its importance is lessening due to the increase in the number of treaties which are codifying custom. Custom, in the international sense, does not equate with custom in Scots law. In public international law there are two elements which must be present for a custom to exist: state practice and the belief that a legal obligation binds you to act in a certain way (referred to as *opinio juris et necessitatis*).

11–24 How is it possible to find evidence of custom? Brownlie states that:

> "The material sources of custom are very numerous and include the following: diplomatic correspondence, policy statements, press releases, the opinions of official legal advisers, official manuals on legal questions, manuals of military law, executive decisions and practices, orders to naval forces, etc., comments by governments on drafts produced by the International Law Commission, state legislation, international and national judicial decisions, recitals in treaties and other international instruments, a pattern of treaties in the same form, the practice of international organs, and resolutions relating to legal questions in the United Nations General Assembly." (I. Brownlie, *Principles of Public International Law*, 8th edn (Oxford: Clarendon Press, 2012, p.5).)

It is obviously easier to find information about some of the above than others. Sources of information about custom include State papers, such as the British and Foreign State Papers produced by the Foreign Office Library between 1812 and 1968. The International Law Commission mentioned above exists under the auspices of the United Nations. Its role is to promote the progressive development of international law and its codification. Information about it and its activities can be found at its website at *http://www.un.org/law/ilc/* [accessed June 24, 2014].

11–25 Sources of current information about State practice can also be gleaned from the "Current Legal Developments" sections in the journal International and Comparative Law Quarterly and the reference work the British Year Book of International Law.

Cases

The International Court of Justice

11–26 The International Court of Justice ("ICJ") and sometimes referred to as the "world court" is situated in The Hague in the Netherlands. It was established at the same time as the UN in 1946. Its predecessor was called the Permanent Court of International Justice, which had been established under the League of Nations. The International Court of Justice derives its mandate from the Statute of the International Court of Justice which is annexed to the Charter of the UN. Article 59 of that Statute states that "the decision of the court has no binding force except between the parties and in respect of that particular case". Although there is no formal doctrine of binding precedent, previous cases are not ignored in the courts deliberations.

International Court Reports (I.C.J. Reports) (1947–)

This is the official series of ICJ law reports which has the full title of Reports of Judgments, **11–27**
Advisory Opinions and Orders of the International Court of Justice. These reports appear in
both English and French. All cases brought before the court since 1946 are available on the
court's website via the homepage at *http://www.icj-cij.org/homepage/index.php* [accessed June
11, 2014].

Pleadings, Oral Arguments and Documents (I.C.J. Pleadings) (1947–)

This resource is also published by the court. The series contains the documentation for each case **11–28**
which is made public after the final decision has been given. These are also available on the
court's website together with the judgment.

Yearbook of the International Court of Justice (I.C.J. Yearbook)

This contains information about the work of the court, its members and activities in a given **11–29**
year. To mark 90 years of the ICJ's existence a free e-book detailing the development of and the
work undertaken by the ICJ and its predecessor (see below) between 1922–2012 was published
in 2012. This text can be accessed here, *http://www.icj-cij.org/pcij/serie_other/cpji-pcij.pdf*
[accessed June 11, 2014].

Reports of Case Law of the Permanent Court of International Justice

The predecessor to the ICJ was the Permanent Court of International Justice (P.C.I.J.). Between **11–30**
1922 and 1946 P.C.I.J. judgments were published in Series A (Nos 1–24): Collection of Judgments (up to and including 1930) and Series A/B (Nos 40–80): Judgments, Orders and Advisory
Opinions (beginning in 1931). These are all available at the ICJ website.

The International Criminal Court

The International Criminal Court ("ICC") came into being in 2002 when 120 States adopted the **11–31**
Rome Statute, the legal basis for establishing the permanent International Criminal Court. The
Court may only exercise jurisdiction if: the accused is a national of a State Party or a State
otherwise accepting the jurisdiction of the Court; the crime took place on the territory of a State
Party or a State otherwise accepting the jurisdiction of the Court; or the United Nations
Security Council has referred the situation to the Prosecutor, irrespective of the nationality of
the accused or the location of the crime. The court is based in The Hague, in the Netherlands.
Information about the ICC is available at its website *http://www.icc-cpi.int/en_menus/icc/Pages/
default.aspx* [accessed June 11, 2014].

The Official Journal of the ICC is available at *http://www.icc-cpi.int/EN_Menus/icc/Pages/* **11–32**
default.aspx [accessed June 24, 2014]. It includes the Statute of Rome, rules of procedure and
evidence and details of the crimes within the ICC's jurisdiction.

International Law Reports ("I.L.R.")

This series started in 1919 and was originally called the Annual Digest of Public International **11–33**
Law Cases. This is the name for volumes 1–16. From Vol.17 (1950) they have been called
International Law Reports. The aim of this series is to provide English-language access to
judicial matters that have a bearing on international law. It covers the International Court of
Justice, European Court of Human Rights, Inter-American Court of Human Rights and other
international tribunals, as well as national decisions from many countries which have a public
international law angle. Cases can be accessed in alphabetical order, by court, by country and by

subject headings. There are several volumes which can be accessed via the JUSTIS subscription database. Electronic versions of the alphabetical consolidated Tables of Cases for Vols 1–125 and 126–150 can be accessed free of charge on the Lauterpacht Centre for International Law website at *http://www.lcil.cam.ac.uk/publications/international-law-reports* [accessed June 11, 2014].

International Legal Materials (1962–) 📖 and ⌁

11–34 This is a bi-monthly publication produced by the American Society of International Law. (see *http://www.eisil.org/* [accessed June 11, 2014]). It provides wide coverage of developments in international law. The main criterion for selection is that the documents are of substantial interest to legal researchers, practising lawyers and officials dealing with public and private international law. This is a very useful source of information. It is usually the first available source of full text information about key documents. There is a subject index at the end of each annual volume. The entries are arranged under the following headings:

> ➢ Resolutions, declarations and other documents;
> ➢ Treaties and agreements;
> ➢ Judicial and similar proceedings;
> ➢ Legislation;
> ➢ Judicial and similar proceedings;
> ➢ Briefs; and
> ➢ Other documents received.

This publication is also available via LexisNexis and Westlaw.

Secondary sources of international law

Textbooks and bibliographies

11–35 There are several text books and reference works of relevance to international law and most academic libraries will hold copies of one or more of the following:

> ➢ R. Jennings (ed.), *Oppenheim's International Law*, 9th edn (Harlow: Pearson, 1992);
> ➢ I. Brownlie, *Principles of Public International Law*, 8th edn (Oxford: Clarendon Press 2012);
> ➢ A. Boyle and C. Chinkin, *The Making of International Law* (Oxford: OUP, 2007);
> ➢ M. Dixon, *Textbook on International Law*, 7th edn (Oxford: OUP, 2013);
> ➢ R.M.M. Wallace, *International Law*, 6th edn (London: Sweet & Maxwell, 2009);
> ➢ Dingle L, *Guide to electronic sources of International Law* in Crawford J and Koskenniemi M (eds), *The Cambridge Companion to International Law* (2012).

Bibliographies include:

> ➢ E.G. Schaffer and R.J. Snyder (eds), *Contemporary Practice of Public International Law* (Dobbs Ferry NY: Oceana Publications, 1997);
> ➢ *Public International Law—A Current Bibliography of Books and Articles* (1975–). See the for Comparative Public Law and International Law website for further information, *http://www.mpil.de/en/pub/research/details/publications/institute/pil.cfm* [accessed June 13, 2014];
> ➢ E. Beyerly, *Public International Law—A Guide to Information Sources* (London: Mansell, 1991);
> ➢ J.G. Merrills, *A Current Bibliography of International Law* (London: Butterworths, 1978).

Journals

The most widely available journals are: **11–36**

> ➤ International and Comparative Law Quarterly (I.C.L.Q.);
> ➤ American Journal of International Law (A.J.I.L.); and
> ➤ European Journal of International Law (E.J.I.L.).

There are many more international law journals, especially in the US. There are also an increasing number of journals relating to specialist areas of international law, e.g. Journal of Air Law and Commerce. This publication is available via the Heinonline subscription database.

British Yearbook of International Law (B.Y.I.L.) (1920–present)

This publication contains the in-depth articles, detailed book reviews, decisions of British courts **11–37** involving questions of international law; decisions on the European Convention on Human Rights, decisions of the Court of Justice of the EU and UK materials on international law cited from a wide range of sources and arranged by subject within the realm of international law.

Finding journal articles

Public International Law: A Current Bibliography of Books and Articles 📖
This journal is published twice a year. Over 1,400 journals, yearbooks and commemorative **11–38** compilations are regularly evaluated for this bibliography.

Index to Legal Periodicals and Books 📖 and ⌁ subscription indexing service
This index, which is updated daily, references legal periodicals and books which are published in **11–39** the UK, Ireland, US, Canada, Australia and New Zealand. It is an American publication and the majority of material is American. The online version holds materials from 1982 onwards and allows access to some journals in full text. Pre-1981 articles are referenced in the bound volumes. For further information see *http://www.ebscohost.com/corporate-research/index-to-legal-periodicals-books* [accessed June 13, 2014].

Index to Foreign Legal Periodicals 📖 and ⌁ subscription indexing service
This is another US based index. It covers selected international law and comparative law **11–40** periodicals and collections of essays. The paper volumes begin in 1960 and the online version contain material from 1985 onwards. This publication is available via the Heinonline subscription database.

Electronic Resource Guide

This resource is provided by the American Society for International Law. It provides an **11–41** overview of and search strategies for the undernoted subject areas. In addition, each guide lists many other electronic sources and gives hyperlinks to the home pages for same. See *http://www.asil.org/resources/electronic-resource-guide-erg* [accessed June 13, 2014].

> ➤ European Union;
> ➤ International Commercial Arbitration;
> ➤ International Criminal Law;
> ➤ International Economic Law;
> ➤ International Environmental Law;
> ➤ International Human Rights;
> ➤ International Humanitarian Law;

> ➤ International Intellectual Property Law;
> ➤ International Organisations;
> ➤ Law of the Sea;
> ➤ Public International Law;
> ➤ Private International Law; and
> ➤ United Nations.

Westlaw ✐ subscription database

11–42 Westlaw Journals contains the Legal Journals Index and a number of full-text articles. The LJI currently indexes hundreds of legal journals from the UK and English language European journals. See para.8–69.

Foreign Law Guide ("FLAG") database ✐ free

11–43 FLAG is an inventory of the collections of foreign, comparative and international law materials in UK universities and the British Library. It describes the contents of different collections noting shelf marks and providing web links to each of the libraries included in the database. It is not intended to indicate who holds the issues of a particular serial but it will tell you which libraries house certain collections. See *http://ials.sas.ac.uk/library/flag/flag.htm* [accessed June 13, 2014].

Sources of current awareness

11–44
> ➤ Bulletin of International Legal Developments ✐ subscription;
>   This published fortnightly by the British Institute of International & Comparative Law.
>   See *http://www.biicl.org/publications/bild/* [accessed June 13, 2014];
> ➤ Foreign and Commonwealth Office ✐ free
>   This site is updated throughout the day with speeches, transcripts and press releases.
>   See *https://www.gov.uk/government/announcements?departments%5B%5D=foreign-commonwealth-office* [accessed June 13, 2014];
> ➤ International Court of Justice—latest press releases ✐ free
>   See *http://www.icj-cij.org/presscom/index.php?p1=6&p2=1* [accessed June 13, 2014];
> ➤ International Criminal Court homepage has latest news, highlights and recent updates sections ✐ free
>   *http://www.icc-cpi.int/EN_Menus/icc/Pages/default.aspx* [accessed June 24, 2014];
> ➤ BBC News (World) ✐ free
>   This site allows all BBC News online stories since November 1997 to be searched for.
>   See *http://www.bbc.co.uk/news/world/* [accessed June 13, 2014];
> ➤ Keesing's Record of World Events (originally known as Keesing's Contemporary Archives) 📖 and ✐ subscription
>   See *http://www.keesings.com/* [accessed June 13, 2014] .

Selected online legal gateways to international law materials—all free

11–45
> ➤ Access to Law—International Law Materials. See *http://www.accesstolaw.com/other-jurisdictions/world-law/* [accessed June 13, 2014];
> ➤ Electronic Information System for International Law. This is a US based website produced by the American Society of International Law. It provides links to primary materials and websites incorporating many aspects of international law and also lists useful ancillary information about the resources it contains. See *http://www.eisil.org/* [accessed June 13, 2014];
> ➤ GlobaLex. This website includes research guides to many aspects of international law. See *http://www.nyulawglobal.org/globalex/* [accessed June 13, 2014].

➢ Eagle-I is provided by the Institute of Advanced Legal Studies. This website provides links to and introductory information about a host of sources of International law sources. See *http://ials.sas.ac.uk/eaglei/project/eiproject.htm* [accessed June 13, 2014].

➢ *WorldLII*. The website is not, strictly speaking, a direct gateway to international legal resources. However, the "International law" hyperlink on the left hand side of the homepage links, in turn, to the jurisprudence of selected national and international courts. This website also provides hyperlinks to certain International Treaties and a limited selection of online law journals. See *http://www.worldlii.org/* [accessed June 13, 2014].

International Legal Research Online Tutorial

This US-based resource is designed to instruct students and practitioners on: (i) International **11–46** law basics; (ii) research strategies; and (iii) research methodologies to enable them to efficiently search both paper and electronic sources of International legal materials. See *http://www.law.-duke.edu/ilrt/* [accessed June 13, 2014].

Human rights law

Public international law can be sub-divided into discrete areas, e.g. the law of the sea, inter- **11–47** national environmental law, world trade law and international criminal law. One area of international law which is increasingly important is that of human rights law. The European Convention on Human Rights (whose proper title is The Convention for the Protection of Human Rights and Fundamental Freedoms) was adopted by the Council of Europe in 1950 and entered into force in 1953. The European Court of Human Rights ("ECHR") was set up in 1959. It is located in Strasbourg. Originally there was a European Commission on Human Rights (formed in 1953) whose role was to examine cases with regard to admissibility. Following Protocol No.11 the Commission was disbanded.

The ECHR is an International convention which became part of UK law after the enactment of **11–48** the Human Rights Act 1998 (the domestic instrument of ratification). This innovation has had an impact on almost every area of national law and it is vital that the Scots lawyer can locate primary and secondary sources of human rights law materials.

Human rights jurisprudence developed over decades in the European Court of Human Rights **11–49** (ECtHR) now forms part of UK domestic common law. Article 1 of the Convention requires all signatory states to "secure to everyone within their jurisdiction the rights and freedoms ... of this Convention" and s.2 of the Human Rights Act 1998 makes it clear that any UK court or tribunal (determining a question which has arisen in connection with a Convention right) must take into account any "judgment, decision, declaration or advisory opinion of the European Court of Human Rights". All UK courts and tribunals have a statutory duty to interpret domestic legislation and the common law in a way that is compatible with Convention rights, they must also ensure that public authorities do not, through an act or omission, act in such a way as to breach convention rights.

Section 57(2) of the Scotland Act 1998 states that "a member of the Scottish Government **11–50** (previously Executive) has no power to make any ... legislation, or to do any other act, so far as the legislation or act is incompatible with any of the Convention rights".

The 1998 Act does not specify who or what is a public authority beyond stipulating in s.2 that **11–51** courts and tribunals qualify as such. However, the Liberty Guide to Human Rights, at *http://yourrights.org.uk/yourrights/the-human-rights-act/how-does-the-human-rights-act-1998-work-*

.html [accessed June 11, 2014], suggests that "bodies like the police, local councils and government departments and agencies are all public authorities". Case law has determined when a body is, for the purposes of the 1998 Act, considered to be a public body and this will always be the primary question to be answered when a dispute arises. The UK Ministry of Justice website contains an abundance of materials aimed at both members of the public and public bodies. One such publication "Human Rights: Human Lives—A Handbook for Public Authorities" can be accessed here, *http://www.justice.gov.uk/downloads/human-rights/human-rights-handbook-for-public-authorities.pdf* [accessed June 13, 2014].

11–52 The Human Rights Act 1998 is widely published on the internet, with the *legislation.gov.uk* website publishing the official version currently in force here; *http://www.legislation.gov.uk/ukpga/1998/42/contents* [accessed June 11, 2014].

Primary sources of human rights law

The European Convention on Human Rights

11–53   ➤   The Council of Europe (CoE) European Treaties website allows free access to full text versions of all CoE Conventions, protocols and the status of these instruments, including the dates signed and ratified by the various signatory states, date of coming into force and any reservations or declarations. Click on *http://conventions.coe.int/Treaty/Commun/ListeTraites.asp?CM = 8&CL = ENG* [accessed June 11, 2014] to access the ECHR. It is the third instrument listed;

  ➤   Alternatively, the ECHR can be accessed elsewhere on the CoE site at *http://www.hri.org/docs/ECHR50.html* [accessed June 11, 2014];

  ➤   The ECtHR website, at *http://www.echr.coe.int/* [accessed June 24, 2014], also provides a link to the ECHR from its homepage.

Case law from the European Court of Human Rights

The European Court of Human Rights website ⌐ free
11–54 The ECtHR website contains:

  ➤   Information for applicants and the general public about the court, and its procedures;

  ➤   The text of the ECHR and additional protocols;

  ➤   Case law database. This vital resource contains lists of recent judgments and decisions which can be searched using HUDOC;

  ➤   Pending cases; and

  ➤   Press information which contains a calendar of scheduled hearings and press releases.

Case law from UK Courts

11–55 The resources generally available to locate human rights case law litigated before UK courts are the same as for UK cases (see Ch.4). The volume of Human Rights cases in the UK has now spawned law reports which solely cover human rights cases:

European Human Rights Reports 📖 and ⌐ subscription
11–56 The leading paper source for the decisions of the ECtHR is the commercially produced European Human Rights Reports (E.H.R.R.) (published by Sweet and Maxwell since 1979 onwards). This publication, which is also available on Westlaw, provides full text judgments.

Human Rights Law Reports—UK Cases (H.R.L.R.) 📖 and ⌐ subscription
This publication is also produced by Sweet and Maxwell and focuses entirely on the application **11–57**
of the Convention and the 1998 Act as interpreted by UK courts. For each reported case, a
headnote containing keywords, a synopsis of the human rights issue(s) before the court and a
summary of the decision precedes the full transcript of the judgment.

Secondary sources of human rights law

Text books

> ➤ S. Foster, *Human Rights and Civil Liberties* (Cambridge: Pearson Publishing, 2011);   **11–58**
> ➤ R. Reed and J. Murdoch, *Human Rights Law in Scotland*, 3rd edn (London: Bloomsbury, 2011);
> ➤ A selection of Human Rights e-books with an international perspective or specific focus, e.g., crimes against humanity, is provided free by the E-books Directory. This resource can be accessed here; *http://www.e-booksdirectory.com/listing.php?category=345* [accessed June 13, 2014].

Journals

> ➤ *European Human Rights Law Review* (E.H.R.L.R.) is published six times a year;   **11–59**
> ➤ *Human Rights Law Review* (H.R.L.Rev.) is published three times a year;
> ➤ The CoE's Yearbook of the European Convention on Human Rights provides an account of both case law and general developments in the human rights arena in a given year. Certain older Yearbooks are available free on Google Books. *http://books.google.com/* [accessed June 13, 2014].

Finding journal articles

Westlaw ⌐ subscription database
Westlaw's LJI lists relevant publications and provides to links to a number of full-text articles. **11–60**

Current awareness websites (all free)

The following websites are recommended in terms of coverage and the depth with which specific **11–61**
human rights issues are discussed or reported.

> ➤ Amnesty International UK. See *http://www.amnesty.org.uk/* [accessed June 13, 2014];
> ➤ CoE Commissioner for Human Rights. The office of the Commissioner is an independent institution within the CoE mandated to promote the awareness of and respect for human rights in all CoE member states. See *http://www.coe.int/web/commissioner* [accessed July 16, 2014];
> ➤ Equality and Human Rights Commission (UK) is a publicly funded statutory body with the remit to, inter alia, promote and monitor human rights. See *http://www.equalityhumanrights.com/* [accessed June 13, 2014]. This website has a specific page detailing the work of this body in Scotland at *http://www.equalityhumanrights.com/scotland/* [accessed June 13, 2014];
> ➤ Liberty is a campaigning organisation also known as the National Council for Civil Liberties. See *http://www.liberty-human-rights.org.uk/index.shtml* [accessed June 13, 2014];
> ➤ One Crown Office Row—Human Rights Update. This service is provided by barristers of Crown Office Row, based in Temple, London. It contains over a thousand reports and commentaries, from 1998 onwards, on human rights cases. The website at, *http://www.1cor.com/humanrights* [accessed June 13, 2014], is updated weekly and provides

practical guidance on the ECHR, the Human Rights Act 1998 Act and publishes articles on human rights issues. To access contemporary content registration is required;

> Ministry for Justice (Westminster). See *http://www.justice.gov.uk/human-rights* [accessed June 13, 2014];
> Scottish Human Rights Commission. See *http://scottishhumanrights.com/* [accessed June 13, 2014];
> Parliamentary Joint Committee on Human Rights (Westminster). See *http://www.parliament.uk/business/committees/committees-a-z/joint-select/human-rights-committee/* [accessed July 16, 2014].

Chapter 12
Topic Based Research and the Legal Investigation Process

This chapter considers topic-based research and the legal investigation process. In doing so, it **12–01** initially discusses a model search strategy for the efficient gathering of relevant information thereby inviting the researcher to hone research skills and knowledge gained from their reading of previous chapters by reprising: (i) which resources provide an authoritative version of primary and secondary sources; and (ii) where best to locate these sources. How to present the fruits of a research project in a coherent and legalistic way (in both written and oral form) is discussed in Ch.14.

However, legal research can involve more than focusing on finding the substantive or "black **12–02** letter" rules of law in a given area. Thus the term "legal research" is not restricted to considering these rules alone or in isolation. Beyond the confines of black letter law there exists socio-legal research which examines how law operates or impacts in a variety of social spheres. It seeks to determine whether specific rules of law have changed societal attitudes and/or behaviour and also consider, as does analytical black letter law research, whether existing rules are fit for purpose or whether further or new rules are required. Accordingly, this chapter concludes with a brief discussion of selected methods of data collection that are common to all the social sciences; questionnaires, interviews and observational studies and highlights the different ethical considerations each method presents.

LITERATURE-BASES RESEARCH

Topic based research:

Primary issues

As stated throughout this text, "finding the law" on a particular topic has in some ways become **12–03** much easier with the increased availability of online materials and legal databases which allow the researcher to search through and across large amounts of different data using elementary or increasingly more sophisticated search techniques. However, it is essential at this point to reiterate that all research projects undertaken must be focussed, comprise valid (authoritative) primary and secondary resources representing the current (not historic) law and proceed on the basis of a proper understanding of the task that has been set.

The perils of over-reliance on the internet as a research tool are detailed throughout Ch.2. The **12–04** main issues of concern are restated below:

> ➤ The sheer availability of information on the internet means that even the narrowest of search terms will retrieve a large number of irrelevant hits;

➢ There is no quality control, therefore the accuracy of any information retrieved or the weight to be attached to it cannot be discerned without validating such information with an official source;

➢ The vast majority of free primary and secondary sources will be out-of-date when accessed, thus proving irrelevant unless an historical piece of research is being undertaken; and

➢ General internet subject searches increasingly retrieve Wikipedia or paid for advertising websites high in the ranking order of search results. Such web pages lack authority and accuracy, and in some instances veracity, and should never feature in a legal research project.

12–05 To ensure efficient and meaningful use of open source internet resources, legal databases and information gateways ought to be located and used in preference to undertaking a general search using a commercial search engine. Subscription databases, like Westlaw, offer superior search facilities which allow a search to be undertaken across both primary materials, such as cases and legislation, and secondary materials, e.g. legal journals and legal commentary, using Boolean searching (see para.2–58), which will generally reduce the time (and effort) taken to locate relevant materials. Certain open source resources, e.g. the HUDOC database (see para.11–54) do likewise.

12–06 Therefore, the first issue a topic-based researcher should consider before a word is written is what (re)sources will be required to successfully complete a given research project.

Using paper and electronic sources

12–07 It should also be remembered that it can be more efficient on many occasions to consult paper sources, such as encyclopaedias and reference works as detailed throughout Ch.8, at the outset to gain general information about a topic. Such resources should not be overlooked merely on the basis that they may only be available in paper form and that an internet search will yield a large amount of background information in an instant.

12–08 The major benefits derived from consulting these resources are as follows:

➢ Legal encyclopaedias and reference works are written by experts and are specifically designed to discuss and update the law on a subject by subject basis;

➢ Whilst legal databases provide a list of hits that are linked to the words in any search term(s) used, they may or may not provide detailed background information, the legal context or how the different pieces of information relate to one another. Sources such as the *Stair Memorial Encyclopaedia* (or other major reference works) will not just identify a piece of legislation or a case, they will place it in context in the development of the relevant area of law. This means such sources will: explain the background to any innovation and how it fits in to the area of law concerned; discuss how it has been interpreted; offer critical comment on it; and consider how/why the law has developed and how it might develop in the future;

➢ Most encyclopaedias are updated on a regular basis either in paper (loose-leaf) and/or online formats.

Consulting an encyclopaedia or major reference work is therefore to be recommended as a starting point for research. Such initial enquiry allows the researcher to use the information obtained to construct more appropriate search terms when subsequently searching full text databases.

Devising a search strategy

It is rather unhelpful (but nonetheless true) to say that the precise search strategy to be adopted **12–09**
will depend on what exactly the researcher has been asked to find and then do with the information retrieved. However, a general search strategy and methodology for undertaking legal
research is outlined below.

At the outset, a firm focus on the particular issue or issues raised by the topic-based title set by **12–10**
the tutor is required. First consider if the work to be undertaken relates to substantive (black
letter) law or if it is to be approached on a more theoretical level. If the title of the project is, e.g.
"Explain and contrast the defences of self-defence and provocation" it is clear that a substantive
discussion is required and that two distinct criminal defences are to be "explained and contrasted". This may seem to be stating the obvious. However, students can fall into error simply
by not reading the question carefully and "go off on a frolic of their own", meaning that,
although the separate topics may be "explained" by the researcher, if they are not "contrasted"
(i.e. compared with the differences isolated then highlighted) the actual title set will not be fully
addressed. Essay writing techniques and techniques for answering "problem" questions are
discussed, respectively, in paras 14–24—14–34 and paras 14–50—14–58.

Getting started

Two issues in particular require to be resolved at the outset to define the search parameters of **12–11**
the project. It is crucial that this is done timeously to ensure that the range of sources consulted
is appropriate and sufficient.

> ➢ Jurisdiction: does the title require a discussion of Scots law only or is there a UK, EU
>   or international dimension?
> ➢ Time period to be covered: does the title require an analysis of the current law or does it
>   also include a historical study? If it is the latter, which time period? Undergraduate and
>   post-graduate students may be advised, particularly if research is to be undertaken over
>   a period of several months, that the project must reflect the law in force up to a certain
>   date.

Initial search

As suggested in para.12–07, it is productive to initially locate a source that will provide a general **12–12**
overview of the subject and identify relevant primary materials and further reading. Encyclopaedias and reference works are an ideal starting point. If the available resources do not extend
to such publications, a research project should commence by consulting a tutor recommended
textbook and any materials on a reading list (comprising both library-based paper and electronic sources) regarding the subject area/topic. These resources should be followed up as far as
possible for, in addition to detailing the undernoted materials, they will make reference to other
textbooks and/or journal articles in their respective bibliographies, further reading sections or
footnotes/endnotes and assist greatly in collating a longer list of other potential sources. If any
difficulty is encountered in locating such resources make use of one of the best resources in a
library—the law librarian.

Having begun the investigation process by looking at general information about the topic **12–13**
necessary to become familiar with the subject area, the search can be gradually narrowed to
focus on more specific material as demanded by the title, e.g.:

> ➢ Cases which are directly relevant to the subject under scrutiny (see para.4–58);

> ➤ Cases which have interpreted certain words in a legislative provision in a particular way (see para.4–72);
> ➤ Bills before the Westminster Parliament (see para.6–03) and/or the Holyrood Parliament (see para.7–12);
> ➤ Acts of the Westminster Parliament and/or Acts of the Holyrood Parliament;
> ➤ SIs (see para.6–118) and/or Scottish SIs (see para.7–69);
> ➤ Relevant debates in the Westminster Parliament (see para.6–17) and/or the Holyrood Parliament (see para.7–23);
> ➤ EU legislation (see Ch.10);
> ➤ UK (see paras 8–109—8–135) and/or Scottish, (see paras 8–136—8–152) and/or EU, (see Ch.10 generally) official publications;
> ➤ Scottish Law Commission reports (see para.8–149);
> ➤ Law Commission (England and Wales) reports (see para.8–149); and
> ➤ Journal articles concerning the topic under investigation.

As detailed throughout Ch.2, when using electronic sources to locate all or any of the above, the selection of appropriate search terms is vital. Restricting a search to one or two terms will most likely exclude germane material. Synonyms should also be used, e.g. if the title concerns the regulation of agricultural pollution in the UK, a search should be undertaken by using inter alia the following terms: environmental protection; pollution; agricultural pollution; water pollution; waste disposal; farm waste; nitrates; silage; slurry; run-off, etc.

12–14 As the search progresses it may prove necessary to alter the search terms or the original search parameters if too few resources are located. If this proves to be the case, broaden out the search by using a more general term or terms. In the example given above, the following terms could be used to extend a current search: agricultural pollution and Wales; agricultural pollution and farm waste; environmental protection and nitrates; EU and nitrates, and so on. Boolean and/or keyword search techniques can be used depending upon the electronic source consulted (see paras 2–58—2–59).

Updating an initial literature search

12–15 Given the passage of time between a research project commencing and concluding (this may be a matter of weeks or months), further primary and secondary materials will likely have been enacted/decided/published since the materials initially consulted were last updated, particularly if they are paper sources. Therefore it is vital to check for recently decided cases, any legislative developments and journal articles published in the intervening period prior to submitting the research project. The actual steps required will depend on the project title and the sources identified during the initial search, but these could involve accessing:

> ➤ Subscription databases, e.g. Westlaw and LexisNexis, which are updated on a daily basis;
> ➤ Official and unofficial websites that contain information on current legal developments in the subject area, such as the Scottish Parliament, Scottish Government, House of Commons Weekly Information Bulletin, *Hansard*, The Stationery Office Daily List;
> ➤ Current Law Monthly Digest/Statutes Service File which are updated on a monthly basis (see para.8–19 et al);
> ➤ Updating services available for various sources. Always check the frequency with which a specific service is updated and the date of the last update. Some services are only updated on a six-monthly basis; and
> ➤ News and media organisations.

It is important to be systematic when undertaking a research project and stay in control of the material collected. When relevant material has been located and is under consideration for inclusion in the work, the researcher should ensure that the full bibliographic reference for each source is noted accurately at that time it is consulted. This approach will save a lot of time (and frustration) when both footnotes/endnotes and the finalised bibliography are being compiled and checked for accuracy prior to submission. To do this efficiently and effectively, a "personal bibliography", in essence a "live" database of references, can be constructed. In addition to recording the full citations for materials already consulted, adopting this methodology allows the researcher to record under separate headings;

> ➢ Sources which have been located but are still to be read;
> ➢ Sources requested via the library on inter-library loan and awaited;
> ➢ Sources sought but still to be located; and
> ➢ Sources where the citation is uncertain. This may be the case when an internet-based source, without an obvious citation, has been found. See paras 2–95—2–99 for guidance on citing internet sources.

The importance of compiling accurate bibliographic references prior to submitting a research project is discussed more fully in paras 13–60—13–120.

EMPIRICAL RESEARCH METHODS

Beyond a literature only research project

Legal research may involve researching beyond the substantive law found in various types of **12–16** legal literature to gain information about the views of selected individuals, groups or a section of the public on a particular aspect of the law or legal system. This is achieved by direct or indirect observation or personal contact with the subjects concerned. Whilst it is still the case that most undergraduate law students will conduct research purely within the confines of a literature-based search, postgraduate students, particularly if their thesis cuts across disciplines, e.g. law and criminology or law and politics, may be required to undertake empirical research to successfully complete their higher degree. The word "empirical" is usually defined as a methodology or source of knowledge "derived from or relating to experiment and observation rather than theory".

The remainder of this chapter considers three established empirical methods of collecting pri- **12–17** mary (raw) data: questionnaires, interviews and observational studies. Although the methods are dealt with separately, in practice, the researcher may use more than one method when conducting a single piece of research. Each method in itself gives rise to general concerns about the ethical nature or otherwise of its use in a given project in tandem with ethical issues raised by the nature of a specific research project at the outset. It is common for law students to underestimate the difficulties, both practical and ethical, that present when carrying out this type of research.

Research ethics—obtaining clearance to proceed with a research project

If the research project is purely literature based, i.e. does not involve empirical research, it is **12–18** unlikely that research ethics clearance by an institution's research ethics body will be required before the project can commence. However, many institutions may require undergraduate students engaged in solo project or dissertation work to complete a research ethics form (with the help of their supervisor) to confirm that this is the case.

12–19   If the research project or part of it is to proceed on the basis of empirical study, guidance on the relevant institution's policies in this regard should be consulted prior to framing the proposal. Whilst each institution's policies will differ, all will be broadly aligned with the contents of six key principles identified by the Economic and Social Research Council which, the Council suggests, ought to underpin the notion of ethical research (see *http://ethicsguidebook.ac.uk/* [accessed June 13, 2014]).

12–20   The Economic and Social Research Council key principles:

> ➢ *Research should be designed, reviewed and undertaken to ensure integrity and quality*, i.e. is the research study worth doing? Can the integrity and quality of the research be ensured?
> ➢ *Research staff and subjects must be informed fully about the purpose, methods and intended possible uses of the research, what their participation in the research entails and what risks, if any, are involved. Some variation is allowed in very specific and exceptional research contexts for which detailed guidance is provided in the policy guidelines*, i.e. can the researcher ensure that any potential participants will be fully informed of the purpose, methods and intended possible uses of the research? If not, can an ethics committee be convinced that the project is justifiable?
> ➢ *The confidentiality of information supplied by research subjects and the anonymity of respondents must be respected*, i.e. is it possible to maintain participant confidentiality and anonymity within the study?
> ➢ *Research participants must participate in a voluntary way, free from any coercion*, i.e. can the researcher guarantee that participants involvement in the research is truly voluntary?
> ➢ *Harm to research participants must be avoided*, i.e. can the researcher guarantee the absence of harm to the research participants? In social science research, "harm" is taken to mean more than just physical harm and can refer to emotional harm and risk of upset, as well as to reputational damage.
> ➢ *The independence of research must be clear, and any conflicts of interest or partiality must be explicit*, i.e. will the research design enable the researcher to remain independent throughout the process? Are there any conflicts of interest?

These principles make it clear that the onus is firmly on the researcher to fully consider the issues and risks posed by engaging in empirical research at the outset and that a negative response to any one of the questions posed above will likely lead to ethical research clearance being denied unless the research proposal can be amended to the satisfaction of the relevant ethics committee in light of the specific concerns it has about a particular part of the proposal.

12–21   As detailed above, it is vital in all projects where empirical research is involved to be clear about the aims, objectives and risks posed by the proposed research to gain research ethics clearance. However, such clarity is also required to ensure, once the project has been approved, that the effort that will require to be expended to collect the data using a particular empirical method is justified.

12–22   The methodology chosen will depend on factors, such as:

> ➢ The purpose of the study;

> The type of information sought;
> Accessibility of the subject(s) of the research;
> The age/sex/other characteristics etc of the subject(s);
> Time constraints. Every research project has a deadline;
> Cost; and
> The researcher's skills set, e.g. if s/he has no aptitude for figures, questionnaires where numerical calculations and statistical analysis post data collection are required ought to be avoided unless absolutely essential.

Questionnaires

A questionnaire is data collection tool which involves creating a set of questions which will then **12–23** be put to each participant via a survey. The survey may be carried out by post, email, telephone or via a face-to-face meeting, either in person or using an internet tool, such as Skype. Questionnaires tend to be used for large-scale surveys, particularly those involving a geographically scattered population. Questionnaires have become increasingly easy to construct and distribute with the advent of specialised free software, e.g. SurveyMonkey *https://www.surveymonkey.com/* [accessed June 13, 2014]. However, questionnaires will only prove to be an effective tool if the "right" questions are asked, i.e. the questions posed are carefully designed to elicit responses that will meet the research objectives.

Advantages of using questionnaires as a method of data collection

> Questionnaires are an efficient way of gathering information from respondents who are **12–24** widely dispersed geographically or who live in inaccessible places;
> The cost of using questionnaires is low compared with carrying out interviews or observational studies;
> Questionnaires enable the researcher to gather information from a large number of people in a resource (time and cost) efficient way;
> The collection of standardised data which can then be analysed quantitatively using software, such as Excel or predictive analytic software such as SPSS, and presented using tables, graphs, diagrams, etc.

Disadvantages of questionnaires as a data collection method

> The major disadvantage is the low level of response rates generally achieved. This is **12–25** important because of the bias that can result. Bias occurs because the respondents may not be representative of the sample, i.e. they may have a particular interest in the specific topic;
> There is no opportunity to probe beyond the answers received on the questionnaire;
> There is no opportunity to clarify an ambiguous answer;
> There is no opportunity to check either the accuracy or truthfulness of any answer given;
> The researcher cannot be sure who, within an organisation, has answered the questionnaire;
> The researcher has no control over the order in which questions are answered;
> The researcher has no way of ensuring that all the questions are answered;
> Questionnaires are unsuitable for certain groups of respondents, e.g. people with poor literacy skills or poor sight.

In addition to the issues raised above, it is essential that the questions asked are interpreted by the respondents in the way the researcher intend so that the data collected will, by and large, answer the research questions posed. One way to help ensure that this will happen in the majority of cases is to pilot the questionnaire. Getting real responses at a formative stage in the data collection process will help the researcher to gauge if the wording of any particular question needs to be changed (in which case the amended questionnaire should again be piloted) and analysing the data obtained should indicate whether it will achieve the research objectives.

Interviews

12–26 Interviews should not just be viewed as a chat with someone about the research being undertaken. In order for the information obtained to be useful and useable, the researcher must carefully plan the interview and think deeply about exactly what information s/he wishes to obtain from the interviewee. Part of this process involves the preparation of detailed questions, thinking about possible answers that could be given by the interviewee and then thinking about subsidiary questions to the main questions in case the initial question does not elicit the information desired. The researcher must also be fully aware that the interviewee is doing them a great service by allowing themselves to be interviewed and that on no account should the interviewee be argued with or badgered into answering a question or questions s/he does not wish to answer.

12–27 There are four different types of interview:

- ➤ The "structured" interview where a questionnaire checklist is completed by the researcher/interviewer, not the interviewee;
- ➤ The "semi-structured" interview where questions are normally specified by the researcher but the researcher/interviewer is free to probe beyond the initial answers given by the interviewee;
- ➤ The "informal" interview where the interviewee is allowed to talk about the issue(s) in any way s/he chooses; and
- ➤ The "group" interview where the researcher/interviewer focuses on group values and the group dynamic per the issue(s) under scrutiny

Advantages of using interviews as a data collection method

12–28
- ➤ The response rate will tend to be better than that achievable by using questionnaires;
- ➤ The researcher/interviewer can ensure that the interviewee understands what they are being asked by the repetition of or rephrasing of questions;
- ➤ An interview ensures that the interviewee answers the questions in the sequence intended;
- ➤ There is an opportunity to probe beyond an answer;
- ➤ The interviewee has scope to talk about issues in more detail than it would be possible to write down in response to a questionnaire;
- ➤ Interviewees who cannot write fluently are able to express their opinions more readily; and
- ➤ The interview situation allows data to be collected not only from the answers provided by interviewees but also from how they gave their answers. This includes factors such as body language and the sincerity of the answers given.

Disadvantages of using interviews as a data collection method

12–29
- ➤ Interviews can be very time-consuming;
- ➤ Interviews can be costly. Travel costs depend on the location of the interviewees and whether or not they are being paid expenses for taking part in the research project;
- ➤ If too little structure or consistency is maintained it becomes difficult to use the data in a comparative exercise; and

> ➢ The possibility of bias being introduced by the interviewer. An interviewee can be influenced by the way a question is asked. This does not just involve the language used, but the inflection of the voice and body language.

Observational studies (also referred to as "Field" research)

> "The distinguishing feature of observation … is that the information required is obtained **12–30** directly, rather than through the reports of others; in the area of behaviour one finds out what the individual does, rather than what he says he does." (C.A. Moser and G. Kalton, *Survey Methods in Social Investigation*, 2nd edn (Heinemann Educational, 1971) p.245.)

Observation, which can be covert or overt, not only involves watching, recording and analysing events of interest, but also includes talking to people and examining relevant documents such as diaries or records. Thus interviews and observational studies can take place simultaneously. In general terms, much information is yielded via an observational study thus it is vital that the researcher adopts a clear and systematic approach to data collection so that what is noted down is always relevant to the research objective(s).

Advantages of using observational studies as a data collection method

> ➢ It allows the spontaneous element of the data to be captured because behaviour is being **12–31** recorded behaviour as it takes place;
> ➢ It enables the study of those who are unable to comprehend and provide accurate answers to questions in questionnaires or interviews, e.g. young children; and
> ➢ It is not dependent on memory. People can distort past events either intentionally or unintentionally. Observation allows the researcher to witness events at first hand.

Disadvantages of using observational studies as a data collection method

> ➢ The subjectivity/bias of the researcher/observer must be guarded against. Empathy **12–32** with those observed must also be avoided;
> ➢ Undertaking an observational study can be very time-consuming;
> ➢ A false environment rather than a real one may end up being measured if observation is overt due to people's tendency to behave differently if they are aware they are being observed;
> ➢ It is only possible to observe events which have a set duration, thus an observational study is usually not an appropriate way of measuring opinions and attitudes. This disadvantage may be mitigated by combining the use of an observational study with one of the other methods of data collection;
> ➢ There are some situations where observation may not be possible, desirable or ethical, e.g. doctor/patient consultations, covert/overt observation in dangerous locations or situations; and
> ➢ The success or otherwise of the research project in terms of the data collected is almost wholly dependent on the personality of the researcher. S/he needs to be able to communicate effectively with, be accepted by and build up a relationship with those being observed.

Further issues

Once raw data has been collected it has to be organised, analysed and interpreted. Organising **12–33** data can be repetitive and boring; however it is a most important part of the research process. It must be done consistently, e.g. the way raw data is categorised must be uniform, to ensure that the data collected is not misreported. Thus, attention to detail is of the utmost importance.

Initial organisation of the data will be followed by analysis. This involves examining the raw data and looking for patterns, similarities, differences, groupings and items of particular significance. The analytical techniques used will depend on the type and quantity of data collected. If only a small number of questionnaires have been used the raw data collected can most likely be analysed manually. However, if a large scale questionnaire was used the raw data obtained may have to be entered into a suitable computer package. There are many software packages currently available for statistical analysis and the choice will depend on the level of statistical sophistication the researcher wishes to achieve. If carrying out basic statistical tests, an Excel spreadsheet may suffice. However, to generate more sophisticated statistics access to specialist software, such as SPSS, may be required. If interviews or an observational study were undertaken the appropriate analytical techniques will depend on the form the raw data has taken, e.g. if structured or semi-structured interviews were conducted the data will probably be able to be presented in numeric form. On the other hand, if informal or group interviews were conducted, non-numeric analysis techniques more suitable to qualitative data would most likely have to be considered which would involve the selection of relevant, illustrative or interesting material and quotations gained from the interviewees.

Further reading per empirical research

12–34　　➤　J. Bell, *Doing Your Research Project*, 4th edn (Buckingham: Open University Press, 2005)

➤　A. Bryman, *Social Research Methods*, 3rd edn (Oxford: Oxford University Press, 2008)

➤　S. Cottrell, *Dissertations and Project Reports* (London: Palgrave, 2014)

➤　M. Denscombe, *The Good Research Guide for Small-Scale Research Projects*, 2nd edn (Buckingham: Open University Press, 2003)

➤　D. de Vaus, *Surveys in Social Research*, 6th edn (London: UCL Press, 2013)

➤　T. May, *Social Research*, 4th edn (Buckingham: Open University Press, 2011)

Chapter 13
Cultivating Study Skills and Research Skills: Making Effective Use of Information

Significant abbreviations used in this chapter

- *Ibid. (Ibidem)*—meaning "the same"
- *Loc. Cit. (Loco citro)*—meaning "in the place cited"
- *Op. Cit. (Opere citaro)*—meaning "in the work previously cited"
- OSCOLA—Oxford Standard for Citation of Legal Authorities PDP; Personal Development Planning
- SI—Statutory Instrument
- SPICe—Scottish Parliament Information Centre

This chapter is written with the first year law student firmly in mind. Whilst it cannot provide an **13–01** exhaustive guide to the academic life that awaits a first year law student as s/he embarks upon the study of Scots law or reflect the first year syllabus or practices and procedures of particular institutions, it can give guidance on specific goals common to all students new to academia. Primarily, this chapter advises on the acquisition of generic skills every law student is working towards attaining during their first year of study. Accordingly, it begins by discussing the vital skill of time management and how to get the most out of structured class meetings, such as lectures and tutorials. Thereafter, it concentrates on good learning practice and the cultivation of the core study skills, including effective reading and note-taking. The benefits gained from reflecting on feedback from tutors are also discussed. It concludes by providing guidance on the evaluation of documentary material, record-keeping, referencing conventions for different sources of information and how to construct a bibliography.

In essence, this chapter suggests how the student new to the study of law can become an active, **13–02** rather than passive, participant in the process of teaching and learning as they acquire a body of legal knowledge and skills and how they should then, as assessment and examination deadlines approach, prepare to express that knowledge. Assessment techniques are discussed in Ch.14.

That said, both undergraduate and post-graduate students, whatever the stage of study, will **13–03** wish to remind themselves from time to time of essential study skills.

Studying law

"Law is different". This is a phrase the student will likely hear uttered by their tutors more than **13–04** once in the course of their legal studies. But what does it mean? Why is law different? What is it different from or to? Is it how lawyers study that marks them out from their fellow undergraduates? Is it what they study, a body of rules and principles which are then to be relied upon to provide the "right answer" to determine disputes between private citizens or punish criminal acts? Or is it the fact that law impacts upon practically every human relationship or transaction which sets law apart from the study of, for example, physics or fine art? Unhelpfully, nowhere is it written down or agreed, even between lawyers, what it is that makes the study of law different. So, it can be argued, on the one hand, there is no rationale or basis for perpetuating the myth that law is in a class of its own and encouraging, perhaps, the cultivation of a superiority complex amongst law students! On the other hand, law is different from other academic disciplines in that it cannot be categorised either as the study of a science, such as biology, or a humanity, such as sociology. Rather, it is a hybrid discipline being systematic, objective and logical to the extent that defined rules of law are applied to factual situations, as in science. Yet such rules may come into conflict with one another and their competing principles must be balanced, with one eventually gaining the upper hand to allow a judge to reach a decision in a particular case. Therefore, law can also be said to be pragmatic, practical and even intuitive in nature.

13–05 For example, a court given the unpalatable task of deciding where the child of legally separated parents should live is required to make a decision in the best interests of the child concerned. In doing so s/he will take the subjective view of the child into account along with objective legal arguments made on behalf of the parents before reaching a decision. So to the extent that law is required to find the "right answer" to the myriad complex and conflicting questions posed by a variety of human relationships, it is arguable that law and the study of law and its practice is unique and quite simply sui generis, i.e. in a class of its own. In any event, each and every law student will form their own opinion as to the nature of law as they progress through their programme of study and beyond. However, it is quite common for that opinion to change, perhaps more than once, with the passage of time.

Induction

13–06 Most institutions provide some form of induction event for new students immediately before the academic year commences. This may be a dedicated day where students meet academic staff and are given an opportunity to ask questions about their degree programme. Induction can also be extended over several days or even a week with a programme of events being provided where the procedures and policies of the institution will be explained in addition to a general introduction to the subjects that will be studied that academic year. Registration may also take place at this time. Whatever form induction takes, it provides a good opportunity to get to know academic staff and fellow students and find out more about the institution. A personal or academic tutor may also be made known to students at this time. S/he will be a member of academic staff who will take a direct interest in the academic development, performance and personal welfare of tutees.

13–07 Most institutions follow the modular approach to teaching law. A module is simply a discrete subject area, e.g. the law of contract, which is taught in a block of a number of weeks during an academic term or semester. In addition to the core law modules which must be studied, students may be offered options, also known as electives, which allow for the study of a subject from a different, but related discipline. Finding out about any options before making a final selection is to be advised as a bare modular title, e.g. "Forensic Science" will rarely describe its actual content. If the name of the member of academic staff delivering an optional module is not readily apparent, ask a member of the law academic staff for advice on how to contact the relevant person to discuss the module before registering for it.

Embarking on the study of law

There is a Chinese proverb of unknown origin that neatly encapsulates the teaching and learning **13–08** experience of any academic discipline, "Teachers open the door—you enter by yourself".

Thus, the student's input to the process of teaching and learning is pivotal. **13–09**

The narrative below illustrates behaviours that evidence engagement, or otherwise, with the **13–10** process:

Positive learning behaviours *(active and engaged learning—making the experience profitable and enjoyable)*	**Negative learning behaviours** *(passive and detached learning—making the experience difficult and potentially stressful)*
➢ Reading through/considering module booklets/materials/specific guidance given by tutors and referring to these resources when necessary thereafter.	➢ Making no effort whatsoever at the outset to discover what each module is about.
➢ Finding out what is to be achieved and the deadline(s) involved, i.e. the objectives of and the inputs/outputs required by each module).	➢ Not knowing what is to be achieved or when.
➢ Considering why each module is important and what knowledge will be gained from it.	➢ Deciding at the outset that a module or certain modules are just a compulsory part of the course and of no real interest or use.
➢ Attending class meetings regularly and participating in discussions and debates.	➢ Attending classes sporadically and, when in attendance, sitting passively, detached from what is being said or done.
➢ Preparing for and identifying the purpose of each class meeting and then reflecting on what has been learnt in/from it. Thereafter, considering how each topic studied relates to other topics taught on a particular module or topics studied in another module.	➢ Attending class meetings without knowing the point of the lecture/tutorial having failed to do the recommended reading.
➢ Using all available primary/secondary sources of information, i.e. reading widely.	➢ Complaining that the library does not have copies of a core textbooks. **NB** students are expected to purchase some.
➢ Approaching academic staff with any problems encountered.	➢ Making no use of academic staff to overcome problems encountered.
➢ Getting assessment tasks, where possible, ready before schedule.	➢ Submitting ill-informed, sloppy last-minute work.
➢ Going over what has been learnt on a regular basis to consolidate knowledge with the aim of achieving the best grade possible for each piece of work.	➢ Exiting each module with a bare pass/fail, having no real understanding of the subject(s) studied.

Time management

13–11 The hours of class contact will vary slightly from institution to institution, but the average student "working" week will comprise 40 hours which will be split between attendance at classes, research and private study. One of the most productive things you can do at the start of each session is to get yourself organised and consider carefully how these 40 hours will be spent. This is vital given that several different subjects are to be studied at the same time and different activities will also require to be undertaken simultaneously, e.g. attendance at lectures, preparing for tutorials, writing assessments and revising for exams. The level of activity for each specific task will not be the same therefore it is essential to plan for periods referred to as "pinch points" when many different and competing demands coincide. To do so effectively, a time management plan is essential.

13–12 The development of time management skills has become increasingly important in a world where the majority of students are employed in part-time or, more rarely, full-time work. Whilst it is vital to maintain a balance between the demands of "life" and "study", there is no "right" way to achieve this. However, forward planning is the key to making sure that every waking hour, whether for the purposes of study, work or personal life is factored in to a realistic time management plan—a plan that will be as individual as the person it applies to.

13–13 Cultivating the following educational habits will ensure that a time management plan commences on a firm footing:

> ➢ Quickly become familiar with the university timetable and know when and where classes are held. Universities number the weeks of each term/semester in an academic calendar and use this document to refer to specific events/deadlines for students and staff. Mark up or note the numbers/weeks in a diary/wall chart/electronic calendar and then enter class meetings/events/deadlines/when assessments are due to be submitted, etc. Failure to do this can easily result in classes or assessments being missed and lingering uncertainty about whether a resit opportunity may be offered;
> ➢ Set target dates for achieving set tasks. Choose dates which are well in advance of any deadline (such as a submission date for an assessment or tutorial preparation), but ensure that target dates are realistic, i.e. achievable. Organise each "university week" around these target dates. However, build in some leeway to allow for the unexpected. Prioritise work depending on its urgency. Make a list of specific goals and cross off each one as and when it is achieved. Review and update the list on a regular basis;
> ➢ Establish a routine and a study schedule. Be flexible. Make good use of downtime, e.g. bus/train journeys and breaks between classes;
> ➢ Develop a system for filing lecture and study notes. Revision is made much easier when faced with a neat and coherent body of work rather than a large, unstructured file of disorganised notes. Do not rely purely on the desktop/hard drive of a PC, etc. as a storage facility—back up notes and assessments regularly on a USB, external hard drive or other removable device or in the "Cloud";
> ➢ Do not put off doing something because it appears difficult initially. Make a plan for each piece of work. Break up the task set into small parts. It is much less daunting to start a small portion than to tackle the whole task at once. It is also far more productive and less stressful to work in short, but consistent bursts of activity than to work through a whole day and into the night to begin and complete a piece of work, e.g. if the task is a 1,000 word essay begin by drafting a structure (see paras 14–36—14–42). Then consider the resources required. Next, locate the resources over a set period of time and consult them. If unsure about a specific issue try to resolve this through further reading or seek guidance from the relevant tutor. Draft the essay. Compiling

work within a structured environment over a designated period of time allows the author to think more carefully about each element and also to reflect on what element(s) can be improved prior to the submission date;

➢ Build variety into a study schedule. Do not spend an entire day/evening on one task;
➢ Give all tasks equal attention. It is human nature to put off the task least understood or enjoyed and it is for these reasons that it should be given equal priority. All assessments count towards the overall grade achieved for a module and all modules count towards gaining a degree. Therefore, consider why a certain task appears unpalatable and resolve the issue(s) at the outset rather than procrastinate and submit ill-informed and/ or error-ridden work at the last gasp; and
➢ When studying take short breaks to refresh the mind and spirit.

Personal development planning ("PDP")

Skills development

In addition to acquiring a growing body of legal knowledge students are expected to develop a **13–14** portfolio of personal transferable skills (also known as life skills) to aid personal and academic development. The Higher Education Academy defines PDP as "a structured and supported process undertaken by an individual to reflect upon their own learning, performance and/or achievement and to plan for their personal, educational and career development" (see *http:// www.heacademy.ac.uk/resources/detail/pdp/pdp* [accessed June 13, 2014]. Thus PDP is a long term activity that involves the identification of goals—both short and long term ones—and considering how each goal, from passing a particular assessment to graduating with a first class honours degree and securing a good job, is to be achieved through reflection and self-evaluation of personal progress.

Many institutions use a software package, such as Pebble +, to enable students to begin the **13–15** PDP process from day one, year one of undergraduate study by recording achievements, reflections on, inter alia, feedback received and how best to improve future performance. Further information on the concept and value of PDP can be gained from consulting Stella Cottrell's text, *Skills for Success Personal Development and Employability*, published by Palgrave Macmillan in 2011. Chapter 1 of this text can be downloaded free of charge from the publisher's webpage at *http://www.palgrave.com/products/title.aspx?PID=404590* [accessed June 13, 2014].

Developing essential study skills

In the first year of study, and periodically thereafter, most institutions will provide timetabled **13–16** seminars or lab-based events focused on developing skills in, inter alia, the following areas:

➢ **Research**: Good research skills are an essential tool in the armoury of any law student or practitioner which can only be honed by practice. Research should not be viewed simply as a means to an end, e.g. gathering materials for a particular assessment, but rather an on-going learning process in itself. One undisputed fact about law is that it changes and keeping up-to-date through research is of the utmost importance;
➢ **Communication**: The ability to express ideas and concepts clearly and confidently in both written and oral form when explaining the law is an essential legal skill. This skill will be continuously developed by attendance at classes, particularly tutorials, and through preparation for oral assessments. How to prepare for oral assessments/presentations is discussed in paras 14–61—14–80;
➢ **IT**: Most students arrive at university with the ability to confidently and competently use a variety of IT platforms. However, if e-information literacy seminars are offered, either as a core part of a module or as a separate teaching block, do not view these

classes as optional extras where nothing new can be learnt. Any instruction given will be designed to develop research skills;

 ➢ **Problem Solving**: Law students are required to identify the main features of a given problem and provide a reasoned legal response. Specifically, they are asked to define the boundaries of the problem, analyse the various parts and identify the various options. Legal problems will require to be resolved in all modules of study and a suggested approach to tackling problem questions in an exam setting is discussed in paras 14–50—14–58;

However, problem solving is also about self-evaluation. This is the ability to objectively assess your personal inputs, the outcomes achieved and then identify areas or skills where improvement is required.

13–17 The questionnaire below is designed to aid self-evaluation of core study and study-related skills and offers the opportunity to rate your current skills level and monitor progress in these areas throughout the first stage of study. Remember, some of the skills that need to be acquired during the first stage of a law degree will be new ones and an initial self-rating of weak, or just OK, should be expected in such areas. It is what is done thereafter to improve upon any current perceived weakness that is important.

13–18 Repeat this exercise on a regular basis to evaluate progress.

	Self rating 1 – weak 2 – OK 3 – good 4 – very good 5 – excellent
I persevere with tasks.	
I can keep to deadlines.	
I have the confidence to express my own ideas in front of an audience.	
I can read texts and find then explain the essential points.	
I can retrieve information from different sources and carry out meaningful research.	
I can write up research in my own words.	
I learn from and reflect upon my experiences.	
I can construct a Word document.	
I can insert page numbers in documents.	
I can insert footnotes/endnotes in documents.	
I can create a PowerPoint presentation.	
I can create an email and send it.	
I can attach a file to an email.	
I can organise emails in files.	
I can use the email calendar function to set meetings and classes and assessment deadline reminders.	

I can access and navigate my institution's webpage and intranet.	
I can access any learning resources made available on-line by my institution.	
I can find my timetable online.	
I can navigate my institution's library intranet pages.	
I can use the library catalogue on-line.	
I can access and confidently navigate legal databases, e.g. Westlaw and LexisNexis via my institution's library intranet pages.	
I know which librarian to contact regarding legal resources.	
I can find Scottish case law.	
I can find English case law.	
I can find UK statutes.	
I can find Scottish statutes.	
I can find EU legislation.	
I can find journal articles.	
I can find textbooks.	
I know the library opening hours.	
I know what structure I should adopt for a particular coursework.	
I know the style of writing I should use for a particular coursework.	
I know how to structure the legal argument(s) I wish to make.	
I know the style of referencing I must use.	
I know how long it is going to take me to research and write a particular coursework.	
I understand my institution's policy on plagiarism.	
I know how to construct a bibliography in the approved style.	
I know how I am required to submit a particular coursework e.g. in hard copy and/or electronic format.	
I know what structure I should adopt when writing exam answers.	
I know what additional materials I am allowed to take into a particular class test/examination.	
I feel confident when making an oral presentation.	

Further Reading

13–19   ➤ S. Cottrell, *The Study Skills Handbook*, 4th edn (London: Palgrave, 2013)
           ➤ P. McMurray, *Study Skills Essentials Effective Study Skills Publications* (Effective Study Skills Publication: N Ireland, 2011)
           ➤ K. Williams, M. Reid, *Time Management Pocket Study Skills* (Basingstoke: MacMillan, 2011)

LECTURES

13–20 Lectures are a vital part of university study and should not be viewed as an optional extra. Whilst they are a positive learning experience in themselves, attendance at lectures will also provide the quickest and easiest way of obtaining relevant information about a topic. The information given in an hour long lecture would take the student far longer than one hour to find themselves in a paper and/or virtual library. The perennial minority of new law students who believe that they can "get through" a degree by skipping lectures and just reading a book instead will find that they have chosen the difficult and stressful and generally doomed way to study any subject. It is like looking for buried treasure on an island without the assistance of an accurate map as the prime purpose of a lecture is to put a given topic into context by identifying important areas to be followed up thereafter. The information given in lectures has been selected and structured by the tutor and tailored to the module's learning outcomes which means it is taught at a level required by a particular stage of study. Attendance at lectures also allows students to gain first-hand experience of the way legal material should be presented or discussed, e.g. the way the tutor refers to legal principles or cites case law and legislation.

How to get the most out of a lecture

13–21 It should never be doubted that lectures are only ever an introduction to a topic. The tutor will explain the concepts and principles underpinning a particular area of law with the expectation that the student will then put "flesh on the bones" by taking notes and undertaking the recommended reading. During lectures tutors will also give weight to certain elements, indicating those areas which are of greater importance.

13–22 It is good practice and more productive to do the recommended reading before and after the relevant lecture. This allows you to attend with some understanding of the topic and thereafter to better consolidate knowledge and identify any areas of outstanding uncertainty more readily. Preparation for and active participation in lectures will make the activity much more memorable and easier to recall when compiling course works or revising for exams.

13–23 Make sure to arrive in good time for the start of a lecture. If you arrive late the outline and structure of the lecture and any important announcements will have been missed and it may prove to be an uphill battle to fully understand what is going on. Arriving late is also disruptive to other students and many institutions have policies in place decreeing that late arrival after a certain time will see the late-coming student being denied entry to that class meeting.

13–24 Writing down every word spoken by the tutor like an automaton is inefficient and unnecessary. This modus operandi may yield a record of everything that was said but will be unlikely to note whether everything said was of equal importance. It is good practice to underline or annotate in same way what the tutor highlighted or emphasised. Another result of trying to write down every word will probably be completely illegible thus poor quality or even unusable notes. It is much better practice to take an active role in the lecturing process. This involves thinking about what is being said, asking questions and considering whether a particular point is important and, pivotally, whether the point is fully grasped and understood. If not, make a note and check the point in the recommended reading and raise it again in a tutorial if any uncertainty lingers thereafter.

At the beginning of a lecture the tutor may outline the structure of the lecture and/or at the end **13–25** may summarise the material covered. Alternatively, an outline or summary may be provided in the module handbook or materials.

Learning to recognise what is important in each lecture

➢ The emphasis given by the tutor, e.g. s/he may say directly that something is important **13–26** or use terms such as "a leading case" or "when looking at past papers you will notice that this topic is frequently examined";
➢ The time devoted to a topic. If something is only mentioned briefly it is probably a minor point; and
➢ If material covered in a lecture is the subject of subsequent tutorial preparation and discussion then the topic(s) concerned should be viewed as of the upmost importance.

Lecture notes

As stated above in para.13–24, it is very tempting to write down everything said by the tutor, **13–27** especially at the beginning of a university career. As time goes by students gradually build up confidence in their own note-taking abilities and develop shorthand or précis versions of words or phrases, e.g. there is no need to write out UK Supreme Court in full every time it is referred to—simply write UKSC. Likewise, use the abbreviation EU for the European Union. Nor is there any need to write continuous prose or to cram everything written down in to a small space in an attempt to save paper. Rather, break up the text with headings or numerals and use a new page for each separate topic or point. Note-taking techniques per se are covered in more detail below.

Re-read any lecture notes taken for, (i) accuracy and (ii) coherence while the contents of the **13–28** lecture are still fresh in your mind. If they prove to be vague on a certain point or unclear in any way, ask a fellow student for sight of their notes to check what has been missed or misunderstood. Note-taking is, however, a subjective process, thus reliance on someone else's notes is no substitute for attending the lecture and taking personal notes. If lending lecture notes to a fellow student, make sure that a copy is kept. In any event, it is good practice to type up any hand written notes and back these up electronically. Notes taken on a PC should also be backed up.

Follow up the lecture by re-reading any materials recommended by the tutor. Do not try to read **13–29** everything on a reading list or in the library—there will never to sufficient time to do so. Select the most important materials based on the emphasis accorded by and the recommendation of the tutor.

Do not regard lecture notes as all that will be needed to pass exams or write-up coursework. **13–30** Lecture notes are just one source of material and must be allied with notes taken from texts and from primary and secondary sources. If specific cases or statutes are discussed in a lecture, these must be read in their original, or in the case of legislation, amended form with appropriate notes taken whilst doing so. This practice will not only aid understanding of the topic, but will create further materials for revision purposes.

13–31 Lecture material will be more up-to-date than that contained in textbooks. Lectures will include developments which have taken place up to the previous day, whereas textbooks are likely to be several months out of date by the time they are published. Likewise, lecture notes will go out of date and cannot be relied upon with the passage of time to reflect the actual law. However, for the purposes of assessments, the law as taught in class meetings will be the law you are examined on.

TUTORIALS

How to get the most out of a tutorial

13–32 Tutorials involve small groups of students having a discussion with the tutor about a topic which has previously been introduced in lectures. Tutorials are a crucial part of the teaching and learning process. It is therefore important to attend all scheduled tutorials. If a lecture is missed notes can be borrowed and may prove useful, up to a point. Tutorials, on the other hand, tend to yield fewer notes as they are discursive and interactive in nature. Above all, tutorials are the forum for testing understanding and contributing in a direct way to the academic working environment.

13–33 The more effort put into tutorial preparation, the more that will be gained. Preparation will be required for most tutorials, with the tutor typically providing a set exercise to be completed prior to the tutorial and directed reading from a textbook as an aid to a discussion. If no preparation has been undertaken it will prove hard to understand the discussion and take part in the proceedings in any meaningful way.

13–34 Although tutorials are led, by definition, by the tutor, all students should be ready, willing and able to participate in the discussion by asking questions, listening to other people's contributions and responding to issues raised. Tutorials thus provide a first class opportunity to improve your cognitive and oral communication skills. At first, the thought of speaking in front of an audience may be nerve-wracking, but the more experience gained in the small (and friendly) tutorial setting the more confident the novice speaker will become. This will help you to display more confidence when required to give assessed oral presentations.

13–35 Tutorials are an important point of contact, not only with the tutor, but also with fellow students. It is always useful to share ideas and it can also be reassuring to discover that other students are finding a topic or area of law challenging too. Use tutorials as a forum to raise questions about anything not fully understood in lectures or to seek further guidance on the assessments for a particular module.

13–36 It is also generally through contact in tutorials that students decide to set up independent study groups.

13–37 In tutorials brief notes only should be taken of anything said that proves helpful or thought provoking or if the tutor stresses a particular point. Otherwise concentrate on participating and not writing. Shortly after the tutorial, write up salient points.

13–38 Tutorials are where the problem-solving skills required to tackle certain exam questions and the practice of law generally are introduced and developed. Whereas lectures tend to introduce the content of the law in a given area, tutorials are where students learn how to apply that law. The ability to apply the law to factual situations is a fundamental and essential legal skill. Thus it is through preparation for and participation in tutorials that the ability to analyse given facts in order to identify the relevant legal issues arising from them will be acquired. Once relevant legal principles have been identified they can then be applied to relevant facts in order to assess possible outcomes and, in doing so, give accurate legal advice. How best to approach a problem question is discussed further in paras 14–50—14–58.

Tutorials and receiving feedback

Tutorials also tend to be the setting for receiving generic oral feedback on how the class overall **13–39** fared in a particular assessment. Written and/or oral feedback as appropriate on individual performance and attainment in a unit of assessment will be given separately and will remain confidential between the student and the tutor. Tutorials may also be utilised to provide "feedforward" prior to assessments. This includes: indicating where previously submitted student work could have been improved upon; providing a very good example of a previous submission; or using tutorial exercises to work through forthcoming assessment topics. Feedforward is thus designed to give comment on previous submissions of varying quality or your draft work and how it can be improved.

EFFECTIVE READING TECHNIQUES

Students are required to "read" for their degree, thus consulting written material will take up **13–40** the majority of time spent outwith the classroom setting. Prior to reading a textbook or journal article, it is the best use of time to consider at the outset the reason or reasons for reading a particular publication.

Reasons for reading a book or article include: **13–41**

- ➢ The factual content;
- ➢ To gain an insight into the author's interpretation of the law/events;
- ➢ To give consideration to the author's style of writing; and
- ➢ To discover which sources the author has used.

Do not feel compelled to read every text from cover to cover. Use the contents page and the index to identify chapters or shorter sections of the text which are relevant to the task at hand. Assess what is being read by posing the following questions:

i. Is it easy to understand and follow the author's arguments?
ii. Are the arguments backed up by reference to primary and secondary legal authority?
iii. Do I agree with the arguments? If yes, why? If no, why not? Whatever opinion is reached this will, in turn, require to be backed up with primary and secondary legal authority to validate the opposing argument(s).

Make notes of what is read to retain the essential points. Taking notes (see paras 13–45—13–54 for further detail) ensures that the mind stays active whilst reading is undertaken. Reading without taking any notes is generally a waste of time and effort as the majority of what is read be forgotten or vaguely recalled even only a few hours after the event, requiring the reader to re-read the materials and take notes at the second time of asking.

One method of making notes is to mark a personal copy of a text—never a library book or a text **13–42** borrowed from a fellow student—by highlighting or underlining sections. This focuses attention on the relevant passages and gives a permanent reminder of initial thoughts as the remainder of the text is read and then revisited prior to an assessment falling due for submission.

13–43 Notes made while reading should not be a shorthand copy of the text. Notes should be clear and concise as it is essential that the author can discern what has been recorded weeks or perhaps months after the event. This is not as straightforward as it sounds. It is easy to become familiar with a text and grow tired of making full notes and end up with a series of cryptic scribbles that make little sense.

13–44 It is also vital to ensure that sufficient details about the material consulted are recorded at the same time as the reading is undertaken. See paras 13–60—13–120 on referencing conventions and constructing a bibliography. In addition, it is advisable to note down the library reference. These precautions enable the reader to reference the material in a piece of coursework or find it again with a minimum of difficulty. It is extremely frustrating to find a quotation for inclusion in an essay that has to be removed at the last minute simply because the author has no idea where s/he found it. It is even more frustrating to finally finish an essay only to discover that salient and required bibliographic details of a text, case or legislation have not been noted down accurately or at all and that valuable time will have to be spent checking or finding the details.

NOTE-TAKING

13–45 When taking notes, do not merely copy out passages verbatim. Try to think about what the material is saying and then put it into your own words. If actual words from a source are used make this clear by putting them in quotation marks. This will help avoid unwitting plagiarism (see paras 14–14—14–18). There is no right way to take notes and various styles or methods can be employed. You should quickly discern which style suits you best and adopt this approach thereafter.

13–46 To capture the essence of the following statement, experiment with the undernoted methods of note-taking.

> "There are five formal sources of Scots law. The most important of the sources is legislation. The second most important is case law. The institutional writers were very important but their influence has diminished with the passage of time. Custom and equity are the other recognised formal sources of Scots law."

Précis

13–47 Prose, as above, may be appropriate where you want to abstract important details of key facts/principles/ideas, etc. The disadvantage of using continuous prose is that it is rarely easy to scan. Breaking the text up by using paragraphs helps to make it easier to read.

Headings and sub-headings

13–48 Formal sources of Scots law:

  ➢ Legislation. (Add basic detail here);
  ➢ Case law. (Add basic detail here);
  ➢ Institutional Writers. (Add basic detail here);
  ➢ Custom. (Add basic detail here);
  ➢ Equity. (Add basic detail here).

Numbered sections

> ➢ 1.1 Legislation. (Add basic detail here);   **13–49**
> ➢ 1.2 Case law. (Add basic detail here);
> ➢ 1.3 Institutional Writers. (Add basic detail here);
> ➢ 1.4 Custom. (Add basic detail here);
> ➢ 1.5 Equity. (Add basic detail here).

Annotation

Annotation can involve marking up or adding comments to texts, journal articles, etc. or notes   **13–50**
taken in classes. The purpose of an annotation is to place emphasis on specific passages, phrases
or words to aid understanding and act as a prompt or aide memoire when re-reading a passage.
Annotation may also involve making a skeleton or bullet point diagram in the margins to
capture the main points. If this method is used it can also prove useful to use the headings and
sub-headings or numbered sections method to construct your marginal diagram.

Annotated photocopied material

This approach involves marking up a photocopy with your own comments. If this method is   **13–51**
used be careful not to fall into the trap of photocopying and filing efficiently, but failing to
actually read the material.

Colour code

Using different colours for the formal sources of Scots law. This approach is also useful when   **13–52**
taking notes about: case names, details of cases, titles of statutes, etc.

Direct entry into a PC

This method can make it easier to manipulate the material using cut and paste functions.   **13–53**
However, it does not remove the issue of how the material should be arranged or marked up. A
filing system of some description will be required, as will a method of highlighting essential
features of the material.

Card index system

Notes of specific items can be recorded on and in a small card index which can then be stored   **13–54**
alphabetically, by subject or both. Many students use this method for collating case notes. Using
this method has the added benefit of forcing you to make any notes concise as they are required
to fit on to the card—typically 3" x 5", (7.6 x 12.7 cm).

EVALUATION OF DOCUMENTARY SOURCES ONCE THEY ARE LOCATED

Once information has been located, the next step in the legal investigation process is to evaluate   **13–55**
it. Information sources, as detailed throughout this text, are divided into primary and secondary
sources. Primary sources include legislation and case law, i.e. sources which state the law.
Secondary sources include textbooks, journal articles, Government statistics, White and Green
Papers, etc. A document which has been compiled "about" the law or a legal issue can only ever
provide opinion or evidence for conclusions reached by its author. For example, the separate
crime statistics published annually by the UK and Scottish Governments can be open to criticism for failing, inter alia, to reveal the true extent of crime in the respective jurisdictions.

Reasons for the number of reported crimes being an underestimation of the real extent of crime include:

> ➢ A large amount of crime is not reported to the police for a variety of reasons;
> ➢ Official statistics may reflect specific activities undertaken by a police authority, e.g. if the authorities decide to concentrate on breath testing drivers the number of reported crimes of drink-driving will invariably increase.

Given this inherent weakness, the official statistics can only be used as a piece of evidence about trends rather than definitively represent the extent of crime in a given year.

13–56 As a general rule, no matter the type of secondary sources being cited, the researcher should be alert to any possible bias or distortion that it may contain. The distortion need not be deliberate, but could be due to the way the information is collected, categorised and interpreted. However, even if bias is detected that does not render the whole document worthless. It may still contain some useful information which then requires cautious and careful examination. The important point is that the reader and any subsequent audience are aware of the bias and take it into account when giving credence or otherwise to the information in the document concerned.

13–57 When a document is being read consider various questions. The relevancy of the questions will depend on the nature of the document under consideration, e.g.:

> ➢ Who is the author? What are their qualifications for writing on the subject? Are they well respected? What else have they written on the subject? Are they legally qualified? If they are an academic, what is his/her reputation in academic circles? If the subject matter is practical, has the author qualified as a lawyer or are they an academic lawyer who might fail to identify practical issues?
> ➢ What is the date of the publication? Always check this to ensure that the most up-to-date information possible is gathered. If there is more than one edition of a text, check that the latest edition is consulted as the law will likely have changed since a previous or earlier editions were published.
> ➢ Which jurisdiction(s) is the work purporting to cover? Is it referring to Scots law or English law or is it an area of law that applies on a UK-wide basis? Is a comparative jurisdiction being discussed? If so, how does that jurisdiction differ from the applicable law in Scotland?
> ➢ Why was it produced? Has any funding been obtained to write-up the research? If so, from whom? The preface or introduction may contain details of the purpose/objective of the work. Bear in mind that this will be the publicly declared purpose, whereas the real purpose may be very different.
> ➢ Is any bias declared? For example membership of a particular political party or pressure group?
> ➢ How was the research carried out? If the document presents results of research, how much information is given about the research process and the methodologies employed? Can the methodology be justified? Has the methodology been used appropriately? Has it been used according to convention, i.e. followed current guidelines? Is it an established methodology? Is it experimental? Further relevant questions would depend on the methodology employed, but might include: is there a copy of the questionnaire, details of sample size or mention of the response rate? Are the results produced in a way which allows the reader to assess their validity e.g. if percentages are used, is there sufficient information to allow the reader to convert them to real numbers?

> ➢ How well has the document been researched? NB Footnotes/references will provide an indication.
> ➢ What are its underlying assumptions?
> ➢ How is the argument presented? How well supported and convincing is its argument?
> ➢ Are any conclusions which have been reached based on the evidence presented?
> ➢ What does the document not say? Are there any omissions?
> ➢ How does the document relate to other works? Does it follow on from previous works? Is it part of a trend? Has it disagreed with all previous work? How does it relate to later works? Has anyone taken the research further? Have they confirmed this work or have they contradicted it?
> ➢ What do other sources have to say about it? Has it received critical reviews? If it has, who has been criticising it—experts in the field or competitors?

RECORD-KEEPING

Whatever the type of legal research being undertaken, it is vital that sufficient details are written **13–58** down regarding each source to enable the researcher to locate the reference again and to use it in a bibliography. For the specific details required for the different types of sources of information, see paras 13–60—13–120 below.

It is important to be systematic and thorough when checking sources of information and **13–59** obtaining relevant items. A check on the sources already consulted, those still to be read and a list of items requested via the library on inter-library loan will enable you to remain in control throughout the currency of a research project.

BIBLIOGRAPHIC REFERENCING CONVENTIONS

A bibliography is a list of books, journal articles, reports, theses or any other secondary sources **13–60** of information consulted during the preparation of a piece of research and is required to: (i) acknowledge the sources which have been consulted; and (ii) enable readers of the research to access the materials cited. References in a bibliography therefore must convey certain details which should be accurate, complete and presented in a consistent style.

An excellent referencing guide is the 4th edition of the *Oxford Standard for Citation of Legal* **13–61** *Authorities* ("OSCOLA"). This can be found at, *http://denning.law.ox.ac.uk/published/oscola.shtml* [accessed June 14, 2014]. However, accepted styles will vary from publication to publication, due principally to different publishers adopting different house styles. While there is no single and agreed method of referencing legal authorities OSCOLA is generally accepted in academic circles. However, this style does not include many distinctively Scottish materials.

Each institution will provide specific training and guidance on how primary and secondary **13–62** sources are to be referenced when submitting written pieces of work and it is vital that any instruction offered is taken and followed as such "house styles" too will vary.

Primary sources of information, such as cases and statutes, are not included in a bibliography. **13–63** They should be listed in separate tables of cases or statutes as dictated by institutional policy. Guidance as to the more common types of bibliographic references is given below. It should be noted at this point that elsewhere in this text the conventions referred to below have not been adhered to because of the need to conform to the publisher's house style.

13–64 When referring to a source always reference the source actually used. If, for example, a primary source was not consulted but instead was read about in a casebook or an excerpt of an article in a collection of shortened versions (sometimes called "readers") then this must be acknowledged, e.g. J.F. DiMento, "Can Social Science Explain Organisational Non-compliance with Environmental Law?" (1989) 45 (1) *Journal of Social Issues* 109–132 in B. M. Hutter, *A Reader in Environmental Law* (Oxford: OUP, 1999) 218.

13–65 The above illustrates that the first named article by DiMento was not consulted, rather reference to it was made in the 1999 Hutter text which was consulted.

Cases

13–66 Case names (citation) appear in in *italics*. See Ch.3 in general for more details about citations.

13–67 If referring to a particular judgment refer to the name of the judge, the page number of the case report and, where applicable, the corresponding letter in the margin (if included in the series of law reports), e.g. *McNulty v Marshalls Food Group Ltd*, 1999 S.C. 195, per Lord Macfadyen, p.206F.

13–68 If using a media neutral citation (see paras 3–36—3–37) to refer to a post 2005 case in Scotland (post 2001 in England and Wales) also refer to the paragraph number thus, e.g. *Dow v West of Scotland Shipbreaking Company Limited* [2007] CSOH 71 [24].

> **NB** If a case is published in a printed format and also available electronically always reference the printed source for the case.

Legislation

Acts of the Scottish Parliament (pre–1707)—*referred to as Scots Acts*

13–69 The correct citation of Scots Acts is by the short title or by the calendar year and chapter number or by the volume, page and chapter number of the Record edition. The Acts did not originally have short titles, but all surviving Scots Acts were given short titles by Sch.2 of The Statute Law Revision (Scotland) Act 1964. An example from Sch.2 is the Act formerly known by "For pwnishment of personis that contempnandlie remanis rebellis and at the horne". It acquired the short title The Registration Act 1579.

13–70 Prior to 1964 Scots Acts were cited by calendar year and chapter number in the Glendook edition or by the volume and page number of the Record edition. This is still the case for Scots Acts which have been repealed.

Acts of the UK (Westminster) Parliament

13–71 For modern statutes the normal citation is the short title with no comma before the date, e.g. Citizenship (Armed Forces) Act 2014.

13–72 A complete citation for an Act will include the chapter number of the act, e.g. Defamation Act 2013 c.26.

> ➤ If referring to a section cite thus: Defamation Act 2013 s.1;
> ➤ If referring to a subsection cite thus: Defamation Act 2013 s.1(1);
> ➤ If referring to a paragraph in a subsection cite thus: Defamation Act 2013 s.3(4)(a).

For older statutes it is preferable to include the appropriate regnal year and chapter number. In the example below, the information in parentheses indicates that the Act was given Royal Assent in the 20th year of the reign of George II. It was the 43rd Act given the Royal Assent in that Parliament, hence it is called "chapter 43": Heritable Jurisdictions (Scotland) Act 1746 (20 Geo 2 c.43)

If referring to a particular part of an older act Act, indicate which section, etc. is being cited. **13–73**

Local and Personal Acts. Local and Personal Acts are cited in the same way as Public General **13–74** Acts, except that, in order to differentiate them, the chapter number is printed differently.

The chapter numbers of Local Acts appear in lower case roman numerals, e.g. Peterhead **13–75** Harbours Order Confirmation Act 1992 c xii.

The chapter numbers of Personal Acts appear in italicised Arabic figures, e.g. John Francis Dare **13–76** and Gillian Loder Dare (Marriage Enabling) Act 1982 *c 1*.

Statutory Instruments

Title, date and number (if available) or, alternatively, by year and running number, e.g. the **13–77** Financial Services (Banking Reform) Act 2013 (Disclosure of Confidential Information) Regulations 2014/882 or SI 2014/882 (alternatively SI 2014 No.882).

Statutory instruments themselves frequently stipulate the citation by which they should be **13–78** referred e.g. reg.1 of the above states "These Regulations may be cited as the Financial Services (Banking Reform) Act 2013 (Disclosure of Confidential Information) Regulations 2014...".

Acts of the Scottish Parliament (1999–)

Short title with no comma before the date, e.g. Aquaculture and Fisheries (Scotland) Act 2007. **13–79**

A complete citation would also include the asp number, e.g. Aquaculture and Fisheries (Scot- **13–80** land) Act 2007 asp 12.

Private Bills enacted by the Scottish Parliament become Acts of the Scottish Parliament and are **13–81** cited in the same way as Public General Acts, e.g. Stirling-Alloa-Kincardine Railway and Linked Improvements Act 2004 asp 10.

Scottish SI (1999–)

Name, date and number, e.g.: **13–82**

> ➤ The Renewables Obligation (Scotland) Amendment Order 2014 SSI 2014/94; or
> ➤ SSI 2014/94 (alternatively SSI 2014 No.294).

The instruments themselves frequently stipulate the citation by which they should be referred, e.g. art.1(1) of the above order states "This Order may be cited as the Renewables Obligation (Scotland) Amendment Order 2014...".

Books

13–83 Author, surname and initials, *title in italics*, followed by the publication information in parentheses (edition if other than the first edition, publisher, place of publication, date of publication), e.g. J. Thomson, *Delictual Liability* (4th edn, Haywards Heath: Tottel, 2009).

13–84 If a book has three or more authors you should include the first named author and then put "et al" meaning "and the others", e.g. T.H. Jones et al, *Criminal Law* (5th edn, Edinburgh: W. Green, 2012).

Chapters in books

13–85 Author, "title of chapter" in inverted commas, in author/editor of main work, title of main work, followed by the publication information in parentheses (edition if other than the first edition, publisher, place of publication date of publication). The page numbers for the contribution are unnecessary, e.g. W.G. Carson, "Symbolic and Instrumental Dimensions of early Factory legislation: A Case Study in the Social Origins of Criminal Law" in R Hood (ed), *Crime, Criminology and Public Policy* (Heinemann, London 1974).

The Laws of Scotland: Stair Memorial Encyclopaedia

13–86 The style of reference to the *Stair Memorial Encyclopaedia* depends on whether the material is from one of the original volumes or a reissue.

13–87 Material in a title in one of the original volumes should be styled: *The Laws of Scotland: Stair Memorial Encyclopaedia*, Vol.6, paras 896–922

13–88 Material in a title that has been reissued should be styled: *The Laws of Scotland: Stair Memorial Encyclopaedia*, Criminal Procedure Re-issue, para.183.

13–89 Note that there is no need to cite the date of publication given that this encyclopaedia is updated on an ongoing basis.

Journal articles

13–90 Author, "title of the article" in inverted commas, followed by the publication date and volume number, title of the journal and the page number marking the first page of the article, e.g. V. Aubert, "Some Social Functions of Legislation" (1966) 10 Acta Sociologica 97.

13–91 Points to note:

> ➤ If the publication date identifies the volume, the year reference should not be in brackets, unless it is an English journal in which case it should appear in square brackets, e.g. D.M. Walker, "The Importance of Stair's Work for the Modern Lawyer",1981 JR 161; C. Boch, "The Enforcement of the Environmental Assessment Directive in the National Courts: A Breach in the 'Dyke'" [1997] JEL 129;
> ➤ Normal practice is to abbreviate journal titles, but if you are referring to a lesser known or foreign journal you should provide its full title;
> ➤ If you are referring to a particular page within the article you should put a comma between the first page of the article and the particular page number. If you are referring to a paragraph number as opposed to a page number it should appear in square brackets.

Electronic journal articles

If an article is published in a printed format and also available electronically, the printed source **13–92** for the article only should be cited.

Some journals are only published electronically in which case they should be referenced as **13–93** above, but with the following additional details: the website address within angled brackets and most recent date of access, e.g. M. Kumza, "Regulatory Compliance and Web Accessibility of UK Parliament Sites" [2009] 2 JILT < http://www2.warwick.ac.uk/fac/soc/law/elj/jilt/2009_2/kuzma > accessed April 2, 2014.

Law Commission Materials

Scottish Law Commission

Scottish Law Commission Reports should be referenced by title followed by the following **13–94** details in parenthesis (number, any Scottish Executive or House of Commons paper numbers as appropriate and the year), e.g. Report on Judicial Factors (Scot Law Com No.233, SG/2013/152, 2013).

The reference for Scottish Law Commission Discussion Papers should include the DP number **13–95** which indicates that it is a discussion paper as opposed to a final report, e.g. Discussion Paper on Review of Contract Law: Third Party Rights in Contract (Scot Law Com DP No.157, 2014).

English Law Commission

The following referencing conventions ought to be adopted: **13–96**

> ➢ Report on Renting Homes in Wales (Law Com No.337, 2013);
> ➢ Consultation Paper on Contempt of Court (Law Com No.209, 2013).

NB Joint reports of the Scottish and English Law Commissions are cited thus:
Report on Level Crossings (Law Com No 339) (Scot Law Com No 234) 2013

UK Government Publications

UK Parliament Bills

Each Bill is given a number. However, if the Bill is reprinted it will be given a new number. The **13–97** number of a Bill has no connection with the chapter number that will be allocated when it becomes an Act.

The elements of the citation of a Bill are: the initials of the House (e.g. HC or HL), the session of **13–98** Parliament (e.g. 2013–14) and the Bill number which will be in square brackets if it is being considered by the House of Commons. An example of a Bill being considered by the House of Commons: Access to Mental Health Services Bill HC 2013–14 [106].

An example of a Bill being considered by the House of Lords: Forced Marriage (Civil Pro- **13–99** tection) Bill HL 2006–07 70 (this is the Bill as reprinted following amendments, the Bill was originally introduced as the Forced Marriage (Civil Protection) Bill HL 2006–07 3).

Command Papers

13–100 Name of author/department/institution/body, "title of report" in inverted commas followed by the (Command number and date) in parenthesis, e.g. The Scottish Office, "Scotland's Parliament" (Cm 3658, 1997).

> **NB** How the reference to Command papers is styled depends on the year of publication. See paras 8–111—8–114. From 1986 onwards the appropriate abbreviation is Cm.

Hansard

13–101 Cite thus: *Hansard*, the appropriate abbreviation for the House, full details of the date and column number, e.g. Hansard HC 31 March 2014, Col 577.

Scottish Parliament materials

13–102 The citations given below should be used for both electronic and print versions of the documents, etc. listed.

Bills

13–103 Bills should be referenced by Scottish Parliament (SP) Bill number, title, [printing], session, (year), e.g.:

> ➤ SP Bill 75 Rights of Relatives to Damages (Mesothelioma) (Scotland) Bill [as introduced] Session 2 (2006).
> ➤ SP Bill 58A Edinburgh Airport Rail Link Bill [as amended at Consideration stage] Session 2 (2007).
> ➤ SP Bill 59-ML2 Christmas Day and New Year's Day Trading (Scotland) Bill [Marshalled List of Amendments selected for Stage 3] Session 2 (2007).

Unlike UK Parliament Bills, Scottish Parliament Bills keep the original numbering. Subsequent revisions are indicated as follows:

SP Bill 1	Bill as introduced
SP Bill 1A	Bill as amended at Stage 2

Accompanying documentation and lists of amendments are given references which are linked to the citation of the Bill.

SP Bill 1- PM	Policy memorandum
SP Bill 1-EN	Explanatory notes and other accompanying documents
SP Bill 1-ML	Marshalled list of amendments to the Bill as introduced—if there are several marshalled lists of amendments then they are numbered SP Bill 1-ML1, SP Bill 1-ML2 etc
SP Bill 1A-ML	Marshalled list of amendments to the Bill as amended at Stage 2
SP Bill 1A-EN	Supplementary explanatory notes for the Bill as amended at Stage 2
SP Bill 1A-FM	Supplementary financial memorandum for the Bill as amended at Stage 2
SP Bill 1-G	Groupings of amendments—if there are several groupings then they are numbered SP Bill 1-G1, SP Bill 1-G2 etc

SP Bill 1-DPM   Delegated powers memorandum
SP Bill 1B   Bill as passed

Official Report

The reference for the Official Report for meetings of the Parliament should include SP OR **13–104** followed by full details of the date and column numbers, e.g. SP OR 29 March 2007, col 33710–33712.

The reference for the Official Report for Committee meetings should include SP OR followed by **13–105** the appropriate committee abbreviation, the date and column numbers, e.g. SP OR ERD 24 April 2006, col 3061–3104.

The reference for the Official Report for written answers should include SP WA followed by the **13–106** date and parliamentary question number, e.g. SP WA 28 March 2007, S2W-32485.

Committee abbreviations

Below is a list of all Scottish Parliament committees since 1999.   **13–107**

Committee Name	Abbreviation
Ad Hoc Standards	AHS
Audit	AU
Airdrie-Bathgate Railway and Linked Improvements Bill	AB
Baird Trust Reorganisation Bill	BAIRD
Burrell Collection(Lending and Borrowing) (Scotland) Bill	BC
City of Edinburgh Council (Portobello Park) Bill	EPP
City of Edinburgh Council (Leith Links and Surplus Fire Fund) Bill	LLI
Commissioner for Children and Young People (Scotland) Bill	CC
Communities	COM
Delegated Powers and Law Reports	DPLR
Economy, Energy and Tourism	EET
Edinburgh Airport Rail Link Bill	EARL
Edinburgh Tram (Line One) Bill	ED1
Edinburgh Tram (Line Two) Bill	ED2
Education	ED
Education and Culture	EC
Education, Culture and Sport	ED
Education, Lifelong Learning and Culture	ELLC
End of Life Assistance (Scotland) Bill	ELA
Enterprise and Culture	EC
Enterprise and Lifelong Learning	EL
Environment and Rural Development	ERD
Equal Opportunities	EO
European	EU
European and External Relations	EU
Finance	FI
Forth Crossing Bill	FCB
Glasgow Airport Rail Link Bill	GARL
Health	HC
Health and Community Care	HE

Health and Sport	HS
Infrastructure and Capital Investment	ICI
Interests of Members of the Scottish Parliament Bill	MI
Justice	J
Justice and Home Affairs	JH
Justice 1	J1
Justice 2	J2
Justice Sub-Committee on Policing	JSP
Local Government	LG
Local Government and Communities	LGC
Local Government and Regeneration	LGR
Local Government and Transport	LGT
National Galleries of Scotland Bill	NG
National Trust for Scotland (Governance etc.) Bill	NTS
Procedures	PR
Public Audit	PA
Public Petitions	PE
Public Petitions	PPC
Referendum (Scotland) Bill	REF
Review of SPCB Supported Bodies	RSSB
Robin Rigg Offshore Wind Farm (Navigation and Fishing)(Scotland) Bill	RR
Rural Affairs	RA
Rural Affairs, Climate Change and Environment	RACCE
Rural Affairs and Environment	RAE
Rural Development	RD
Salmon and Freshwater Fisheries (Consolidation) (Scotland) Bill	SF
Scotland Bill	SCO
Scottish Parliamentary Pensions Bill	SPPB
Scottish Parliamentary Pension Scheme	SPPS
Scottish Parliamentary Standards Commissioner Bill	SC
Social Inclusion, Housing and Voluntary Sector	HS
Social Justice	SJ
Standards	ST
Standards and Public Appointments	ST
Standards, Procedures and Public Appointments	SPPA
Stirling-Alloa-Kincardine Railway and LinkedImprovements Bill	SAK
Subordinate Legislation	SL
Transport and the Environment	TE
Transport, Infrastructure and Climate Change	TIC
Ure Elder Fund Transfer and Dissolution Bill	URE
Waverley Railway (Scotland) Bill	WAV
Welfare Reform	WR
William Simpson's Home (Transfer of Property etc.) (Scotland) Bill	WSH

Minutes of Committees

13–108 Minutes of Committees should be referenced as follows: SP M followed by the appropriate committee abbreviation and the date, e.g. SP M SL 29 November 2005.

Minutes of Proceedings

Minutes of Proceedings should be referenced as follows: SP MOP, volume, number, session and **13–109** date, e.g. SP MOP vol 4 no 41 Session 2, 14 December 2006.

Public petitions

Petitions are referenced according to their PE number, e.g. PE975. Each public petition before **13–110** Parliament is numbered sequentially. No year number is given.

Scottish Parliament papers

These should be referenced as follows: author/committee/body, report number, year, title (SPP **13–111** number) in parenthesis, e.g. Environment and Rural Development Committee 1st Report, 2006, Stage 1 Report on the Animal Health and Welfare (Scotland) Bill (SPP 502).

Scottish Parliament Information Centre (SPICe) Publications

These should be referenced as follows: title, series in abbreviated form, number, date. The **13–112** abbreviations for the various series are below:

Series name	Abbreviation
Fact Sheet	FS
IPRN Briefing	IPRN
Research Note (until 31 December 2001)	RN
Research Paper (until 31 December 2001)	RP
SPICe Briefing	SB
Subject Map. Comparative Series	SM CS
Subject Map. Devolved Area Series	SM DA
Subject Map. Scottish Parliament Series	SM SP

Examples include:

> ➤ Labour Market Update, SB 14/25, 20 March 2014
> ➤ Allotments, RN 00/102, 23 November 2000
> ➤ The Water Industry, SM DA21, 21 December 1999

Scottish Government papers

Scottish Government papers are given a running number as they are published within a calendar **13–113** year, e.g. SE 2014/19.

NB More information about referencing material from the Scottish Parliament can be found in "A Guide to Recommended Citations for Scottish Parliament Publications" , FS3-12, 17 September 2013 which is available here *http://www.scottish.parliament.uk/ parliamentarybusiness/15984.aspx* [accessed June 26, 2014].

Conference proceedings

13–114 The form of citation will depend on whether the conference proceedings have been published. If this is the case the following details should be included: author(s), "title" (of specific paper), conference title, publisher; place of publication, date, paper number of specific paper, if given. For example, A. Murray, "The Nature of Law", Proceedings of the Conference on Legal Things, Research Association, Dundee 2006, Paper 3.

13–115 If the conference proceedings are only available at a conference or directly from the author they should be referenced by author, title, conference title and date.

13–116 If the conference proceedings are only available online the reference should include the additional details of the web address and date of access.

Theses

13–117 Author, "title" in inverted commas, followed by the remaining information in parentheses (degree or award, university or other institution, year), e.g. A.D. Smith, "Some Comparative Aspects of Specific Implement in Scots Law" (PhD thesis, Edinburgh University, 1989).

Newspaper articles

13–118 Author/editorial/anon as appropriate, "title of article" in inverted commas, name of *newspaper in italics,* followed by the publication details in parenthesis (city of publication, the full date), page number, e.g. I. Bell, "Springtime in Quangopolis", *The Scotsman* (Edinburgh, March 17, 1999) 19.

13–119 If the article is from a newspaper's web site and there is no page number, the reference should include the website address and date of access, e.g. K. Rawlinson, "Court to decide whether mentally ill woman should have hysterectomy", *The Guardian* (London, March 31, 2014) < http://www.theguardian.com/law/2014/mar/31/court-decide-mentally-ill-woman-hyster-ectomy > accessed April 29, 2014.

Online and CD Rom materials

13–120 See paras 2–95—2–100.

REFERENCING SYSTEMS

13–121 There are three main referencing systems which are used to link statements made in academic work to bibliographic details of documents which support these statements. The choice of which system is to be used will likely be determined by each institution—only in rare circumstance will the choice be a free one. The important point is that one system (whether mandatory is not) is used consistently.

13–122 The systems are:

Running notes

13–123 With running notes, numerals in the text, [in brackets] or [superscript], refer to notes numbered in the order they occur which contain references and sometimes other information. Multiple citations of the same document receive separate numbers. Details of the documents referred to (e.g. page references) should be given in the notes. This system can be used to incorporate explanatory footnotes, as well as bibliographic references and is widely used in UK legal journals. Running notes can be listed at the foot of the page where reference is made to them (footnotes) or in numerical sequence at the end of the work (endnotes).

In the list of references/bibliography the works cited are listed in numerical order.   **13–124**

If more than one reference is made to a document when running notes are used, it is possible to **13–125** avoid a full reciting of the document by using the following terms:

> ➤ *Ibid* (*Ibidem*—meaning "the same") can be used if successive references are made to the same document. Each use of "ibid" should be followed by the page number;
> ➤ *Op.Cit.* (*Opere citato*—meaning "in the work previously cited") where the document has been cited at an earlier point, but not immediately before this reference. The author's name and page number are required. The original citation should contain full bibliographic information;

The numeric system

Documents are numbered in the order in which they are first referred to in the text. At each **13–126** point in the text at which a reference is required, its number is inserted, [in brackets] or in superscript. Subsequent citations of a particular document receive the same number as the first citation. If details of a particular document, e.g. page number, are required they should be given after the reference number.

In the list of references/bibliography the works cited are listed in numerical order.   **13–127**

This system produces a list of references which is easy to prepare and easy to look up whilst **13–128** reading the text, but it is not in any useful order as a bibliography. This system ought to be coupled with a separate bibliography in alphabetical order of author name(s).

Example

Recent research [1] has shown that ... however a respected author [2] has put forward a further theory. After much debate the findings of both works [1] have now been accepted as representing the law on this point.
[Excerpt from list of references:]
    1. Lloyd I. *Information Technology Law Oxford*: OUP, 2011
    2. Murray A. *Information Technology Law* Oxford: OUP, 2013

The name and date system (also known as the "Harvard System")

This system is widely used in Scottish universities across many disciplines, including law. The **13–129** author's name and date of publication are inserted in brackets at each point in the text where reference to the particular document is required. If the author's name occurs naturally in the text, the date only should be in brackets. If reference is made to different works by the same author in the same year, distinguish them by small case letters after the year.

The works cited would be listed alphabetically by author in the references/bibliography. The **13–130** date is given after the name and not repeated at the end of the reference. If there are several works by the same author, they should be listed in chronological order.

Example

Recent research (Wallace 2006) has shown that ... however a respected author (Bruce 2007) has disagreed. After much debate the findings of the original work (Wallace 2006) have now been accepted.

[Excerpt from list of references:]
1. Bruce R. (2007) *Even Newer Law Book*, Edinburgh: W. Green.
2. Wallace W. (2006) *New Law Book*, Edinburgh: W. Green.

Additional reading

13–131
➤ David P. Bosworth, *Citing your references: a guide for authors of journal articles and students writing theses or dissertations* (Underhill Press, Thirsk, 1992)
➤ D. French, *How to Cite Legal Authorities* (Blackstone Press, London, 1996)

CONSTRUCTING A BIBLIOGRAPHY

13–132 The purpose of recording all references that have been found during a research project is twofold. In the first instance, full references are required so that the author can incorporate them into his/her bibliography for a specific piece of work to comply with usual academic practice, e.g. as there will tend to be a time gap between collecting the references, making use of the information and finally submitting the work it is best practice to reference all materials at the point of use. If footnotes are to be used, a full reference given there can be harvested for the construction of the bibliography once the piece of work is complete. The second reason for accurately recording references is that it enables the researcher to build up their own research database for other work undertaken at some point in the future.

13–133 Various ways of constructing a bibliography can be considered and tried. Experience will dictate which method best suits the individual researcher:

➤ A manual record card system maintained in alphabetical order of the author's surname;
➤ A database in electronic form. This can be achieved by constructing a table in Word or by using a spreadsheet, such as Excel. There are also a number of specialist database software packages, such as Microsoft Access, RefWorks, Endnote and Reference Manager designed to aid researchers when storing references and generating bibliographic details

In either case it is useful to adopt a keyword system describing the contents of each item. The inclusion of supplementary information may also prove useful, e.g. author's surname given in alphabetical order with full citation; the keyword(s) could be "criminal" or "criminal law" with the supplementary information briefly recording the researcher's comments on the work or the passages cited.

Chapter 14
How to Use your Research to Produce
High Quality Work

This chapter provides practical advice on using your research to produce work of a high **14–01** standard whilst at university. It starts by providing guidance on the appropriate use of authority, use of quotations and how to avoid plagiarism. The chapter then looks at preparing assessments and how best to structure essays, answers to problem questions and oral presentations. Construction of research projects is also discussed. The chapter concludes with discussion of how to evaluate your own research followed by guidance on revision strategies for exams and exam technique.

APPROPRIATE USE OF AUTHORITY

When making specific points or arguments in any piece of academic work you must back them **14–02** up with supporting authority. At a general level, authority means the provision of reasons, evidence or justification for the propositions given by making reference to the originator of the idea, statement, etc. When discussing legal issues, you must also refer to relevant primary and secondary legal authority. Primary authority comprises cases, legislation or another source of law, such as a statement by one of the Institutional Writers. Secondary authority refers to journal articles or other publications of merit, e.g. a Scottish Law Commission Report or government policy paper.

The best way of developing the technique of using authority is to look at and then consider how **14–03** it has been used by other lawyers in a variety of circumstance.

Judges in their opinions

Chalmers v HMA [2014] HCJAC 24 Opinion of the Lord Justice General (Lord Wheatley) at **14–04** paras [5], [7] and [8]:

> [5] "The principal issue in this appeal concerns the extent, if any, to which, when imposing a life sentence and fixing the punishment part, the sentencing judge should take account of the accused's conviction on another offence that is libelled on the same indictment. That requires us yet again to visit section 2, as amended, of the Prisoners and Criminal Proceedings (Scotland) Act 1993 (the 1993 Act). A separate aspect of it exercised the minds of five judges in *Ansari* v *HM Adv* (2003 JC 105) and of seven judges in *Petch v HM Adv* (2011 JC 210)."
>
> "Murder (Abolition of Death Penalty) Act 1965.
>
> [7] Section 1(2) of the 1965 Act permitted the sentencing judge, at his discretion, to recommend a minimum period that a convicted murderer should serve before release. In making a recommendation the sentencing judge could take into account the consideration

of public protection. Therefore he almost inevitably took into account any other offences of which the accused was convicted on the same indictment (e.g. *Casey* v *HM Adv* 1993 SCCR 453, at p 458B–D)".

8] "The judge's recommendation was persuasive only. The Secretary of State could release the prisoner before or after the expiry of any recommended minimum term, after consultation with the sentencing judge and the Lord Justice General in every case. The decision of the Secretary of State was based on an assessment of the public interest (*cf R (Anderson)* v *Secretary of State for the Home Department* 2003 1 AC 837 at para.[14]). That remained the position until 1993."

Legal writers in texts

14–05 R. Conway, *Personal Injury Practice in the Sheriff Courts*, 3rd edn, W. Green, Ch.15 2011, [15–02] [15–03]

"**[15–02]** The sheriff's written judgment will not normally deal with expenses, but will fix a date for a hearing on expenses.[1] You should send the judgment to the client immediately. If you have lost on the merits or a significant aspect of the case you will have to consider whether to appeal. The interlocutor will become final after expenses have been dealt with, and you will have a 14-day time limit in which to mark a note of appeal running from the date of that interlocutor.[2] The immediate post-judgment period will therefore provide a breathing space in which a considered decision can be taken with the client. Almost all clients who have been unsuccessful on the merits want to go to appeal, which they think will be a re-run of the facts. Your job is to assess and advise on the realistic prospects. Where the finding complained of relates to an ancillary matter such as quantum or contributory negligence you should always remember that your appeal will open up the whole matter to a cross-appeal from the defender which is not limited to the points which you have taken. If your client has a civil legal aid certificate, then a meeting to consider an appeal will be covered under that certificate. You require a fresh civil legal aid application for the appeal itself, and preliminary matters require cover under Legal Advice and Assistance. Where you conclude that there are no reasonable prospects on appeal, you must write to the client advising him and also point out the expiry date for marking an appeal."

"**[15–03]** Think twice before making any appeal based purely on a supposed error of finding in fact. As noted below, the adjudication privileges which attach to a judge at first instance are well nigh impenetrable, unless you can show that he or she is "plainly wrong".[3] The traditional framework for appeals is contained in the speech of Lord Thankerton in *Thomas v Thomas*,[4] where he said as follows:

'(1) Where a question of fact has been tried by a Judge without a jury, and there is no question of misdirection of himself by the Judge, an appellate Court which is disposed to come to a different conclusion on the printed evidence should not do so unless it is satisfied that any advantage enjoyed by the trial Judge by reason of having seen and heard the witnesses could not be sufficient to explain or justify the trial Judge's conclusion. (2) The appellate Court may take the view that, without having seen or heard the witnesses, it is not in a position to come to any satisfactory conclusion on the printed evidence. (3) The appellate Court, either because the reasons given by the trial Judge are not satisfactory, or because it unmistakably so appears from the evidence, may be satisfied that he has not taken proper advantage of having seen and heard the witnesses, and the matter will then become at large for the appellate Court. It is obvious that the value and importance of having seen and heard the witnesses will vary according to the class of case, and, it may be, the individual case in question.'

The sheriff principal will expect you to know this and be prepared to argue with reference to this passage that the matter is at large for the appellate court.

¹ See, e.g. practice note 1988 to this effect for South Strathclyde Dumfries and Galloway.
² OCR 31.1.
³ *Thomson v Kvaerner*, 2004 S.C. (H.L.) 1.
⁴ *Thomas v Thomas*, 1947 S.C. (H.L.) 45 at [54]."
⁵ See also the case of *Sunderland*, 1992 S.L.T. 1146 and the decision of Sheriff Principal McLeod in *Durham v Gateway Food Market*, 1992 S.L.T. 83, (Sh. Ct)."

Tutors in their lecture notes

F. Grant, Lecture Notes Intellectual Property Law, 2013.　　　**14–06**

"The work undertaken by the EU High Level Expert Group (Copyright Subgroup)¹ which issued its final report in June 2008 presaged the proposal for a Directive on certain permitted uses of orphan works.² Although the Directive is limited in effect, liberating only orphan works of cultural significance it does not preclude licensing of works of economic value by member states. Accordingly, the response to the consultation questions must be considered in light of the provisions detailed therein. The proposal for a Directive envisages online intra-EEA cross-border access to orphan works held in archives/libraries et al first published of broadcast in a member state. Indeed, the preamble to the Directive amplifies the rationale of the proposed legislation by making clear that few member states have followed the lead given by the Commission's 2006 Recommendation on the digitisation and online accessibility of cultural content and digital preservation,³ inviting them at the time of writing to take interim legislative measure to authorise the use of orphan works. It is further noted [and lamented] in the proposal for a Directive that those member states who have acted to liberate orphan works do not permit online access to non- residents of that state. There is nothing in the proposal for a Directive to suggest constraints on member states wishing to widen the authorisation mechanism or licensing regime per extra EU/EEA online access to orphan works.⁴ Indeed, Article 7 of the proposed Directive is permissive in that it enables Member States to authorise the use of orphan work for purposes '*other than those referred to in Article 6(2)*'.

The creation of a legal framework to facilitate the cross-border digitisation and dissemination of orphan works in the single market is also one of the key action points identified in the Digital Agenda for Europe (part of the Europe 2020 Strategy).⁵

¹ *i2010: Digital Libraries Report on Digital Preservation, Orphan Works, and Out-of-Print Works.* Adopted 18.4.2007
² European Commission, 2011. *Proposal for a Directive of the European Parliament and of the Council on certain permitted uses of orphan works* (COM(2011)289 final 2011/0136 (COD). Hereinafter referred to as *the proposal for a Directive.*
³ Commission Recommendation 2006/585/EC of 24 August 2006 on the digitisation and online accessibility of cultural content and digital preservation.
⁴ See Recital 21.
⁵ Communication from the Commission (26/08/2010)."

Substantiating your assertions with authority

A statement such as "Distances mentioned in Acts of Parliament should be measured in a **14–07** straight line" is an unsubstantiated assertion as no evidence has been produced to back up the statement. Such a statement is described as a "bare" statement.

An acceptable level of reference to authority would be, "Unless specifically stated otherwise, **14–08** references to distance in Acts of Parliament should be measured in a straight line (Interpretation Act 1978, s.8)".

14–09 An authoritative reference could consist of the following, "Section 8 of The Interpretation Act 1978 states that distances referred to in Acts of Parliament 'shall, unless the contrary intention appears, be measured in a straight line on a horizontal plane'".

14–10 This statement has quoted words from the relevant statute in order to make the position absolutely clear, as a matter of law. You may wish to quote from the actual words of the statute if you feel that they would make your point more clearly. However, you should rarely need to write out the entire statutory provision. This generally adds little to any piece of academic work and simply wastes words in any coursework, constrained as it will be by a word count.

14–11 When using a case as authority it will rarely be sufficient to simply cite the case concerned, e.g. "The offence of causing pollution contained in s.85(1) of the Water Resources Act 1991 should be regarded as a strict liability offence—*Alphacell v Woodward* [1972] A.C. 824".

14–12 The narration of excessive factual detail about a case is not appropriate either, e.g.:

> "The offence of causing pollution contained in s.85 (1) of the Water Resources Act 1991 should be regarded as a strict liability offence—*Alphacell v Woodward* [1972] A.C. 824. This case concerned a company who had premises on the banks of the River Irwell. They treated manila fibres as part of the process of manufacturing paper. The fibres had to be boiled and the water in which they were boiled became seriously polluted. This water was drained into two settling tanks on the edge of the river. One settling tank was higher than the other and the overflow from the higher tank went into the lower. In a shed nearby, there were two pumps which ensured that there was no overflow from the lower tank. If the pumps failed the liquid went straight into the river. This happened one day in November 1969. The court found Alphacell guilty."

Best practice is to detail what is relevant about the authority to illustrate your point. This means providing a summary of the ratio decidendi of a case (the reason(s), as a matter of law, for the decision in a specific case—see paras 3–07—3–08) either in your own words or in the form of a brief quotation:

> "The offence of causing pollution contained in s.85(1) of the Water Resources Act 1991 should be regarded as a strict liability offence, *Alphacell v Woodward* [1972] A.C. 824. This House of Lords case examined the concept of causation and decided that the word 'cause' should be given its common, everyday meaning. Negligence, knowledge and intention were all regarded as irrelevant. The important factor was that an active operation had resulted in polluting matter entering a river, thus 'causing' the damage levelled in the charge'."

The above illustrates the importance of following the advice given in paras 3–49—3–52 about writing a case note to isolate the ratio decidendi of leading cases highlighted in class meetings before or shortly after the event.

QUOTATIONS

14–13 If you want to repeat the exact words used in one of the sources consulted you must use quotation marks. Everything between quotation marks, including punctuation, should be exactly as it appeared in the original text. If you wish to add something to the quotation you should put it in square brackets, [ ]. If you omit something you should mark this by adding an ellipsis (...). The quote should be referenced and, in addition, the page from which it was taken should be included in the reference, e.g.:

> "In homicide, it is not an offence to kill whether intentionally or recklessly, by omission, unless one is under a duty to act ... In the pollution cases,(where a statutory provision applies), the courts have attempted to make a similar distinction." (N. Padfield, "Clean Water and Muddy Causation: Is Causation a Question of Law or Fact, or Just a Way of Allocating Blame", Crim L.R. [1995] 683 at p.690.)

PLAGIARISM

University study is all about exploring literature and being influenced by new and different **14–14** ideas. However, there is a fine dividing line between being influenced by the academic sources to which you are exposed and plagiarism.

The Oxford English Dictionary defines plagiarism as, "The action or practice of taking someone **14–15** else's work, idea, etc., and passing it off as one's own; literary theft". Thus expressing someone else's ideas and presenting them as your own in a piece of work is plagiarism. Plagiarism includes copying out chunks of or an entire article, section of a book or another student's work without due acknowledgement. Plagiarism is not an acceptable academic practice. If you resort to including unacknowledged sources in your work you will be penalised to the extent that you may well be awarded no marks at all for the submission concerned and/or face disciplinary action.

It is also salutary to note at this point that law students, post-graduation from the Diploma in **14–16** Legal Practice wishing to embark upon a traineeship are required to apply for an entrance certificate to the profession. The Law Society of Scotland advises that, "An Entrance Certificate is the certificate issued by the Society which certifies that an individual is a fit and proper person to enter into a traineeship" (see *http://www.lawscot.org.uk/education-and-careers/the-traineeship/ starting-a-traineeship-soon/entrance-certificate-and-training-contract-faqs* [accessed June 14, 2014]).

At the time of writing, the guidance notes published by the Council of the Law Society of **14–17** Scotland for applicants state that s/he must disclose inter alia " ... any past behaviour indicating a lack of probity including ... any conscious act or omission which might mislead another person including plagiarism or cheating in an academic setting" (see *http://www.law scot.org.uk/media/526068/fitandproperguidanceoct2013.pdf* [accessed June 14, 2014]).

In order to avoid plagiarism: **14–18**

> ➢ Familiarise yourself at the start of your studies with your institution's plagiarism documentation and policies. Many institutions provide a hard copy during induction or in the first few weeks of study, with an electronic copy being available on the institution's intranet;
> ➢ Attend any classes/labs/seminars devoted to the pursuit of good academic practice. These may be offered as part of a particular module and/or your institution may routinely offer refresher classes which are open to all students;
> ➢ Ensure that you always acknowledge the sources which you have used. See paras 13–60—13–68 per techniques for collating references and constructing a bibliography;

> ➤ If you wish to paraphrase, i.e. express ideas from someone else's work in your own words where the source clearly identified, make sure you refer to it as, "X's view of Y" to ensure the opinion given is clearly denoted as that of another;
> ➤ If you wish to use the exact words of an author/judge in a prior work or case report, use a brief quotation.

NB Block quoting, i.e. taking chunks of the work of various authors and incorporating them into a coursework with appropriate references given, comes into the category of bad academic practice, i.e. whilst there is no intention to deceive or pass the work off as your own, it is not acceptable to submit work where there is little (if any) original expression, i.e. your work. Work coming into this category will rarely be awarded a passing grade.

UNIVERSITY ASSESSMENTS

14–19 No two institutions will assess students in the same way. A module may be continuously assessed, meaning there is no terminal exam. If this is the case, students are required to submit items of coursework during the period of teaching. On the other hand, a module may be assessed by a coursework which is submitted during the teaching period and an exam which will take place once teaching has concluded. Or you may be assessed via an oral presentation and coursework. The possible permutations are endless, therefore it is essential to make a point of finding out at the start of each module how and when you will be assessed. The main types of assessment used consistently throughout each stage of an undergraduate law degree include: essays/research projects, oral presentations, multiple choice questions and exams. These are discussed in turn below.

14–20 It is vital to be aware at the outset that the study of law is not simply a memory test. You will be required to display more than knowledge of the law in a particular area and apply legal rules and principles to particular situations and also to develop analytical and critical thinking when presenting and communicating legal argument in a clear and logical manner.

14–21 A key part of the assessment process is the feedforward and/or feedback you receive from tutors (see para.13–39).

14–22 After each piece of work has been marked you will generally receive a feedback sheet where particular skills have been graded in accordance with the criteria for that assessment. A feedback sheet, as in the example given below, may also contain general comments on how future performance in the areas tested can be improved.

	A	B	C	D	F
Knowledge of the relevant law demonstrated.	☐	☐	☐	☐	☐
Awareness of the context in which the relevant law operates displayed.	☐	☐	☐	☐	☐
Topic(s) covered in appropriate depth.	☐	☐	☐	☐	☐
Sufficient and proper use of primary authority.	☐	☐	☐	☐	☐
Sufficient and proper use of secondary authority.	☐	☐	☐	☐	☐
Spelling, grammar and presentation of the paper of a high standard.	☐	☐	☐	☐	☐
A coherent and structured argument given.	☐	☐	☐	☐	☐
Referenced in accordance with good academic practice/adherence to the university referencing style.	☐	☐	☐	☐	☐

Demonstrates sound legal reasoning to support the conclusion(s) reached

Comments: Your essay whilst well-structured and well written does not fully address the title. Accordingly, the grade awarded reflects the fact that only two out of the three issues which ought to have been discussed were explored in any meaningful way. Your use of primary authority could have been enhanced my making reference to judicial comment to explain salient points rather than relying on quotes from text books. For future submissions please revisit the module handbook where further guidance is given on the proper use of both primary and secondary authority.

If, after having read the comments for a particular piece of work, you do not understand where you went wrong, make an appointment with the tutor who marked it. It is vital to find out how to improve your work so that you can ensure that you will perform better in the future. It is never pleasant to receive criticism, but all criticism given will be constructive and it is in your best interests to take it on board, reflect on it and learn from it.

General points for all types of assessments

> ➢ Make sure that you understand what is expected of you. You should read and if **14–23** necessary re-read the assessment criteria to be adopted;
> ➢ Ensure that you answer the question set and do so fully. A partial answer, even a very good one, will seriously impact upon the grade awarded;
> ➢ Do not include unsubstantiated (subjective) personal opinion;
> ➢ Always back up your arguments/conclusions with reference to primary and, where appropriate, secondary authority;
> ➢ It is best practice to reference the person who originated the idea than the people who have written about it subsequently;
> ➢ Do not include substantive points in footnotes to get round the word limit. Under no circumstances should the footnotes on any one page exceed the amount of substantive text, i.e. the essay/report, etc. itself;

> ➢ Your work should be intelligible at first reading. It is important to ensure that your meaning is clearly communicated to the reader; and
> ➢ Make sure that your grammar and spelling is correct. If necessary make use of spell-check, a thesaurus or a dictionary. However, bear in mind if using spell-check that it is not infallible and may fail to recognise certain legal words, e.g. the word "delict" is a stranger to this facility. Words such as this can be added manually to a spell-check dictionary. If using spell-check also ensure that the language setting is "English UK" not "US". Also ensure that the Word package used is set for English UK.

Essay Writing Techniques

14–24 Essays are one of the ways in which students are required to express themselves and present information in written form. Essays are likely to feature as a prominent part of the assessment regime you encounter at university either as coursework or as part of an exam. This section is designed to help you enhance your essay writing skills.

Compliance with requirements

14–25 The handbook issued at the start of each academic year and/or other materials issued by individual module tutors will contain information about the university's assessment criteria for essays. Make sure that you familiarise yourself with these. If you do not understand what any of the criteria means or requires contact the relevant tutor to discuss what is expected.

14–26 Make sure that you are aware of any special requirements, such as word limits or format stipulations. Word counts or limits may be given as guidelines or as upper and lower limits for a particular essay, e.g. if the instruction is to author an essay in "no more than 1,500 words", no lower limit has been set, although it would be a foolish student who decided to submit a work comprising half of the permitted word count. On the other hand if the instruction is to author and essay "between 1,200 and 1,500 words" there is some flexibility and autonomy built in and an informed choice can be made as to whether the lower or upper limit is the one which ought to be achieved. In both circumstances, provide an accurate word count (excluding footnotes unless instructed to do so). In general, under or over-length submissions will be penalised so ensure that any instructions in this regard are also read and followed.

14–27 If you are having difficulty finding enough material for the essay and are woefully short of the word limit, you may be searching under the wrong terms or you may have misunderstood the question. If you have written far in excess of the word limit, you have likely included extraneous material. Re-read your work and remove material that does not directly relate to the question or questions posed by the essay title.

Considering the question

14–28 Examine the wording of the question carefully and decide what you are being asked to do. On occasion this is more easily said than done. One way to help focus your thoughts is to underline key words in the question. You should be aware that essay titles are always carefully chosen to elicit a specific outcome. The basic topic may be narrow, e.g. "Explain the defence of self-defence as it is understood in Scotland".

14–29 This title makes it crystal clear than one topic is under scrutiny and that only the Scottish jurisdiction is be considered. The word "explain" denotes that the author is to confine them-selves to outlining the rules defining the defence by giving examples of when it has been successfully or unsuccessfully pled and why, i.e. by providing an explanation as to the court's reasoning when considering the defence in specific cases by making reference to both primary and secondary authority.

On the other hand, if the title is, "Critically analyse the defence of self-defence as it is under- **14–30** stood in Scotland and England", a comparative analysis of how the defence operates in these separate jurisdictions is required. To do this, the rules in each jurisdiction have to be isolated prior to comparing and contrasting any differences. Again, reference to primary authority will be crucial, as will reference to relevant secondary sources.

Some essay titles may prove to be broader in nature, e.g. "The threat to the environment can **14–31** only be reduced by strengthening the existing legal controls. Discuss."

It is a common mistake for students to read a title like this and to conclude that they are being **14–32** asked to write as much as they know on "the environment" or "strengthening the existing legal controls". These factors are relevant, but they are not the major focus of the question. With titles such as this it is helpful to consider which of the words used will assist in narrow the essay's scope. Here, the title is asking you to identify the most probable ways of "reducing" the "threat" to the environment and then to assess whether "strengthening" existing legal controls is more effective than any of the other possible options. For further guidance consult, S. Drew and R. Bingham, *Key Words in Essay Questions* (based on a table by *The Student Skills Guide*, 2nd edn (Aldershot: Gower, 2001)).

The title always determines what is going to be relevant to the essay. Your answer must address **14–33** the question(s). Accordingly, everything you write should be relevant to answering the specific question(s) asked. You will not gain any marks for irrelevant material—no matter how accurate or interesting it may be. The inclusion of irrelevant material will detract from your answer. If you ensure that you understand the question then you should be able to identify what is relevant from the material you have been directed to by the tutor. If you are unsure of what is relevant you need to take a step back and reconsider the question and clarify your understanding.

As detailed above, an essay title can be framed in different ways. You will become familiar with **14–34** the subtle differences between the words listed below as they will feature in essay titles repeatedly throughout your undergraduate career.

Analyse:	Break up ... into component parts and examine each part.
Compare:	Look for similarities and differences between ...
Contrast:	Bring out the differences between ...
Criticise:	Present and evaluate evidence before reaching a judgement about ...
Define:	Set out the precise meaning of ...
Describe:	A detailed account of ...
Discuss:	Explain the meaning of ... and examine the reasons for and against ...
Evaluate:	What is the value/worth of ...
Explain:	Make ... plain and understandable and account for it.
Identify:	Establish the nature of ...
Illustrate:	Make clear by giving examples.
Interpret:	Use your judgement to make clear the meaning of ...
Justify:	Use arguments to make a case for ...
Review:	Make a survey of ... and examine it critically.

COLLECTING RELEVANT MATERIAL

14–35 Once you have decided what the question is asking you to do, you can begin gather relevant materials (see paras 12–09—12–15).

Planning the essay

14–36 Examine all the material you have gathered and decide which sources, both primary and secondary ought to be included in your essay. You should always keep the essay title uppermost in your mind when doing so. Do not be tempted to try to use all of the material you have gathered. Some of it may prove irrelevant and even material you consider to be relevant may have to be omitted. The next step is to construct an essay plan outlining the basic structure of the essay. Essays tend to conform to a basic framework which consists of three parts: introduction, discussion and conclusion. It is important, however, to adhere to any specific guidance given by a tutor with regard to a particular piece of work.

Introduction

14–37 In your introduction you essentially set out how you are going to tackle the essay. You might include:

> ➤ How to interpret any ambiguous terms in the title, e.g. what you understand by "the threat to the environment");
> ➤ Any assumptions you are going to make rather than argue in detail;
> ➤ The criteria you are going to use to reach your conclusions, e.g. "the environment is so important that I shall assume that anything which has an unknown effect must be assumed to have a bad effect");
> ➤ How you are going to structure your essay.

It is often a good idea to write your introduction after you have completed the discussion that will form the majority of the essay. This will ensure that your introduction matches what you have actually done.

Discussion

14–38 This is the most significant portion of the essay. Each paragraph should deal with a single point. Each main point should be considered, developed and justified by reference to relevant authority.

14–39 Do not include unsubstantiated (subjective) opinion. Avoid phrases such as "it is obvious that" or "most people would agree". Such comment is devoid of authority. Authority should be either a case, a piece of legislation or a secondary source, such as a journal article or an extract from a legal encyclopaedia.

14–40 You should not present only one side of an argument. You should show the reader that you have taken account of any apparently conflicting evidence. An outline of a discussion might be Brown's theory of X is well-founded because of (a), (b) and (c). However, it can also be said, as argued by Grey, that (d), (e) and (f) may also be applicable.

Conclusion

Your conclusion should bring your whole argument together into a set of points that you want **14–41** the reader to retain. These points are to be presented in paragraphs, never bullet points. Your conclusion is based on your arguments as detailed in the discussion part of the essay and should not include any new material. Do not confuse "conclusion" with "summary". You do need to summarise all your arguments.

Bibliography

It is vital to include a bibliography. Failure to do so will result in marks being deducted. This **14–42** should include references to all the materials you have used in preparation of the piece of work. Lecture notes and primary sources, such as cases and legislation, should not be included. Neither should you refer to online databases, such as Westlaw or LexisNexis. This would be the equivalent of referring to a law library! See paras 13–60—13–68 for further guidance on bibliographic references.

Writing the essay

The thought of the whole process of writing an essay and even planning the essay can be **14–43** daunting. You may find it easier if you break the overall task down into smaller component parts, e.g.:

- ➢ Analyse the title and decide what exactly you are being asked to do;
- ➢ Consider all possible approaches;
- ➢ Collect relevant material;
- ➢ Decide on an appropriate structure;
- ➢ Write the discussion section;
- ➢ Write the conclusion; and
- ➢ Write the introduction.

Make sure you do not fall into error by making any of these common mistakes:

- ➢ Regurgitation of lecture notes/books;
- ➢ Failure to address the question asked;
- ➢ The inclusion of material without linking it to the essay question;
- ➢ Failure to back up arguments with legal authority;
- ➢ The inclusion of too much description and too little analysis;
- ➢ Use of colloquial terms;
- ➢ Using words inappropriately;
- ➢ Inclusion of unsubstantiated personal opinion;
- ➢ Failure to communicate ideas clearly; and
- ➢ Poor use of the English language.

Drafts

Write a draft of the essay which conforms to your essay plan. Do not expect to hand in the first **14–44** or even second draft. Do not just put down everything you know and presume that the marker will extract the relevant/correct sections. You should identify the relevant/correct material and excise the irrelevant, as the inclusion of extraneous material detracts from the appropriate material you have presented.

14-45 You should aim to present a clear and concise discussion of the topic. Try to use simple straightforward language. Flowery words and phrases generally add nothing to legal argument and have a tendency to encompass subjective comment. Use short sentences. Avoid using words you do not understand. Employing complicated language will not give a favourable impression if it is obvious that the writer does not understand its meaning. If you are in doubt about the meaning of a word, check a dictionary or a thesaurus.

14-46 Ultimately, you should view your draft work as a basis for refining your arguments/and or supplementing them if you discover that a relevant issue has not been included or has not been fully explored. If time permits, lay draft work aside for a few days before reviewing what you have written. It is good practice to re-read the draft as if it was the first time you had seen the work. This will enable you to consider if from the perspective of the intended audience, the tutor. Are your propositions clearly stated? Has sufficient authority been given to underpin points and arguments made? Is your structure linear, i.e. one point made links with the next in a logical and coherent way? Are your references in the required form? Are they sufficient? If the answer to any of these questions is no, remedy any deficiencies you have identified.

14-47 Before submitting your essay you should:

> ➢ Re-read the essay to ensure that you have answered the question(s) set;
> ➢ Check spelling and punctuation;
> ➢ Check that all your references are accurate;
> ➢ Ensure that essay is in the required format, e.g. font, font size, indented paragraphs, spacing, etc.; and
> ➢ Consult paras 14–104—14–106 "Evaluation of your own Research".

Receiving feedback

14-48 One of the most valuable parts of the essay writing process is receiving summative (after the event) feedback from whoever marked it. You should fully take on board any comments to help you improve your work in the future.

Further reading

14-49
> ➢ J. Godfrey, *How to Use Your Reading in Your Essays* (Basingstoke: Palgrave McMillan 2009)
> ➢ J. Godwin, *Planning Your Essay* (Oxford: Oxford Brookes 2009)
> ➢ B. Greetham, *How to Write Better Essays*, 2nd edn (Basingstoke: Palgrave McMillan, 2008)
> ➢ H.S.I. Strong, *How to Write Law Essays & Exams*, 3rd edn (Oxford: OUP, 2010).

TECHNIQUES FOR TACKLING PROBLEM QUESTIONS

14-50 Problem questions (also known as case studies or scenarios) are popular forms of assessment at university because problem solving is one of the essential skills for a lawyer. The problem question format is used most frequently in tutorial exercises, coursework and exams. A problem question will provide a set of facts. Being presented with a set of facts and asked to give accurate advice on their legal implications is an everyday activity of the practising lawyer. As a student, you will be expected to identify and apply the relevant law to these facts. You will then usually be asked to come to some form of conclusion. This will depend on the question, but may involve advising one or more of the parties as to the legal remedies available to them.

Problem questions differ from essay questions in that they are far more specific. You are not **14–51** provided with a general topic area for discussion, instead there are particular questions to address in logical order. When you construct your answer to a problem question you should not include a long introduction. There is no need to start with a general discussion of the area of law. Rather, you should identify the area(s) of law under discussion and then begin to deal with the specific issues raised by the question, e.g. "This scenario concerns my client's position with regard to compliance with ss.19, 20 and 21 of The Money Laundering Regulations 2007".

Read the question carefully to ensure that you understand it. Problem questions are often quite **14–52** detailed. Make sure that you have not misread or overlooked any details. This is particularly easy to do under exam conditions. Never write out the question. This is a waste of time and if you are required to keep to a word limit it will eat into a given word count. Rather, underline key words to help focus your thoughts.

The answer to a problem question is rarely "yes" or "no". If you think the answer is **14–53** straightforward, re-read the question because you have probably missed something vital.

Problem questions tend to concentrate on one area of law, e.g. money laundering, but that does **14–54** not mean that they contain just one issue—they may contain several different issues that require to be addressed, one after the other.

Identify the legal issues raised by the facts. Do not invent "facts" or add "arms and legs" to the **14–55** narrative given in the problem question. If you do so, you will be embarking on a "frolic of your own", meaning that you are answering a completely different question from the one actually posed.

However, in problem questions, which are required to be necessarily brief, you may believe that **14–56** the complete factual picture has yet to emerge. This is a legitimate consideration. Therefore it is appropriate, if this is the case, to present your answer thus:

> "Without full information as to my client's status within the company (whether he is a relevant person per s.19 of The Money Laundering Regulations 2007) a definitive answer cannot be given at this stage. However, if he is a relevant person then the likely outcome will be X ... if he is not a relevant person then they likely outcome will be Y ..." (All propositions given having been backed up with primary and, where relevant, secondary authority.)

When you are sure you have detected the legal issues to be addressed you should then begin your answer, if an exam, or, if a coursework, your literature search.

Structuring your answer

It is essential to devise a logical structure. The actual structure will depend, however, on the **14–57** nature of the problem/area of law it pertains to. In the case of a delictual problem concerned with the law of negligence the approach might be:

> ➢ Is there a duty of care owed?
> ➢ Has that duty been breached?
> ➢ Did the breach cause the harm and loss complained of?

➤ Is the loss quantifiable? and
➤ Are there any defences, partial or complete, upon which the defender can seek to rely?

Summary of the approach to be taken when faced with a problem question

14–58
Examine the available facts

Identify the legal issue(s) raised by the facts

Identify the *material* facts

Be aware of the omission of any material facts. But do not speculate and "go off on a frolic of your own"

Carry out a literature search to find the current legal position

Apply the relevant law to the factual scenario

Advise client on available options/remedies

NB Always ensure that your answer is relevant to the question. Credit will only be given for the appropriate application of the relevant law to the factual scenario. Do not be tempted to include long descriptive passages.

➤ Do not write a general introduction about the particular area of law;
➤ Never just provide an answer to the question-you must justify your position and back up your arguments by reference to authority (see paras 14–07—14–12);
➤ You have to apply the law as you find it. If you personally disagree with it or find it unfair, that is irrelevant to answering the question. Subjective (personal) opinion must never feature.
➤ Make sure that you do what has been asked of you. If you are asked to advise X, make sure that you advise X. This does not mean ignoring arguments against X's position. You should take into account any counter-arguments against your adopted position;
➤ Do not spend ages agonising over the conclusion to the problem. There is indeed unlikely to be one correct answer. If you feel that there is no one answer to the problem, discuss the possible alternatives. At university the conclusion that you reach is not the most significant part of your answer. You will receive credit for the presentation of relevant and cogent arguments, backed up by authority. For the practitioner dealing with real life situations the conclusion is, of course, very important.

Further Reading

➢ E. Finch & S. Fafinski, *Legal Skills*, 4th edn (Oxford: OUP, 2013)   **14–59**
➢ C. Turner, J. Boylan-Kemp, *Unlocking Legal Learning*, 3rd edn (Abingdon, Routledge/Hodder 2013) Ch.7
➢ A.T.H. Smith, Glanville Williams, *Learning the Law*, 15th edn (London: Sweet & Maxwell, 2013) Ch.8

MULTIPLE CHOICE QUESTIONS

Multiple choice questions may feature in a class test or, more rarely, in an exam. On the face of **14–60** it, multiple choice questions may seem an attractive form of assessment from the student's point of view given that they present options, i.e. give you a one in three, one in four or one in five "chance" of providing the right answer. However, on the law of averages, if the answer to a question is not known a student is more likely to pick the wrong answer than the right one. If you do not know the answer to a question the following technique should be followed:

➢ Exclude any answer you know to be incorrect;
➢ Re-read the question;
➢ Then focus on the remaining options. Re-read them carefully. Do any of the remaining options now appear to be incorrect? If so, exclude them; and
➢ Consider the remaining answers. If left with two options you now have a 50/50 chance (if you have correctly excluded the other possible answers) of answering the question correctly.

For example, consider the following multiple choice question.

Which one of the following statements is true?

a) The institutional writers are appointed by the Lord President of the Court of Session.
b) Where there is a conflict between case law and institutional writings, the law as stated by the institutional writer applies.
c) A court may strike down a statute in conflict with an institutional writing.
d) Where there is a conflict between a statute and institutional writings, the law as stated in the statute applies.
e) New institutional writings are formulated by the Lord President of the Court of Session.

If unsure of the correct answer you should consider what you do know about the Institutional Writers/Writings. If you recall that the works of these writers are historic (being authored between the 17th and 19th century) you can discount option (a) given the phrase "are appointed". If you remember that Institutional writings are regarded as a "closed category of law", i.e. no further legal works, however worthy, can be added to Institutional writings, you can discount option (e). The remaining options require you to consider the hierarchy of the sources of Scots Law. If you know that the hierarchy, in descending order is: Legislation (statutory law); Case Law; Institutional Writings; Custom and Equity; you would be able to conclude that the correct answer is option (d).

ORAL PRESENTATIONS

14–61 Oral presentations are increasingly used as a form of assessment at university. You may be asked to give a presentation as an individual, as part of a group, or you may be required to moot, i.e. debate a legal issue with another student or group of students. Mooting may or may not involve role play, i.e. you may assume the role of the prosecutor or defence counsel and address a mock court (with your tutors acting as the judges) on a specific legal point. For example, you may be required to make a submission as to the competency or otherwise of judicial review in light of the information given in a previously circulated case study. In this example you may be allowed to rebut your opponent's arguments and you will most likely be asked questions by the bench (your tutors) about your submission. The advice given in the following paragraphs will, in general, apply when preparing to moot. However, a moot is a specialised form of presentation given it simulates professional practice, thus specific instructions on court room etiquette and procedure will given by the tutor in each instance. Given the specific nature of this form of assessment and to avoid unhelpful generalisation, advice on mooting per se is not given below.

Initial preparation

14–62 Make sure that you know:

> ➤ **Who** your audience will be. Will it just be the tutor(s) or will fellow students also be present?
> ➤ **What** your audience is expecting from you. Is it just a presentation or will the audience ask questions after the event?
> ➤ **How long** the presentation is to last. This is vital given that under/over length presentations will be penalised. Always check whether the time specified includes questions.
> ➤ **When** the presentation will take place. Diary the date and time well in advance.
> ➤ **Where** the presentation is to take place. Diary the room/lab/theatre, etc. and check there has been no last minute change on the actual day.

Construction of an oral presentation

14–63 Careful planning is the key to a successful presentation. Once you have fully considered the title given and identified its parameters, the next step is to identify the resources you will need to consult. Once the information sought has been collected and collated you should:

> ➤ Establish the main points you want to make;
> ➤ Ensure that you have relevant and sufficient primary and secondary sources to support these points (e.g. cases, statutory provisions, statistics or a quotation from a journal article, etc.); and
> ➤ Structure your main points and supporting material into a clear and logical order.

The structure of the presentation should conform to the essay model and have an introduction, discussion of the main points and a conclusion (see paras 14–36—14–42).

14–64 The beginning and end of the presentation require special attention. At the beginning you want to command your audience's attention. You will do this by introducing yourself, explaining the subject-matter and title of your presentation and giving a clear outline of what will be covered in your presentation. If necessary, for the purposes of clarification or the avoidance of doubt, it is appropriate to say what will not be covered and, in brief, say why.

At the conclusion of the presentation you want to ensure that your audience goes away with a **14–65** firm understanding of the main points and issues raised so provide a brief summary of these points and your associated findings.

Using notes

No matter how good your memory, you will find that you will need some form of notes to guide **14–66** you through the presentation. Notes help ensure that you do not omit anything from your talk. Some students write or type out everything they are going to say, others use small cards which contain only the main points and act as an aide memoire rather than a script. There is no right or wrong method; it is up to you to choose whichever approach makes you feel comfortable and confident.

If you are inexperienced at giving presentations you may feel happier writing out the full text. If **14–67** you elect to do this:

- ➢ Use large writing or typeface;
- ➢ Use double line spacing;
- ➢ Use only one side of a piece of paper; and
- ➢ Number the pages (just in case you drop them).

The main disadvantage of this method is that you will have difficulty maintaining eye contact with your audience. There is also a natural tendency to mumble if looking down at hand held notes and for your voice to become indistinct because your chin is resting on your voice box and vocal cords. If selecting this method, enquire in advance whether a lectern or some form of stand is available for use on the day of the presentation.

Delivery of the presentation

Timing

Make sure that you are familiar with the entire contents of your presentation. Practice speaking **14–68** it out loud at a measured pace—not too fast, not too slow—ideally in the room where you are to give the presentation. This will help you to judge the length of the talk and whether it can be delivered within the time allocated. If it is delivered with minutes still to spare you do not have enough material. Organise any visual aids that you are permitted to use. Only use visual aids that you feel happy operating unless a mandatory aid has been stipulated. If the latter scenario presents make sure that you know how to operate the visual aid concerned When you are nervous it may not be very clear, especially using unfamiliar equipment, how to, for example, start a PowerPoint presentation on full screen. A few moments familiarising yourself with any equipment beforehand will be time well spent.

If you use PowerPoint make sure that the slides are not too crowded. Short summaries or bullet **14–69** points should be used. Do not include large sections of prose. This only results in a loss of visual impact as key sections disappear in the middle of the detail. The font should be large enough to be read from the back of the room.

Visual aids commonly used in presentations: **14–70**

- ➢ PowerPoint slides;
- ➢ Black or white boards;
- ➢ Flip charts;
- ➢ Physical objects; and
- ➢ Handouts.

Handouts

14–71 If you are required to produce a handout or copies of PowerPoint slides do not include every word of your talk on the slides or the notes page. If you do, you run the risk of your audience paying more attention to the papers in front of them than to the presenter. A handout should summarise the main points of your talk. Try and make it as attractive as possible. Pay attention to design and layout, include slides numbers and ensure that proper spelling and grammar are maintained throughout.

On the day of the presentation

14–72 Do not read your presentation out word for word. It is important to maintain eye contact thus a connection with your audience. Try and look at your script, memorise the next few words and then look at members of the audience while you are speaking. They will quickly become disengaged if you merely read out material in a stilted voice so try to vary the tone of your voice and put some feeling into your presentation.

14–73 Be aware of your body language. Good posture shows the audience that you are relaxed and confident. Do not fold your arms or stand with your hands behind your back. Try to avoid waving your arms around—it is very distracting for the audience.

14–74 The pace at which you speak is very important. Remember that your audience does not know what you are going to say and will need time to listen to and digest your words. At the start of the presentation, make a conscious effort to slow down your speech pattern. Do not talk too quickly or you will lose coherence—and your audience.

14–75 Make sure that you speak loud enough so that the people at the back of the room can hear you.

14–76 Make sure that you keep to time by putting your watch (not a mobile phone) on the table or lectern or somewhere you can see it easily. You should try and work out beforehand which section you could cut from your presentation if you find yourself running out of time. It is also prudent to have some additional material which would fit in nicely towards the end of your presentation just in case you find you have time left to fill.

Questions

14–77 Waiting for questions can be daunting, however the more prepared you are, the easier it will be to answer them. You should consider in advance what questions you may be asked. The best way to do this is to put yourself in the shoes of your audience. What question(s) would you ask if you had just heard the material being delivered?

14–78 Is there any part of the presentation where you skimmed over a particular issue by stating rather than explaining it? If so, a tutor will likely ask you to expand on what was said. Was there a glaring omission in your presentation? If so, the ability to answer a question about same can serve to mitigate.

14–79 If asked a question which you do not understand, say so. Ask the questioner to repeat the question or to clarify exactly what they mean. By doing this you give yourself an extra few seconds to think of and structure an answer. If asked something that you do not know the answer to it is better to admit it rather than give a "waffly" and totally irrelevant answer.

Nerves

Everybody is nervous before making a presentation, even seasoned presenters. Whilst there is no **14–80** magic formula for banishing you can control your nerves by:

- ➢ Being well prepared, having gone over the materials and practiced your presentation many times;
- ➢ Remembering that you may be only too aware of your nerves, but your audience will probably not notice that you are nervous;
- ➢ Being confident that you will know more about the topic than your audience;
- ➢ Continuing undeterred if you drop your notes or lose your place, pause, get yourself organised and take a deep breath. You may feel that the whole process took an hour, but the audience will not perceive the delay as anything but minimal;
- ➢ Pausing momentarily if you become short of breath during the presentation. Take a deep breath. Then continue at a more moderate pace.

Further Reading

- ➢ A. Bradbury, *Successful Presentation Skills*, 4th edn (London: The Sunday Times, **14–81** 2010)
- ➢ J. Snape, G. Watt, *How to Moot: A Student Guide to Mooting*, 2nd edn (Oxford: OUP 2010)
- ➢ J. Van Emden, L. Becker, *Presentation Skills for Students*, 2nd edn (London: Palgrave MacMillan, 2010)

UNDERGRADUATE RESEARCH PROJECTS

Most undergraduate students are required to submit a research project, generally referred to as **14–82** a dissertation, in their honours year. However, it is becoming increasing common for institutions to offer research project modules in earlier stages of study. Undergraduate research projects differ from essays and other coursework in that the title of the project will be self-selected and agreed with a tutor who will then act as your personal supervisor for the duration of the project.

Research project modules are not generally taught modules, i.e. class meetings with the tutor in **14–83** charge of a project module will focus on and outline what you are required to do or achieve for the currency of the module. S/he will not "teach" you what to do, as such. Rather, you will likely be offered refresher skills classes covering core academic skills, such as referencing, research methods and techniques and long document formatting.

Research projects are therefore the product of personal research and evaluation of the materials **14–84** consulted with guidance only being given by your supervisor. S/he will not routinely direct you to recommended reading or suitable materials. Nor will s/he demand or schedule regular meetings. It is up to you to seek guidance and meetings.

Research projects also tend to demand a longer of piece of work. They will typically be between **14–85** 3,000 and 10,000 words (excluding footnotes and bibliography), whereas a typical undergraduate essay will require a submission of 1,000 and 2,000 words (excluding footnotes and bibliography).

14–86 While the assessed component parts of a particular research project will vary, the following may feature at an early stage in the process:

Abstract

14–87 An abstract is: (i) a concise overview of your research, highlighting any important findings at the time of writing. You may be required to submit a written abstract when you present your initial findings in oral form as a discrete part of the assessment process, or you may be required to provide an abstract when you submit your completed project. Abstracts are also (ii) submitted to conference organisers or journal editors by academics for the purpose of potential publication of their finished paper or article.

Poster

14–88 A poster is a more detailed form of abstract. It is generally shorter than a coursework or academic paper (usually about six to eight sheets of A4). It is presented as a wall chart, literally a poster. Posters are generally used to present preliminary results and are used as a form of assessment at undergraduate level. Post-graduate students and academic lawyers will display posters at conferences where there will be set sessions in the programme in which delegates can inspect the posters. During this period the researcher has to be present to answer any questions about their research. This can be a very useful exercise in that it enables the researcher to receive advice, as well as to advertise their work and also to network with other academics working in a particular area.

Conference or seminar paper

14–89 Delivering a paper at a conference is equivalent to giving a short lecture on your research. Undergraduate students are unlikely to do this, but, as stated in paras 14–61—14–67, students undertaking a research project module may be required, as part of the assessment process, to deliver an oral presentation (often in a seminar setting) as their research progresses and answer questions from tutors and fellow students about their initial findings.

Presenting your research findings in writing

14–90 Presentation of research in written form is the principal method of assessing research project outcomes at both undergraduate and postgraduate level. The exact structure of the paper you are to submit will be subject to the requirements of your institution but the following features represent the conventional form of presenting research:

Title page

14–91 This page should include the title of your work, your name, institution, date and, if the work is being submitted for a particular qualification, you should include the relevant details. The title should be concise and provide an accurate impression of the nature of your work.

Acknowledgements

14–92 It is usual to include any acknowledgements and thanks after the title page. Undergraduate and postgraduate students generally thank their supervisor and any other member of staff who has assisted them in some way throughout the research and writing-up process.

Abstract

An abstract is usually required. It should be regarded as independent of the research and should **14–93** not be referred to in the text. The purpose of the abstract is to provide a brief and concise overview of the research and to highlight any important findings.

Contents page

This should include a list of chapter headings and page numbers along with details of any **14–94** appendices.

Chapter 1—Introduction

This should include: **14–95**

> ➢ Aims;
> ➢ Objectives;
> ➢ Research questions or hypotheses which have been investigated;
> ➢ Proposed methodology (if relevant);
> ➢ Indication of why the research topic was chosen; and
> ➢ The scope of the work.

Chapter 2—Literature review

This should contain a review of previous academic work on the topic. It should not be a **14–96** descriptive account of every work published on the topic. You should display skills of critical analysis by commenting on previous works, selecting only relevant material and organising its presentation in an appropriate way.

Chapter 3—Methodology

This should include a discussion of the methodology(ies) adopted and a justification of your **14–97** choice. Another important element of this chapter is to discuss any limitations in the methods employed. The research instruments which were used should be included in an appendix, e.g. the questionnaire or interview schedule or descriptions of various statistical tests.

Chapter 4—Presentation of results or findings

Presentation of results should be accurate and clear. Detailed comment and interpretation **14–98** should be left until the following chapter.

Chapter 5—Discussion

This is the key section of the work. It should start by detailing your research questions or **14–99** hypotheses, as outlined in your first chapter. You should then make use of the results or findings from your fourth chapter to back up the strands of your argument. You should then tie in these lines of argument with your research questions/hypotheses. You should also detail how your research relates to previous work undertaken in the area discussed in your second chapter. Any limitations in the research design should be included along with suggestions of alternative approaches.

Chapter 6—Summary and conclusions

14–100 The purpose of this chapter is to bring all your arguments together and draw detailed conclusions. You should only include conclusions which can justifiably be drawn from your results/findings. You should not introduce new material in this concluding chapter. You should indicate that you are aware of any limitations of the work and steps that you have taken to minimise these. It is a good idea to mention whether your work has implications for further research in the area.

Bibliography

14–101 This should include all the sources which you have consulted during your research.

Appendices

14–102 Appendices may include copies of any research instruments which were used, e.g. the questionnaire or interview schedule or descriptions of various statistical tests.

Further reading

14–103
> J. Bell, *Doing Your Research Project*, 5th edn (Buckingham: Open University Press, 2010)
> L. Blaxter, C. Hughes and M. Tight, *How to Research*, 4th edn (Milton Keynes: Open University Press, 2010)
> M.B. Davies, *Doing a Successful Research Project*, 2nd edn (Basingstoke: Palgrave McMillan, 2014)
> M. Salter, J. Mason, *Writing Law Dissertations: An Introduction to the Conduct of Legal Research* (Harlow: Pearson Longman, 2007)

EVALUATION OF YOUR OWN RESEARCH

14–104 When you write up your research (be it an essay or research project) be prepared to work through several drafts. One draft will not be sufficient for many reasons: your ideas will evolve; you may need to bring the work more up to date; or you may need to either lengthen or shorten it. In order to facilitate revisions to your work, you should insert a header or footer which includes the number of draft and the date. In the unlikely event that you are writing up your research by hand you should leave extra room for alterations and only write on one side of a page.

14–105 Before submitting of a piece of work you should put it to one side and forget about it for a period of time. You should then read it again with fresh eyes. This should enable you to pick up any errors which you might have missed previously because you were too close to the work. This requires you to have produced your draft well in advance of any submission deadline. See paras 13–11—13–13 per time management skills and planning.

14–106 When reviewing your work for the final time prior to submission consider the following:

> Have you answered the question/addressed your research questions?
> Does it have a logical structure?
> Is your meaning clear?
> Are your arguments backed up with authority?

> ➤ Are the most important points sufficiently emphasised?
> ➤ Are there any faults or gaps in your logic/reasoning?
> ➤ Have you taken into account any conflicting arguments?
> ➤ Are the conclusions justified?
> ➤ Does it read well?
> ➤ Are the abbreviations used appropriate and used consistently?
> ➤ Is your spelling accurate? Most word processing software will include a spell-check facility. You should, however, ensure that you adopt the British spelling options and do not slip into American-English spelling. A dictionary and a thesaurus can also be useful.
> ➤ Grammar—is your meaning clear or clouded by clumsy grammatical constructions? Short simple sentences are preferable. It is particularly important to check your use of tenses. It is very easy to slip from one tense to another, especially when you are writing over a long period of time. Most software now has a grammar check facility. However, it is generally not as useful as the spell-check facility.
> ➤ Are your references accurately presented?

REVISION STRATEGY FOR EXAMS

Make sure that you are aware of what is expected of you in the exam. Firstly, find out how **14–107** many questions the paper will contain. Then confirm for each module how many questions you are required to answer, e.g. a choice of three questions from a possible six. Also ascertain whether any particular question in the paper is mandatory and must be answered. Also double-check the duration of the exam and consider, e.g. if three questions are to be answered in a two-hour paper how much time ought to be devoted to each one. It is a common mistake for students to forget that time management in an exam is just as important as time management throughout the semester. If you spend too long on one particular question you run the risk of running out of time and authoring answers to only two out of the three required, or, worse still only answering one question. Exam technique is discussed further below.

If you are allowed to use unannotated statutory materials in the exam it can, on the face of **14–108** things, be reassuring to have a volume of statutes sitting on your desk. However, if you are not familiar with the material you can waste much time simply trying to find the relevant provisions, never mind interpret them. Accordingly, if you know the use of such materials is permitted familiarise yourself with the relevant legislation and, again if permitted, highlight certain sections with a marker pen and/or use different tabs (colour coded labels) for each provision to ensure you can locate each one with the minimum of effort. On no account slavishly copy out statutory provisions. All this shows the examiner is that you are able to copy text from one document to another. Rather, use short excerpts then display your understanding of and analysis of the materials cited.

Early preparation

> ➤ Ensure that you know the extent of the syllabus for the module and which topics are **14–109** examinable. If you have any doubts about what is expected of you, ask your tutor;
> ➤ Obtain copies of past exam papers. The best way to make use of past papers is to work through them attempting to answer the questions. It can be beneficial to do this with another student or in a small study group so you can share your knowledge and understanding of the topics. Whilst past papers are useful for giving guidance do not be tempted to use them to "question spot". This is a very dangerous strategy. If you

concentrate only on a few topics or areas which appear to be examined frequently and they do not appear in the exam, you will likely fail the paper or only achieve a bare pass. Nor can you presume that the exam set for you will be in the same format as in previous years. The type and frequency of question types (essay/short notes/problem, etc.) will change as will the content (issues relevant in the past may no longer exist or a case may have been overruled or a piece of legislation repealed, etc.). Seek guidance from the module tutor as to the types of questions that will feature in the exam and practice the technique for tackling each type.

Make sure that you have all the information you need

14–110 Far in advance of the date of the exam you should ensure that you have a full set of lecture notes and handouts for each subject. Organising these materials in advance (this is ideally done after each class meeting) gives you time to catch up with notes or locate materials for any classes that you have missed. Ideally you should have been undertaking the recommended reading before and after lectures and preparing for tutorials throughout the semester. If you have done this you should have a sufficiency of notes from texts and case notes, etc. to use as a basis for revision purposes and not need to look up textbooks at this stage except to clarify any points that remain unclear. If you have not undertaken the reading at the recommended time or made useful and usable notes along the way what you term as "revision" will actually be learning about a topic rather than revising it. If this is so, you have made life much harder and stressful for yourself that it need have been at this point in the academic year.

14–111 Reflect and act on feedback/feedforward received from the tutor from any tutorial exercise or previous assessment.

The process of revising

14–112 Do not sit and look at a thick file of notes. If you do that you will find yourself putting off the evil hour when you have to start revising. All sorts of jobs around the house will suddenly appear far more appealing than sitting and opening this awful file. The way around this is to start by consulting the syllabus for the module. You will find that it can be broken down into several topics or parts. Pick the topic you are most interested in and start with that. Try to get a grasp of the major topics. Then move on to the less important points. Once you have identified, for example, six topics, gather together all your material on the topics. This will include lecture notes, tutorial preparation, notes made from independent reading, case notes, notes from statutes, notes from journal articles, etc. Read all the material you have gathered for one topic then re-read it to ensure you have identified the key points. Then make revision notes for the topic. These should contain the essential points from all your materials. These notes should not be very long (four to five sides of A4) and should consist of lists with various headings, categories and sub-categories. Base your future revision on this précis version of the topic.

14–113 Some students like to make notes from notes until they end up with a list of bullet points of vital issues. Others prefer just to read their original notes over and over again whilst a few prefer to dictate revision notes and to listen to them over and over again.

14–114 Exams aim to test knowledge and the application of that knowledge in a variety of contexts. When revising ask yourself:

> ➤ What are the key points?
> ➤ What source or sources provide the best authority/evidence/argument for each proposition I wish to make?

> ➤ Is there a counter argument? If so, what source or sources provide the best authority/evidence/argument for each proposition I wish to make?

➤ Test yourself by drafting brief outline answers to questions from old exam papers;

➤ Build periods of free time into any revision schedule. You need to maintain a balance between work and normal life;

➤ Do not sit up all night the night before an exam. You will end up being exhausted and jaded the following day and likely perform poorly, no matter how much you know. It is far better to organise your revision timetable so that the evening before an exam you can relax. You will then perform much better the next day. If you have revised the materials and understand the topics, your knowledge and understanding will not disappear overnight;

➤ Do not worry because you do not "know everything". No one ever does. Constantly remind yourself of what you do know rather than worrying about what you do not know; and

➤ Finally, make sure that you know the correct date, time and location of the exam.

EXAM TECHNIQUES

➤ Arrive in good time for the exam. Ensure your phone, etc. is switched off before you **14–115** enter the room. *Remember to conform to any university requirements, such as bringing your matriculation card for identification purposes;

➤ Read any instructions carefully;

➤ Make sure that you know how many questions you are required to answer and if any questions are compulsory;

➤ Read through the whole paper to get an idea of the content of the questions. Then re-read the paper and decide what each question is actually asking. Underline "key words" which indicate the kind of answer you should give. Only then select the questions that you intend to answer;

➤ Before writing anything, decide on the order you will answer the questions. Some students prefer to answer the question that seems "easiest" first and work through to the "hardest". Others prefer to tackle the hardest question first. It really is a matter of personal preference. The main thing is that you answer the required number of questions even if your last answer is short and far from complete. The few marks you gain may be vital for your final result;

➤ Never leave a question blank. Make sure that you answer all parts of a question;

➤ Do not be phased by students who start to write at speed the second the invigilator announces that the exam is underway. You are better advised to sit and take stock, rather than ploughing straight in and realising later that you have misread or misinterpreted the question;

➤ Make brief notes in bullet point form for each question selected before you start writing your first answer. This technique helps you focus on your subsequent answers at the start of the exam and if time is running short by the time you get to these you have an aide memoire in front of you;

➤ Allocate your time properly. If each question bears an equal number of marks, spend an equal amount of time on each question. If the marks are different for different questions spend an appropriate proportion of your time on each question. If you use up your time-limit on a question you will already have gained most of the marks that you are going to get. Another five or 10 minutes writing is unlikely to get you many more marks. The same time spent concentrating on the key issues in a new question will earn you more marks. Remember that the first few marks in each question are the easiest ones to get;

➢ Do not write out the question—this just wastes valuable time;

➢ Answer the question asked, not the one which you would like to have answered. No credit will be given for irrelevant material, no matter how accurate it may be. For each question, isolate out the main points. Do not attempt to write down everything you know about the topic; expect to have to go into depth on only part of what you know;

➢ Remember to back up your arguments with authority. You will not be required to remember full reference details, e.g. the full citation of a case. Ideally, you should give the names of the parties, e.g. *Gold v Silver*, but in exam conditions it is easy to forget the precise name of a case. As a minimum you should try to write down sufficient details to show the examiner that you have identified the correct case. If you cannot remember the names of either of the parties, you should give some brief detail about the case that identifies it, e.g. "In the case about the snail in the bottle . . .". In a hand-written exam you should underline the names of the parties, e.g. *Donoghue v Stevenson*;

➢ When referring to a case do not include a descriptive account of the facts of the case. The part of the case that you should use is the ratio decidendi. Writing down lots of facts will not gain you any extra marks—it will merely waste precious exam time and detract from the cogency of your answer;

➢ If a student or several students leave the exam early do not read anything into this;

➢ If you miscalculate the time badly, finish the question in note-form. This is better than nothing and may pick up a few valuable marks; and

➢ Re-read your answers to check for errors and inaccuracies.

What not to do in an exam

14–116
➢ Get the date, time and room wrong;
➢ Fail to answer the question asked;
➢ Fail to use authority to back up your arguments;
➢ Include lots of description (e.g. narration of facts of cases) instead of explanation and critical analysis;
➢ Fail to manage your time appropriately;
➢ Fail to write enough, e.g. a question worth 25 marks is not going to be answered sufficiently in six or seven lines;
➢ Make jokes and/or frivolous comments. This is not appropriate;
➢ Fail to express yourself clearly;
➢ Write illegibly. If the marker can't read what you have written they can't mark it; and
➢ Use abbreviated text language, e.g. gr8. This is not appropriate for academic work.

Further Reading

14–117
➢ S. Cottrell, *The Exam Skills Handbook*, 2nd edn (Basingstoke: Palgrave McMillan, 2012)
➢ H. McVea and P. Cumper, *Exam Skills for Law Students*, 2nd edn (Oxford: OUP, 2006)

Appendix
Index of Websites

The website and webpage addresses below as referred to in *Legal Research Skills for Scots Lawyers* are correct at the time of publication. Whilst it is inevitable that such addresses will change, be modified, or otherwise become unavailable with the passage of time, many websites making such changes will provide a "redirect" link to take the viewer to the current landing page for a resource.

If a website or webpage is referred to more than once in this text, only the paragraph in which it was first mentioned in is listed.

A

ABYZ News Links: *http://www.abyznewslinks.com/*
Academic Keyword List: *http://www.uclouvain.be/en-372126.html*
Access to Law—International Law Materials: *http://www.accesstolaw.com/other-jurisdictions/world-law/*
Acts of the (old) Scottish Parliament: *http://www.legislation.gov.uk/aosp*
Acts of the Scottish (Holyrood) Parliament 1999: *http://www.legislation.gov.uk/asp*
Advocates' Library: *http://www.advocates.org.uk/library/index.html*; h
   ttp://voyager.advocates. org.uk/; *http://voyager.advocates.org.uk/*
Amazon: *http://www.amazon.co.uk/*
American Society for International Law: *http://www.eisil.org/*
Amnesty International UK: *http://www.amnesty.org.uk/*
Archive of The Bulletin of the EU: *http://ec.europa.eu/archives/bulletin/en/welcome.htm*
Avizandum: *http://www.avizandum.co.uk/*

B

BAILII: *http://www.bailii.org/*; *http://www.bailii.org/form/search_multidatabase.html*
BBC News: *http://news.bbc.co.uk/*; *http://www.bbc.co.uk/news/politics/*; *http://news.bbc.co.uk/*
BBC News (World): *http://www.bbc.co.uk/news/world/*
BBC World Service Europe Today: *http://www.bbc.co.uk/worldservice/programmes/europe today/index.shtml*
Bills Before Parliament: (Westminster) *http://services.parliament.uk/bills/*
British Humanities Index: *http://www.csa.com/factsheets/bhi-set-c.php*
British Library: *http://www.bl.uk/bibliographic/natbibweekly.html*
British Official Publications Collaborative Reader Information Service (BOPCRIS): *http://www.southampton.ac.uk/library/ldu/projects.html#18C*
Bulletin of International Legal Developments: *http://www.biicl.org/publications/bild/*
Bulletin of the EU (archive): *http://ec.europa.eu/archives/bulletin/en/welcome.htm*
Business Bulletin (Holyrood):
   http://www.scottish.parliament.uk/parliamentarybusiness/BusinessBulletin.aspx;
   http://www.scottish.parliament.uk/parliamentarybusiness/eBulletin.aspx

C

Cardiff Index to Legal Abbreviations *http://www.legalabbrevs.cardiff.ac.uk*
Casecheck: *http://www.casecheck.co.uk/CaseLaw.aspx?BlogID = 700*
Cats Protection: *http://www.cats.org.uk/what-we-do/about-us-index/annual-review/*
CELEX: *http://eur-lex.europa.eu/Result.do?code = 32007R0967&Submit = Search&RechType = RECH;*
  http://eur-lex.europa.eu/RECH_celex.do?ihmlang = en
Chronological Tables of Local Acts and of Private and Personal Acts
  http://www.legislation.gov.uk/changes/chron-tables/local/intro;
   http://www.legislation.gov.uk/changes/chron-tables/chron-table-abbreviations.pdf
Civil Service Year Book: *http://www.tsoshop.co.uk/parliament/bookstore.asp?DI = 328151*
Committee of the Regions (EU): *http://cor.europa.eu/en/about/Pages/index.aspx*
COPAC: *http://www.copac.ac.uk/*
Council of the EU and European Council: *http://www.consilium.europa.eu/homepage?lang = en*
Council of Europe: *http://www.coe.int/aboutCoe/index.asp?page = nepasconfondre&l = en*
Council of Europe Commissioner for Human Rights: *www.coe.int/web/commissioner*
Council of Europe Convention on Cybercrime: *http://conventions.coe.int/Treaty/Commun/print/*
  ChercheSig.asp?NT = 185&CL = ENG
Council of Europe Convention on Human Rights:
  http://conventions.coe.int/Treaty/Commun/ListeTraites.asp?CM = 8&CL = ENG;
  http://www.hri.org/docs/ECHR50.html
Council of Europe Treaty Office: *http://conventions.coe.int/*
Council of Europe Yearbook: *http://books.google.com/*
Court of Justice of the European Union: *http://europa.eu/about-eu/institutions-bodies/court-*
  justice/index_en.htm
Court of the Lord Lyon: *http://www.lyon-court.com/lordlyon/CCC_FirstPage.jsp*
Crown Office and Procurator Fiscal Service: *http://www.copfs.gov.uk/*
CURIA: *http://curia.europa.eu/; http://curia.europa.eu/jcms/jcms/Jo2_6999/; http://curia.europa.eu/*

D

Daily List: *http://www.tso.co.uk/daily_list/issues.htm*
Delia Venables' Portal to Legal Resources in the UK and Ireland: *http://www.venables.co.uk/*
  scotland.htm
Diana Botluk Strategies for Online Legal Research: *http://www.llrx.com/features/strategy.htm*
Digest (formerly the English & Empire Digest) *http://www.law.ox.ac.uk/lrsp/print/*
  case_law_indexes5.php
Directory of EU Legislation and Agreements: *http://eur-lex.europa.eu/en/legis/index.htm*
Directory of EU Legislation in Force: *http://eur-lex.europa.eu/en/legis/latest/index.htm*
Draft Statutory Instruments (UK): *http://www.legislation.gov.uk/draft/2014*
Draft Statutory Instruments (Scotland): *http://www.legislation.gov.uk/sdsi*

E

Eagle-I: *http://ials.sas.ac.uk/eaglei/project/eiproject.htm*
Ebookee: *http://ebookee.org/law.html*
E-books Directory: *http://www.e-booksdirectory.com/listing.php?category = 345*
E-bookspdf.org: *http://www.e-bookspdf.org/*
Economic and Social Research Council: *http://ethicsguidebook.ac.uk/*
Electronic Information System for International Law: *http://www.eisil.org/*
Electronic Resource Guide: *http://www.asil.org/resources/electronic-resource-guide-erg*
Employment Appeal Tribunal: *http://www.justice.gov.uk/tribunals/employment-appeals/judgments*

European Voice: *http://www.europeanvoice.com/*
Eurostat Statistical Office: *http://epp.eurostat.ec.europa.eu/portal/page/portal/eurostat/home/*

F

Faculty of Advocates: *http://www.advocates.org.uk/*
Findlaw.com: *http://www.findlaw.com/*
First-tier Tribunal (Information Rights): *http://www.justice.gov.uk/tribunals/general-regulatory-chamber/hearings-and-decisions*; *http://www.justice.gov.uk/about/hmcts/tribunals*
Flare Index to Treaties: *http://193.62.18.232/dbtw-wpd/textbase/treatysearch.htm*
Foreign and Commonwealth Office: *https://www.gov.uk/government/announcements?departments %5B%5D=foreign-commonwealth-office*
Foreign Law Guide (FLAG): *http://ials.sas.ac.uk/library/flag/flag.htm*

G

General Report—Activities of the EU *http://europa.eu/publications/reports-booklets/general-report/index_en.htm*
Global Legal Information Network (GLIN): *http://www.loc.gov/law/news/glin/*
GlobaLex: *http://www.nyulawglobal.org/globalex/*
Google Books: *http://books.google.com/*
GoogleGuide: *http://www.googleguide.com/google_works.html/*
Google Researcher: *http://www.mygooglest.com/*
GOV.UK: *https://www.gov.uk/*;   *https://www.gov.uk/searchq=british+official+publications +not+published https://www.gov.uk/government/organisations*
Guidance on Private Bills (Holyrood): *http://www.scottish.parliament.uk/parliamentarybusiness/ Bills/15709.aspx*

H

Hammicks Legal Information Bookshop: *http://www.hammickslegal.com/live/*
Hansard: *http://www.parliament.uk/business/publications/hansard/*
Heinonline: *http://home.heinonline.org/*
Her Majesty's Court Service: *http://www.justice.gov.uk/courts/glossary-of-terms/glossary-of-terms-legal*; *http://www.justice.gov.uk/courts/glossary-of-terms*
Her Majesty's Stationery Office (HMSO): *http://www.nationalarchives.gov.uk/*
Higher Education Academy: *http://www.heacademy.ac.uk/resources/detail/pdp/pdp*
Historic Hansard: *http://hansard.millbanksystems.com/*
House of Commons European Scrutiny Committee: *http://www.parliament.uk/business/committees/ committees-a-z/commons-select/european-scrutiny-committee/role/*
House of Commons Library: *http://www.parliament.uk/about/how/publications/research/*
House of Commons Papers: *http://www.parliament.uk/business/publications/commons/*
House of Commons Weekly Information Bulletin: *http://www.publications.parliament.uk/pa/cm/ cmwib.htm*
House of Lords EU Select Committee: *http://www.parliament.uk/business/committees/committees-a-z/lords-select/eu-select-committee-/*
HUDOC: *http://hudoc.echr.coe.int/sites/eng/Pages/search.aspx#*
Huffington Post: *http://www.huffingtonpost.co.uk/*
Human Rights Act 1998: *http://www.legislation.gov.uk/ukpga/1998/42/contents*

I

Incorporated Council of Law Reporting for England and Wales (ICLR): *http://www.iclr.co.uk/*
Index to Foreign Legal Periodicals: *http://heinonline.org/HeinDocs/IFLP.pdf*
Index to Legal Periodicals and Books: *http://www.ebscohost.com/corporate-research/index-to-legal-periodicals-books*
Index to Theses *http://www.theses.com/*
Information Commissioner's Office (England and Wales): *http://search.ico.org.uk/ico/search/decisionnotice*; *http://www.ico.org.uk/enforcement/fines*
Inforrm Blog (International Forum for Responsible Media): *http://inforrm.wordpress.com/*
Inner Temple Library: *http://www.innertemplelibrary.org.uk/*
Institute of Advanced Legal Studies: *http://ials.sas.ac.uk/library/guides/docs/guide7_abbreviations.pdf*; *http://ials.sas.ac.uk/eaglei/project/eiproject.htm*
International Court of Justice *http://www.icj-cij.org/homepage/index.php*; *http://www.icj-cij.org/pcij/serie_other/cpji-pcij.pdf*; *http://www.icj-cij.org/presscom/index.php?p1=6&p2=1*
International Court Reports *http://www.icj-cij.org/homepage/index.php*
International Criminal Court *http://www.icc-cpi.int/en_menus/icc/Pages/default.aspx*; *http://www.icc-cpi.int/home.html&l=en*
International Criminal Court Official Journal *http://www.icc-cpi.int/EN_Menus/icc/Pages/default.aspx*
International Labour Organisation (Normlex): *http://www.ilo.org/dyn/normlex/en/f?p=NORMLEXPUB:1:0::NO:::*
International Law Commission: *http://www.un.org/law/ilc/*
International Legal Materials: *http://www.asil.org/resources/international-legal-materials*
International Legal Research Online Tutorial: *http://law.duke.edu/ilrt/*
Internet Corporation for Assigned Names and Numbers (ICANN): *http://www.icann.org/*
Internet for Law: *http://www.vtstutorials.co.uk/ws//tracking/launchcontent.aspx?cv=44F5E07D-4809-4851-93F2-A436C626AE7E&e=A0000&c=8EF8563D-BC82-41D3-8521-045C1F4C830C&SID=bc1afaf0-b200-4c45-afaf-91a36335e691*
IPKat: *http://ipkitten.blogspot.co.uk/*
ISI Web of Knowledge: *http://ip-science.thomsonreuters.com/m/pdfs/wos_workbook_en.pdf*

J

Jean Monnet Center: *http://centers.law.nyu.edu/jeanmonnet/*
Joint Information Systems Committee (JISC): *http://www.jisc.ac.uk/*
Journal of Information Law & Technology (JILT) (renamed European Journal of Law and Technology as of 2010): *http://www2.warwick.ac.uk/fac/soc/law/elj/jilt/*
Journal of the Law Society of Scotland: *http://www.journalonline.co.uk/*
Judicial Committee of the Privy Council: *http://jcpc.uk/decided-cases/index.html*
Judiciary of Scotland: *http://scotland-judiciary.org.uk/29/0/Glossary*
JustCite: *http://www.justcite.com/*
Justis: *http://www.justis.com/*; *http://www.justis.com/titles/daily_cases.html* (

K

Keesing's Record of World Events: *http://www.keesings.com/*

L

Liberty Guide to Human Rights: *http://www.yourrights.org.uk/yourrights/the-human-rights-act/how-does-the-human-rights-act-1998-work-.html*
Labour Research Department *http://www.lrd.org.uk/*

Lands Tribunal for Scotland: *http://www.lands-tribunal-scotland.org.uk/records.html*
Lands Valuation Appeal Court: *http://www.casecheck.co.uk/CaseLaw.aspx?BlogID=700*
Lauterpacht Centre for International Law: *http://www.lcil.cam.ac.uk/publications/international-law-reports*
Law Library of Congress: *http://www.loc.gov/law/find/databases.php*
Latin Abbreviations: *http://latin-phrases.co.uk/abbreviations/*
Law Commission for England and Wales: *http://www.lawcom.gov.uk/*
Lawlinks: *http://www.kent.ac.uk/library/subjects/lawlinks/*
Law Society Gazette: *http://www.lawgazette.co.uk/47152.article*
Law Society of Scotland: *http://www.lawscot.org.uk/*
    http://www.lawscot.org.uk/wcm/lssservices/find_a_solicitor/Core/directory.aspx;
    http://www.lawscot.org.uk/education-and-careers/the-traineeship/starting-a-traineeship-soon/entrance-certificate-and-training-contract-faqs;
    http://www.lawscot.org.uk/media/526068/fitandproperguidanceoct2013.pdf
Lawtel: *http://www.lawtel.com/Login?ReturnUrl=%2fLogin.aspx*
Legal 500 *http://www.legal500.com/assets/pages/ebooks/index.html*
Legal Information Institute (LII): *http://www.law.cornell.edu/*
Legal Resources in the UK and Ireland, Delia Venables: *http://www.venables.co.uk/*
Legislation.gov.uk *http://www.legislation.gov.uk/ukpga;*
    http://www.legislation.gov.uk/ukla; http://www.legislation.gov.uk/aosp
LexisNexis: *https://www.lexisnexis.co.uk/en-uk/home.page*
Liberty Guide to Human Rights: *http://yourrights.org.uk/yourrights/the-human-rights-act/how-does-the-human-rights-act-1998-work-.html;*
    http://www.liberty-human-rights.org.uk/index.shtml
London Gazette: *http://www.london-gazette.co.uk/issues/60448/supplements/2/page.pdf.*

M

Max Planck Institute for Comparative Public Law and International Law: *http://www.mpil.de/en/pub/research/details/publications/institute/pil.cfm*
Ministry of Justice (Westminster): *http://www.justice.gov.uk/downloads/human-rights/human-rights-handbook-for-public-authorities.pdf*
Mitchell Library (Glasgow): *http://www.glasgowlife.org.uk/libraries/the-mitchell-library/Pages/home.aspx*
Money Bills: *http://www.publications.parliament.uk/pa/ld201011/ldselect/ldconst/97/9703.htm*

N

N-Lex: *http://eur-lex.europa.eu/n-lex/index_en.htm*
National Archives: *http://www.nationalarchives.gov.uk/*
    http://tna.europarchive.org/20100402134329/
    http://www.opsi.gov.uk/official-publications/command-papers/index.htm
National Archives Official Documents: *http://www.official-documents.gov.uk/*
National Library of Scotland: *http://www.nls.uk/catalogues/catalogues-plus-databases*
    http://www.nls.uk/catalogues/scottish-bibliographies-online/locations;
    http://main-cat.nls.uk/vwebv/searchBasic?sk=nls_en; http://www.nls.uk/
National Records for Scotland: *http://www.nrscotland.gov.uk/*
NHS Information Services Division: *http://www.isdscotland.org*
NewsNow: *http://www.newsnow.co.uk/h/*
New World Encyclopedia: *http://www.newworldencyclopedia.org/entry/Abstraction*
NoodleTools: *http://www.noodletools.com/tools/index.php*
    http://www.noodletools.com/tools/noodletools_users_guide.pdf

Scots Law Online: *http://www.scottishlaw.org.uk/lawfirms/index.html*

Scottish Committee Administrative Justice & Tribunals Council:
http://ajtc.justice.gov.uk/scottish/publications-scottish.htm

Scottish Council of Law Reporting: *http://www.scottishlawreports.org.uk/resources/open-access.html*

Scottish Courts: *http://www.scotcourts.gov.uk*; *http://www.scotcourts.gov.uk/search-judgments/about-judgments*

Scottish Criminal Cases Review Commission: *http://www.sccrc.org.uk/home.aspx*
http://www.sccrc.org.uk/ViewFile.aspx?id=585

Scottish Environment Protection Agency: *http://sepa.org.uk/about_us/publications/annual_reports.aspx*

Scottish Government Publications: *http://www.scotland.gov.uk/Publications/Recent*

Scottish Government Titles Book Source: *http://www.scotland.gov.uk/About/Information/PublicationCharges*

Scottish Government Statistics: *http://www.scotland.gov.uk/Topics/Statistics/*

Scottish Human Rights Commission: *http://scottishhumanrights.com/*

Scottish Information Commissioner: *http://www.itspublicknowledge.info/ApplicationsandDecisions/Decisions/decisions.php*

Scottish Land Court: *http://www.scottish-land-court.org.uk/digest.html*;
http://www.scottish-land-court.org.uk/recent.htm;
http://www.scottish-land-court.org.uk/;
http://www.scottish-land-court.org.uk/digest.html

Scottish Law Agents Society: *http://www.scottishlawagents.org/*

Scottish Law Commission: *http://www.scotlawcom.gov.uk/*;
http://www.scotlawcom.gov.uk/publications/

Scottish Law Online: *http://www.scottishlaw.org.uk*
http://www.scottishlaw.org.uk/lawfirms/index.html

Scottish Legal Aid Board: *http://www.slab.org.uk/*

Scottish Legal Complaints Commission: *http://www.scottishlegalcomplaints.org.uk/resources/annual-report-accounts.aspx*

Scottish Legal News: *http://www.scottishlegal.com/*

Scottish Legal Services Ombudsman: *http://www.slso.org.uk/*

Scottish Neighbourhood Statistics: *http://www.sns.gov.uk/*

Scottish Paralegal Association: *http://www.scottish-paralegal.org.uk/*

Scottish Parliament: *http://www.scottish.parliament.uk/index.aspx*

Scottish Parliament Business Homepage: *http://www.scottish.parliament.uk/ParliamentaryBusiness.aspx*

Scottish Parliament European and External Relations Committee: *http://www.scottish.parliament.uk/parliamentarybusiness/CurrentCommittees/29814.aspx*

Scottish Parliament Private Bills: *http://www.scottish.parliament.uk/parliamentarybusiness/Bills/15709.aspx*

Scottish Parliament Publications: *http://www.scottish.parliament.uk/abouttheparliament/15018.aspx*

Scottish Parliament Research Briefings/Fact Sheets (SPICe): *http://www.scottish.parliament.uk/parliamentarybusiness/Research.aspx*

Scottish Parliament Factsheet, Guide to Recommended Citations for Scottish Parliament Publications: *http://www.scottish.parliament.uk/parliamentarybusiness/15984.aspx*

Scottish Parliament Subordinate Legislation Committee: *http://www.scottish.parliament.uk/parliamentarybusiness/PreviousCommittees/64264.aspx*

Scottish Parliament Weekly eBulletin: *http://www.scottish.parliament.uk/parliamentarybusiness/eBulletin.aspx*

UK Supreme Court: *http://supremecourt.uk/*
  http://www.supremecourt.gov.uk/docs/jurisdiction-of-the-supreme-court-in-scottish-appeals.pdf;
  http://www.supremecourt.gov.uk/decided-cases/index.html
UK Treaty Series: *https://www.gov.uk/uk-treaties*
United Nations Treaty Collection: *https://treaties.un.org/;* *https://treaties.un.org/Pages/*
  UNTSOnline.aspx?id=1
United Nations Treaty Series: *https://treaties.un.org/Pages/UNTSOnline.aspx?id=1*
Upper Tribunal Administrative Appeals Chamber: *http://www.justice.gov.uk/tribunals/aa*

V

Viviane Reding (Mackenzie-Stewart annual lecture at the University of Cambridge's Faculty of
  Law on February 17, 2014):
  http://www.theguardian.com/world/2014/feb/17/eurozone-countries-united-states-europe-
  viviane-reding

W

Weekly Information Bulletin (Westminster): *http://www.publications.parliament.uk/pa/cm/*
  cmwib.htm
Westlaw: *http://legalresearch.westlaw.co.uk/*
Wildy & Sons Ltd: *http://www.wildy.com/*
Wiley Online Library: *http://onlinelibrary.wiley.com/subject/code/000076*
World Intellectual Property Organization (WIPO): *http://www.wipo.int/wipo_magazine/en/pdf/*
  2013/
World Legal Information Institute (WLII): *www.worldlii.org*

Y

Yearbook of the International Court of Justice: *http://www.icj-cij.org/pcij/serie_other/cpji-*
  pcij.pdf.

Z

Zetoc: *http://zetoc.mimas.ac.uk/*

Index